Teddy Bears
&
Stuffed Animals
by
HERMANN TEDDY ORIGINAL®
1913-1998

Milton R. Friedberg

Schiffer Publishing Ltd

4880 Lower Valley Road, Atglen, PA 19310 USA

Designed by Bonnie M. Hensley
Type set in Geometric 231 Hv BT/Humanist 521 BT

ISBN: 0-7643-0933-1
Printed in China
1 2 3 4

Published by Schiffer Publishing Ltd.
4880 Lower Valley Road
Atglen, PA 19310
Phone: (610) 593-1777; Fax: (610) 593-2002 E-mail: Schifferbk@aol.com

In Europe, Schiffer books are distributed by Bushwood Books
6 Marksbury Avenue Kew Gardens
Surrey TW9 4JF England
Phone: 44 (0)181 392-8585; Fax: 44 (0)181 392-9876 E-mail: Bushwd@aol.com

Please visit our web site catalog at **www.schifferbooks.com**

This book may be purchased from the publisher. Include $3.95 for shipping. Please try your bookstore first.
We are interested in hearing from authors with book ideas on related subjects. You may write for a free printed catalog.

Contents

Acknowledgments

This effort is the result of the insistence and assistance of several friends whose personal knowledge supplied the thread that connected many diverse facts. First there is Ken Yenke and his wife Brenda, who successfully entangled me in the web of Teddy Bear history and secondly, Peter and Anna Kalinke, who supplied the missing links and anecdotes of Hermann Family products and their cross-connections. Renate Riesch and her husband Jurgen went from a commercial relationship to being our very close friend. Among Renate's many accomplishments was turning our 1997 visit to the Hermann Factory from a discourteous disaster to a triumphant success.

Our appreciation is expressed to Margit Drolshagen-Hermann and Traudel Mischner-Hermann for the information they have supplied and for the permission to reproduce "Hermann Teddy Original" copyright and proprietary material.

This document is only completed to ensure the continued approval of my devoted loving wife and couldn't possibly have been attempted without her help. Thank you, Joanne.

Foreword

The intent of this book is to present in one place a comprehensive survey of the Teddy Bears produced under the current trade name of "Hermann Teddy Original®." Previous publications (listed in the included Bibliography) provide a magnificent survey of the history of the company, but fail to adequately detail the products manufactured.

Therefore, this book presents only a brief summary of the company's background, while devoting its efforts to study in depth the company's products and their delineation.

In general, the listings are complicated by two major problems. World War II disrupted not only the company's existence in the Eastern portion of Germany, it forced a move to Western Germany in order to exist. During that move vital historical records were irretrievably lost. The information specifying the era prior to 1982 is vague and has been restored primarily from reasonable deductions and from a few surviving catalog pages.

The second problem is caused by the world wide acceptance of "bar codes" and Universal Product Code (UPC) coding to the International Standards mandated by governments. Prior to 1988, Teddy Original used a continuation of their historic "Number/Size" product identifiers; for example, "62/30" indicated model 62 Teddy Bear in a 30 cm size. During and after 1988, they instituted the new numbering system mandated by the industry, using a five digit number followed by a space and a sixth numeral, e.g., 16230 5. The first three digits represent the model number, the next two represent its size in centimeters, and the last numeral represents a color or variation. During 1988 and 1989, there was considerable confusion in attempting to institute the new system and renumber older products. As a result, there are items in collectors' hands that have an incorrect number on the identity tag and products which have a number duplicating an entirely different item. By 1990, most of these

problems were solved, except in the case of items specifically made for industrial customers (number begins with a zero). By 1997, the management became aware of these difficulties and attempted to correct the numbering problem for the future.

In this book, you will find that old and new style numerical listings and descriptions have been combined, but that the catalog illustrations have been separated by dates "prior to" and "after" the 1988 catalog year. Illustrations have been taken directly from existing catalogs (except for Specials) and unfortunately are not consistent in size or completeness.

If your bear or stuffed animal has an arm or leg tag, an attached booklet, or a hanging logotype, the information on determining age of Teddy Bears will be helpful. If your bear or stuffed animal has a number, it will be listed sequentially in the tabular data found in Part III. Special sections to the tables were added for those animals having "Jesco," "Rubin," or "Kathy Ann" identifiers. The Alphabetical Index is designed to be a quick guide to the more complete detail found in the numerical tables. In the case of named bears, e.g., Anniversary Bear, the index will lead readers to possible listings in the numerical tables.

Some Teddy Bears have been described and priced by various authors in prior publications. Where possible, attributions of model number have been made and entered in the body of the listings. However, many Teddy Bears cannot be specifically identified by model number. These unidentified Bears have been grouped by size in a separate list with the specific Bibliography reference associated with the entry.

M.R. Friedberg
March 1, 1999

Part I
Background

Chapter 1: The Hermann Family Company History

Teddy Bears have universal appeal. Their inherent cuddle-appeal leads to an immediate requirement to permanently embrace them. Age is not a bar to that feeling of affinity, and neither the age nor sex of the Teddy Bear or of the beholder changes that feeling! A 1997 example was the fad phenomenon of the cuddly "Teddy Beanies" distributed by the TY Company. The Beanies first appeared in toy and hobby shops. As word of their acceptance spread, gift and card shops added them to their wares. The manufacturer put his marketing department to work, increased the limited number of models, and—through a combination of clever public relations techniques and a consistently monitored minor shortage of products—gradually accelerated demand until the "Beanies" became a fad. Then, with a masterstroke of marketing, the national chain of McDonald's fast food restaurants added the "Beanie" as a premium in their child's meal package. They limited their selection to ten items that were slightly smaller that those sold by the normal Teddy Bear reseller. Teddy Bears were the original selections of the "Beanies," but the final designs incorporated many other animals and fanciful creatures as well.

The appeal of the toy "Beanie" is a minuscule variation of the lasting appeal of a well designed Teddy Bear carefully assembled by master craftsmen. Several companies have been in existence since the early 1900s and are still producing stuffed animals of world class quality. Many companies have come and gone, merged or been acquired, but the masters are still the outstanding names. Names such as Steiff, Schuco and Teddy-Hermann (Gebrüder Hermann) immediately pop into mind. These names are immediately recognized as established leaders and their products retain the features produced by the original craftsmen. The most recognized name is "Steiff," which is found on the product labels of a family controlled factory originated by a German seamstress back in the 1890s. Her first product was an elephant shaped pin cushion used to hold sewing needles, followed shortly by other small stuffed animals and toys.

The great number of local artisans working from their homes became suppliers to the successful designers with sales personnel. These artisans and crafts-men were part of the cottage industries that were the backbone of the German trades. Many other nearby German cottage industries also supplied stuffed animal and wooden toys to the toy trade. A yearly Exhibition or "Trade Fair" was the meeting place for all the small entrepreneurs to discuss products, methods, and materials. In addition, most small concerns were centered around the town of Sonneberg in Southeastern Germany. Successful new products quickly traveled among the trade and all joined in the success of a product. In addition, many of these manufacturers became inter-related as the children from one family married into the family of another manufacturer. Many of these small firms carried designs for stuffed animals, and as the family joined another family the design passed on as well!

A contemporary family in the Sonneberg area of Germany was the Johann Hermann family. Johann Hermann (1854-1919) was in business in 1907 as "The Johann Hermann Toy Factory." His family consisted of three sons, three daughters, and wife Rosalie (1867-1933). Artur, Bernhard, and Max were the sons and Adelheid, Ottilie, and Ida, the daughters. Ida (1907-1964) and Ottilie (1902-1975) apparently married outside the industry. Arthur carried on the family business, primarily supplying wooden toys, Teddy Bears, and stuffed animals to the toy trade. Sonneberg had become a buying center for the industry and F.A.O. Schwarz, S.S. Kresge, F.W. Woolworth, and other large retailers all had offices in the area.

Bernhard (1888-1959) formed his own toy manufacturing company in 1912 and married Ida Jager (1888-1966) that same year. His company operated under various forms of the Bernhard Hermann name and his products varied from wooden toys to stuffed animals as materials and orders were obtained. In the 1930s, he operated under the logotype "BE-HA" and the company evolved into the "Gebrüder Hermann Company" and then into today's company producing the "Hermann Teddy Original" Teddy Bears.

Adelheid (1891-1939) married into the Bauman family, which still produces the "Baki" line of Teddy Bears.

Artur (1894 -1989) worked in Johann Hermann's toy factory and contributed to the growth of the company. After Johann's death in 1919, Artur took over his father's business and operated under the company name of "Johann Hermann Nachfolger" (Johann Hermann Successor), owner Artur Hermann. The company was sold to Anker of Munich in 1954 and went through a series of metamorphoses until its final closing in 1974.

Max (1899-1955) left the family business in 1920 and started "Max Hermann Company," which eventually became "Max Hermann and Son (MAHESO)," now known as "Hermann Spielwaren" (Hermann Playthings). Hermann Spielwaren uses a bear with a running dog on a triangular tag as a trademark.

The novice Teddy Bear collector is easily confused by this profusion of Teddy Bears bearing the Hermann name in various forms. The novice is further confused by the similarity of appearance in Bears produced prior to 1930 by all the German Teddy Bear producers! The similarity is readily understood when approached from the Johann Hermann family viewpoint and is even more understandable when one realizes that most bears were produced by cottage industry artisans supplying their items to all of the area's manufacturers.

There are, however, very definite distinguishing marks and features that are evident in the products produced after the 1930s.

1910 Family Photograph: Max, Johann, Bernhard, Adelheid, Ida, Artur, Rosalie, Otille

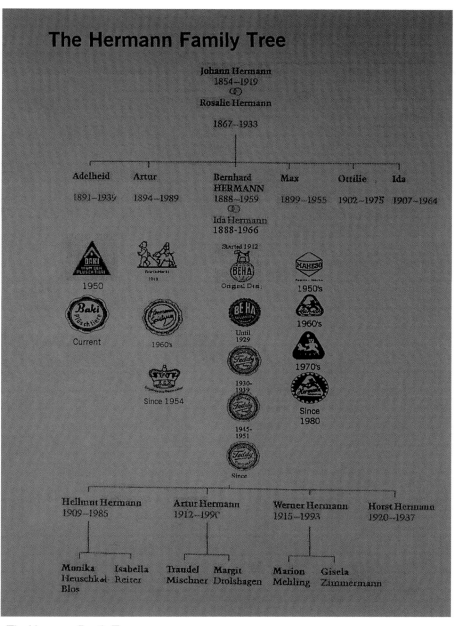

The Hermann Family Tree

Bernhard Before 1953

Although the Johann Hermann family is widely connected to other Teddy Bear brand families, we are only concerned here with the Bernhard Hermann family branch. They are the producers of the Gebrüder Hermann Teddy Bears under the current trade name of "Hermann Teddy Originals." Although the company makes items other than Teddy Bears, this book will ignore those products and concentrate only on the Teddy Bear and stuffed animal production.

Bernhard and Ida's children were Hellmut (1909-1985), Artur (1912-1990), Werner (1915-1993), and Horst (1920-1937).

Hellmut left school in 1923 and began his long career in the production and management of the company. His marriage to Maria in 1934 produced three daughters: Gudrun (1934-1942), Monika (1944), and Isabella (1947). Artur entered the family business in 1932 as a bookkeeper and expanded into Sales and Marketing. Eventually, Artur took over active guidance of the company. In 1939, he married Elisabeth Stöckel. During the war years she too helped in the family business until the birth of their daughters, Traudel in 1942 and Margit in 1949. Werner started to work in the business after finishing school and was intrigued by the design of Teddy Bears and the patterns required to produce them. Werner married Elisabeth Bauer in 1945 and they had two daughters, Marion (1949) and Gisela (1951). Horst died from blood poisoning at age seventeen.

The family actually lived in the town of Neufang, a short distance from Sonneberg. After World War II, this area was a part of the Soviet Zone of East Germany (German Democratic Republic), and was cut off from trade with the West. Obviously, the major market for stuffed animals, Teddy Bears, and other items made from mohair fabrics was the Western sphere of influence. The United States, Canada, and England were essentially impossible to reach with trade goods if you were in the Eastern Zone. Bernhard and his family never spoke openly about a possible relocation from the Soviet Eastern Zone of Germany to the Western Zone (Federal Republic of Germany). Secretly, the family began the quiet unobtrusive move to Hirschaid (Western Zone) in 1948 and by 1949 the company was in full parallel operation in Hirschaid as well as in Sonneberg (Eastern Zone). Hirschaid's first production in 1948 was of Bears with felt paws and sewn ears. They exhibited their first products at a stand during the Leipzig Toy Fair of 1948. Maintaining operations in both areas required great skill in eluding the trade restrictions between the zones while gradually moving the factory totally to the Western Zone.

Hermann Teddy Original

On January 25, 1953, the final break was made and the family departed from Neufang and Sonneberg for the last time. It was necessary to abandon all their possessions and holdings still remaining in the Eastern Zone.

In 1948, the company had been incorporated under Western Zone regulations as "Teddy- Plüschspielwarenfabrik Gebr. Hermann KG.," which translates to "Teddy Plush Toys Factory, Hermann Brothers." In 1952, the company adopted the trade-mark "Hermann Teddy Original" as an identifier for their products. Although the company name has changed since 1952, the trademark has been carefully preserved and promoted. In 1986, both of Artur's daughters and one of Werner's daughters were given formal positions in the operation of the company, with Margit Drolshagen as World Sales and Marketing Manager, Marion Mehling as Purchasing and Administration Manager, and Traudel Mischner-Hermann as Chief Designer. The company has gone through all the struggles, upheavals, and reorganization that accompany growth and survival in the changing economies from 1952 through the present. The study of those activities is not within the scope of this book and the reader is referred to those books detailing the history of the company rather than the delineation of its products. In 1991, the company became a Limited Company, and changed their official name to "Teddy-Hermann GmbH." The three managing Directors are the daughters of Artur (Margit Drolshagen-Hermann), the daughter of Werner (Marion Mehling-Hermann), and the daughter of Hellmut (Isabella Reiter-Hermann). Marion Mehling is responsible for Corporate Management and Isabella Reiter has the responsibility for Production Management.

American Sales

The company's original sales to the US were through American buying offices located in Sonneberg, East Germany until the onset of World War I. After the War, the Americans reopened their buying offices in Germany until the beginning of World War II. After that war, many buying offices were again reopened, but German manufacturers found it advantageous to either open their own US Sales Offices (as did Steiff) or to employ sales representatives in the States.

After the move from Sonneberg to Hirschaid, K. Grabowski of Miami, Florida became the company's American representative from 1948 through 1965. Starting in 1978, a Mr. Rubin and his wife, of Los Angeles, California, ordered special editions of the Standard Hermann product for resale in the states. These items were marked with a special underarm tag that specified they were Rubin Products. Rubin became ill in 1984/1985 and retired.

Rubin sold the product line to Nancy Vilasenor, who operated as "JESCO." She apparently had a partner and they operated successfully for three or four years. A second tag was added to the existing "Rubin" stock to indicate "JESCO" and was finally replaced by a single tag for items made exclusively for JESCO. Vilasenor separated from her partner and the company became defunct in approximately 1988.

Kathy Berman, owner of "Kathy Ann's Imports" in Toledo, Ohio, then took over with the help of Anna Kalinke of Columbus, Ohio, and Anna's husband Peter. They operated as "Kathy Ann Dolls," with Peter Kalinke traveling in the states representing the company to the trade. In 1991, the team was disrupted by an internal argument and disbanded.

Hermann then appointed "Tiderider" to represent them and the arrangement lasted until 1994 when they replaced "Tiderider" with "Euro-Collectibles" of Miami, Florida. Euro-Collectibles is operated by Reiner Lawitska.

Chapter 2: Determining the Age of Teddy Bears

Advertising and legal identifiers attached to the product are some of the items that help determine the date of manufacture of Teddy Bears. These include the logotypes (trademarks) attached to the body as well as the labels and booklets shown by representative samples below. Historical lists follow the illustrations.

Paper Logotypes

Swinging Logotypes

Used for toy production (left: 20 mm square. below: 18 mm square).

1930-52 (25 mm dia.).

Green paper (25 mm dia.).

Metal logo used in back of head (10 mm dia.).

Old and new paper logotypes (both 20 mm dia.).

Metal and paper (12 mm dia.).

Gold plastic (25 mm dia.).

Large red plastic (25 mm dia.).

Special Swinging Logotypes

Special Bears (25 mm dia.).

Bears made with "Dralon" cloth (25 mm dia.).

Special Bears (25 mm dia.).

Early red plastic (25 mm dia.).

Small red plastic (12 mm dia.)

Booklets

Early German language booklet cover (18.5 mm long).

Above & Below: Outside and inside of booklets. Words change with bear materials (18.5 mm long).

One of the current booklet styles (18 mm long).

Arm Tags

Early "Made in West Germany" tag. Green lettering on white cloth (aged yellow). 35 mm long.

Green ink printed on white cloth (16.5 mm long).

Green thread lettering on white cloth: 1945-1985. Brown thread lettering on white cloth: 1985-1988 (16.5 mm long).

Red thread lettering on white cloth: since 1988 (16.5 mm long).

More Identifying Characteristics

Prior to 1960, all Teddy Bears' eyes were either black shoe buttons or were specially made from glass. Hermann uses glass and plastic eyes that have a distinctive reddish brown color and are easily recognizable. Plastic eyes normally have a sharp edge at the back part of the eye where the mold parted. Glass eyes are always smooth at the back of the eye. Running a fingernail over the edge where the curve of the front of the eye meets the flat of the back allows one to quickly determine whether the sharp edge of the plastic eye or the smooth curve of the glass eye is present.

Further identifiers are the typical inset muzzle of the Hermann Bears. They differ from other bears in the shape of the muzzle and in the process used to sew it in place. Most Hermann's have three stitched claws on all paws and the ears are stitched low on the head. Noses have vertical stitches.

Table for Determining Age

Year	Eyes	White Cotton Fabric Arm Tag	Swinging Logotype	Head	Notes
Before 1920	Glass	?	?	No	Company is actually "Bernhard Hermann And Sons"
1920 to 1930	Glass	?	Beha Quality German	No	No identifier tags or logos before 1920
1930 to 1945	Glass	?	Marke Behar Burgt	No	
1945 to 1952	Glass	Green Lettering	Marke Behar Burgt	No	"Gebrüder Hermann" company starts in 1948
1952	Glass	Green Lettering	Hermann Teddy Original	No	
1953	Glass	Green Lettering	Hermann Teddy Original	No	Company moved from Sonnenberg, East Germany to Hirschaid, West Germany
1954	Glass	Green Lettering	Hermann Teddy Original	No	After 1954 all bears up to 8" tall had swinging small gold metal tag with paper insert
1952 to 1960	Glass	Green Lettering	Paper printed in Green	No	Two sizes of logo fastened with yellow cord
1960 to 1970	Glass or Plastic	Green Lettering	Green Paper or Metal	No	Glass eyes were used in the smallest jointed bears until mid-1980s
1970 to 1972	Glass or Plastic	Green Lettering	Green Paper Or Metal	No	
1972 to 1977	Glass or Plastic	Green Lettering	Gold Plastic/Green/Metal	No	Antique gold colored tie. Believe cardboard tags with red printing appeared here.
1977 to 1978	Glass or Plastic	Green Lettering	Red Plastic/Gold Plastic/Green/Metal	No	1.25" Diameter
1978 to 1980	Glass or Plastic	Green Lettering	Red Plastic/Gold Plastic/Green/Metal	No	Early 1980s, small cardboard tags printed in red used for children's toys
1980 to 1985	Glass or Plastic	Green Lettering	Red Plastic/Gold Plastic/Green/Metal	No	
1985 to 1988	Plastic	Brown Lettering	Red Plastic/Gold Plastic/Green/Metal	No	EAN numbers start in 1986, finalized in 1988
1988 to 1990	Plastic	Red Lettering	Red Plastic/Gold Plastoc/Green/Metal	No	
1990 to 1993	Plastic	Red Lettering	Small Red Platic or Large Red	No	Became "Teddy-Hermann Gmbh" in 1991
1993 on	Plastic	Red Lettering	Red Plastic	Metal	Metal logo fastened to back of head for bears taller than 20cm (7.87")

Note: Toy production in the Far East uses a rectangular white label with "Hermann Teddy Original" in red.

Identifying an older Teddy Bear is seldom an easy task. Unfortunately, a well loved bear has often lost his identifying trademarks, arm tags, and logo-types as well as most of his fur! However, certain traits help with identification. Most Bears of German manufacture have a distinctive hump at the back of the neck. All pre-WWII bears are solidly stuffed with excelsior (wood shavings used extensively as a shipping material prior to the invention of foamed plastic). Excelsior is still used in practically all high quality stuffed animals while various plastic materials are used at present to obtain the desired body hardness for less expensive bears.

Hermann Teddy Original Bears have three relatively short claws on each paw. Competitive bears usually have longer claws, no claws, or four claws. The claws are defined by a single strand of thread starting at the seam of the paw pad and extending over the curve of the paw. The top of the hip on Hermann Bears usually has almost a square front and back corner; competition is normally much rounder. The Hermann nose is defined by a series of vertical stitches in the form of an open "V' with a short vertical area finishing the top of the "V." The mouth is usually a single stitch inverted "V" attached to the bottom of the nose "V" with a short stitch. Muzzles (snouts) are a distinguishing feature of many of the early Gebrüder Hermann Bears. Instead of being cut with the face pattern of the bear, they were cut separately and inset to the face. Gebrüder Hermann Bears also have a distinctive curve to the upper surface of the muzzle—it is almost flat, but not quite! The placement of the ears is also important. Gebrüder Hermann ears are located as though the head was a triangle and the ear surrounds the joint of each top corner angle. The ear is usually made of two pieces of material inset to the head seam at each corner. Other manufacturers either follow the same practice or sew the ear to the head. Various manufacturers change ear position so that some ears seem to be level with the top of the head or are mainly above the head.

Additional data used in determining age:

•Plastic eyes were not used until 1960. Glass eyes were still being used in the smallest jointed until mid-1980s.
•White cotton fabric labels (tags) bore the words "HERMANN Teddy ORIGINAL Made in West Germany" printed or woven in green until 1980.
•From 1985-1988 the tags were woven with the same wording in brown letters.
•From 1988 on tags were cream colored with the trademark woven in red (no West Germany identification).
•Since 1993 all mohair Teddy Bears 8" or taller have a brass seal fastened in back of the head.

•In 1920 the company logo was a circular trademark with white lettering on a red background reading "BEHA & Quality Germany."
•By 1930 an irregular shaped rim was used with blue lettering on a gold background reading "Marke BEHA Teddy bürgt für Qualitat."
•In the late 1940s text was changed to "Hermann Teddy bürgt für Qualitat."
•In 1952 text was changed to "HERMANN TEDDY ORIGINAL."
•After 1954 all Teddys up to 8" had a small gold colored metal tag with an inserted paper printed in red "HERMANN Teddy Original."
•From 1952-1980 all Teddys 8"+ had a gold colored cardboard seal printed in green on both sides. Two sizes of the seal were fastened with yellow cord.
•From 1972-1978 a version appeared with a red and brown rim and green lettering on gold plastic. An antique gold colored cord was used as a tie
•In 1977 the first 1.25" red plastic seal with gold letters and brass colored cord was used.
•In the early 1980s red cardboard logos were used for small children.
•During the 1980s metal logo tags, green and gold cardboard labels, and red plastic logos were used.
•From 1990 on a smaller red plastic logo was also used.
•From 1993 on a metal logo was permanently fastened to the lower back of the head. Bears 7.87" (20 cm) tall have the metal logo.
•In 1986 the "EAN" standard for bar code numbering was adopted in Europe and ID #'s were all standardized to show company identity (4004510) plus a 7 digit product identifier. The system was partially implemented in 1987 and fully in place in 1988.
•Items with "/" (62/40) numbers pre-date 1988 and items with 5 digits, a space, and one number (16260 0) post-date 1987. As a result, identical items may have numbers from either numbering system.

Hermann Bears Issued for Distribution at EPCOT Disney World Conventions

Year	Number	Name	Limited Number
1988	#70004/31	Hiking Boy	Limited to 300
1989	#70007/45 3	Never Named	Limited to 500
1990	#05135 0	Daisy	Limited to 500
1991	#05235 7	Pink Blossom of Spring	Limited to 200
1992	#05230 7	Bikini Beach Boy	Limited to 100
1993	#05229 3	Autumn Wind	Limited to 100
1994	#01633 0	Winter Dream	Limited to 100
1995	#01243 2	Herman & Mickey	Limited to 100
1996	#78504 3	Winnie the Pooh	Limited to 250
1997	#02002 8	Winnie the Student	Limited to 300
1998	#02015 8+ #02016 5	"Pooh and Piglet"	Limited to 300

02/60

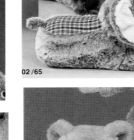

02/65

021/30

021/30/1

03/38 gold

03/38 blau

4/25

4/30

4/35

5/30
Serie 5

500/3

5/50
5/60
5/70

5/60
5/90

5/90/2

6/23
Serie 6
0/4

10/28

11/35

15/28
28

20/28
Serie 20

20/28

30/32
Serie 30

40S/30
Serie 40S

50/15
Serie 50

50/42

51/42

52/42

55/35/1

55/35/2

55 /35 /3

55 /35 /4

56/35/3

56/35/4

61/14

61/25

25

61/36

MOHA

61/50

62/14 caramel

62

62/14 mais

62 /14
62 /17

mais   oder
caramel lieferbar

62/17 caramel
62/20
62/25

62 /20

15

62 /25

62 /30

62/30
62/35

62 /40

62/35/5

62/40
82/50

63/8

63/01

63/14

63/17

63/20
63/25

63/20/2 K

63/20/3 K

63/20/4 K

63/20/5 K

63/20/6 K

63/20/7 K

63/30/1

63/30/2 K

63/30/3

63/30/4

63/30
63/35

63/40
63/50
63/60

64/8
64/14

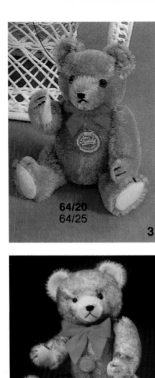

64/20
64/25

3

64/30

62/30
62/35

64/40

66 /35
66 /42

NEU

69/35

MOHAIR

76/50

76/30

76/40

76/50

76/80
76/130
76/150

77/30

77/50
77/80

78/30

78/40

79 /25
79 /30
79 /36
79 /45
79 /55

18

80/24
Serie 80

ollbeweglich

80/40

81/40

81/50

84/18

84/25

84/24
84/28
84/35
84/42
84/50

84/30

84/40

85/18

85/24

2

85/28

85/35

85/24

85/42

85/50

88 /30

88 /38

88 /42

90 /30

90 /38

8 /42

90/42

91 /30
91 /38 91 /42

100/25
Serie 100

100/32

101/22

102/22

103 /40 /1

103 /40 /3

104 /80

106 /60

108 /30
108 /40

61
61
61

/12

108 /45

109 /30 /3

109 /30

109 /30 /1

110/17
Serie 110

0/25
Serie 100

120/22
Serie 120

150/20   150/10
Serie 150

151/32   151/45
Serie 151

152 /18

153/15

153/20

153 /35

154/22

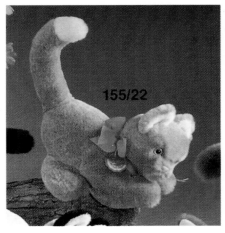

155/22

156/22

157 /22

158 /42

162 /40

159/25   159/30   150

Serie 159

163/40

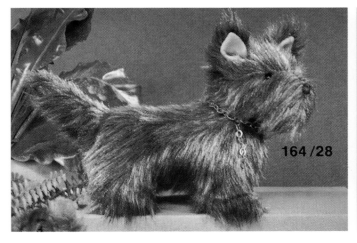

164 /28

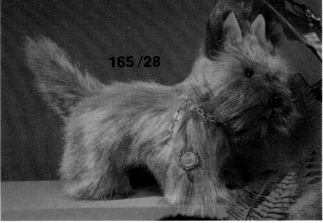

165 /28

166/18

166/25

166/28

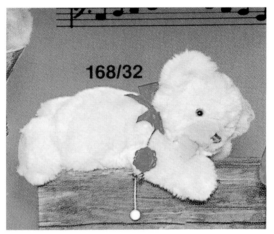

168/32

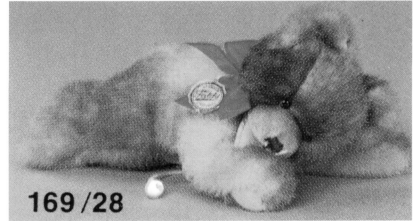

169 /28

169/32

170/30

170/35

174 /30

176 /30

180/25

180/15

1500 Stück

2000 Stück

limitierte Auflagen:

MOHAIR

196 /16

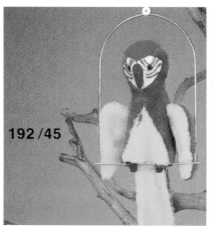

192 /45

196/16   196/18

196 /25

Glockenstimme   197 /18

198/25

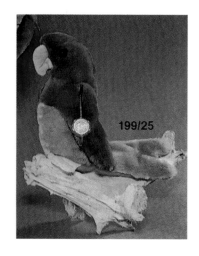

199/25

200/40
Serie 200

210/18

210 /24

210/30

210/38

210/18

210/50

215/40
215/50

218/35
218/45

220/35

232/20

232/20
232/28

250/30   250/20
Serie 250

261/20
Serie 261

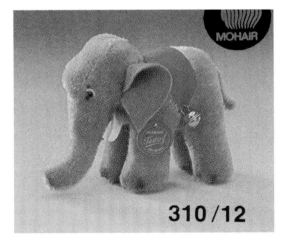

MOHAIR

310/12

312/20

312 /25

321 /32

340/40

330/40/4F

SU70

51/20

330/45
Serie 330

403 /40
403 /55

404 /33

40S/30
Serie 40S

410 /13

410 /14

410 /15

410/16

410/18

410/19

420 /8

420/40
420/50

420/9

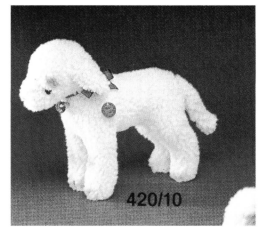

420/10

420/40
420/50

0/10

421 /50

20 /10

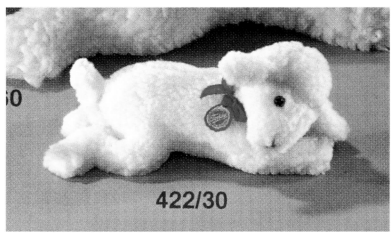

50

422/30

27

422/60

434/16
434/22

MOHAIR

442/20
442/30
442/42

444/30
444/40

DF-Serie „Schwarzwald-Klinik"
rzwald-Klinik"
rzwald-Klinik«

450/35

451/40

452/28

453/1

457/25

459/30

MOHAiR

860/9

460/18

476/18
476/30
476/40
476/50

490/32
Serie 490

495/30

495/45

496/35

499/30
499/42
499/62

200/4
Serie

500/3

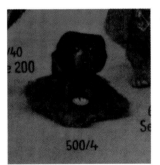

/40
e 200

500/4

510/3

512 /17

512/24

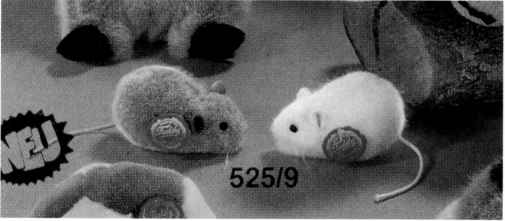

525/9

525 /21

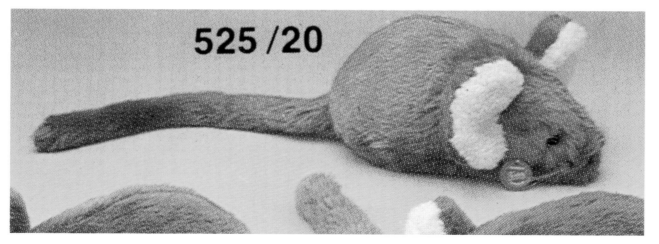

525 /20

525 /22

526/20

527/25

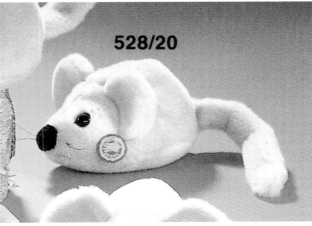

528/20

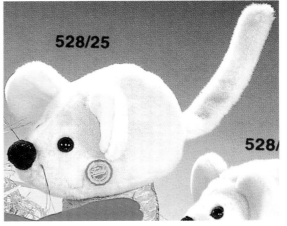

528/25

528/

529/20

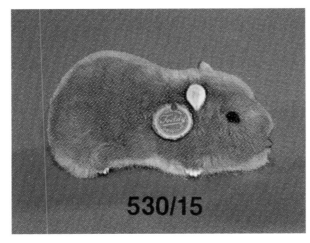

530/15

530/25
gelb

31

530/25
grau

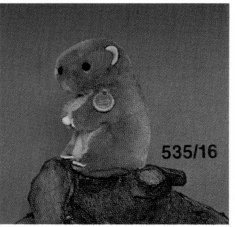

535/16

535/25

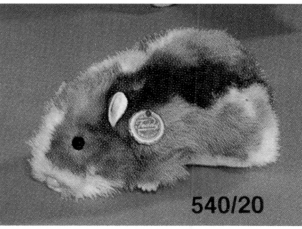

540/20

540/21

550/30
550/80

261/20
Serie 261

551/20
Serie 551

552/25

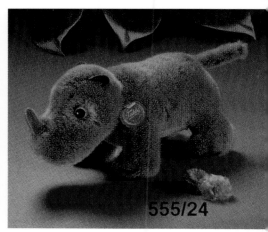

555/24

560/30

571/23
571/30

600/1   600/2   600/3   600/4   600/5   600/6

Serie 600 Familie Langhals

600 /14 *
600 /17 *

604/23   limitierte Auflage: 2000 Stück

607 /21 *

607 /28

600 /14 *
600 /17 *

607 /42

610 /35

616 /26
616 /33

620 /35

33

625 /25 /1

625 /25 /2

62

630 /28
630 /33
630 /40

0600/28

640/38

101

646/30

/30

647/40

647/45

650/18
Serie 650

S

/13
e 650

655/18

655/13

Serie 655

660/13

660/20

Serie 660

S

670/40

705 /20

708 /28

710/21

714/18

715 /25

719 /35

720 /52

722 /35

1352 /12

607 /21 *

725/16

735 /28

736 /24

35

736 /32

736 /42

736 /65

736 /24

737 /32

739 /24

739 /32

739 /42

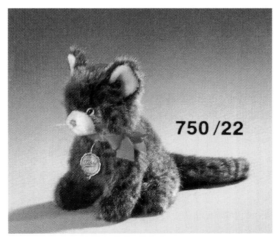

750 /22

757 /22

758 /22

759/22

780/10 sortiert

607 /42

780 /20*

781/15

781/20

NEU

2/20

782/15

783/20

784/20

NEU

796 /32

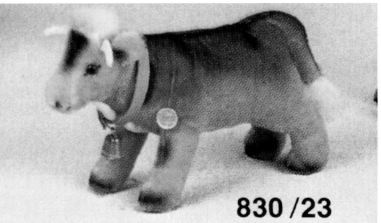

830 /23

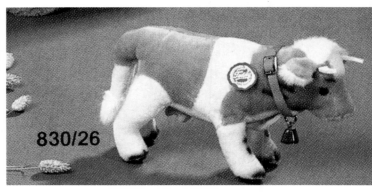

830/26

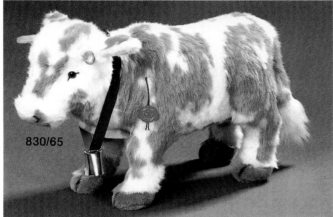

830/65

855 /25
855 /30

860 /7
860 /9

880 /10
880 /16
880 /22

85/12

880/10

885/16

885/22

MOHAIR

886/18

890/20

890 /30

525/9

892/20

900/30   900/40   900/50   900/60

Serie 900

925/40   925/60 B

Serie 925   B=lenk

nkbarer Kopf   960/60 B   960/50

Serie 960

985 /25

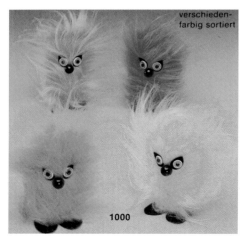

verschieden-
farbig sortiert

1000

39

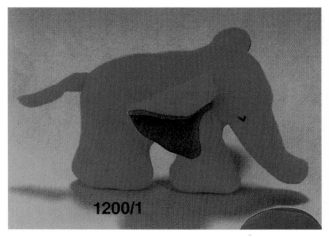

1200/1

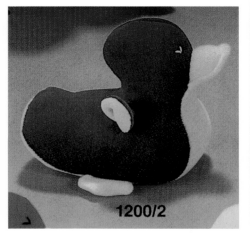

1200/2

1200/3

0/11

1200/4

1200/5

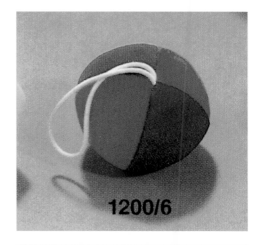

1200/6

1200/13

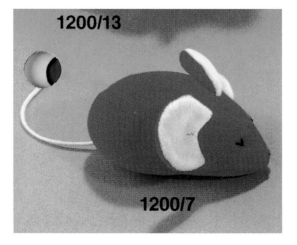

1200/7

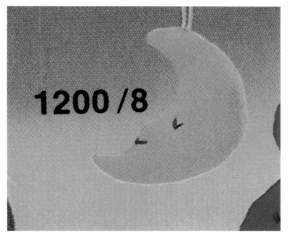

1200 /8

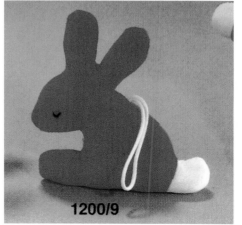

1200/9

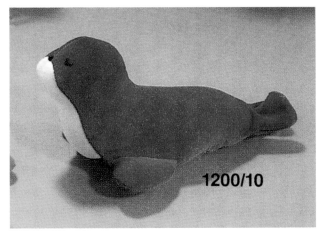

1200/10

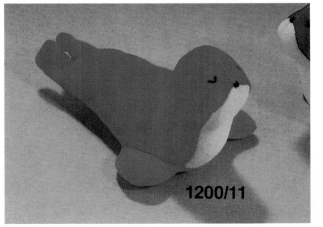

1200/11

1200/12

1200/13

1200/2

1200/14

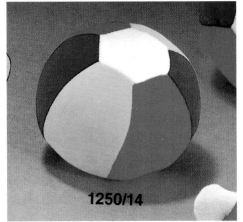

1250/14

1255/16

1300 /22 ohne Korb
1305 /17 mit Korb
1305 /22 mit Korb

1310/22

1316/10/3

1330/24

1350 /25

1352/12

1353/15

1354/20

1355 /18

1356/15

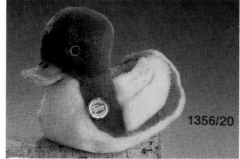
1356/20

1356 /25

1365 /16

1398 /20
1398 /35
1398 /45

1399/22

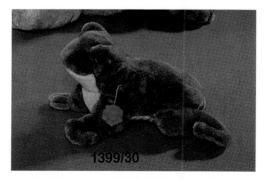
1399/30

1399/40

1399/60
1399/75

1410 /26

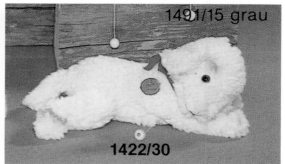
1491/15 grau
1422/30

42

1452/25
schwarz-weiß

1452/25
braun-weiß

37 /18

1480 /14

1481 /14

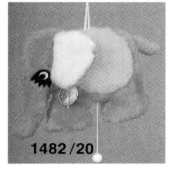

1481/14

1482 /20

1483/14

1484/25

1485 /22

148

1486 /20

1487 /18

1/14

1488/22

1489 /20

1490 /40

4

1492/15
1491/15 grau

1962 /30

1962/48

84090/55
84090/75

1962/60

2017 /60
2017 /80

2000 /33
2000 /58

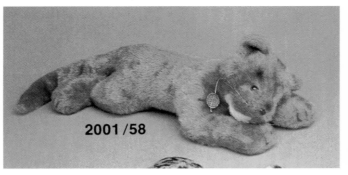

2001 /58

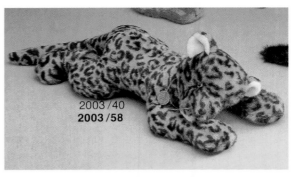

2003 /40
2003 /58

2005/25
2005/35

2014 /35
2014 /45
2014 /60

2016 /35
2016 /45
2016 /60

2017 /45
2017 /60
2017 /80

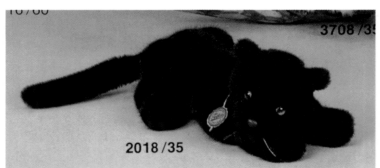

16 /60

3708 /35

2018 /35

2021 /30

2022 /25

2023 /25

2024/20
2024/25

2025/20

2025/25

2026 /25

2028/20

2028/25

2030 / 22

2040/25

2045/30

2040/

2200 /25

2300 /24

862635

2322

2500 /15

2500/25

2500 /35

2550/15

2550/25

3002 /20
3002 /30

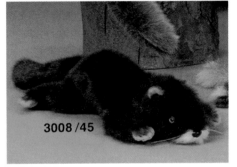

3008 /45

3045 /40

5   3200 /30

3200/44
3200/52

3250 /28

3260/28

3400/26

3400/58

3601 / 15

3602/15

3603/24

3604/15

3605/15

3606/15

3608 /15

3650 /25

80458/31

3660/25

3700 /30

3705 /35

1250 /14
1251 /14
mit
Glocken-
stimme

4001 /30

3708 /35

4010 /30

4010/30 F

4010/30
4020/30

4020/30 F

4030/35
525 / grau
525/9 w

4700/30

5000 /38

5000 /48

6220

6225NSO

6230

6235NSB

6230NSO

6235NWB

6240

6250NSB
83233

5NSO

6250NWB
63205K

6755
76235W

6935

7040

7630W

6225NSO
7650B

7750H
623

7008435

73360F

76235W

NEUHEITEN 1987

80004/25

80004 /30

80005 /48
80005 /60
80005 /70

80006/50

80006/62
80006/72

80007/50

80007/85

80008 /45

80008 /48

49

80008/62

80009/40

80010/26

80011/26

80020/35

80021/35

80022/35

80023/35

80029/41

80029/42

80029/43

80030/28
80030/42
80030/33
80032/42
80032/28
80032/33

50

80031/28

80031/33

80031/42

5/33

80035/28

80035/33

80036/35

80036/42

80041/42

80045/40

80046/40   80047/40

80081/40

80083 /40

80164/35

80166 /40
80166 /50
80166 /65
80166 /95

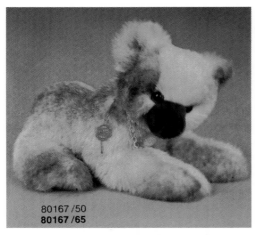

80167 /50
80167 /65

80168 /22

80168/30

80168 /40
80168 /50
80168 /65
80168 /95

169/32

80169/22

80170 /42
80170 /70

80174/35

80175/45

80176/35

80219/40

80219 /52

80219/55
80219/58

80219/75

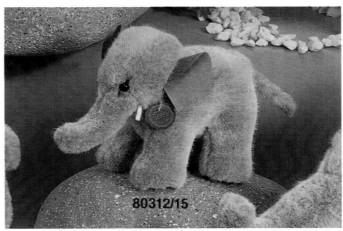

80312/15

80312/20

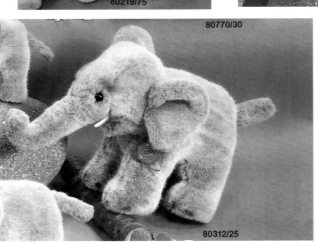

80770/30

80312/25

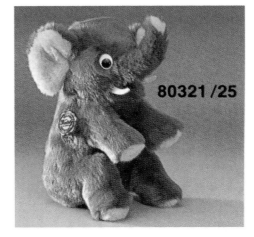

80321 /25

80321 /32

80321/36

80322 /45

80331 /30

80331 /50
80331 /60

80420/30

80425 /40

80425/45

NEU

80436/38

80438/40

80440/50

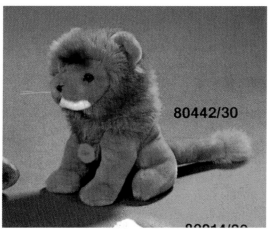

80442/30

80443/38
80443/85

80445 /42

80448/50

80450 /35

80458/30

80458/31

80460/30

80492/52

80492/42

80492/52

80560B

80510/35
80510/50

80600/28

80601/28

80607/28

80607/42

80601/28

80620 /25
80620 /35

80622/35

80625/35

80640 /35

80642/35

80650 /30
80650 /50

80650/35

80651/35

80660/50

80672H

80170/42

80705/20

80709/28

80714/24

80742/40

80742/50

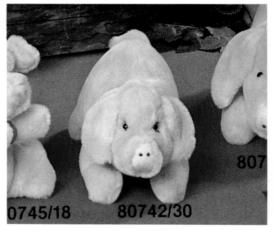

0745/18   80742/30   807

80763/28

80770/75

80785C

816850

80850B

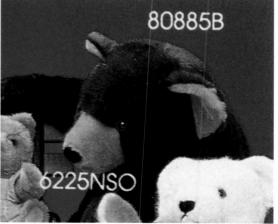

80885B

6225NSO

58

81350/30

81357/30

81358/30

81399/30

83242

816435

816830

816850

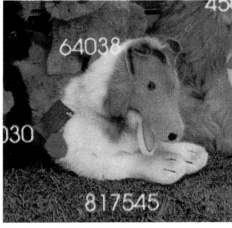

64038

817545

82000/40

82006/28

82006/60

82007 /25
„Schnurz"

82007 /55

82008 /60

82009/30

82009 /30

82009 /40
82009 /60

82010 /35
82010 /55
82010 /75
82010 /100

82012/75

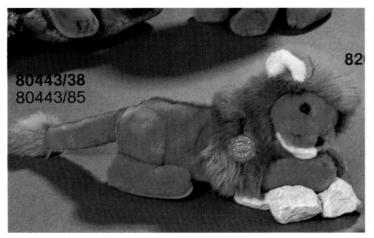

80443/38
80443/85

82015/30

82017 /60
82017 /80

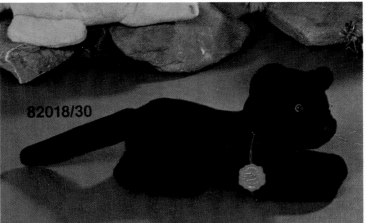

82018/30

82021/30

821430

1942

83

83020 /65

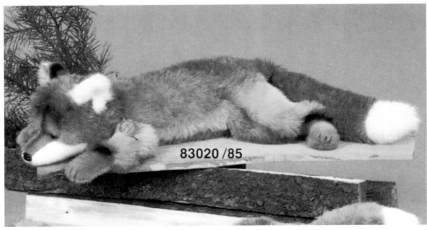

83020 /85

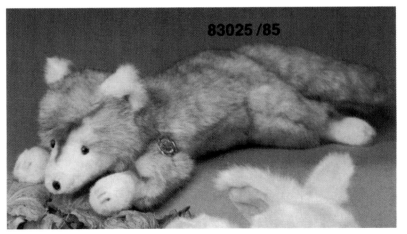

83025 /85

83026

83041 /40

83042H

84060/45

83045/40

8310

83100/40

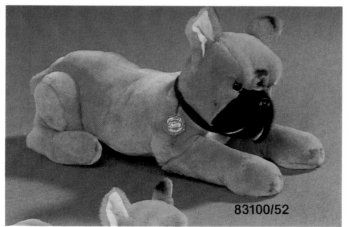

83100/52

83133

83242

83233

62

83242 83233

83603 /35

83605/30

83606/30

83610/40

83615/40

83620/30

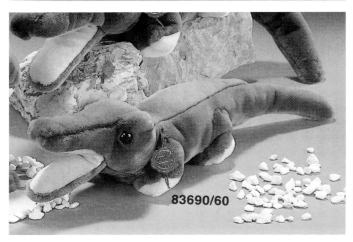

83690/60

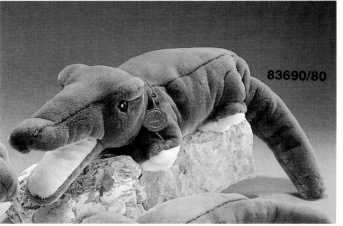

83690/80

83710 /30

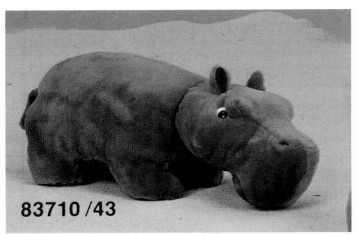

83710 /43

83710 /62
83710 /100

83715 /30

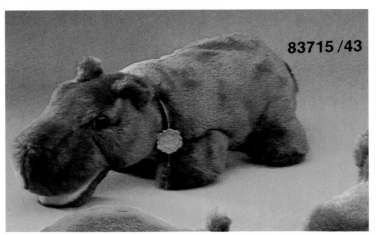

83715 /43

83715 /43

83715 /62
83715 /100

83716/30
83716/43
83716/62
83716/100

83718/30

83720 /42

83725/42

83730 /40

83731 /40

83735/36

84030/40

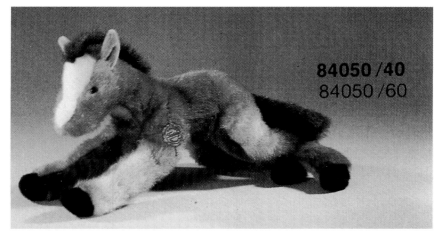

84050 /40
84050 /60

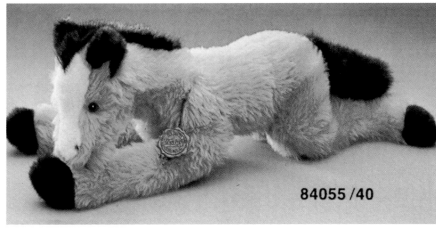

84055 /40

84060 /45
84060 /55

Heidi und ihr treuer Freund **Josef**
... die beiden Stars der neuen 52-teiligen Zeichentrick-Serie, die ab Januar 1987 im ZDF-Fernsehen ausgestrahlt wird.

84070/50

84080/40

84085/55

84090/55
84090/75

84090/110

84095/40

84095/55
84095/75

N 87   **TEDDY-Plüschspielwarenfabrik Gebr. Herma**
Telefon (0 95 43) 91 61 / 91 62, Telex

87730

87750

816830

87928

9000.4

01009 0

01093 5

01193 1

01193 2

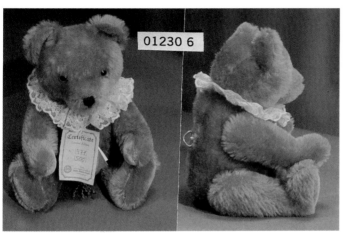

01230 6

01302 9

01303 0

01303 1

01304 0

01333 4

01361 7

01363 1

01363 0

67

01421 4

01423 2

01483 6

01493 5

01512 3

01514 0

01522 5

01563 0

01611 7

01623 0

01632 0

01633 0

01633 0

01633 3

01633 5

01633 6

01634 1

01954 1

01954 29

01954 36

02002 8

02015 8 + 02016 5

02035

03060 7

04025

04035 4

05135 0

05229 3

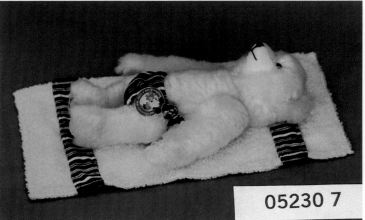

05230 7

05235 7

06220 1   06230 1

062356

06240 0

06240 0

06755

08635 2

10001 0

Left: 08419 8   Right: 08417 4

10002 7

10003

10011 9

10020 1

10021 8   Teddy Nostalgie-Schule
10041 6   ,,Mein Schulfreund ist Ausländer''

10025 6
Miniatur-Teddybären-Schule
Bestückung: 1 Lehrer 8 cm
3 Schüler 5 cm
L 20 cm, B 15 cm, H 12 cm
Limit 1000 Stück

Miniature Teddy Bear School
Equipped with: 1 teacher 8 cms
3 pupils 5 cms
L 20 cms, W 15 cms, H 12 cms
Limited to 1000 pcs.

École miniature
garni avec: 1 maître 8 cm
3 élèves 5 cm
L 20 cms, A 15 cms, H 12 cms
Limitée 1000 pcs.

10031 7

10042 3

10043 0

10044 7

10050 8

10070 6

NEU

10071 3
48 cm
Limit 500 Stück

10075 1
22 cm
Limit 1000 Stück

10076 8
18 cm
Limit 1000 Stück

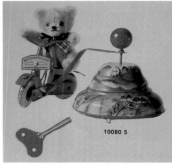

10080 5

10081 2
13 cm
Limit 1000 Stück

10082 9
15 cm
Limit 1000 Stück

10083 6
15 cm
Limit 1000 Stück

10085 0

10090 4

10121 5

10122 2

10123 9

10124 6

10420 9

10221 2

10222 9

10223 6

10224 3

10321 9

10322 6

10421 6

10422 3

10508 4

10514 5

10521 3

NEU

10522 0

10620 3

10720 0

10621 0

10722 4   10622 7

10721 7

10831 3

10832 0

10833 7

10930 9

NEU

10931 0
Limit 2000

10932 7

10940 2

11033 0

11241 9

11121 4　11120 7

11123 8
Limit je 2000

11221 1　11232 7
11220 4

11231 0

11240 2

11241 9

11129 0　11128 3

11331 7
11333 1
11330 0

21 8
11320 1

11321 8
11320 1

11323 2　11322 5　11324 9

11400 0

11404 8　11403 1
11401 7
11402 4

11405 5

11414 7

11415 4

11430 7
11431 4
11434 5
11435 2　11436 9

11433 8

11517 5

11515 1

11516 8

11535 9   Limit 2000

11550 2

11618 9   11617 2

11622 6

11621 9   11620 2

11655 4

11735 3

11741 4

11750 6

11842 8

11843 5

11845 9

12035 3

12040 7
Limit 2000

Ein bäriges,
exklusives Prä
für viele Anlä

12042 1

12041

Bitte beachten Sie hierzu
unseren Sonderprospekt.

-Buch deutsch
-Buch englisch

12050 6

12250 0

BUSSI BAR

12335 4

12350 7

Deb Canham

12530 4

12840 3

12530 3

12620 1   12520 4   12820 5

Deb Canham ①

12727 7

12726 0

Der Marionettenbär ③

NEU

12940 0
Limit 1000

②

12941 7

②

13025 3

13030 7

13130 4

④

13135 9

④

13230 1

13231 8

②

13330 8

②

13331 5   156

①

13417 6

13430 5

②

50630 0

13455 8

13517 3

13530 2

③

13617 0

13625 5

13629 3

13630 9

②

13633 0

13632 3

13631 6

Dekoration

13634 7

13745 0

14038 2

14127 3

NEU

14130 3
Limit 2000

14140 2

142140

Charlie

142300

Teddybären-Serie „Tradition"

14440 3

17320 5

17321 2

11518 9 11617 2

14430 4   14450 2

NEU

14531 8   14530 1
Limit je 2000

14732 9

10932

14740 4

Replika 1994

Original ca. 1930

NEU

14830 2 Limit 2000

14840 1

14945 3   14935 4

14936 1   14946 0

14950 7

spiel gut
von alternativen energie- spielzeug siegerstück

Limit je 3000

②

15030 5

15040 4   15050 3

15130 2
Weihnachtsbär
mit Spieluhr
Limit: 500 Stück

Teddy ORIGINAL

15114 2

15115 9

15140 1

15145 2

VEREINIGUNG 7000

7000

Certificate
1999

15219 4

15221 7

①

MOHAIR

15230 4   15222 4   15223 1

15233 0

15225 5

15229 3
Limit 2000

15231 1

15231 1

15231 1

15232 8

Certificate

15234 7

15245 8

15322 1

1

MOHAIR

15325 2

15345 0

⑪

MOHAIR

15430 8

78

15440 2

15445 7

15545 4

Edwin
6fach gegliedert   15550 8

15630 7

15140 1

2

15445 1

15635 2   15638 3

15701 4   5 cm
Teddy, caramel

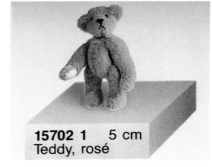

15702 1   5 cm
Teddy, rosé

15703 8   6 cm
Teddy, zimt

15704 5   8 cm
Jester

15705 2   7 cm
Schlafteddy

15706 9   8 cm
Teddy, gold   Limit 3000

15707 6   8 cm
Teddy, nougat   Limit 3000

15708 3   11 cm
Mohairbär, beige

15709 0   6 cm
Teddy, caramel

15712 0   7 cm
Teddy, blau

15713 7   7 cm
Teddy, caramel

15714 4   7 cm
Teddy, braun

15716 8   7 cm
Teddy, gold

15720 5   8 cm
Schüler   Limit 3000

15721 2 9 cm
Semantha

15722 9 9 cm
Zack

15723 6 6 cm
Panda

15724 3 8 cm
Teddy, zimt

15725 0 8 cm
Teddy, schwarz

15726 7 9 cm
Razz

15727 4 9 cm
Matazz

15728 1 6 cm
Teddy, altgold

15730 4 7 cm
Kiki

15731 1 8 cm
Chappy

15732 8 8 cm
Malcolm

15733 5 7 cm
Tabatha

15734 2   7 cm
Toro

15735 9   8 cm
Tina

15736 6   8 cm
Teddy's Bär

15737 3   8 cm
Hotel-Boy

15738 0   8 cm
Teedie, beige

15740 3   7 cm
Buffy

15741 0   7 cm
Fluffy

15742 7   7 cm
Sadie

15743 4   7 cm
Ting Panda

15744 1   11 cm
Teddy, altgold

Teddybären
mit Parfümflakon
im Bärenkörper

mit Kettchen
und Geldbörse

15749 6
Theo   7 cm

15748 9
Floppy 7cm

15746 5
Jasmine   11 cm

15745 8
Carmille   11 cm

15747 2
No-No-Bär   8 cm

15751 9
Setzkasten aus Holz
Glastüre mit Messingknopf,
Spiegelrückwand,
36 x 36 cm mit 2 Hängeösen

Wooden letter-case,
glass door with brass knop, backwall: mirror,
36 x 36 cms with 2 hangers

Casier vitrine
avec fermeture, fond avec une glace, vide

15756 4

Bekleidung

NEU

15757 1

für Bären-Miniaturen 5-8 cm
im Geschenkkarton

15756 4 Kleidchen gehäkelt, 4-farbig sortiert
15757 1 Westen, gestrickt, 4-farbig sortiert

Theken-Glasvitrine, 75 x 37 cm   **15758 8**
incl. 2 Halogenleuchten à 20 Watt mit Trafo.
Schloß, Spiegelboden, 3 drehbare Einlageplatten,
Sicherheitsglas, Sockel u. Blende schwarz

15760 1   7 cm
Amelia m. Teddy

15761 8   7 cm
Bär mit Affe

15762 5   7 cm
Bär mit Panda

15763 2   7 cm
Bär mit Gans

15764 9   7 cm
Dizzy

15766 3   7 cm
Hummel

15767 0   7 cm
Autsch

MOHAIR

15770 0   8 cm
Holly

15769 4

15771 7 8 cm
Ivy

15772 4 8 cm
Nicolas

15773 1 8 cm
Kris+Kringle

15774 8 8 cm
Hansel+Rudy

15780 9 4 cm
Teddy, zimt

15781 6 4 cm
Panda

15782 3 4 cm
Teddy, grün

15783 0 5 cm
Teddy, caramel

15784 7 5 cm
Teddy, braun

15786 1 5 cm
Teddy, gold

15787 8   5 cm
Teddy, rosé

15791 5   5 cm
Teddy, beige

15792 2   5 cm
Teddy, blau

15793 9   5 cm
Teddy, rot

15794 6   5 cm
Teddy, gold

15795 3   5 cm
Teddy, braun

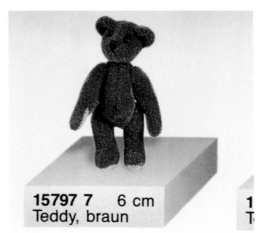

15796 0   6 cm
Teddy, beige

15797 7   6 cm
Teddy, braun

15798 4   5 cm
Teddy, schwarz

15799 1   5 cm
Teddy, grün

Geschenkkarton für Miniaturbären
Gift box for miniatur bears
Boîte pour l'ours miniature
15801 1 für Miniaturbären bis 5 cm,
        small, petite
15802 8 für Miniaturbären über 5 cm,
        large, grande

15822 6   8 cm
Panda, Mohair
Limit 3000 Stück

15827 1   8 cm
Benjie
Limit 3000 Stück

15829 5   9 cm
Belinda

Collection von Deb Canham

Honey Hills

15833 2
Simon   12 cm
Limit 3000 Stück

15834 9
Bratty Butchy   12 cm
Limit 3000 Stück

15831 8
Gerti   12 cm
Limit 3000 Stück

Honig

Dekoration

15830 1
Willyum   12 cm
Limit 3000 Stück

15832 5
Poppo   12 cm
Limit 3000 Stück

15901 8   7 cm
Bluebeary

15902 5   7 cm
Raspbeary

15903 2   7 cm
Bananabeary

15904 9   7 cm
Strawbeary

15910 0   9 cm
Chocolate

15911 7   9 cm
Honey

15913 1   8 cm
Old Fashioned, altgold

15914 8   8 cm
Old Fashioned, zimt

15915 5   8 cm
Old Fashioned, braun

15916 2   7 cm
Marmelade

15917 9   7 cm
Silver

15920 9   9 cm
Jolly Jester

15923 0   7 cm
Spanky

15924 7   7 cm
Jenny+Delia

15925 4   7 cm
Jack+Puff

15930 8   6 cm
Bearfoot and Pregnant

15931 5   5 cm
Zeke

15932 2   3-teilig   je 6 cm
Hear no, See no, Speak no evil

15933 9   8 cm
Sassie

15934 6   9 cm
Fibber

15935 3   8 cm
Magic

15942 1   8 cm
Halloween Cat
Limit 2000 Stück

15945 2   7 cm
Ashley

15946 9   7 cm
Teddy, altgold

15947 6   7 cm
Teddy, braun

15948 3   7 cm
Teddy, beige

15949 0   7 cm
Teddy, braun

15950 6   8 cm
Teddy, rost

15951 3   8 cm
Teddy, braun

15953 7
Chester, 10 cm
braun

15954 4
Chester, 10 cm
beige

15955 1
Tumbler, 6 cm

15952 0
Polarbär, 14 cm

15955 1
Tumbler, 6 cm

1595
Che
beig

16014 4

87

2

16030 4

16150 9   16114 1   16136 3

16210 0   16211 7
Weihnachtszwerge

16340 4

16214 8

1

12640 9

12620 1   12630 0

16250 6

16350 3   16360 2

16308 4   16314 5   16317 6   16320 6

163800

16514 9   16416 2   16420 3

16514 9

16517 0

③

16620 7

16614 6

16630 6

16730 3

16714 3

16720 4

16830 0

16850 8

16840 9

15245 8

16880 5

1000

16914 7

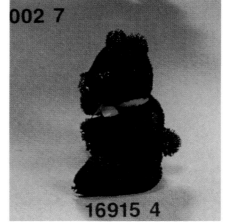

002 7

16915 4

169157

16916 1

16920 8

89

16930 7

16931 4

171454

17221 3

17220 6

17222 0

17225 5

17320 5

17321 2

17328

17225 7

17550 6

17650 3

17640 4

17630 5

09

17730 2

17731 9

17843 9

11414 7

18030 2

18025 8

18040 1

18040 1

16

18122 4

18121 7

18123 1

1

18440 9

18430 0

18425 6

18435 5

18418 8

2

98151 0
englisch

Tales of Teddy Hermann

Die Geschichte der
Original-Hermann-Teddybären

Teddys und Tiere sammeln

98150 3
deutsch

18535 2

18528 4

18450 8

18610 2

18625 0

186304

8   19040 0

① 19047 9

19055 4

NEU

Die Flexiblen von
Teddy HERMANN

19155 1

19156 8

NEU ②

19445 3

③

19540 5

730   196248

⑤

19645 7

⑭

19745 4

①

20030 7

20025 3   20035 2

NEU

20185 4

20250 9

20285 1

2 20430 5

20425 1

20551 7   20571 5   20561 6

20650 7

20660 6

20650 7

20750 4

20750 4

20786 3   20751 1   20185 4

20850 1

93

20885 3

20960 0

21026 9

21126 6

22035 0

22335 1

22135 7

22235 4

spiel gut

22128 9

22133 3

22840 0

22940 7

22740 3

23028 1

23042 7

23228 5

23033 5

spiel gut

23328 2

23333 6

23342 8   2332

NEU   ADAC   HERMANN   23430 2

41230 4   NEU   23430 2

spiel gut
vom arbeitsausschuß
kinderspiel+spielzeug
ausgezeichnet

NEU   23540 8   23530 9

24740 1   24640 4

25635 9   25535 2

25835 3   25735 6

30165 3   30050 2

30065 6

30195 0

30166 0

30141 7

30151 6

NEU

②

30195 0

30142 4

30167 7

30152 3

⑤

30265 0

30250 6

②

NEU

30266 7

30251 3

30241 4

30275 9

30380 0

30360 2

30350 3

31030 3

31020 4

31030 3

31040 2

31130 0

55 5

31540 7

31755 5   31725 8   31628 2   31660 2

31875 0   31897 2

32635 9

32532 1

32728 8

32845 2

32860 5

32875 9

74116 9

33515 3

33625 9

34061 4

34051 5

34031 7

NEU

34116 1

34120 8

075 1

spiel gut
vom arbeitsausschuß
kinderspiel · spielzeug
ausgezeichnet

34121 5

34236 6

34330 1

34350 9

34425 4

34465 0

35030 9

35230 3

35265 5

35145 0

35232 7

35138 2

35232 7

35335 5

36135 0

36030 8

36062 9

36042 1

36060 5

36235 7

36260 9

36570 9

36571 6

36840 3

36860 1

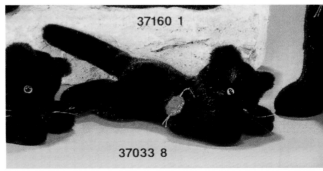

37160 1

37033 8

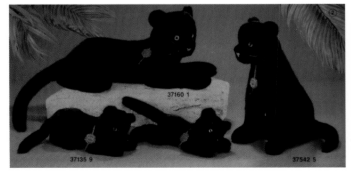

37160 1

37135 9

37542 5

37560 9

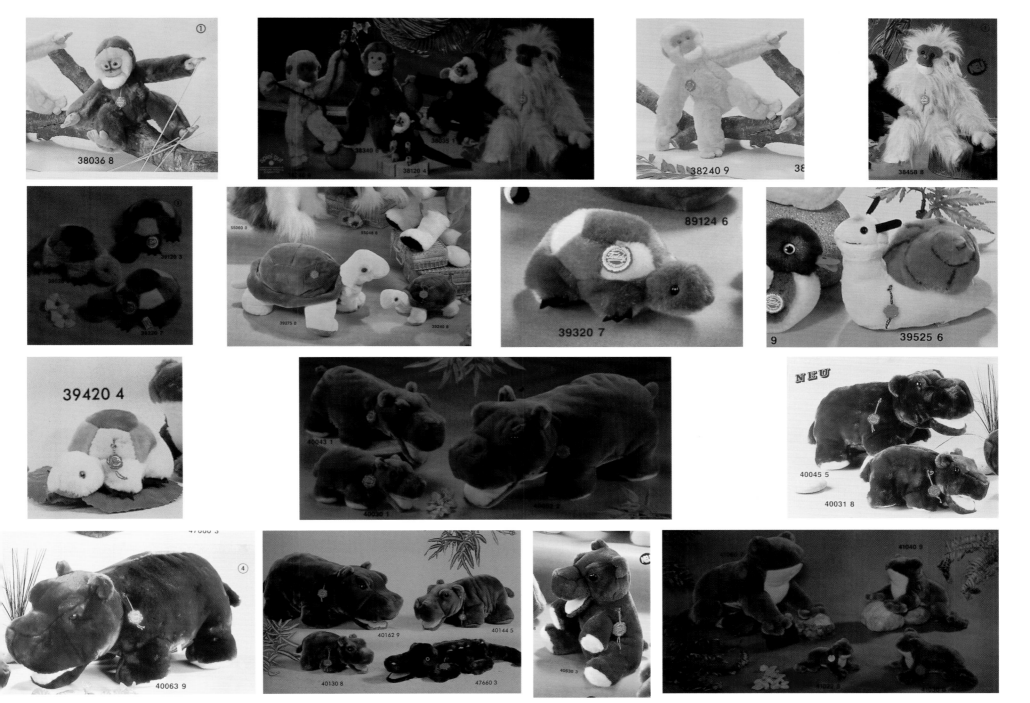

① 38036 8

38340 8 38035 1

38120 4

38240 9 38

38458 8

③
39120 3
39325
39326 7

55060 0 55048 8
39275 0 39240 8

89124 6
39320 7

9 39525 6

39420 4

40043 1
40030 1

NEU
40045 5
40031 8

47080 3 ④
40063 9

40162 9 40144 5
40130 8 47660 3

40630 3

41040 9
41022 5

101

41160 4
41130 7
NEU
41122 2
41140 6

42035 4
42022 4

42022 4
42036 1

41230 4

42036 1

42125 2
42225 9

42330 0

43025 4

43035 3
43185 7

43858 7
43526 6

43460 9

43560 0
43530 3

43858 8
43526 7

44030 7

44530 2

44630 9

44652 1
44644 6
44728 3

44660 4
44732 0
44650 5

N
44732 0

NEU
47825 6
45035 1

45665 0
45526 4

46023 7
46542 3
46030 5

46842 0
46123 4
46170 8

46123 4

4
46148 7

461708
461234

46240 8
46624 6
46250 7
46642 0

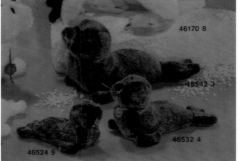

46170 8
46542 3
46532 4
46524 9

46842 0
46148 7
46123 4
46565 5
46532 1
46624 6
46524 9

47560 6

47660 3

NEU
47675 7

NEU
47825 6

47840 9

47850 8

77628 4

47865 2

48030 3

48130 0

48530 8

48660 2

48730 2

50040 7

50140

50235 7

50245 6

50335 4

55060 0

50530 3

50535 8

50630 0

50635 5

50730 7

51035 2

104

51545 6

51550 0

③

52040 5

52145 7

52

52540 0

52552 3

52635 3

NEO

52760 2

51545 6

52145 7

52735 0

53040 4

53050 3

53630 7

53830 1

53730 4

8

53730 4

53530 0

17

53930 8

53830 1

54025 0

54525 5

54515 6

55655 8

55048 8

55760 9

56035 7

56080 7

56081 4

56135 4

56555 0

46123 4   46148 7

57040 0

57050 9

60020 6   60015 2

63130 9

61222 3

61022 9   61122 6

62120 1

62220 8

64231 2

64326 5

62420 2

62320 5

71509 2   71609 9

106

63030 2

63130 9

② 63230 6

63231 3

64231 2

② 63330 3

71509 2

63540 6

64022 6

④ 64325 8 64230 5

② 65040 9

67017 9

6 3 67115 2

67212 8

67316 3

67413 9

67527 3

67613 3

69015 3 69020 7

70001 2 70002 9

70004 3 70003 6

70005 0

70016 6 70017 3 70021 0

70020 3

70022 7

70015 6 70115 8 70415 7 70515 4
70324 2 70215 3 70615 1

711100

71509 2 71609 9

712107

71825 3 71925 0 71920 5
71920 8 72020 1 71720 1

72616 0 74112 1
72515 2

72518 3

72625 8

72616 6

74112 1

73020 0

73022 4

73023 1

73024 8

73040 8

74122 0

74112 1   74116 9

74313 2

74316 3

74322 4

74330 9

74335 4

74528 0   74628 7   74728 4

74828 1

75120 5

74829 8

76414 4

75317 9

76120 4

75418 3

27

75526 5

75724 5

75122 9

75328 5

75220 2

75614 9

75618

75818 1

75420

5

75525 8

75607 1

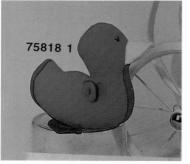

75818 1

75525 8

76020 7

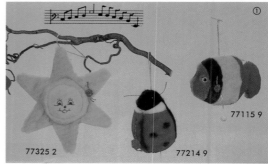

77325 2

77214 9

77115 9

77322 5

77325 2

77031 2

77214 9

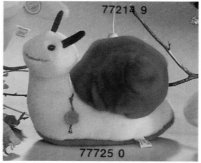

77214 9

77725 0

628 4

77325 2

78925 3

79025 9

78725 9

78825 6

78625 2

78525 5

8003

80535 9

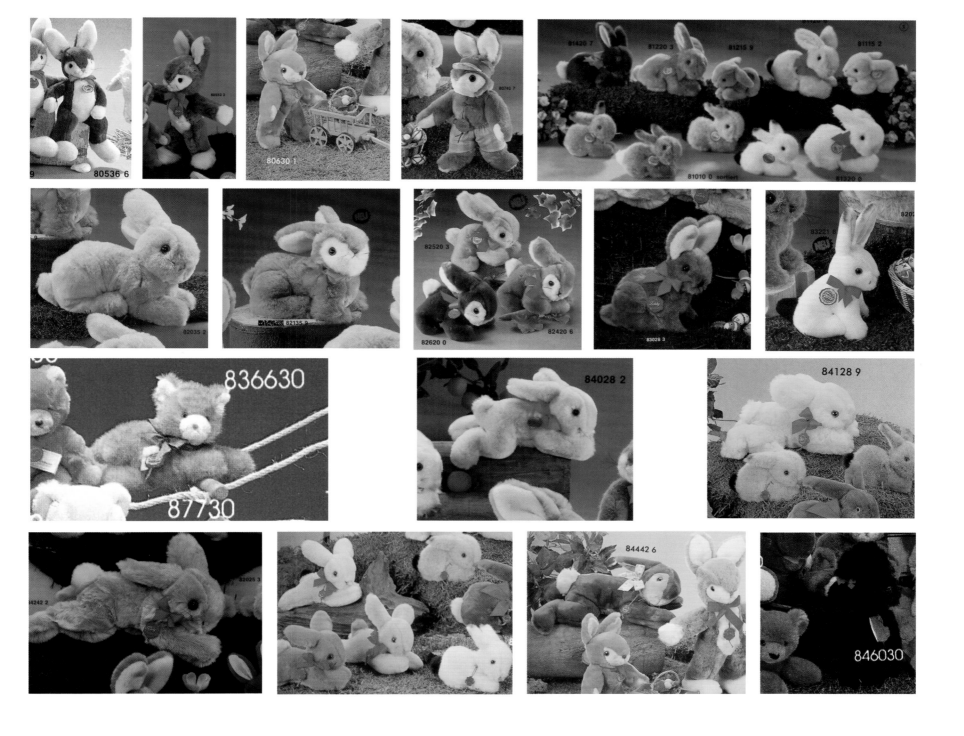

80536 6

80550 2

80630 1

80740 7

81420 7   81220 3   81215 9   81115 2

81010 0 sortiert   81320 0

82035 2

82135 9

82520 3   82420 6   82620 0

83028 3

83221   8202

836630

87730

84028 2

84128 9

84242 2   82025 3

84442 6

846030

85023 6

850236

85025 0

85138 7

86020 4

86012 9

86024 2

86040 2

86160 7

73040 8

86228 4

45035

862635

86530 8

86560 5

86630 5

86732 6

spiel gut

87012 8
4-fach sortiert

87015 9

87020 3

87025 8

87026 5

87116 3

87216 0

87316 7

87015 9

6 3

87416 4

87630 4

88022 6

88035 6

3

88135 3

88225 1

88325 8

88326 5

88350 0

88225 1

88503 0

88510 8

NEU

89055 3

89024 9

89124 6

89530 5

89540 4

89540 4

90012 2

90027 6

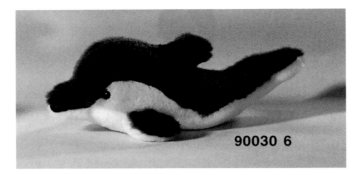

90030 6

90048 1

90065 8

90065 8

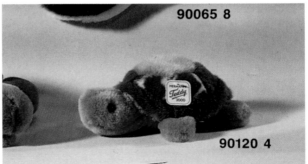

90120 4

90128 0

012 2   90132 7

90240 9

90224 9

90225 6

90225 6

90228 7

90230 0

90231 7

90240 9

114

90250 8

90324 6

90325 3

90355 0

90425 0

90426 7

90430 4

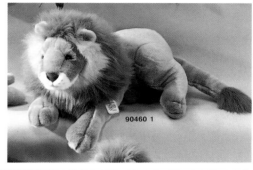

90460 1

90425 0

90426 7

90461 8

90462 5

90468 7

90501 1

90502 8

90510 3 6-fach sortiert

90517 2
4-fach sortier

2

90582 0

90625 4

90634 6

90635 3

90720 6

90730 5

90750 3

90760 2

90824 1

94550 5

94518

90925 5

90825 8

90835 7

90838 8

90932 3

90940 8

91022 0

91035 0

91040 4

91045 9

91070 1

91108 1

9

91115 9

91123 4

91125 8

91129 6

91132 6

91136 4

91220 0

91225 5

91230 9

91238 5

91244 6

91254 5

91268 2

91330 6
beige u. braun
sortiert

91342 9

91420 4

117

91430 3

91432 7

91535 5

91640 6

91730 4

91755 7

91840 0

91916 2

91925 4

91945 2

91965 0

92018 2

92121 9

92222 3

92420 3

91420

92430 2

92440 1

92530 9

09

93022 8

92532 3

92612 2
grau u. weiß
sortiert

92617 7

92625 2

92725 9

92720 4

92725 9

92730 3

92730 3

92825 6

91430 3

92935 2

93020 4

93022 8

93025 9

90250 8

93055 6

93415 8

93112 6

93114 0

93124 9

93125 6

93415 8

93424 0

93630 5

93518 6

93612 1

93618 3

93615 2

93618 3

625 1

936

93630 5

93725 8

94518 5

94

94020 3

94516 1

93020 4

94115 6

94120 0

94516 1

94518 5

120

94550 5

9

MINI · PORZELLAN · SET

95001 1

④

NEU

⑨

95002 5

③

95007 3

95005 9

95006 6

95021 9

HERMANN *Teddy* ORIGINAL

95023 3

③

95204 6

95029 5

95027 1

NEU

NEU

95031 8

95020 1

95022 2

95037 0

95038 7

⑮

95043 9

95042 2

95040 8

95041 5

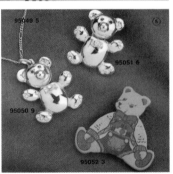

95049 5

Ⓢ

95051 6

95050 9

95052 3

NEU

⑥

95054 7

95053 0

⑤

95101 8

95201 5

95203 9

10833 7

95105 6

95106 3

1511

95120 9   95121 6

95201 5   95203 9

95204 6

95303 6   95302 9   95311 1

95601 3   95602 0   95603 7

NEU

Exklusiv
für unsere Teddys
Strickkleidung passend
für die Bärengrößen
30 cm, 40 cm und 50 cm.

Bärige Teddy-Moden

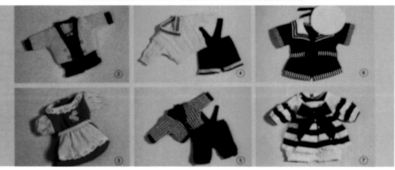

98001 8

98002 5

98003 2

98004 9

NEU

98013 1   98014 8   98007 0   98009 4   98010 0

17841 5   17840 8

98012 4
Poster DIN A2

98150 3 Teddy-Buch deutsch
98151 0 Teddy-Buch englisch

982104   98211 1

98212 8
98230 2

99001 7

98004 9

99002 4

98002 5

99003 1

98003 2

99004 8

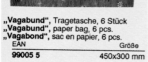

„Vagabund", Tragetasche, 6 Stück
„Vagabund", paper bag, 6 pcs.
„Vagabond", sac en papier, 6 pcs.
EAN   Größe
99005 5   450x300 mm

98001 8

99005 5

98003 2

99006 2

98001 8   98005 6

99008 6   99009 3

98006 3   98004 9

99010 7   99011 4

99016 1
3x 4 Motive sortiert

Chapter 5: Jesco/Rubin and Kathy Ann Dolls Teddy Bears

The first three illustrations show the cloth arm tags found on the Jesco/Rubin products. They are followed by pictures of Jesco/Rubin and Kathy Ann Teddy Bears.

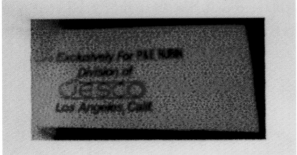

Jesco arm tag.

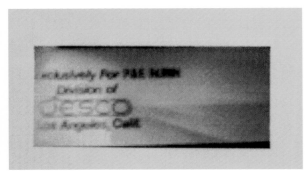

Jesco Division of Rubin arm tag.

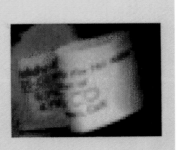

Combination of Teddy Hermann and Jesco arm tags.

CA140

CH80

CH140

CI80

CI140

733

GO80

GR140

GR100

GR80

HOOO1

HOOO2

. . . Home for the Holidays . .

LI40

LI 75

LI140

55

LI140N

340

GR80

NO70

NO75

S 0002

S0003

SU40

SU55

SU

SU70

SU

SU 70

SU75

SU 75

SU80

SU 80LI

SU100

SU 100LI

SU120

SU140

SU 140W

SU190

SU240

TS001

Chapter 6: Bears with Unidentified Model Numbers

MRF "B"

MRF "C"

MRF "D"

MRF "E"

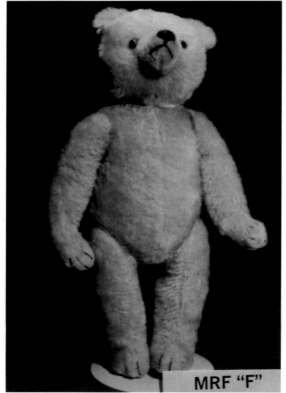

MRF "F"

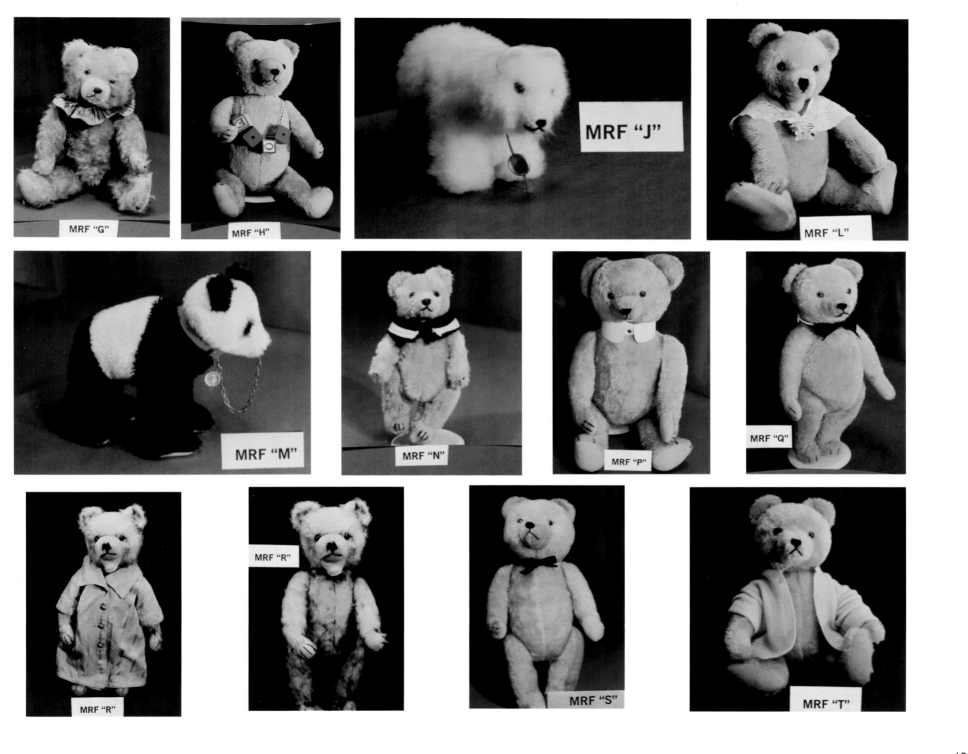

MRF "G"

MRF "H"

MRF "J"

MRF "L"

MRF "M"

MRF "N"

MRF "P"

MRF "Q"

MRF "R"

MRF "R"

MRF "S"

MRF "T"

MRF "Z"

MRF "AA"

MRF "AB"

MRF "AE"

MRF "AF"

MRF "AG"

MRF "AH"

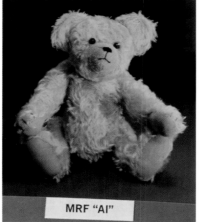

MRF "AI"

MRF "AJ"

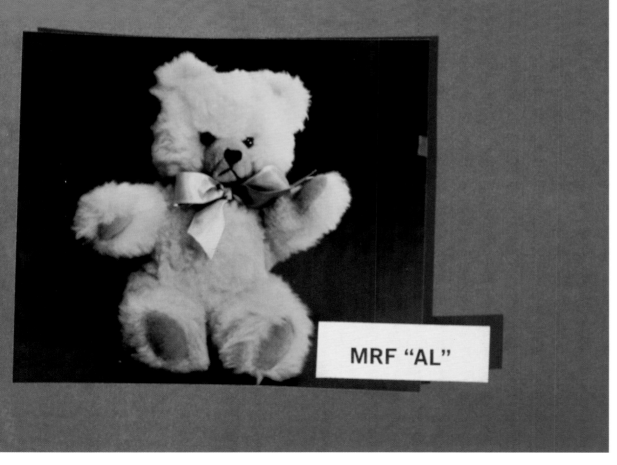

MRF "AL"

MRF "AM"

MRF "AN"

MRF "AO"

MRF "AP"

Listings

Chapter 7: Numerical Listing of Teddy Bears

"Book" refers to *Tales of Teddy Hermann* (see Bibliography for other abbreviations), "K" in number refers to transparent plastic packaging, and "MRF" refers to the author's initials.

Many times the same "EAN #" or "OLD #" was used more than once for different bears. In addition, the same bear design can have many different numbers, either in "EAN #" or "OLD #". Refer to 060/33, for example.

"EAN" numbers starting with zero are special occasion issues, are for someone else, or were sold under someone else's name

REF #	EAN #	HERMANN OLD #	ALSO SEE	LIMITED NUMBER	DATA FROM	NAME	INCHES TALL	DESCRIPTION	VOICE	HANGING BOOKLET	ARM TAG	COMPANY LOGO	CURRENT RETAIL
5	No #			UNIQUE	HERMANN 1997 DATA	PETER PAN	7.87	DRESSED AS PETER PAN; FOR LASTING OF JAPAN, NEVER PRODUCED - SAMPLE ONLY					NA
6	No #			UNIQUE	HERMANN 1997 DATA	ONE-OF-A-KIND	19.69	BLK EYES, BURGUNDY PADS, ROSE TIPPED MOHAIR, LEFT PAW PAD EMBROIDERED; FOR HUIS TEN BOSCH, JAPAN			RED	HD+RED PL	NA
7	01009 0			2	HERMANN 1998 DATA	SCHOOLHOUSE, 2 STORY		SPECIAL EXHIBITION SCHOOLHOUSE FOR DISPLAY; FOR GERMAN DEP'T STORE DEALER & THIS AUTHOR			RED	HD+RED PL	$3,600
8	01014 0			300	HERMANN 1998 DATA	ROSABELLE	15.75	ROSE MOHAIR W/EXCELSIOR STUFFING, BRN NOSE, BLK EYES, SPECIAL FOR JAPAN		YES	YES	HD+RED PL	$250
9	01092 9			500	HERMANN 1998 DATA	KATHLEEN	13.8	W/MUSIC BOX "I WILL TAKE YOU HOME AGAIN, KATHLEEN"; FOR TEL OF IRELAND	MUSIC	YES	RED	HD+RED PL	$250/$350
10	01093 5			300	HERMANN 1998 DATA	DANNY BOY	13.8	GRN ENGLISH MOHAIR W/BLK EYES, WHT PAWS, ORANGE BOW; FOR TEL OF IRELAND	MUSIC	YES	RED	HD+RED PL	$250/$350
11	01150 1			50	HERMANN 1998 DATA	IRISH TEDDY BEAR	5.9	WHT MOHAIR W/BLK EYES, ORANGE NOSE, GRN BOW; FOR TEL OF IRELAND	NONE	YES	RED	RED PLASTIC	$100/$200
12	01151 7K			300	HERMANN 1995 DATA	COFFEE BEAN BEAR	6.69	11517 5 W/BURLAP PANTS, HAT & SACK; FOR TEL OF IRELAND	NONE	YES	RED	RED PLASTIC	$150/200
13	01182 5			200	HERMANN 1997 DATA	TEDDY BEAR	9.84	ROSE PLUSH, BLK EYES, BURGUNDY SOLES, LTD # IN LEFT SOLE; FOR JAPANESE FIRM LASTING					$200/300
14	01193 1			100	HERMANN 1996 DATA	TEDDY BEAR	11.8	ROSE MOHAIR, BLK EYES, "IZU MUSEUM 1ST ANNIV" ON SOLE; FOR IZU MUSEUM, JAPAN					$250/350
15	01193 1			150	HERMANN 1995	COCOA, TOLEDO TOY STORE	11.8	DARK BRN LONG PILE, FELT PADS, FULLY JTD, TAN POLKA DOT TIE; HERMANN SISTERS TOUR OF USA, 1995	NONE	NONE	RED	HD+RED PL	$180
16	01193 2			75	HERMANN 1997 DATA	HENNEF (TOTAL SHOW)	11.8	LT BEIGE W/GRN STRIPED OVERALLS; FOR "TEDDYBEAR TOTAL" 1997	NONE	YES	RED	HD+RED PL	$250
17	01204 0			500	HERMANN 1994 DATA	HARRY	15.75	PLAID SMOCK W/GOLD PAD; FOR ASQUITH OF HENLEY	GROWLER		RED	RED PLASTIC	$350
18	01204 1			200	HERMANN 1997 DATA	ROSE	15.75	ROSE MOHAIR, WHT SATIN PADS, LTD # IN LEFT SOLE; FOR TAKASHIMAYA OF JAPAN		YES	RED	HD+RED PL	$350
19	01204 2			200	HERMANN 1997 DATA	GRANDPA	15.75	OLD GOLD MOHAIR VEST, GLASSES, NAME & # ON SOLE; FOR ASQUITH OF HENLEY			RED	HD+RED PL	$350
20	01204 3			250	HERMANN 1998 DATA	GRANDMA	15.75	GOLD DISTRESSED MOHAIR, CHECKED SHAWL, W/GLASSES; SPECIAL FOR ASQUITHS		YES	RED	HD+RED PL	$250
21	01230 6			500	GROVE	TEDDY BEAR, MUSICAL	12	RUST 100 % MOHAIR, W/PINK LACE COLLAR, PLAYS TB PICNIC; KATHY ANN IMPORT	MUSIC	YES	RED	RED PLASTIC	$180
22	01243 2			150	1995 DISNEY CONV	HERMANN & MICKEY	17?	HERMANN BEAR PLUS SMALL MICKEY MOUSE					$300/400
23	01245 5			UNIQUE	1995 DISNEY CONV	INT'L PLAYMATES	???	1995 DISNEY CONVENTION AUCTION PIECE; UNIQUE					$1,000+
24	01302 5			200	HERMANN 1998 DATA	TEDDY BEAR	9.8	GOLD DISTRESSED MOHAIR, CINNAMON EMBROIDERED PAWS; FOR LASTING		YES	RED	HD+RED PL	$75
25	01302 9			300	HERMANN 1997 DATA	GARTNERBEAR	11.8	BRN MOHAIR SPECIAL, DRESSED AS GARDENER W/RAKE; FOR KARSTADT	NONE	YES	SPECIAL	RED PLASTIC	$250
26	01303 0			100	HERMANN 1996 DATA	HANS IM GLUCK	11.8	LT BEIGE W/RED BLOUSE & HANDKERCHIEF TIED TO WALKING STICK; FOR KARSTADT	NONE	YES	RED	HD+RED PL	$200
27	01303 1			300	HERMANN 1997 DATA	TEDDY BEAR	11.8	LT GOLDEN BLOND W/GRN RIBBON, BLK PLASTIC SHOE BUTTON EYES; FOR HANLEY OF LONDON	NONE	YES	RED+ HANLEY	HD+RED PL	$162

REF #	EAN #	HERMANN OLD #	ALSO SEE	LIMITED NUMBER	DATA FROM	NAME	INCHES TALL	DESCRIPTION	VOICE	HANGING BOOKLET	ARM TAG	COMPANY LOGO	CURRENT RETAIL
28	01303 2			3000	HERMANN 1998 DATA	FIRE BEAR	11.8	GOLD DISTRESSED MOHAIR IN SOCCER OUTFIT, EMBROIDERED PAWS; FOR LASTING OF JAPAN		YES	RED	HD+RED PL	$195
29	01304 0			500	HERMANN 1997 DATA	BURGFRAÜLEIN	11.8	BROCADE DRESS, CONE SHAPED HAT W/STAND; FOR HUIS TEN BOSCH OF JAPAN	NONE	YES	RED	HD+RED PL	$195
30	01333 4			???	HERMANN 1998 DATA	WANDSBEKER HUSAR	11.8	OLD GOLD MOHAIR IN BLK & GOLD BRAID "DRUM MAJOR" COSTUME					$150/200
31	01361 7			500	HERMANN 1994 DATA	TEDDY BEAR	7.87	ROSE MOHAIR W/LONG DARK BOW, ROSE IN HAIR; NEUSTADTER BARENFESTIVAL '94	NONE	TAG	RED	SML RED PL	$250
32	01363 0			250	HERMANN 1997 DATA	HEART TO HEART	11.8	RED, AS PAIR W/01363 1, BLK SUEDE CLOTH PAWS; ANIMAL KINGDOM, HONG KONG	NONE	YES	RED	HD+RED PL	$165
33	01363 1			250	HERMANN 1997 DATA	HEART TO HEART	11.8	ROSE, AS PAIR W/01363 0, PURPLE SUEDE CLOTH PAWS; ANIMAL KINGDOM, HONG KONG	NONE	YES	RED	HD+RED PL	$165
34	01421 4		14214 0	400	HERMANN 1997	ROSENKAVALIER	5	OLD GOLD CARRYING BOUQUET OF ROSES, WEARS STRAW HAT	NONE	YES	RED	RED PLASTIC	$165
35	01423 2			2,000	HERMANN 1997 DATA	ROSENKAVALIER	11.8	OLD GOLD CARRYING BOUQUET OF ROSES, WEARS STRAW HAT; FOR HERTIE, GERMANY	GROWLER	YES	RED	HD+RED PL	$250
36	01432 5			200	HERMANN 1997 DATA	NIEDIEK	9.8	CURLY MOHAIR, SOLE EMBROIDERED W NAME; FOR GRIMES IN GREFORTH					$275
37	01473 2			300	HERMANN 1996 DATA	TEDDY BEAR	11.8	CURLY MOHAIR, CLIPPED MUZZLE, BRN EYES, # ON SOLE; FOR BOTTJER FIRM	?	YES	RED	HD+RED PL	$300
38	01483 0			50	HERMANN 1994 DATA	TEDDY BEAR	11.8	DATA EMBROIDERED ON FELT APRON, SEE PG 159 OF "BIG BEAR BOOK"; FOR ROTHENBERG DOLL & TOY MUSEUM	?	NO	RED	RED PLASTIC	$300
39	01483 6		14836 4	150	HERMANN 1995	HALLOWEEN WITCH	11.8	GOLD, POINTED BARE MUZZLE, DRESSED AS WITCH, W/EXTERNAL SQUEAKER, EMBROIDERED ON PAD	GROWLER	YES	RED	HD+RED PL	$299
40	01493 5			150	HERMANN 1996 DATA	PEACH FUZZ	13.9	PEACH MOHAIR, BLK EYES, EMBROIDERED PAW W/JUNIPER TREE; FOR JUNIPER TREE, ATLANTA, GA	GROWLER	YES	RED	HD+RED PL	$230
41	01493 6			300	HERMANN 1998 DATA	TEDDY BEAR	13.8	MOHAIR W/GRN SUEDE EMBROIDERED PAWS, GRN/GOLD BOW; FOR BENTALLS OF LONDON		YES	RED	HD+RED PL	$250
42	01495 0			200	HERMANN 1996 DATA	TEDDY BEAR	11.8	"TATESHINA 1ST ANNIV 1996/7/21" ON SOLE, SMOKY BLUE MOHAIR; FOR TATESHINA MUSEUM, JAPAN	?	YES	RED	HD+RED PL	$250
43		015/30			1983 PRICE LIST	BISON							
44	01512 3				HERMANN	POLDI BEAR	8.7	CURLY MOHAIR CINNAMON, PLAID LONG RIBBON ENDING IN BELL AT EACH END	NONE	YES	RED	HEAD	$130
45	01514 0			50	HERMANN 1995	WEINBRANDT	15.75	CARAMEL MOHAIR W/STRIPED GREY/BLK VEST & BEAR PIN; USA ONLY	GROWLER	NONE	RED	HD+SM RD PL	$275
46	01522 5			300	HERMANN 1997 DATA	KUSCHWEBEL "OLLI"	7.9	PLAID TIE, CURLY MOHAIR, BEIGE PADS; FOR KARSTADT	NONE	YES	SPECIAL	HD+SM RD PL	$199
47	01522 9			300	HERMANN 1997 DATA	BOTTJER BEAR	11.8	BIG BLK EYES W/ SHAVED NOSE, NUMBERED ON RT PAW; FOR BOTTJER FIRM		YES	RED	HD+RED PL	$250
48	01523 2			100	HERMANN 1997 DATA	PALLI-TEDDY	11.8	BLK MOHAIR, "DAS SPIELHAUS" ON ONE PAD, 1957-1997 ON OTHER; FOR PALLENDORF IN VIENNA	?	CERT.	RED	HD+RED PL	$250
49	01563 0				HERMANN 1996 BEAR	NEUSTADT BEAR	11.8	ROSE MOHAIR, "BAREN FESTIVAL / 1996" ON RT PAW, LTD DATA EMBROIDERED ON LEFT PAW	NONE	YES	RED	HD+RED PL	$150
50	01611 7			300	HERMANN 1995	TEDDYBAR TOTAL 95	6.5	NOUGAT HEAD, ARMS & LEGS, YELLOW BODY, 15703 8 ATTACHED	NONE	LTD ONLY	BRN	SML RD PL	$100
51	01623 0			500	HERMANN 1996 DATA	ETERNITY BEAR	11.8	PURPLE CURLY MOHAIR, BLK EYES, NAME EMBROIDERED ON SOLE; FOR CALVIN LI (ANIMAL KINGDOM), HONG KONG	GROWLER	YES	RED	HD+RED PL	$165
52	01623 1			1950	HERMANN 1998 DATA	STRATFORD UPON AVON	15.75	FULLY JTD, MOHAIR, BLK/GOLD COLLAR, EMBROIDERED PAWS; FOR TEDDY BEAR MUSEUM		YES	RED	HD+RED PL	$250
53	01623 8			NO LIMIT	HERMANN 1997 DATA	LINA	11.8	STRAW HAT/STRIPED DRESS, GIVEN AWAY AT HOSPITALS; FOR FRAU MARKERT TO DISTRIBUTE			RED	RED PLASTIC	$125
54	01624 1			50	HERMANN 1998 DATA	STRATFORD UPON AVON	11.8	FULLY JTD, MOHAIR, BLK/GOLD COLLAR, EMBROIDERED PAWS; FOR TEDDY BEAR MUSEUM		YES	RED	HD+RED PL	$180
55	01628 0		70007/45	UNIQUE	1989 DISNEY CONV	TEDDY BEAR	31.5	AUCTION PIECE, NO DETAILED INFO					
56	01632?		16913 0	300	HERMANN 1997 DATA	HUMMEL-HUMMEL	13.4	SAME AS 16913 0, ALSO FOR KARSTADT; FOR KARSTADT OF HAMBURG	?	YES	RED	?	$300
57	01632 0			1,000	BOOK PG 85, 1993 MFD	MÜNCHNER KINDL	7.87	ANT. GOLD BEAR IN HACKER-PSCHORR MUG, CAPUCHIN CLOAK; KARSTADT DEPT STORE	NONE	NO	RED	HD+RED PL	$171
58	01633 0			100	1994 DISNEY COVER LETTER	WINTER DREAM	11.8	ANT GOLD DRESSED IN SANTA COAT W/MUFF	NONE	NO	RED	HD+RED PL	$195
59	01633 0			200	HERMANN 1998 DATA	GOLD-WORKER	11.8	FULLY JTD MOHAIR BEAR W/LT SUEDE PAWS, GOLDSCHLAGERS OUTFIT, FOR POLSTER OF SCHWABACH		YES	YES	HD+RED PL	$180
60	01633 1			1,000	HERMANN	TEDDY BEAR	11.8	ANTIQUE GOLD, W/BELL ON VELVET TIE	GROWLER	YES	RED	HD+RED PL	$100
61	01633 3			100	HERMANN 1993	BIMBO "ERICA"	11.8	ANTIQUE GOLD, PAW EMBROIDERED "BIMBO 5.10.93"; FOR APELDORN HOLLAND	GROWLER	YES	RED	HD+RED PL	$200/300
62	01633 5			???	HERMANN 1998 DATA	KOLNER-DOMBAU-BEAR	11.8	ANT GOLD, STONE MASON COSTUME; COLOGNE CATHEDRAL WORKER			RED	HD+RED PL	$200/300

REF #	EAN #	HERMANN OLD #	ALSO SEE	LIMITED NUMBER	DATA FROM	NAME	INCHES TALL	DESCRIPTION	VOICE	HANGING BOOKLET	ARM TAG	COMPANY LOGO	CURRENT RETAIL
63	01633 6			888	HERMANN 1996 DATA	SINGAPORE LION BEAR	14.2	ANTIQUE GOLD W/RED + WHT RIBBON, EMBROIDERED PAWS; FOR CLASSIC TEDDY BEARS, SINGAPORE	GROWLER	YES	RED	MTL HEAD	$211
64	01634-1			500	DISCONTINUED 1995	BERLIN "4-SECTIONS BEAR"	15	ANTIQUE GOLD W/CROWN + 4 SECTOR FLAGS ON EACH PAW	GROWLER	NO	RED	HD+RED PL	$250
65	01635 1		01633 0		1994 DISNEY CONV	TEDDY BEAR	14.2	AUCTION PIECE FOR 1994 DISNEY			RED	HD+RED PL	
66	01769 9			UNIQUE	HERMANN 1996 DATA	TEDDY FOR AUCTION	59	MOHAIR, BRN EYES, BLK NOSE, SINGAPORE LION; FOR CLASSIC TEDDY BEARS, SINGAPORE	?	?	RED	HD+RED PL	
67	01803 7			300	HERMANN 1997 DATA	KLINGENBERG MUSEUM	15.75	THEIR DESIGN, DARK BRN MOHAIR OPEN MOUTH, BLK EYES, BRN & WHT CORD BOW	?	YES	RED	HD+RED PL	$250
68	01954 1			50	HERMANN 1996 DATA	TEDDY COUGAR	15.75	BRN SPOTTED MOHAIR, BRN EYES, BEIGE BOW; FOR 1996 TEDDYBEAR TOTAL, HENNEF	GROWLER	YES	RED	RED PLASTIC	$140
69	01954 29			50	HERMANN 1996 DATA	TEDDY TIGER	15.75	WHT STRIPED MOHAIR, BRN EYES, RED SUEDE BOW; FOR 1996 TEDDYBEAR TOTAL, HENNEF	GROWLER	YES	RED	GOLD PLASTIC	$140
70	01954 36			50	HERMANN 1996 DATA	TEDDY LEOPARD	15.75	SPOTTED MOHAIR, BRN EYES, BEIGE SUEDE BOW; FOR 1996 TEDDYBEAR TOTAL, HENNEF	GROWLER	YES	RED	RED PLASTIC	$140
71	02002 8			300	1997 DISNEY CONV	WINNIE THE STUDENT	9.84	ANTIQUE GOLD W/RED SWEATER, SEATED AT DESK W/SLATE & BACKPACK; 1997 DISNEY CONVENTION	NONE	YES	RED	HD+RED PL	$264
72	02003			UNIQUE	HERMANN 1997 DATA	DISNEY AUCTION PIECE	?	WINNIE'S TREE HOUSE W/WINNIE, PIGLET, DONKEY, ETC.; UNIQUE FOR DISNEY AUCTION					
73	02010			500	1997 DISNEY CONV	WINNIE	11.8	POOH BEAR W/RED T-SHIRT & CERAMIC HONEY POT; FOR PANG OF SINGAPORE	?	?	RED	HD+RED PL	$275
74	O2015 8		02016 5	300	1998 DISNEY CONV	WINNIE, THE SAILOR	12.6	POOH BEAR W/ SAILOR SUIT AND PIGLET (02016 5); SOLD AS A PAIR, DBL TAG DISNEY & HERMANN	NONE	YES	DBL	HD+RED PL.	$283
75	02016 5		02015 8	300	1998 DISNEY CONV	PIGLET	7.9	PIGLET W/SAILOR HAT & COLLAR AND POOH (02015 8); SOLD AS A PAIR, DBL TAG DISNEY & HERMANN	NONE	YES	DBL	HD+RED PL.	NA
76	02035		020/35	200	1985 BEAR	TEDDY BEAR 1985 CONF	11	GREY LLAMA WOOL (62% LLAMA W/38% C) FOR 1ST ANNUAL ARTISTS CONF; SIMILAR TO 1985 ROWBEAR LOWMAN	GROWLER	YES	GRN	RED PLASTIC	$275
77		02/60			1982 PRICE LIST	DONKEY	23.62						$50
78		02/65			1982 PRICE LIST	ELEPHANT	25.6						$50
79		021/30			1986 PRICE LIST	KIWI BIRD	11.8	GOLD					$50
80		021/30/3			1986 PRICE LIST	KIWI BIRD	11.8	BRN					$50
81		03/38			1982 PRICE LIST	CHILD'S CUSHION	14.2	BLUE					$50
82		03/38			1982 PRICE LIST	CHILD'S CUSHION	15	GOLD					$50
83	03060 7		73360F	500	KATHY ANN CAT 1989	RIDING BEAR	23.62	DARK BRN MOHAIR ON WOODEN WHEELS; ALSO SEE 70330/60		YES	RED	RED PLASTIC	$275
84		4/25	20025 3		1982 PRICE LIST	TEDDY BEAR	10.2	WASHABLE, MINK PLUSH					$25
85	04025		040/25		SEE 70062/20	SWEETHEART BEAR	7.75	RED					$25
86		4/30			1982 PRICE LIST	TEDDY BEAR	11.8	SEE 20030 7					$25
87		4/35			1982 PRICE LIST	TEDDY BEAR	14.2	SEE 20035 2					$25
88	04035 4		70084/35	500	HERMANN 1987/LTR	ZOTTY, USA EXCLUSIVE	14.2	BRN TIPPED, TAUPE PADS AND MUZZLE, ARM PADS ON BOTTOM SEAM; SPECIAL MOHAIR	GROWLER	YES	RED	RED PLASTIC	$150
89		5/23			BEHA CATALOG 1927	YOUNGBEAR	8.66	COMIC EYES & SHAPE W/PACIFIER, SOFT STUFFING, WOOL PLUSH, GOLDEN YELLOW?	GROWLER		RED		
90		5/26			BEHA CATALOG 1927	YOUNGBEAR	10.2	COMIC EYES & SHAPE W/PACIFIER, SOFT STUFFING, WOOL PLUSH, GOLDEN YELLOW?	GROWLER		RED		
91		5/30			BEHA CATALOG 1927	YOUNGBEAR	11.8	COMIC EYES & SHAPE W/PACIFIER, SOFT STUFFING, WOOL PLUSH, GOLDEN YELLOW?	GROWLER		RED		
92		5/34			BEHA CATALOG 1927	YOUNGBEAR	12.6	COMIC EYES & SHAPE W/PACIFIER, SOFT STUFFING, WOOL PLUSH, GOLDEN YELLOW?	GROWLER		RED		
93		5/50			1982 PRICE LIST	TEDDY, LARGE	19.7	CINNAMON TIPPED MOHAIR, FULLY JTD, RED BOW TIE				RED PLASTIC	$26
94		5/60			1982 PRICE LIST	TEDDY, LARGE	23.6	CINNAMON TIPPED MOHAIR, FULLY JTD, RED BOW TIE	NONE	YES	NONE	GRN PAPER	$35
95		5/70			1982 PRICE LIST	TEDDY, LARGE	27.6	CINNAMON TIPPED MOHAIR, FULLY JTD, RED BOW TIE					$43
96		5/90			1986 CATALOG	TEDDY, LARGE	35.5	CINNAMON TIPPED MOHAIR, FULLY JTD, RED BOW TIE				RED PLASTIC	$45
97		5/90/2			1982 PRICE LIST	TEDDY, LARGE	35.5	CINNAMON TIPPED MOHAIR, FULLY JTD, RED BOW TIE					$45
98	05135 0		06380 7	500	1990 DISNEY CONV	DAISY	12.6	CREAM W/CONVENTION MEDALLION; CONVENTION BEAR	GROWLER	YES	RED	RED PLASTIC	$150
99	05229 3			100	1993 DISNEY CONV	AUTUMN WIND	11.8	CINNAMON TIPPED MOHAIR, 1993 DISNEY CONVENTION MEDAL; CONVENTION BEAR	NONE	YES	RED	RED PLASTIC	$300
100	05230 7			100	1992 DISNEY CONV	SUMMER JOY	11.8	BEACH BOY IN BIKINI W/TOWEL, CREAM W/CONVENTION MEDALLION, SIGNED PAW	NONE	YES	RED	RED PLASTIC	$175
101	05235 7			200	1991 DISNEY CONV	PINK BLOSSOM	14.2	"PINK BLOSSOM OF SPRING", IVORY MOHAIR, PINK DRESS & ROSES, CONV MEDALLIONS	GROWLER	NONE	RED	RED PLASTIC	$150
102	05260 9		05235 7	UNIQUE	1991 DISNEY	TEDDY BEAR	23.6	AUCTION PIECE FOR 1991 DISNEY CONVENTION					$1,000+
103		6/23			BEHA CATALOG 1940'S	YOUNGBEAR	8.8	COMIC EYES & SHAPE, WOOL PLUSH, SOFT STUFFED IN REMOVABLE PANTALOONS OR APRON	GROWLER			HANGING	$400/500

REF #	EAN #	HERMANN OLD #	ALSO SEE	LIMITED NUMBER	DATA FROM	NAME	INCHES TALL	DESCRIPTION	VOICE	HANGING BOOKLET	ARM TAG	COMPANY LOGO	CURRENT RETAIL
104		6/23			BEHA CATALOG 1940'S	YOUNGBEAR	9.8	COMIC EYES & SHAPE, WOOL PLUSH, SOFT STUFFED IN REMOVABLE PANTALOONS OR APRON	GROWLER			HANGING	$400/500
105		6/23			BEHA CATALOG 1940'S	YOUNGBEAR	11.8	COMIC EYES & SHAPE, WOOL PLUSH, SOFT STUFFED IN REMOVABLE PANTALOONS OR APRON	GROWLER			HANGING	$400/500
106		6/23			BEHA CATALOG 1940'S	YOUNGBEAR	13.4	COMIC EYES & SHAPE, WOOL PLUSH, SOFT STUFFED IN REMOVABLE PANTALOONS OR APRON	GROWLER			HANGING	$400/500
107		060/33		3,000	HERMANN 1986	HELEN SIEVERLING	13	CREAM MOHAIR, ALSO SEE 60/33 & 861/30, SIGNED TAG; 1930 REPLICA	GROWLER	YES	BRN	RED PLASTIC	$150
108	06017 2			500	HERMANN 1992 DATA	FELDHAUS	6.69	CINNAMON MOHAIR, IN PLASTIC BOX W/HANGING TAG; FOR SPIELWAREN FELDHAUS 150TH ANNIVERSARY		YES	RED	RED PLASTIC	
109	06220 1	CAT SAYS 06220 2?		2,000	MRF COLLECTION	ORIGINAL HERMANN	7.9	BRN	NONE	YES	RED	SML RED PL	$75
110	06220 2			2,000	KATHY ANN CAT 1989	ORIGINAL HERMANN	7.9	BRN	NONE	YES	RED	SML RED PL	$75
111	06230 1			2,000	KATHY ANN CAT 1989	ORIGINAL HERMANN	11.8	BRN MOHAIR WITH PLAID TIE, LIGHT TAN PADS	GROWLER	YES	RED	RED PLASTIC	$75
112	06235 6			2,000	KATHY ANN CAT 1989	TOUGH RUDY	13.8	BRN DISTRESSED MOHAIR W/BRN & WHT CORD TIE, GRAY FELT PADS	GROWLER	YES	RED	RED PLASTIC	$140
113	06240 0			2,000	MRF COLLECTION	LEO BEAR	15.8	DARK BRN MOHAIR W/BEIGE SUEDE PADS, PLAID BOW; DEPT STORE SPECIAL	GROWLER	YES	RED	MTL+RED PL	$195
114	06240 0				KATHY ANN CAT 1989	TEDDY BEAR	15.8	BRN MOHAIR W/PLAID TIE, LT TAN PADS					$150
115	06380 0		16380 0	500	KATHY ANN CAT 1989	TEDDY BEAR	31.5	OLD GOLD MOHAIR, FULLY JTD, RED BOW TIE, ORANGE-TAN PAWS	GROWLER	YES	RED	RED PLASTIC	$250/350
116	06380 7		05135 0	UNIQUE	1990 DISNEY AUCTION	DAISY'S PICNIC	31.5	RD HAT, WHT LACE COLLAR ON CHECKED CLOTH W/PICNIC BASKET					$1,000+
117	06755				1990? JESCO	TEDDY BEAR	22	HONEY W/VEST					$200
118	07223			1,000	HOCKENBERRY	TEDDY BEAR	7.9	TIPPED MOHAIR, ILLUSTRATED PG 156 OF HOCKENBERRY'S *BIG BEAR BOOK*, 1994 WENZ CO.	?	YES	RED	RED PLASTIC	$125
119	07225			1,000	BIG BEAR BK, PG 156	TEDDY BEAR CIRCA '94	7.9	TIPPED MOHAIR, PLASTIC EYES		YES	YES	PLASTIC	$125
120	08417 4			500	WOLFF	BRN BEAR	7.5	DARK BRN WITH TAN MUZZLE	NONE	YES	RED	RED PLASTIC	$79
121	08419 8			500	WOLFF	WHT BEAR	7.5	WHT W/BLUE PAW PADS	NONE	YES	RED	RED PLASTIC	$89
122	08635 2			3,000	WOLFF	PANDA BEAR	15	BLK & WHT, OPEN MOUTH	GROWLER	YES	RED	RED PLASTIC	$150
123	095408			500	OWNER + M. HERMANN	TEDDY BEAR	11.8	1992 BLK BEAR W/TAN MOHAIR PAWS, FUNCHIELLO EAR TAG "LORENZ BOLZ, ZIRNDORF TAG", #67 OF 500, 70% ACRYLIC W/DISNEYLAND PRICE TAG					$375
124		10/28			HERMANN CAT 1982	PETZI	14	STORY BOOK FIGURE, SEE BOOK FOR ILLUSTRATION	NONE	PETZI	GRN	PETZI ONLY	$250
125		100/17			BEHA 1927 CATALOG	CAT	6.69	COLORED ARTIFICIAL SILK-PLUSH, ARTIFICIAL SILK RIBBON					$250/350
126		100/20			BEHA 1927 CATALOG	CAT	7.87	COLORED ARTIFICIAL SILK-PLUSH, ARTIFICIAL SILK RIBBON					$250/350
127		100/22			BEHA 1927 CATALOG	CAT	8.66	COLORED ARTIFICIAL SILK-PLUSH, ARTIFICIAL SILK RIBBON					$250/350
128		100/32	80032 3		1985 PRICE LIST	MOTHER RABBIT	12.6						$175
129		100/40/1			HERMANN CAT 1982	TEDDY BEAR	15.75	HONEY W\DARK BRN SNOUT, ARMS AND LOWER TRUNK, UPPER TRUNK IS RED VEST				MTL W/PAPER INSERT	$350
130		1000			1982 PRICE LIST	OWL							$100
131	100010		63/01		HERMANN CAT 1986	NOSTALGIC TEDDY SCHOOL	47 X 21.6 X 12.5	8" BEARS W/DESKS, 6 PUPILS + TEACHER; INCLS 2 BLACKBOARDS; WITH SCHOOLROOM					$750
132	100010		274/100		1988 KATHY ANN	NOSTALGIC TEDDY SCHOOL	47 X 21.6 X 12.5	8" BEARS W/DESKS, 6 PUPILS + TEACHER INCLS 1 BLACKBOARD; NO SCHOOLROOM					$450/550
133	100027	62/14	100034	3,000	BOOK 1989 PG 88	MEIN TEDDYBAR	5.5	DARK BRN PLUSH BEAR IN BOOK, GERMAN					$112
134	100034	62/14	100027	3,000	KATHY ANN CAT 1989	MY TEDDY BEAR BOOK	5.5	DARK BRN PLUSH BEAR IN BOOK, ENGLISH	NONE	BOOK	RED	SML RD PL	$112
135	100119				1992 PRICE LIST	SAILOR BEAR SCHOOL	7.9	1 TEACHER, 6 PUPILS, 15 ITEMS FURNITURE, 2 SCHOOL BAGS, 2 BAGS CANDY					$750
136	100201			500	1995 PRICE LIST	COUNTRY SCHOOL	15.7 X 8.5 X 9.5	1 TEACHER, 3 PUPILS DESKS, ETC.	NONE	NO	RED	SML RED PL	$576
137	100218			1,000	1993 PRICE LIST	MINI TEDDY SCHOOL	24 X 12 X 11	SCHOOLROOM + 7 BEARS, 6" BEARS					$1,102
138	100256			1,000	1996 PRICE LIST	MINI TEDDY SCHOOL	8 X 5 X 5	SCHOOL ROOM + 8CM TEACHER +3 PUPILS 5CM	NONE	NO	NO	SML METAL(1)	$375
139	100258			1,000	1996 PRICE LIST	MINI TEDDY SCHOOL	7.8 L X W X 5.1H	SCHOOL ROOM + 8CM TEACHER +3PUPILS 5CM					$450
140	100263			300	1997 PRICE LIST	FONDUE HALL	15.7 X 8.5 X 9.5	FONDUE PARLOR WITH 3 DIFFERENT COLORED POSEABLE BEARS	NONE	NO	RED	RED PLASTIC	$495
141	100317			1,000	1993 PRICE LIST	MINI TEDDY WORKSHOP	24 X 12 X 11	WORKSHOP + 4 BEARS	NONE	NO	RED	SML RD PL	$1,249
142	100409			50	1997 XMAS FLYER	MINI TEDDY XMAS SCENE	234 X 10 X 11	XMAS FIRESIDE SCENE W/XMAS TREE & 2 BEARS	NONE	NO	RED	RED PLASTIC	$695

REF #	EAN #	HERMANN OLD #	ALSO SEE	LIMITED NUMBER	DATA FROM	NAME	INCHES TALL	DESCRIPTION	VOICE	HANGING BOOKLET	ARM TAG	COMPANY LOGO	CURRENT RETAIL
143	10041 6			333	1993 PRICE LIST	MINI TEDDY SCHOOL	24 X 12 X 11	"MY FRIEND IS A FOREIGNER"	NONE	NO	RED	SML RED PL	$1,500
144	10042 3			1,000	1998 PRICE LIST	PLAY ROOM	7.8L X 6 W X 5.1H	FURNITURE, WOODEN TOYS +2 BEARS	NONE	NO	RED	SML RED PL	$246
145	10043 0			500	1998 PRICE LIST	JOINER'S WORKSHOP	11 X 7.8 X 8	WORKSHOP+1 BEAR	NONE	NO	RED	SML RED PL	$491
146	10044 7			500	1998 PRICE LIST	TEDDY SCHOOL	15.7 X 8.5 X 9.5	SCHOOLROOM+2 STUDENTS+TEACHER	NONE	NO	RED	SML RED PL	$481
147	10050 8			2,000	1995 CATALOG	RATSKELLAR	7.75 X 8 X 10	RATSKELLAR COMPLETE W/ 4 BEARS					$487
148	10051 5			500	1994 PRICE LIST	ELECTION MTG IN RATSKELLAR	7.75 X 8 X 10	RATSKELLAR COMPLETE W/ 4 BEARS	NONE	NO	RED	SML RD PL	$514
149	10060 7			500	HERMANN 1995	BEARY-GO-ROUND	4	3 DIFFERENT COLORS; INCLS 3 BEARS	NONE	NO	RED	SML RD PL	$637
150	10070 6			500	1996 PRICE LIST	FERRIS WHEEL	14.5H	ROTATING MECHANISM W/4 6CM BEARS	MUSIC	NO	NO	SML MTL	$967
151	10071 3			500	1998 PRICE LIST	MINI RR "ADLER"	NA	DESIGNED BY "TUCHER & WALTHER", FOR HERMANN; INCLS 5 MINI BEARS	NONE	NO	NO	SML MTL	$825
152	10075 1				1997 PRICE LIST	AIRPLANE & PILOT		TAIWAN MINIATURE					$248
153	10076 8				1997 PRICE LIST	FIRE DEPT AUTO W/DRIVER		TAIWAN MINIATURE					$210
154	10080 5			1,000	1996 PRICE LIST	TEDDY ON SCOOTER	3	ROTATING SCOOTER, OLD GOLD BEAR, SMALL METAL LOGO ON MECHANISM	NONE	YES	RED	MTL+SML RD	$216
155	10081 2				1997 PRICE LIST	CYCLIST W/SIDECAR	1.5	MINIATURE, IMPORTS FROM CHINA					$165
156	10082 9				1997 PRICE LIST	AUTO RACER	1.5	MINIATURE, IMPORTS FROM CHINA					$230
157	10083 6				1997 PRICE LIST	AUTO RACER	1.5	MINIATURE, IMPORTS FROM CHINA					$165
158	10085 0			1,000	1996 PRICE LIST	SCOOTERIST "ROLFI"	7.5	RIDING ON SCOOTER, OLD GOLD	NONE	YES	RED	MTL+SML RD	$168
159	10090 4			1,000	1997 PRICE LIST	CHINESE BEAR W/BIKE	7 + 3	RIDING ON TRIKE	NONE	YES	RED	MTL+SML RD	$237
160		101/22	80022 4		1985 PRICE LIST	RABBIT, BABY	8.66	RED					$75
161	10120 0					DRESSED GIRL	8	RED DRESS ON OLD GOLD MOHAIR BEAR	NONE	YES	RED	RED PAPER	$85
162	10121 5				1992 PRICE LIST	DRESSED GIRL	8						$85
163	10122 2				TEDDY & CO	HIKING BOY	8.5						$115
164	10123 9				1994 PRICE LIST	DIRNDL	7.9	GOLD W/CHECKED OUTFIT W/LEATHER BACKPACK					$167
165	10124 6				1994 PRICE LIST	SEPPL	7.9	GOLD W/CHECKED OUTFIT W/LEATHER BACKPACK					$167
166		102/22	80122 1		1985 PRICE LIST	RABBIT, BABY	8.66	GOLD					$75
167	10220 5		63/20/2K		1988 CATALOG	SCHOOLGIRL PLASTIC BOX	7.9	OLD MOHAIR PLUSH W/GRN DRESS AND CONE IN PLASTIC BOX	NONE	YES	BRN	RED PAPER	$125
168	10221 2				1992 PRICE LIST	SAILOR GIRL	7.9						$125
169	10222 9				1992 PRICE LIST	SAILOR GIRL	7.9						$125
170	10223 6				1994 PRICE LIST	SCHOOLGIRL	7.9	OLD GOLD, CHECKED APRON BLUE-GRN PLAID DRESS, W/LEATHER KNAPSACK	NONE	YES	RED	HD+SML RD	$167
171	10224 3				1994 PRICE LIST	FAMILY, GIRL	7.9	OLD GOLD, PINK CHECKED DRESS					$167
172		103/40/1			1982 PRICE LIST	BEAR	15.75						$250/350
173		103/40/3			1982 PRICE LIST	MONKEY	15.75						$75/125
174	10320 2		63/20/3K		1988 CATALOG	BOY BEAR PLASTIC BOX	7.9	GOLD MOHAIR IN BLUE PANTS					$167
175	10321 9				1992 PRICE LIST	SAILOR BOY	7.9						$122
176	10322 6				1994 PRICE LIST	FAMILY, BOY	7.9	OLD GOLD, BLUE-GRN PLAID PANTS, W/LEATHER KNAPSACK	NONE	YES	RED	HD+SML RD	$167
177		104/80			1982 PRICE LIST	HARE	31.5						$250/350
178	10420 9		63/20/4K		1988 CATALOG	BABY BEAR PLASTIC BOX	7.9	ANT GOLD MOHAIR IN ROMPER SUIT W/NAVY ANCHOR EMBROIDERY, W/LEATHER KNAPSACK	NONE	YES	BRN	RED PAPER	$167
179	10421 6				1992 PRICE LIST	SAILOR BOY 1994	7.9	ANT GOLD MOHAIR IN ROMPER SUIT W/NAVY ANCHOR EMBROIDERY, W/LEATHER KNAPSACK	NONE	YES	RED	RED PLASTIC	$125
180	10422 3				1994 PRICE LIST	FAMILY, GIRL	7.9	OLD GOLD, PINK CHECKED BLOOMERS					$167
181	10508 4			3,000	1993 PRICE LIST	TEDDY PUPIL W/DESK	4	HONEY	NONE	NO	RED	SML RED PL	$75
182	10514 5			3,000	1994 PRICE LIST	PUPIL AT DESK	5.5	OLD GOLD MOHAIR PLUSH					$149
183	10520 6		63/20/5K		1988 CATALOG	GIRL TEDDY @ DESK,	7.9	GOLD 53% W 47%C MOHAIR, CHECKED ROMPERS, LEATHER BACK PACK, NO LTD MARKINGS, PLASTIC BOX		YES	BRN	RED PLASTIC	$160
184	10521 3				1992 PRICE LIST	TEDDY @ DESK	7.9	IN PLASTIC BOX					$173
185	10522 0				1994 PRICE LIST	PUPIL AT BENCH	7.9	OLD GOLD W/PLAID CLOTHES W/LEATHER BACKPACK					$237
186	10525 1			1,000	1995 PRICE LIST	PIANIST AT PIANO	6	CINNAMON, W/PIANO & BENCH	NONE	NO	RED	SML RED PL	$239
187		106/60			1982 PRICE LIST	HARE	23.6						$200/300
188	10620 3		63/20/6K		1988 CATALOG	HIKING GIRL	7.9	GOLD MOHAIR DRESSED W/ BACK PACK					$150
189	10621 0				1992 PRICE LIST	HIKING GIRL	7.9	MOHAIR DRESSED IN HIKING DRESS IN GLASSINE CASE	NONE	YES	RED	RED PAPER	$121
190	10622 7				1994 PRICE LIST	HIKING GIRL	7.9	GOLD W/CHECKED OUTFIT W/RED SUITCASE	NONE	YES	RED	SML RED PL	$151
191	10720 0		63/20/7K		1988 CATALOG	HIKING BOY	7.9	GOLD MOHAIR DRESSED W/ BACK PACK					$150
192	10721 7				1992 PRICE LIST	HIKING BOY	7.9	MOHAIR DRESSED IN HIKING OUTFIT IN GLASSINE CASE	NONE	YES	RED	RED PAPER	$121
193	10722 4				1994 PRICE LIST	HIKING BOY	7.9	GOLD W/CHECKED OUTFIT W/WHT BACKPACK IN PLASTIC CASE	NONE	YES	RED	RED PLASTIC	$151
194		108/30			1982 PRICE LIST	HARE	11.8						$75/125

REF #	EAN #	HERMANN OLD #	ALSO SEE	LIMITED NUMBER	DATA FROM	NAME	INCHES TALL	DESCRIPTION	VOICE	HANGING BOOKLET	ARM TAG	COMPANY LOGO	CURRENT RETAIL
195		108/40			1982 PRICE LIST	HARE	15.75						$100/150
196		108/45			1982 PRICE LIST	HARE	17.7						$125/175
197	10830 6		63/30/2K		1988 CATALOG	FATHER BEAR PLASTIC BOX	11.8	GOLD MOHAIR					$200/300
198	10831 3				1992 PRICE LIST	TEACHER	11.8	ANTIQUE GOLD, WHT SHIRT, TIE, RED CORDUROY VEST, W/BLUE TROUSERS IN PLASTIC BOX	GROWLER	YES	RED	RED PLASTIC	$150
199	10832 0				1994 PRICE LIST	FAMILY, GIRL	7.9	OLD GOLD, PINKISH DRESS W/RED VEST					$224
200	10833 7				1994 PRICE LIST	TEACHER	12	OLD GOLD, W/GLASSES, RED VEST BRN TROUSERS	GROWLER	YES	RED	HD+SM RD PL	$224
201		109/30			1982 PRICE LIST	HARE, RED	11.8						$100/150
202		109/30/1			1982 PRICE LIST	HARE, GRN	11.8						$100/150
203		109/30/3			1982 PRICE LIST	HARE, VARIEGATED GRN	11.8						$100/150
204	10930 3		63/30/3		1988 CATALOG	NOSTALGIC TEDDY BEAR	11.8	GOLD MOHAIR PLUSH, FULLY JTD, MUSICAL (TEDDY BEAR PICNIC)	MUSIC BOX	YES	BRN	RED PLASTIC	$125
205	10931 0			2,000	1995 CATALOG	NOSTALGIC MUSICAL TEDDY	11.8	GOLD MOHAIR PLUSH W/PRTD RED BOW					$185
206	10932 7			2,000	1996 PRICE LIST	NOSTALGIC MUSICAL TEDDY	11.8	MUSICAL DARK BRN MOHAIR PLUSH, PAW EMBROIDERED	MUSIC	YES	RED	HD+SM RD PL	$185
207	10940 2			1,000	1998 PRICE LIST	NOSTALGIC MUSICAL TEDDY	15.8	MUSICAL OLD GOLD MOHAIR PLUSH, PAW EMBROIDERED	MUSIC	YES	RED	HD+SM RD PL	$202
208		11/35			1982 PRICE LIST	PETZI	14.2	STORY BOOK FIGURE, SEE BOOK FOR ILLUSTRATION					$20
209		110/15			BEHA 1927 CATALOG	CAT AND BALL	6	COLORED ARTIFICIAL SILK-PLUSH					$125/200
210		110/18?			BEHA 1927 CATALOG	CAT AND BALL	7	COLORED ARTIFICIAL SILK-PLUSH					$125/200
211		110/20?			BEHA 1927 CATALOG	CAT AND BALL	7.87	COLORED ARTIFICIAL SILK-PLUSH					$125/200
212		110/23			BEHA 1927 CATALOG	CAT AND BALL	8.66	COLORED ARTIFICIAL SILK-PLUSH					$125/200
213	11028 6			2,000	1997 PRICE LIST	MUSICAL W/TURNING HEAD	11.4	BRN TIPPED MOHAIR, REPLICA 1950S, TURNING HD MUSICAL					$170
214	11033 0			1,500	1998 PRICE LIST	MUSICAL W/TURNING HEAD	11.8	OLD GOLD MOHAIR, REPLICA 1950S, TURNING HD MUSICAL	MUSIC	YES	RED	HD+SML RD	$265
215	11040 8			1,500	1997 PRICE LIST	MUSICAL W/TURNING HEAD	15.75	OLD GOLD MOHAIR, REPLICA 1950S, TURNING HD MUSICAL					$269
216	11200 4			1,000	1996 PRICE LIST	SAILOR GIRL	7.9	DRESSED	NONE	YES	RED	HD+SM RD PL	$135
217	11120 7			1,000	1992 PRICE LIST	SAILOR GIRL	7.9	OLD GOLD IN SAILOR DRESS	NONE	YES	RED	MISSING	$120
218	11121 1			1,000	1996 PRICE LIST	SAILOR BOY	7.9	DRESSED WITH CAP	NONE	YES	RED	HD+SM RD PL	$137
219	11121 4			1,000	1992 PRICE LIST	SAILOR BOY	7.9	OLD GOLD IN SAILOR SUIT					$137
220	11122 1			1,000	1994 PRICE LIST	SAILOR GIRL	7.9	OLD GOLD IN SAILOR DRESS	NONE	YES	RED	HD+SML RD	$137
221	11123 8			2,000	1994 PRICE LIST	SAILOR BOY	7.9	OLD GOLD IN SAILOR SUIT					$137
222	11128 3			2,000	1993 PRICE LIST	BIEDERMEIER WOMEN	11	CARAMEL MOHAIR PLUSH W/DRESS	NONE	YES	RED	HD+SML RD	$180
223	11129 0			2,000	1993 PRICE LIST	BIEDERMEIER MAN	11	CARAMEL MOHAIR PLUSH W/BLUE STRIPED PANTS	NONE	YES	RED	HD+SML RD	$180
224	11220 4			1,000	1996 CATALOG	SAILOR GIRL	7.9	YELLOW MOHAIR PLUSH IN SAILOR SUIT	NONE	YES	RED	HD+SML RD	$180
225	11221 1			1,000	1996 CATALOG	SAILOR BOY	7.9	YELLOW MOHAIR PLUSH IN SAILOR SUIT	NONE	YES	RED	HD+SML RD	$180
226	11230 3				1994 PRICE LIST	SAILOR GIRL	11.8	OLD GOLD DRESSED IN SAILOR DRESS	GROWLER	YES	RED	HD+SML RD	$181
227	11231 0				1994 PRICE LIST	SAILOR BOY	11.8	OLD GOLD DRESSED IN SAILOR SUIT	GROWLER	YES	RED	RED PLASTIC	$200
228	11232 7			1,000	1996 PRICE LIST	CABIN BOY "HEIN"	11.8	W/ BLUE STRIPED SMOCK, BLUE TROUSERS, GREEK STYLE CAP	GROWLER	YES	RED	HD + SML RD	$208
229	11240 2				1992 PRICE LIST	SAILOR MOTHER	15.75	OLD GOLD DRESSED IN SAILOR DRESS; KATHY ANN DSTRS TAGGED	GROWLER	YES	RED	RED PLASTIC	$200
230	11241 9				1992 PRICE LIST	SAILOR FATHER	15.75	OLD GOLD DRESSED IN SAILOR SUIT; KATHY ANN DSTRS TAGGED	GROWLER	YES	RED	RED PLASTIC	$200
231	11320 1			1,000	1997 PRICE LIST	AGNES	7	OLD GOLD MOHAIR PLUSH IN WHT DRESS; SHAVED MUZZLE	NONE	YES	RED	SML RD PL	$98
232	11321 8			1,000	1997 PRICE LIST	FLEA MARKET BEAR	7.6	BRN COTTON PLUSH IN PURPLE STRIPED OVERALLS, BLK EYES	NONE	YES	RED	HD+SML RD	$104
233	11322 5			1,500	1998 PRICE LIST	KUNIBERT	7	OLD GOLD MOHAIR IN COSTUME	NONE	YES	RED	SML RED PL	$155
234	11323 2			1,500	1998 PRICE LIST	ROSAMUNDE	7	OLD GOLD MOHAIR IN COSTUME	NONE	YES	RED	SML RED PL	$155
235	11324 9			1,500	1998 PRICE LIST	HOFNAR (JESTER)	7	OLD GOLD MOHAIR IN COSTUME	NONE	YES	RED	SML RED PL	$155
236	11330 0				1992 PRICE LIST	BAVARIAN GIRL	11.8	OLD GOLD DRESSED					$155
237	11331 7				1992 PRICE LIST	BAVARIAN BOY	11.8	OLD GOLD DRESSED					$155
238	11332 4				1992 PRICE LIST	BAVARIAN GIRL	11.8	OLD GOLD DRESSED IN RED KNIT DRESS W/EMBROIDERED DAISY'S; KATHY ANN TAGGED	GROWLER	YES	RED	RED PLASTIC	$155
239	11333 1				1992 PRICE LIST	BAVARIAN BOY	11.8	OLD GOLD DRESSED					$155
240	11400 0			200	1998 PRICE LIST	HOCHZEITSLADER	39.4	CINNAMON MOHAIR, DRESSED EMBROIDERED PAW; STANDING BEAR	NONE	YES	RED	HD+RED PL	$1,173
241	11401 7				1992 PRICE LIST	TEA PARTY TEDDYS	4.7	CINNAMON MOHAIR, DRESSED	NONE	YES	RED	SML RD PL	$95
242	11402 4				1992 PRICE LIST	TEA PARTY TEDDYS	4.7	CINNAMON MOHAIR, DRESSED	NONE	YES	RED	SML RD PL	$95
243	11403 1				1992 PRICE LIST	TEA PARTY TEDDYS	4.7	WHT MOHAIR, DRESSED	NONE	YES	RED	SML RD PL	$95
244	11404 8				1992 PRICE LIST	TEA PARTY TEDDYS	4.7	GREY					$95
245	11405 5			3,000	1993 PRICE LIST	BRIDE AND GROOM	5.5	HONEY BRIDE AND GROOM IN PLASTIC BOX	NONE	YES	RED	SML RD PL	$269
246	11414 7			1,500	1998 PRICE LIST	BABY ON CUSHION	5.9	BABY DRESSED IN WHT ON FANCY CUSHION	NONE	YES	RED	SML RD PL	$125
247	11415 4			1,500	1998 PRICE LIST	BABY ON CUSHION	5.9	BABY IN DIAPERS ON QUILTED CUSHION	NONE	YES	RED	SML RD PL	$125
248	11420 8			500	1995 PRICE LIST	NOSTALGIC TEDDY	7.9	OLD GOLD PLUSH W/LEDERHOSEN & KNITTED VEST	NONE	YES	RED	HD+SM RD PL	$256
249	11429 1			300	1995 PRICE LIST	NOSTALGIC TEDDY	11.8	OLD GOLD PLUSH W/LEDERHOSEN & KNITTED VEST	GROWLER	YES	RED	HD+SM RD PL	$367
250	11430 7				1994 PRICE LIST	NOSTALGIC TEDDY	11.8	OLD GOLD MOHAIR PLUSH DRESSED IN TRACHTENENZUG; TYROLEAN KNIT MALE					$178
251	11431 4				1994 PRICE LIST	NOSTALGIC TEDDY	11.8	OLD GOLD MOHAIR PLUSH DRESSED IN DIRNDL; TYROLEAN FEMALE RED SKIRT					$178
252	11432 1				1994 PRICE LIST	NOSTALGIC TEDDY	11.8	OLD GOLD MOHAIR PLUSH DRESSED CHILD WITH KNIT BEIGE SWEATER & BRN PANTALOONS	GROWLER	YES	RED	HD+SM RD PL	$178

REF #	EAN #	HERMANN OLD #	ALSO SEE	LIMITED NUMBER	DATA FROM	NAME	INCHES TALL	DESCRIPTION	VOICE	HANGING BOOKLET	ARM TAG	COMPANY LOGO	CURRENT RETAIL
253	11433 8				1994 PRICE LIST	NOSTALGIC TEDDY	11.8	OLD GOLD MOHAIR PLUSH DRESSED W/JACKET AND HOSE; RED KNIT SHORTS & SWEATER					$178
254	11434 5				1996 PRICE LIST	NOSTALGIC TEDDY	11.8	OLD GOLD MOHAIR PLUSH DRESSED W/OVERALLS					
255	11435 2				1996 PRICE LIST	NOSTALGIC TEDDY	11.8	OLD GOLD MOHAIR PLUSH DRESSED GIRL W/BEIGE APRON; GRN SLEEVES, RED HEM	GROWLER	YES	RED	HD+SML RD	$182
256	11436 9				1996 PRICE LIST	NOSTALGIC TEDDY	11.8	OLD GOLD MOHAIR PLUSH DRESSED BOY W/HEAVY KNIT SWEATER	GROWLER	YES	RED	HD+SML RD	$182
257	11515 1				1994 PRICE LIST	HERMANNCHEN	6.69	YELLOW W/MAROON BOW TIE	NONE	YES	RED	SML RD PL	$75
258	11515 1M			200	1996 SPECIAL	SAILOR BOY	6.69	YELLOW DRESSED IN SAILOR SUIT W/SEABAG; FOR PUPPENSTUBE MUSEUM, HAMBURG	NONE	YES	RED	SML RD PL	$300
259	11516 8				1994 PRICE LIST	HERMANNCHEN	6.69	CINNAMON W/BLUE BOW TIE	NONE	YES	RED	SML RD PL	$75
260	11517 5				1994 PRICE LIST	HERMANNCHEN	6.69	DARK BRN W/SUEDE TAN BOW	NONE	YES	RED	SML RD PL	$75
261	11520 5			1,000	1995 PRICE LIST	BABY IN CRADLE W/MUSIC	6.69	OLD GOLD MOHAIR PLUSH BABY IN ROCKING CRADLE W MUSIC BOX	MUSIC	YES	RED	SML RD PL	$209
262	11535 9			2,000	1994 PRICE LIST	MOTHER & BABY	13	OLD GOLD W/WHT SILK BOW + BABY + BABY'S PAD	NONE	YES	RED	HD+RED PL	$315
263	11550 2			2,000	1993 PRICE LIST	"OMA" (GRANDMOTHER)	20	CARAMEL MOHAIR PLUSH W/MAROON DRESS	GROWLER	YES	RED	HD+RED PL	$373
264	11555 7		67/55	2,000	1988 CATALOG	PROF BERNHARD	21.6	OLD GOLD MOHAIR EXCELSIOR FILLING, STRIPED VEST W/RED BOW	GROWLER	YES, SGD	RED	RED PLASTIC	$350
266	11615 8			5,000	1995 PRICE LIST	FLOH	5.5	WILD YELLOW MOHAIR PLUSH, FULLY JTD, W/BLUE STRING TIE	NONE	YES	RED	SML RD PL	$93
267	11616 5			1,500	1995 PRICE LIST	FLORI	5.5	BRASS COLORED MOHAIR PLUSH	NONE	YES	RED	SML RD PL	$93
268	11617 2			1,500	1996 PRICE LIST	FIPPS	7.9	CINNAMON MOHAIR PLUSH, FULLY JTD	NONE	YES	RED	SML RD PL	$96
269	11618 9			1,500	1996 PRICE LIST	FREDDY	7.9	PUTTY COLORED MOHAIR PLUSH, FULLY JTD	NONE	YES	RED	SML RD PL	$96
270	11620 2			1,000	1998 PRICE LIST	TIGER EYE	6.3	TIGER EYE QUARTZ COLORED W/STONE MOHAIR FULLY JTD	NONE	YES	RED	SML RD PL	$105
271	11621 9			1,000	1998 PRICE LIST	JADE	6.3	JADE COLOR W/STONE MOHAIR FULLY JTD	NONE	YES	RED	SML RD PL	$105
272	11622 6			1,000	1998 PRICE LIST	ROSE QUARTZ	6.3	ROSE QUARTZ COLOR W/STONE MOHAIR FULLY JTD	NONE	YES	RED	SML RD PL	$105
273	11655 4			3,000	BOOK 1990 PG 88	COUNTRY BEAR	22	LT. BUFF CURLED MOHAIR, 1918 REPLICA	GROWLER	YES	RED	RED PLASTIC	$275
274	11735 3			3,000	1991 PRICE LIST	BEAR W/SHAVED SNOUT	14.2	BRN TIPPED GOLD MOHAIR, REPLICA 1925	GROWLER	YES	RED	RED PLASTIC	$190
275	11741 4			1,000	1996 PRICE LIST	FISHERMAN	15.75	WITH FISHING TACKLE, BRN MOHAIR PLUSH	GROWLER	YES	RED	RED PLASTIC	$388
276	11750 6			2,000	1991 PRICE LIST	BEAR W/SHAVED SNOUT	19.7	BRN TIPPED GOLD MOHAIR, REPLICA 1925	GROWLER	YES	RED	RED PLASTIC	$240
277	11825 1 (A+B)			1,000	1995 PRICE LIST	EMIL & EMILY TWINS	10.2	PAIR OF BEARS, HONEY CURLY MOHAIR, NAME & LTD # ON FOOT PAD	NONE	YES	RED	SML RD PL	$285
278	11825 1A	11825 1		1,000	1995 PRICE LIST	EMIL OF TWINS ABOVE	10.2	PAIR OF BEARS, HONEY CURLY MOHAIR, NAME & LTD # ON FOOT PAD	NONE	YES	RED	SML RD PL	$150
279	11825 1B	11825 1		1,000	1995 PRICE LIST	EMILY OF TWINS ABOVE	10.2	PAIR OF BEARS, HONEY CURLY MOHAIR, NAME & LTD # ON FOOT PAD	NONE	YES	RED	SML RD PL	$150
280	11840 4			1,000	1995 PRICE LIST	SAM	15.75	OLD GOLD MOHAIR PLUSH W/RED VEST & BOW TIE	GROWLER	YES	RED	HD+RD PL	$250
281	11841 1			1,000	1995 PRICE LIST	GEORANGEE	15.75	BRN MOHAIR PLUSH, DRESSED W/CAP, ON STAND	GROWLER	YES	RED	HD+RD PL	$334
282	11842 8			1,000	1995 PRICE LIST	ARTIST BEAR CANDY	15.75	OLD GOLD MOHAIR PLUSH, DESIGNED BY JOYCE ANN HAUGHEY	GROWLER	YES	RED	HD+RD PL	$244
283	11843 5			1,000	1995 PRICE LIST	ARTIST BEAR BONNIE	15.75	BEIGE MOHAIR PLUSH, DESIGNED BY BONNIE WINDELL	GROWLER	YES	RED	HD+RD PL	$248
284	11845 9			3,000	1993 PRICE LIST	SIR ARTHUR	18.1	ANTIQUE BEIGE CURLY MOHAIR, SOFT FILLING W/STRIPED VEST W/STRING TIE	NONE	YES	RED	RED PLASTIC	$296
285	11930 2			1,000	1995 PRICE LIST	PAULY	11.8	BEIGE MOHAIR PLUSH W RED BOW TIE					$153
286	11935 7			1,000	1995 PRICE LIST	PAUL	13.4	BEIGE MOHAIR PLUSH W RED BOW TIE	NONE	YES	RED	HD+RD PL	$176
287		120/17			BEHA 1927 CATALOG	CAT, RUNNING	6.7	WHEELS ON BACK FEET. PAINTED & SPRAYED, MOVEABLE HEAD, WOOL PLUSH & ARTIFICIAL SILK PLUSH					$200/350
288		120/22			BEHA 1927 CATALOG	CAT, RUNNING	8.7	WHEELS ON BACK FEET. PAINTED & SPRAYED, MOVEABLE HEAD, WOOL PLUSH & ARTIFICIAL SILK PLUSH					$200/350
289		1200/1	75120 5		1982 PRICE LIST	ELEPHANT, BABY'S	7.9						$200/350
290		1200/2			1982 PRICE LIST	DUCKLING, BABYS	?						$200/350
291		1200/3	75317 9		1982 PRICE LIST	FISH, BABY'S	6.7						$200/350
292		1200/4	75418 3		1982 PRICE LIST	DOG, BABY'S	6.7						$200/350
293		1200/5	75525 8		1982 PRICE LIST	TEDDY, BABY'S	9.8	RED SOFT TOY W\WHT PADS, SNOUT, EARS					$200/350
294		1200/6	75607 1		1982 PRICE LIST	BABY'S BALL	2.8						$200/350
295		1200/7	75712 2		1982 PRICE LIST	MOUSE, BABY'S	4.7						$200/350
296		1200/8			1982 PRICE LIST	MOON, BABY'S	3.2						$200/350
297		1200/9			1982 PRICE LIST	BUNNY, BABY'S	3.5						$200/350
298		1200/10	76020 7		1982 PRICE LIST	SEA LION, BABY'S	7.9						$200/350
299		1200/11	76120 4		1982 PRICE LIST	SEA LION, BABY'S	7.9						$200/350
300		1200/12	76226 3		1984 PRICE LIST	PUNCH	10.2						$200/350
301		1200/13	76314 7		1983 PRICE LIST	DUCK, RED-GOLD	5.5						$200/350
302		1200/14	76414 4		1983 PRICE LIST	DUCK, GOLD-WHT	5.5						$200/350
303	12035 3	62/35/5			1988 CATALOG	SHEPHERD SET	14.2	CREAM MOHAIR PLUSH, DRESSED, + 2 LAMBS	GROWLER	YES	BRN	RED PLASTIC	$245
304	12040 7			2,000	1994 PRICE LIST	HANS	15.75	TAN MOHAIR PLUSH W/PRTD BEIGE BOW					$200
305	12041 4				1997 PRICE LIST	CONGRATULATORY PAIR	15.75	GOLD MOHAIR PLUSH W/ MESSAGE EMBROIDERED ON PAW	GROWLER	YES	RED	HD+RD PL	$265

REF #	EAN #	HERMANN OLD #	ALSO SEE	LIMITED NUMBER	DATA FROM	NAME	INCHES TALL	DESCRIPTION	VOICE	HANGING BOOKLET	ARM TAG	COMPANY LOGO	CURRENT RETAIL
306	12042 1				1998 PRICE LIST	ROSA	15.75	ROSE MOHAIR PLUSH W/ MESSAGE EMBROIDERED ON PAW	GROWLER	YES	RED	HD+RD PL	$265
307	12050 6			2,000	1994 PRICE LIST	JOHANN	18.1	CURLY BEIGE MOHAIR, REPLICA OF 1970 ISSUE LISTED ABOVE	GROWLER	YES	RED	RED PLASTIC	$275
308	12250 0			4,000	1991 PRICE LIST	SONNENBERG	19.7	CARAMEL MOHAIR PLUSH W/WHT BOW, SHAVED MUZZLE, REPLICA 1922	GROWLER	YES	RED	RED PLASTIC	$251
309	12335 4			1,000	1997 PRICE LIST	BUSSI BEAR	14.2	GOLD MOHAIR	NONE	YES	RED	RED PLASTIC	$190
310	12350 7			2,000	1993 PRICE LIST	TEDDY BEAR, REPL. '25	18.9	GREY TIPPED MOHAIR PLUSH W/BLUE BOW	GROWLER	YES	RED	RED PLASTIC	$291
311	12430 6			1,000	1995 PRICE LIST	NOSTALGIC TEDDYBEAR	11.8	LT BEIGE MOHAIR PLUSH REPLICA 1932	GROWLER	YES	RED	HD+RED PL	$159
312	12450 4			500	1995 PRICE LIST	NOSTALGIC TEDDYBEAR	21.2	LT BEIGE LONG CURLY MOHAIR PLUSH REPLICA 1932	GROWLER	YES	RED	RED PLASTIC	$290
313		1250/14	76516 5		1982 PRICE LIST	BALL, PLUSH	5.5						$50/125
314		1250/16			1984 PRICE LIST	BALL, PLUSH	6.3						$50/125
315		1251/14			1982 PRICE LIST	BALL W/MUSIC BOX	5.5						$50/125
316	12520 4			2,000	1996 PRICE LIST	BARNABY	7.9	PUTTY COLORED MOHAIR PLUSH BARNABY; ARTIST "D. CANHAM"					$138
317	12530 3			2,000	1996 PRICE LIST	ANTHONY	11.8	PUTTY COLORED MOHAIR PLUSH ANTHONY; ARTIST "D. CANHAM"					$173
318	12540 2			2,000	1996 PRICE LIST	ERNEST	15.75	PUTTY COLORED MOHAIR PLUSH ERNEST; ARTIST "D. CANHAM"					$226
319		1255/14			1985 PRICE LIST	BALL, PLUSH	5.5						$50/125
320		1255/16	76620 9		1988 PRICE LIST	BALL W/MUSIC BOX	6.3						$50/125
321	12620 1			2,000	1996 PRICE LIST	JEREMY	7.9	CINNAMON MOHAIR PLUSH JEREMY; ARTIST "D. CANHAM"					$138
322	12630 0			2,000	1996 PRICE LIST	RICHARD	11.8	CINNAMON MOHAIR PLUSH RICHARD; ARTIST "D. CANHAM"					$195
323	12640 9			2,000	1996 PRICE LIST	ALBERT	15.75	CINNAMON MOHAIR PLUSH ALBERT; ARTIST "D. CANHAM"					$224
324	12726 0			1,500	1997 PRICE LIST	MILLICENT	10.6	BEIGE MOHAIR PLUSH MILLICENT, DRESSED IN GRN PLAID DRESS W/BOW IN HAIR; ARTIST "D. CANHAM"	NONE	YES	RED	HD+SM RD PL	$168
325	12727 7			1,500	1997 PRICE LIST	CHARLES	10.6	BEIGE MOHAIR PLUSH CHARLES; ARTIST "D. CANHAM"					$168
326	12820 5			2,000	1998 PRICE LIST	RUDY	7.9	LT BRN MOHAIR PLUSH, RUDY; ARTIST "D. CANHAM"					$138
327	12830 4			2,000	1998 PRICE LIST	ANDREW	11.8	LT BRN MOHAIR PLUSH, ANDREW; ARTIST "D. CANHAM"					$173
328	12840 3			2,000	1998 PRICE LIST	CALVIN	15.75	LT BRN MOHAIR PLUSH, CALVIN; ARTIST "D. CANHAM"					$202
329	12940 0			1,500	1994 PRICE LIST	MARIONETTE	15.75	OLD GOLD MOHAIR PLUSH W/RED PLAID VEST BLUE PANTS					$475
330	12941 7			500	1996 PRICE LIST	MARIONETTE PLAYER	15.75	MARIONETTE W/SML MARIONETTE OLD GOLD MOHAIR	GROWLER	YES	RED	HD+LG RD	$528
331		1300/22			1982 PRICE LIST	HEN	8.7						$150/300
332	13025 3			1,000	1997 PRICE LIST	FRITZ, SON	8.7	LT BRN MOHAIR PLUSH W/GLASSES & PURSE	NONE	YES	RED	MTL HD PIN	$145
333	13030 7			1,000	1997 PRICE LIST	FRANZ, FATHER	11.8	LT BRN MOHAIR PLUSH IN WOOL PANTS	NONE	YES	RED	HD+SML PL	$189
334	13035 2			4,000	1990 PRICE LIST	SWEET ROSE	14.2	SOFT ROSE COLOR DISTRESSED MOHAIR W/LT SUEDE PADS, WHT FEATHER BOA	GROWLER	YES	RED	RED PLASTIC	$165
335		1305/17			1982 PRICE LIST	HEN W/ BASKET	6.7						$100/200
336		1305/22			1982 PRICE LIST	HEN W/ BASKET	8.7						$100/200
337		1310/22	88022 6		1982 PRICE LIST	HEN	8.7						$100/200
338	13130 4			800	1997 PRICE LIST	HONEY	11.8	GOLD MOHAIR PLUSH, W/BEEHIVE AND BEES	NONE	YES	RED	HD+SML PL	$169
339	13135 9			4,000	1990 PRICE LIST	WILLY	14.2	DARK BRN CURLED DISTRESSED MOHAIR, PLAID BOW, LT SUEDE PADS	GROWLER	YES	RED	RED PLASTIC	$160
340		1315/13			1983 PRICE LIST	CHICK	5.1						$50/100
341		1316/10	88510 8		1988 PRICE LIST	CHICK	3.9						$50/100
342		1316/10/3	88503 0		1986 PRICE LIST	CHICKS(3) IN A BASKET	3.9						$50/100
343	13230 1			500	1997 PRICE LIST	WALDGEIST	11.8	OLIVE MOHAIR PLUSH W/ BASKET	NONE	YES	RED	HD+SML PL	$161
344	13230 1			2,000	1990 PRICE LIST	HARLEQUIN	11.8	BLK MOHAIR	GROWLER	YES	RED	RED PLASTIC	$140
345	13231 8			2,000	1991 PRICE LIST	HARLEQUIN LADY	11.8	WHT W/BLK/WHT NECK RUFFLE	GROWLER	YES	RED	RED PLASTIC	$144
346	13260 8			500	1992 PRICE LIST	HARLEQUIN	23.6	BLK MOHAIR	GROWLER	NO-LTD TAG	RED	RED PLASTIC	$480
347	13261 6			500	1992 PRICE LIST	HARLEQUIN LADY	23.6	WHT W/BLK/WHT NECK RUFFLE	GROWLER	NO-LTD TAG	RED	RED PLASTIC	$480
348		1330/24	89024 9		1982 PRICE LIST	SWAN, WHT	9.5						$100/250
349		1331/24	89124 6		1988 PRICE LIST	SWAN, OLD ROSE	9.5						$100/250
350	13330 8			2,000	1990 PRICE LIST	CHEF "OTTO"	11.8	HONEY MOHAIR	GROWLER	YES	RED	RED PLASTIC	$150
351	13331 5			1,000	1998 PRICE LIST	CHIMNEY SWEEP	11.8	HONEY MOHAIR, FULLY JTD, W/LADDER & BROOM	GROWLER	YES	RED	HD+RED PL	$202
352	13417 6			2,000	1990 PRICE LIST	' VIOLET"	6.75	TAN MOHAIR	NONE	YES	RED	SML RD PL	$150
353	13430 5			1,000	1997 PRICE LIST	GOLFER	11.8	LT BRN MOHAIR PLUSH W/GOLF CLUB AND STAND	NONE	YES	RED	HD+RD PL	$230
354	13455 8			200	1997 PRICE LIST	GOLFER	22	OLD GOLD MOHAIR PLUSH W/GOLF BAG & 14 CLUBS					$798
355		1350/25			1982 PRICE LIST	DUCKLING	9.8						$100/175
356	13517 3			2,000	1991 PRICE LIST	DAISY	6.5	OLD GOLD MOHAIR W/WHT DRESS, PINK BOW FLOWERS & LACE HEADDRESS	NONE	YES	RED	SML RD PL	$150
357		1350/15			1984 PRICE LIST	DUCKLING	5.9	ROSE					$50/100
358		1350/25			1982 PRICE LIST	DUCKLING	9.8						$75/150
359		1351/15			1984 PRICE LIST	DUCKLING	5.9	LT. BLUE					$50/100
360		1352/12			1982 PRICE LIST	DUCKLING	4.7						$50/100
361		1353/15	87515 4		1984 PRICE LIST	DUCK, GOLD	5.9						$50/100

REF #	EAN #	HERMANN OLD #	ALSO SEE	LIMITED NUMBER	DATA FROM	NAME	INCHES TALL	DESCRIPTION	VOICE	HANGING BOOKLET	ARM TAG	COMPANY LOGO	CURRENT RETAIL
362		1354/20			1983 PRICE LIST	DUCK	7.9						$75/150
363		1355/18			1982 PRICE LIST	DUCKLING	7						$60/120
364		1356/15	87015 9		1988 PRICE LIST	DUCK, WILD	4.7						$50/100
365		1356/20	87020 3		1983 PRICE LIST	DUCK, WILD	7.9						$75/150
366		1356/25			1982 PRICE LIST	DUCK, WILD	9.8						$75/150
367	13530 2			1,000	1997 PRICE LIST	WASTL	11	BRN MOHAIR PLUSH IN LEDERHOSEN W/ NAME & # EMBROIDERED ON PAW	NONE	YES	RED	HD+RD PL	$214
368		1357/16/1	87116 3		1998 PRICE LIST	DUCK, RED	6.3						$50/100
369		1357/16/2	87216 0		1998 PRICE LIST	DUCK, LIGHT BLUE	6.3						$50/100
370		1357/16/3	87316 7		1998 PRICE LIST	DUCK, GRN	6.3						$50/100
371		1357/16/4	87416 4		1998 PRICE LIST	DUCK, BLUE	6.3						$50/100
372	13617 0			2,000	1992 PRICE LIST	ROSE	6.5	LT PINK IN RED FLOWING DRESS W/ROSE IN EAR	NONE	YES	RED	SML RD PL	$150
373	13625 5			2,000	1998 PRICE LIST	TOOTH ACHE BEAR	9.8	OLD GOLD MOHAIR, FULLY JTD, EMBROIDERED ON PAW	NONE	YES	RED	HD+RD PL	$153
374	13629 3			500	1998 PRICE LIST	ALOIS	11	OLD GOLD MOHAIR, FULLY JTD, W/VEST, EMBROIDERED PAW	NONE	YES	RED	HD+RD PL	$201
375	13630 9			2,000	1997 PRICE LIST	SHADOW	11.5	BLK MOHAIR PLUSH, NAME & # EMBROIDERED ON PAW	NONE	YES	RED	HD+RD PL	$169
376	13631 6			1,000	1998 PRICE LIST	SUNBEAM	12.6	YELLOW MOHAIR, FULLY JTD, PAW EMBROIDERED	NONE	YES	RED	HD+RD PL	$180
377	13632 3			1,000	1998 PRICE LIST	MOONLIGHT	12.6	GREY MOHAIR, FULLY JTD, PAW EMBROIDERED	NONE	YES	RED	HD+RD PL	$180
378	13633 0			1,000	1998 PRICE LIST	BEAUTY	12.6	BLK MOHAIR, WHT PAWS, PAW EMBROIDERED, FULLY JTD	NONE	YES	RED	HD+RD PL	$195
379	13634 7			1,000	1998 PRICE LIST	SWEETHEART	11.8	RED MOHAIR, FULLY JTD, W/DECORATION, PAW EMBROIDERED	NONE	YES	RED	HD+RD PL	$200
380		1365/16			1982 PRICE LIST	SNOWMAN W/MUSIC	6.3						$50/100
381		1370/30	89530 5		1989 PRICE LIST	CHICK	11.8						$75/150
382		1370/40	89540 4		1989 PRICE LIST	CHICK	15.75						$100/200
383	13745 0			1,500	1998 PRICE LIST	VAGABOND	15.75	OLD GOLD MOHAIR W/RED NOSE DRESSED W/RUCKSACK	GROWLER	YES	RED	HD+RD PL	$276
384		1398/20			1982 PRICE LIST	FROG	7.9						$75/150
385		1398/35			1982 PRICE LIST	FROG	13.8						$100/200
386		1398/45			1982 PRICE LIST	FROG	17.7						$200/400
387		1399/22	41022 5		1984 PRICE LIST	FROG	8.7						$75/150
388		1399/30	41030 0		1984 PRICE LIST	FROG	11.8						$100/200
389		1399/40	41040 9		1984 PRICE LIST	FROG	15.75						$150/300
390		1399/60	41067 7		1984 PRICE LIST	FROG	23.6						$200/400
391		1399/75			1984 PRICE LIST	FROG	29.5						$250/500
392	14038 2			2,000	1991 PRICE LIST	GOLFER	15	OLD GOLD MOHAIR, DRESSED, W/GOLF CART	GROWLER	YES	RED	RED PLASTIC	$230
393		1410/26			1982 PRICE LIST	RABBIT	10.2						$60/120
394	14127 3			1,500	1998 PRICE LIST	LADY BLUE	10.8	BLUE MOHAIR, W/HAT, FULLY JTD, PAW EMBROIDERED	NONE	YES	RED	HD+RD PL	$175
395	14130 3			2,000	1994 PRICE LIST	SOCCER PLAYER	11.8	OLD GOLD MOHAIR PLUSH W/SOCCER UNIFORM	GROWLER	YES	RED	HD+RD PL	$200
396	14140 2			1,000	1998 PRICE LIST	ANNABELL	15.75	OLD GOLD MOHAIR FULLY JTD, EMBROIDERED PAW, BENT KNEES	NONE	YES	RED	HD+RD PL	$200
397	14214 0		01421 4	2,000	1997 PRICE LIST	BIRTHDAY CHARLIE	5.5	DRESSED WITH STRAW HAT & FLOWERS, ANTIQUE GOLD MOHAIR	NONE	YES	RED	SML RD PL	$107
398		1422/30	77030 5		1982 PRICE LIST	LAMB W/MUSIC	11.8						$100/200
399	14230 0			1,000	1996 PRICE LIST	BIRTHDAY CHARLIE	11.8	DRESSED WITH STRAW HAT & FLOWERS, ANTIQUE GOLD MOHAIR	GROWLER	YES	RED	HD+RD PL	$210
400	14280 5			100	1997 TB & MEHR	BIRTHDAY CHARLIE	31.5	SAME EXCEPT MOHAIR IS CURLY, PAW EMBROIDERED WITH #	NONE	YES	RED	HD+RD PL	$960
401	14325 3			3,000	1996 PRICE LIST	TRADITIONAL BEAR	9.84	GOLD MOHAIR PLUSH, FULLY JTD	NONE	YES	RED	HD+RD PL	$125
402	14330 7			3,000	1996 PRICE LIST	TRADITIONAL BEAR	14.2	GOLD MOHAIR PLUSH, FULLY JTD	GROWLER	YES	RED	HD+RD PL	$168
403	14340 6			3,000	1996 PRICE LIST	TRADITIONAL BEAR	15.75	GOLD MOHAIR PLUSH, FULLY JTD	GROWLER	YES	RED	HD+RD PL	$211
404	14350 5			2,000	1996 PRICE LIST	TRADITIONAL BEAR	19.7	GOLD MOHAIR PLUSH, FULLY JTD					$300
405	14360 4			1,000	1996 PRICE LIST	TRADITIONAL BEAR	23.6	GOLD MOHAIR PLUSH, FULLY JTD					$400
406	14380 2			500	1996 PRICE LIST	TRADITIONAL BEAR	31.5	GOLD MOHAIR PLUSH, FULLY JTD					$685
407	14430 4			2,000	1996 PRICE LIST	TEDDY BEAR	118	GOLD MOHAIR PLUSH, FULLY JTD					$165
408	14431 1			1,500	HERMANN 1998 DATA	SPECIAL BEAR FOR U.K.	11.8	WHEAT DISTRESSED MOHAIR, BLK EYES & NOSE, GRN SUEDE PAWS, EMBROIDERED PAWS		YES	RED	HD+RED PL	$150
409	14440 3			1,000	1996 PRICE LIST	TEDDY BEAR	15.75	GOLD MOHAIR PLUSH, FULLY JTD					$180
410	14441 0			1,000	HERMANN 1998 DATA	SPECIAL BEAR FOR U.K.	15.75	WHEAT DISTRESSED MOHAIR, BLK EYES & NOSE, GRN SUEDE PAWS, EMBROIDERED PAWS		YES	RED	HD+RED PL	$180
411	14450 2			1,000	1996 PRICE LIST	TEDDY BEAR	19.7	GOLD MOHAIR PLUSH, FULLY JTD					$245
412		1452/25	88225 1		1982 PRICE LIST	STANDING GOAT	9.8	BLK & WHT					$75/150
413		1452/25			1982 PRICE LIST	STANDING GOAT	9.8	BRN & WHT					$75/150
414	14525 7			1,000	1997 PRICE LIST	ANNIV BEAR, 90 YEAR	10.2	GOLD MOHAIR PLUSH, FULLY JTD, NO VOICE					$139
415	14530 1			2,000	1994 PRICE LIST	CLOWN	11.8	WHT MOHAIR PLUSH W/HEART EYES, TYROLEAN RED HAT, GRN OUTFIT	NONE	YES	RED	HD+RED PL	$181
416	14531 8			2,000	1994 PRICE LIST	AUGUST	11	ROSE' MOHAIR PLUSH W/RED DRESS, BLK HAT, WHT FLOWER	NONE	YES	RED	HD+RED PL	$181
417	14532 5			1,000	1997 PRICE LIST	ANNIV BEAR, 90 YEAR	12.6	GOLD MOHAIR PLUSH, FULLY JTD	GROWLER				$157
418	14540 0			1,000	1997 PRICE LIST	ANNIV BEAR, 90 YEAR	15.75	GOLD MOHAIR PLUSH, FULLY JTD	GROWLER	YES	RED	HD+RED PL	$177
419	14732 9			1,000	1996 PRICE LIST	NOSTALGIC 1930 REPLICA	12.6	BRASS COLORED, CURLY LONG MOHAIR	GROWLER	YES	RED	HD+RED PL	$180
420	14740 4			1,000	1996 PRICE LIST	NOSTALGIC 1930 REPLICA	15.75	BRASS COLORED, CURLY LONG MOHAIR	GROWLER	YES	RED	HD+RED PL	$170
421		1480/14			1982 PRICE LIST	LADYBUG W/MUSIC	5.5						$50/100

REF #	EAN #	HERMANN OLD #	ALSO SEE	LIMITED NUMBER	DATA FROM	NAME	INCHES TALL	DESCRIPTION	VOICE	HANGING BOOKLET	ARM TAG	COMPANY LOGO	CURRENT RETAIL
422		1481/14	771149		1982 PRICE LIST	MOONFISH W/MUSIC	5.5						$50/100
423		1482/20			1982 PRICE LIST	ELEPHANT W/MUSIC	7.9						$50/125
424		1483/14	772149		1983 PRICE LIST	LADYBUG W/MUSIC	5.5						$50/100
425	14830 2			2,000	1994 PRICE LIST	TEDDY BEAR	11.8	GOLDEN-YELLOW MOHAIR PLUSH, W/PRINTED RED BOW; 1994 REPLICA OF 1930 BEAR	NONE	YES	RED	HD+RD PL	$140
426	14831 9			800	1998 PRICE LIST	GOOSEBERRY	11.8	GRNISH MOHAIR W/EMBROIDERED LEAVES OF FELT	NONE	YES	RED	HD+RD PL	$210
427	14836 4		01483 6	500	1995 FLYER CATALOG	HALLOWEEN WITCH	11.8	DIFFERENCE IS THEORETICALLY IN TYPE OF MOHAIR USED! SEE 01483 6 WHICH HAD 150 LIMIT					$299
428		1484/25	77325 2		1985 PRICE LIST	SUN W/MUSIC	9.8						$75/150
429	14840 1			800	1997 FLYER CATALOG	STRAWBEARY	15.75	RED MOHAIR WITH GRN STEM HAT; EMBROIDERED PAW	NONE	YES	RED	HD+SML RD	$263
430		1485/22	77422 8		1982 PRICE LIST	HEDGEHOG W/MUSIC	8.7						$50/100
431		1486/20			1982 PRICE LIST	GUINEA PIG W/MUSIC	7.9						$50/100
432		1487/18			1982 PRICE LIST	OWL W/MUSIC	7						$50/100
433		1488/22	77522 5		1985 PRICE LIST	TURTLE W/MUSIC	8.7						$50/100
434		1489/20			1982 PRICE LIST	TURTLE W/MUSIC	7.9						$50/100
435		1490/40			1982 PRICE LIST	PARROT W/MUSIC	15.75						$100/150
436		1491/15			1984 PRICE LIST	DUCK WITH MUSIC BOX	5.9	ROSE					$50/100
437		1492/15			1984 PRICE LIST	DUCK WITH MUSIC BOX	5.9	LIGHT BLUE					$50/100
438	14935 4			1,000	1996 PRICE LIST	DESIGNER BEAR	13.78	BY TRAUDEL MISCHNER-HERMANN, GOLD MOHAIR PLUSH	GROWLER	YES	RED	HD+SML RD	$260
439	14936 1			1,000	1998 PRICE LIST	DESIGNER BEAR	13.78	BY TRAUDEL MISCHNER-HERMANN, GOLD MOHAIR PLUSH	GROWLER	YES	RED	HD+SML RD	$182
440	14945 3			1,000	1996 PRICE LIST	DESIGNER BEAR	17.72	BY TRAUDEL MISCHNER-HERMANN, GOLD MOHAIR PLUSH	GROWLER	YES	RED	HD+SML RD	$311
441	14946 0			1,000	1998 PRICE LIST	DESIGNER BEAR	17.72	BY TRAUDEL MISCHNER-HERMANN, GOLD MOHAIR PLUSH	GROWLER	YES	RED	HD+SML RD	$229
442	14950 7			500	1996 PRICE LIST	BLUEBEARY	15.75	SMOKY BLUE MOHAIR PLUSH W/CAP & NECK ORNAMENTS	GROWLER	YES	RED	HD+LG RD	$296
443		15/28			1982 PRICE LIST	"OLD SALT"	11						$25
444		150/10			BEHA 1927 CATALOG	BONZO DOG	3.9	STANDING, SOFT STUFFED, VELVET					$200/300
445		150/15			BEHA 1927 CATALOG	BONZO DOG	5.9	STANDING, SOFT STUFFED, VELVET					$200/300
446		150/20			BEHA 1927 CATALOG	BONZO DOG	7.9	STANDING, SOFT STUFFED, VELVET					$250/350
447	15030 5			3,000	CATALOG 1994/95	NOSTALGIC TEDDY	11.8	BEIGE MOHAIR PLUSH W/TAN PLAID BOW	GROWLER	YES	RED	RED PLASTIC	$130
448	15040 4			3,000	CATALOG 1994/95	NOSTALGIC TEDDY	15.75	BEIGE MOHAIR PLUSH W/TAN PLAID BOW	GROWLER	YES	RED	RED PLASTIC	$198
449	15050 3			3,000	CATALOG 1994/95	NOSTALGIC TEDDY	19.7	BEIGE MOHAIR PLUSH W/TAN PLAID BOW	GROWLER	YES	RED	RED PLASTIC	$275
450		151/22			BEHA 1927 CATALOG	BULLDOG	8.7	SOFT STUFFED, MADE OF MOLTON, SITTING					$250/350
451		151/28?			BEHA 1927 CATALOG	BULLDOG	11	SOFT STUFFED, MADE OF MOLTON, SITTING					$250/350
452		151/33?			BEHA 1927 CATALOG	BULLDOG	12.6	SOFT STUFFED, MADE OF MOLTON, SITTING					$300/400
453		151/40?			BEHA 1927 CATALOG	BULLDOG	15.75	SOFT STUFFED, MADE OF MOLTON, SITTING					$300/400
454		151/45			BEHA 1927 CATALOG	BULLDOG	18	SOFT STUFFED, MADE OF MOLTON, SITTING					$300/400
455		151/52			BEHA 1927 CATALOG	BULLDOG	20.5	SOFT STUFFED, MADE OF MOLTON, SITTING					$400/500
456	15114 2				1997 XMAS FLYER	XMAS ELF, OLD GOLD	5.5	MOHAIR DRESSED AS XMAS ELF	NONE	YES	RED	SML PLASTIC	$80
457	15115 9				1997 XMAS FLYER	XMAS ELF, WHT	5.5	MOHAIR DRESSED AS XMAS ELF	NONE	YES	RED	SML PLASTIC	$80
458	15120 3			500	1995 FLYER CATALOG	XMAS BEAR W SLED	7.9	WHT BEAR ON SLED W/RED HOLLY BOW & PADS	NONE	YES	RED	MTL+SML PL	$218
459	15125 8			300	1997 FLYER	XMAS BEAR W/HORSE	10.2	OLD GOLD MOHAIR BEAR ON WOODEN ROCKING HORSE "NICKY"	NONE	YES	RED	MTL+SML PL	$105
460	15130 2			500	1995 FLYER CATALOG	XMAS BEAR W/MUSIC	11.8	LT BEIGE BEAR W/JINGLE BELLS MUSIC BOX RED HOLLY LEAF BOW & PADS	MUSIC	YES	RED	MTL+SML PL	$254
461	15135 3			300	1996 FLYER	SANTA W/MUSIC 1996	14.2	OLD GOLD MOHAIR IN SANTA SUIT W/MUSIC "SILENT NIGHT" IN BAG	GROWLER	YES	RED	MTL+SML PL	$225
462	15140 1			1,000	1997 XMAS FLYER	XMAS BEAR	14	HEAD IN CINNAMON, BODY IN RED, LEGS IN BLK BOOTS+ST. NICK HAT	YES	YES	RED	HD+RED PL	$255
463	15145 2			4,000	1991 PRICE LIST	REUNIFICATION BEAR	18.1	BUFF MOHAIR	GROWLER	YES	RED	RED PLASTIC	$275
464		152/18			1982 PRICE LIST	STANDING CAT	7						$200/300
465	15217 0			1,000	BOOK PG 82	RUHRLI 1991/92	7	DARK PEARL GRAY 100% MOHAIR, FULLY JTD; SPECIAL FOR RUHRLAND MUSEUM	NONE	NONE	RED	SML RED PL	$200
466		152/18			1983 PRICE LIST	CAT	7						$200/300
467	15219 4			1,000	1996 PRICE LIST	BILLY	7.9	BLK MOHAIR PLUSH, FULLY JTD, MAROON FELT PADS	NONE	YES	RED	HD+SML PL	$100
468	15221 7			3,000	1993 PRICE LIST	NOSTALGIC TEDDY	8.5	BRN TIPPED MOHAIR PLUSH W/LAVENDER BOW	NONE	YES	RED	HD+SML PL	$133
469	15222 4			2,000	1992 PRICE LIST	NOSTALGIC TEDDY	8.5	CREAM MOHAIR W/LAVENDER PADS AND PAWS, SHARP NOSE	NONE	YES	RED	SML RD PL	$130
470	15223 1			2,000	1992 PRICE LIST	NOSTALGIC TEDDY	8.5	FASHION GREY MOHAIR W/LAVENDER PADS AND PAWS, SHARP NOSE	NONE	YES	RED	SML RD PL	$120
471	15224 8			2,000	1993 PRICE LIST	NOSTALGIC TEDDY	8.5	BURGUNDY MOHAIR PLUSH W/PINK BOW					$127
472	15225 5			2,000	1993 PRICE LIST	NOSTALGIC TEDDY	8.5	DARK BRN MOHAIR PLUSH W/WHT BOW					$127
473	15226 2			500	1998 PRICE LIST	SUNNY	8.5	DRESSED IN BIKINI W/SUN GLASSES ON AIR FLOAT	NONE	YES	RED	HD+SML RD	$150
474	15229 3			2,000	1994 PRICE LIST	ROSALIE	11.8	ANTIQUE ROSE W/BRN HAT + BRN SCARF					$199
475	15230 4			2,000	1992 PRICE LIST	NOSTALGIC TEDDY	11.5	ANTIQUE ROSE MOHAIR	NONE	YES	RED	RED PLASTIC	$125
476	15231 1/6?			2,000	1993 PRICE LIST	NOSTALGIC TEDDY	11.8	WHT MOHAIR PLUSH W/LAVENDER BOW; 1 IN 1993, 6 IN 1994 PRICE LIST					$171

REF #	EAN #	HERMANN OLD #	ALSO SEE	LIMITED NUMBER	DATA FROM	NAME	INCHES TALL	DESCRIPTION	VOICE	HANGING BOOKLET	ARM TAG	COMPANY LOGO	CURRENT RETAIL
477	15232 8/3?			2,000	1993 PRICE LIST	NOSTALGIC TEDDY	11.8	DARK BRN MOHAIR PLUSH W/PLAID BOW					$171
478	15233 5/0?			3,000	1993 PRICE LIST	NOSTALGIC TEDDY	11.8	OLD GOLD					$171
479	15233 0			3,000	BOOK 1993 PG 92	NOSTALGIC TEDDY	11.8	ANTIQUE GOLD MOHAIR PLUSH W/PLAID TIE - SHARP NOSE	NONE	YES	RED	RED PLASTIC	$171
480	15233 0	SPECIAL			PURCHASED 1997	TEDDY BEAR - MISTAKE	11.8	SHAVED NOSE W/GRN JUMP SUIT (MISTAKE AT HOTEL GROLLER); EMBARRASSMENT TO HERMANN	NONE	YES	RED	RED PLASTIC	$171
481	15234 7			500	1996 PRICE LIST	TREVOR	11.8	BLK MOHAIR PLUSH, FULLY JTD, RED PAW PADS, BLK EYES	NONE	YES	RED	HD+SM RD PL	$125
482	15245 8			2,000	1993 PRICE LIST	NOSTALGIC TEDDY	18.1	ANTIQUE ROSE MOHAIR PLUSH W/LAVENDER BOW	NONE	YES	RED	RED PLASTIC	$264
483		153/15	60015 2		1982 PRICE LIST	CAT, BLK	5.91						$150/200
484		153/20	60020 6		1982 PRICE LIST	CAT, BLK	7.9						$200/300
485		153/35			1982 PRICE LIST	BLK CAT	13.8						$250/350
486	15322 1			2,000	1995 PRICE LIST	ROBIN HOOD, LITTLE	8.5	GOLD MOHAIR PLUSH DESIGNED BY JOYCE ANN HAUGHEY; #782 OF 2000	NONE	YES	RED	HD+SML RD	$137
487	15325 2			2,000	1992 PRICE LIST	SALLY	10.2	LT CREAM CURLED MOHAIR ARTIST BEAR BY JENNY KRANTZ	NONE	YES	RED	SML RD PL	$170
488	15345 0			2,000	1992 PRICE LIST	ROBIN HOOD	18.1	BRN CURLED MOHAIR ARTIST BEAR BY JOYCE ANN HAUGHEY	NONE	YES	RED	RED PLASTIC	$225
489		154/22			1986 PRICE LIST	CAT	8.7	BEIGE					$200/300
490		154/22			1986 PRICE LIST	CAT	8.7	GRAY					$200/300
491		154/22			1986 PRICE LIST	CAT	8.7	WHT					$200/300
492		154/22			BEHA 1927 CATALOG	BULLDOG	8.7	SOFT STUFFED, VELVET, SITTING					$200/300
493		154/28?			BEHA 1927 CATALOG	BULLDOG	11	SOFT STUFFED, VELVET, SITTING					$250/350
494		154/33?			BEHA 1927 CATALOG	BULLDOG	12.6	SOFT STUFFED, VELVET, SITTING					$250/350
495		154/40?			BEHA 1927 CATALOG	BULLDOG	15.75	SOFT STUFFED, VELVET, SITTING					$300/400
496		154/45			BEHA 1927 CATALOG	BULLDOG	18.1	SOFT STUFFED, VELVET, SITTING					$300/400
497		154/52			BEHA 1927 CATALOG	BULLDOG	20.5	SOFT STUFFED, VELVET, SITTING					$500/600
498	15428 0			1,000	1995 PRICE LIST	JENNY	11	CARAMEL MOHAIR PLUSH DESIGNED BY JENNY KRANTZ	NONE	YES	RED	HD+SML RD	$187
499	15430 8			2,000	1993 PRICE LIST	NICOLAUS	11.8	ANTIQUE GOLD MOHAIR PLUSH DESIGNED BY JOYCE ANN HAUGHEY	NONE	YES	RED	RED PLASTIC	$200
500	15431 5			1,000	1995 PRICE LIST	BALLERINA	11.8	ANTIQUE ROSE MOHAIR PLUSH DESIGNED BY JENNY KRANTZ	NONE	YES	RED	HD+SML RD	$238
501	15440 2			1,000	1997 PRICE LIST	PIERRE	15.75	REDDISH BRN MOHAIR PLUSH, FULLY JTD W/STAND	GROWLER	YES	RED	HD+SML RD	$293
502	15445 7			2,000	1993 PRICE LIST	JACK	18.1	OLD GOLD MOHAIR PLUSH W/SHAVED MUZZLE BY JENNY KRANTZ	NONE	YES	RED	RED PLASTIC	$252
503		155/22	61022 9		1988 PRICE LIST	CAT	8.7						$150/200
504		156/22	61122 6		1988 PRICE LIST	CAT	8.7						$150/200
505	15545 4			3,000	1994 PRICE LIST	ELIZABETH	18.1	BRN MOHAIR PLUSH, 9 JOINTS	NONE	YES	RED	RED PLASTIC	$340
506	15550 8			2,000	1998 PRICE LIST	EDWIN	19.7	BRN MOHAIR, 6 JOINTS, HEATHER LYELL DESIGNER	NONE	YES	RED	RED PLASTIC	$307
507	15630 7		DUPL. #	1,500	1998 PRICE LIST	PHILLIPP	11.8	BEIGE MOHAIR FULLY JTD, GRN SCOTCH PLAID SCARF; DUPL #	GROWLER	YES	RED	HD+RD PL	$142
508	15630 7		DUPL. #	1,000	1995 PRICE LIST	GLOBETROTTER	11.8	HONEY MOHAIR PLUSH W/RUCKSACK & PAN W/RED BOW; DUPL #	NONE	YES	RED	HD+SML RD	$233
509	15631 4			500	1996 PRICE LIST	XAVER	11.8	HONEY MOHAIR PLUSH DRESSED IN BAVARIAN CLOTHES WITH HAT, INCLS SLED	NONE	YES	RED	HD+SML RD	$432
510	15635 2			1,500	1998 PRICE LIST	AGATHE	13.8	CREAM MOHAIR W/BLK MOHAIR COAT, FULLY JTD	NONE	YES	RED	HD+RD PL	$201
511	15638 3			1,500	1998 PRICE LIST	LUCKY BEATLE BEAR	13.8	BLK MOHAIR W/RED BEATLE COAT, FULLY JTD	NONE	YES	RED	HD+RD PL	$201
512	15645 1			1,500	1998 PRICE LIST	GUSTAV	17.7	DARK BRN MOHAIR WITH YELLOW MOHAIR IN VEST REGION, ARMS & KNEES BENT	NONE	YES	RED	HD+RD PL	$249
513		157/22			1982 PRICE LIST	CAT, BLK	8.7						$150/200
514	15701 4				1995 PRICE LIST	MINI FROM TAIWAN	2.4	TEDDY, CARAMEL SIGNED ON FOOT PAW	NONE	NO	NO	CHEST MTL	$61
515	15702 1				1995 PRICE LIST	MINI FROM TAIWAN	2.4	TEDDY, ROSE					$61
516	15703 8				1995 PRICE LIST	MINI FROM TAIWAN	2.4	TEDDY, CINNAMON (ZIMT), ATTACHED TO & PART OF 01611 7	NONE	ON PAW	NO	NO	$61
517	15704 5				1995 PRICE LIST	MINI FROM TAIWAN	3.15	JESTER, OLD GOLD					$110
518	15705 2				1995 PRICE LIST	MINI FROM TAIWAN	2.75	SLEEPY TEDDY W/TOY (SCHLAFTEDDY)					$110
519	15706 9			3,000	1995 PRICE LIST	MINI FROM TAIWAN	3.15	TEDDY, GOLD SIGNED ON FOOT PAWS	NONE	NO	NO	CHEST MTL	$110
520	15707 6			3,000	1995 PRICE LIST	MINI FROM TAIWAN	3.15	TEDDY, NOUGAT					$110
521	15708 3			3,000	1995 PRICE LIST	MINI FROM TAIWAN	4.3	MINIATURE IMPORTED FROM TAIWAN					$110
521a	15709 0			3,000	1996 PRICE LIST	MINI FROM TAIWAN	4.3	MINIATURE IMPORTED FROM TAIWAN					$75
522	15712 0				1996 CATALOG FLYER	MINI TEDDY	1.5	MINIATURE IMPORTED FROM TAIWAN					$50
523	15713 7				1996 CATALOG FLYER	MINI TEDDY	1.5	MINIATURE IMPORTED FROM TAIWAN					$50
524	15714 4				1996 CATALOG FLYER	MINI TEDDY	1.5	MINIATURE IMPORTED FROM TAIWAN					$50
525	15715 1				1996 CATALOG FLYER	MINI TEDDY	1.5	MINIATURE IMPORTED FROM TAIWAN					$50
526	15716 8				1996 CATALOG FLYER	MINI TEDDY	1.5	MINIATURE IMPORTED FROM TAIWAN					$50
527	15719 9				1996 CATALOG FLYER	MINI TEDDY	1.5	MINIATURE IMPORTED FROM TAIWAN					$50
528	15720 5			3,000	1996 CATALOG	MINI TEDDY	3	STUDENT, CINNAMON					$100
529	15721 2				1996 CATALOG	MINI TEDDY	3.5	SEMENTHA, DRESSED WITH SUNFLOWER HAT					$100
530	15722 9				1996 CATALOG	MINI TEDDY	3.5	ZAK, DRESSED WITH OPEN STRAW HAT					$100
531	15723 6				1996 CATALOG	MINI TEDDY	2.4	PANDA	NONE	NO	NO	NO	$60
532	15724 3				1996 CATALOG	MINI TEDDY	3.15	TEDDY, CINNAMON (ZIMT) WOOL MOHAIR					$100
533	15725 3				1996 CATALOG	MINI TEDDY	3.15	TEDDY, BLK					$100
534	15726 7				1996 CATALOG	MINI TEDDY	4	RAZZ, A GOLLIWOG					$60

REF #	EAN #	HERMANN OLD #	ALSO SEE	LIMITED NUMBER	DATA FROM	NAME	INCHES TALL	DESCRIPTION	VOICE	HANGING BOOKLET	ARM TAG	COMPANY LOGO	CURRENT RETAIL
535	15727 4				1996 CATALOG	MINI TEDDY	4	MATAZZ, A GOLLIWOG					$60
536	15728 1				1996 CATALOG	MINI TEDDY	2.4	TEDDY, OLD GOLD	NONE	NO	NO	NO	$50
537	15730 4				1995 FLYER CATALOG	KIKI W/BASE	2.8	CINNAMON DRESSED AS BIRD					$100
538	15731 4				1995 FLYER CATALOG	CHAPPY W/BASE	3.2	BRN DRESSED					$100
539	15732 8				1995 FLYER CATALOG	MALCOM W/BASE	3.2	GREY DRESSED AS REINDEER					$100
540	15733 5				1995 FLYER CATALOG	TABATHA W/BASE	2.8	WHT DRESSED AS CAT					$100
541	15734 2				1995 FLYER CATALOG	TORO W/BASE	2.8	BRN DRESSED AS BULL					$100
542	15740 3				1996 MINI CATALOG	BUFFY RABBIT	2.8	NOT A BEAR					$100
543	15741 0				1996 MINI CATALOG	FLUFFY RABBIT	2.8	NOT A BEAR					$100
544	15742 7				1996 MINI CATALOG	SADIE	2.8	GREY DRESSED IN HAT AND COLLAR					$100
545	15743 4				1996 MINI CATALOG	TING PANDA	2.8	DRESSED IN OVERALLS	NONE	NO	NO	ARM METAL	$100
546	15744 1				1996 MINI CATALOG	TEDDY	4.3	OLD GOLD WOOL MOHAIR; NOT PRODUCED, ORDERS RETURNED					$100
547	15745 8			3,000	1997 MINI CATALOG	CAMILLE, PERFUME BOTTLE	4.3	CONTAINS A PERFUME BOTTLE; MADE BY "LITTLE GEM"	NONE	NO	NO	ARM METAL	$115
548	15747 2			3,000	1997 MINI CATALOG	AMBER, NO-NO	3.3	NO-NO BEAR, BEIGE MOHAIR	NONE	NO	NO	ARM METAL	$115
549	15750 2				1995 PRICE LIST	WALL CASE W/MINI BEARS	LARGE	INCLUDES 8 MINI TEDDIES					$833
550	15751 9				1996 PRICE LIST	DISPLAY CASE	15 X 15	OCTAGONAL WOODEN LETTER CASE					$100
551	15755 7				1996 PRICE LIST	DISPLAY CASE W/BEARS	15X15	OCTAGONAL WOODEN LETTER CASE WITH 22 MINI BEARS					$1,750
552	15760 1				1996 MINI CATALOG	AMEILIA W/TEDDY	2.8	WHT DRESSED WITH SMALL GREY TEDDY					$100
553	15761 8				1996 MINI CATALOG	BEAR W/APE	2.8	OLD GOLD WITH SMALL APE					$100
554	15762 5				1996 MINI CATALOG	BEAR W/PANDA	2.8	CINNAMON WITH SMALL PANDA ON BACK	NONE	NO	NO	ARM METAL	$100
555	15763 2				1996 MINI CATALOG	BEAR W/DUCK	2.8	HPONEY DRESSED WITH DUCK					$100
556	15764 9				1996 CATALOG FLYER	MINI TEDDY	1.5	IMPORTED FROM TAIWAN					$80
557	15765 6				1996 CATALOG FLYER	MINI TEDDY	1.5	IMPORTED FROM TAIWAN					$95
558	15766 3				1996 CATALOG FLYER	MINI TEDDY	1.5	IMPORTED FROM TAIWAN					$95
559	15767 0				1996 CATALOG FLYER	MINI TEDDY	1.5	IMPORTED FROM TAIWAN					$80
560	15769 4				1996 CATALOG FLYER	MINI TEDDY	1.5	IMPORTED FROM TAIWAN					$95
561	15770 0				1995 FLYER CATALOG	HOLLY	3.1	WHT HEAD & PADS, RED BODY	NONE	NO	NO	ARM METAL	$89
562	15771 7				1995 FLYER CATALOG	IVY	3.1	WHT HEAD & PADS, GRN BODY	NONE	NO	NO	ARM METAL	$89
563	15772 4				1995 FLYER CATALOG	NICHOLAS W/BASE	3.1	HONEY DRESSED IN GRN XMAS OUTFIT W/WHT SML BEAR IN RED HAT					$100
564	15773 1				1995 FLYER CATALOG	KRIS + KRINGLE W/BASE	3.1	BLK BEAR W/ SANTA HAT HOLLY BOW W/SMALL WHT SNOWMAN					$100
565	15774 8				1995 FLYER CATALOG	HANSEL + RUDY W/BASE	3.1	BEIGE "JACK" W/WHT BIB & SMALL BEAR					$100
566	15775 5				1997 FLYER	FELIX	3.1	FELIX THE CAT					$90
567	15776 2				1997 FLYER	TOPSY	3.1	RABBIT					$90
568	15777 9				1997 FLYER	COTTONTAIL	3.1	RABBIT					$90
569	15778 6				1997 FLYER	CHRISTOPHER	3.1	BEAR IN PJ'S W/SML BEAR					$90
570	15780 9				1996 MINI CATALOG	TEDDY	1.6	TEDDY, CINNAMON					$50
571	15781 6				1996 MINI CATALOG	TEDDY	1.6	PANDA	NONE	NO	NO	NO	$50
572	15782 3				1996 MINI CATALOG	TEDDY	1.6	TEDDY, GRN					$50
573	15783 0				1996 CATALOG FLYER	MINI TEDDY	1.5	MINIATURE IMPORTED FROM TAIWAN					$50
574	15784 7				1996 CATALOG FLYER	MINI TEDDY	1.5	MINIATURE IMPORTED FROM TAIWAN					$50
575	15785 4				1996 CATALOG FLYER	MINI TEDDY	1.5	MINIATURE IMPORTED FROM TAIWAN					$50
576	15786 1				1996 CATALOG FLYER	MINI TEDDY	1.5	MINIATURE IMPORTED FROM TAIWAN					$50
577	15787 8				1996 CATALOG FLYER	MINI TEDDY	1.5	MINIATURE IMPORTED FROM TAIWAN					$50
578	15788 5				1996 CATALOG FLYER	MINI TEDDY	1.5	MINIATURE IMPORTED FROM TAIWAN					$50
579	15791 5				1996 MINI CATALOG	TEDDY	2	TEDDY, BEIGE					$50
580	15792 2				1996 MINI CATALOG	TEDDY	2	TEDDY, BLUE					$50
581	15793 9				1996 MINI CATALOG	TEDDY	2	TEDDY, RED					$50
582	15794 6				1996 MINI CATALOG	TEDDY	2	TEDDY, GOLD SIGNED ON FOOT PAD	NONE	NO	NO	NO	$50
583	15795 3				1996 MINI CATALOG	TEDDY	2	TEDDY, BRN					$50
584	15796 0				1996 MINI CATALOG	TEDDY	2.4	TEDDY, BEIGE					$50
585	15797 7				1996 MINI CATALOG	TEDDY	2.4	TEDDY, BRN					$50
586	15798 4				1996 MINI CATALOG	TEDDY	2	TEDDY, BLK					$50
587	15799 1				1996 MINI CATALOG	TEDDY	2	TEDDY, GRN					$50
588		158/42			1982 PRICE LIST	GROWLING TOMCAT	16.54						$400/500
589	15811 0				1996 CATALOG FLYER	MINI TEDDY	1.5	MINIATURE IMPORTED FROM TAIWAN					$95
590	15812 7				1996 CATALOG FLYER	MINI TEDDY	1.5	MINIATURE IMPORTED FROM TAIWAN					$95
591	15813 4				1996 CATALOG FLYER	MINI TEDDY	1.5	MINIATURE IMPORTED FROM TAIWAN					$95
592	15814 1				1996 CATALOG FLYER	MINI TEDDY	1.5	MINIATURE IMPORTED FROM TAIWAN					$95
593	15815 8				1995 PRICE LIST	TEDDY TREND COLLECTION	5.5	CARAMEL WOOL PLUSH W/LAVENDER BOW & CLAWS SEWN INTO BOTTOM FOOTPAD				TREND	$29
594	15820 2				1996 CATALOG FLYER	MINI TEDDY	1.5	MINIATURE IMPORTED FROM TAIWAN					$95

REF #	EAN #	HERMANN OLD #	ALSO SEE	LIMITED NUMBER	DATA FROM	NAME	INCHES TALL	DESCRIPTION	VOICE	HANGING BOOKLET	ARM TAG	COMPANY LOGO	CURRENT RETAIL
595	15821 9				1996 CATALOG FLYER	MINI TEDDY	1.5	MINIATURE IMPORTED FROM TAIWAN					$95
596	15822 6				1996 CATALOG FLYER	MINI TEDDY	1.5	MINIATURE IMPORTED FROM TAIWAN					$95
597	15823 3				1996 CATALOG FLYER	MINI TEDDY	1.5	MINIATURE IMPORTED FROM TAIWAN					$95
598	15824 0				1996 CATALOG FLYER	MINI TEDDY	1.5	MINIATURE IMPORTED FROM TAIWAN					$95
599	15825 7				1996 CATALOG FLYER	MINI TEDDY	1.5	MINIATURE IMPORTED FROM TAIWAN					$95
600	15826 4				1995 PRICE LIST	TEDDY TREND COLLECTION	10	CARAMEL WOVEN FUR WITH PULLOVER SWEATER				TREND	$37
601	15830 1			3,000	1997 FLYER	WILLYUM	4.7	DEB CANAHAN DESIGNS					$125
602	15831 8			3,000	1997 FLYER	GERTIE	4.7	DEB CANAHAN DESIGNS					$125
603	15832 5			3,000	1997 FLYER	POPPO	4.7	DEB CANAHAN DESIGNS					$125
605	15833 2			3,000	1995 PRICE LIST	SIMON	4.7	DEB CANAHAN DESIGNS					$125
606	15834 9			3,000	1997 FLYER	BRATTY BUTCHY	4.7	DEB CANAHAN DESIGNS					$125
607	15835 6			3,000	1995 PRICE LIST	TEDDY TREND COLLECTION	13.8	MOHAIR PLUSH, SURFACE WASHABLE, 5 JOINTS				TREND	$83
608	15840 0			2,000	1997 FLYER CATALOG	HATTIE	3	DEB CANAHAN DESIGNS					$95
609	15841 7			2,000	1997 FLYER CATALOG	HERSCHEL	3	DEB CANAHAN DESIGNS, BEIGE MOHAIR W/ BLUE FELT JACKET	NONE	NO	NO	HANGING MTL	$100
610		159/20			BEHA 1927 CATALOG	BONZO-DOG	7.9	STANDING, SOFT STUFFED, WITH RUFFLE, SQUINT EYES, MADE OF MOLTON					$200/300
611		159/25			BEHA 1927 CATALOG	BONZO-DOG	9.8	STANDING, SOFT STUFFED, WITH RUFFLE, SQUINT EYES, MADE OF MOLTON					$200/300
612		159/30			BEHA 1927 CATALOG	BONZO-DOG	11.8	STANDING, SOFT STUFFED, WITH RUFFLE, SQUINT EYES, MADE OF MOLTON					$200/300
613	15910 0				1997 FLYER CATALOG	CHOCOLATE	3.5	WHT COLLAR					$75
614	15911 7				1997 FLYER CATALOG	HONEY	3.5	WHT COLLAR					$75
615	15915 5				1997 FLYER CATALOG	OLD FASHIONED	3	MINIATURES					$75
616	15916 2				1997 FLYER CATALOG	MARMELADE	2.8	MINIATURES					$75
617	15917 9				1997 FLYER CATALOG	SILVER	2.8	MINIATURES					$75
618	15920 9				1997 FLYER CATALOG	JOLLY JESTER	2.8	MINIATURES					$75
619	15921 6				1997 FLYER CATALOG	CUDDLES	2.8	MINIATURES					$75
620	15922 3				1997 FLYER CATALOG	HUGGIE	2.8	MINIATURES					$75
621	15923 0				1997 FLYER CATALOG	SPANKY	2.8	MINIATURES					$75
622	15924 7				1997 FLYER CATALOG	JENNIE+DELIA	2.8	MINIATURES					$75
623	15925 4				1997 FLYER CATALOG	JACK+PUFF	2.8	MINIATURES					$75
624	15930 8				1997 XMAS FLYER	BEARFOOT & PREGNANT	2.4	MINIATURES					$75
625	15931 5				1997 XMAS FLYER	ZEKE	2	MINIATURES					$75
626	15932 2				1997 XMAS FLYER	NO SEE, NO HEAR, NO TELL	2.4	MINIATURES; 3 BEARS ON BENCH					$75
627	15933 9				1997 XMAS FLYER	SASSIE	3.2	MINIATURES					$75
628	15934 6				1997 XMAS FLYER	FIBBER	3.5	MINIATURES					$75
629	15935 3				1997 XMAS FLYER	MAGIC	3.2	MINIATURES					$75
630	15940 7				1997 XMAS FLYER	SANTA CLAUS	4	ARTIST MINIATURES CANHAM & SPIEGEL	NONE	NO			$75
631	15941 4				1997 XMAS FLYER	GOOSE W/RIDER	4	ARTIST MINIATURES CANHAM & SPIEGEL	NONE	NO			$75
632	15942 1				1997 XMAS FLYER	HALLOWEEN CAT	3.1	ARTIST MINIATURES CANHAM & SPIEGEL	NONE	NO			$75
633	15943 8				1997 XMAS FLYER	XMAS JESTER	3.1	ARTIST MINIATURES CANHAM & SPIEGEL	NONE	NO			$75
634		160/35	50235 7		1988 PRICE LIST	YORKSHIRE-TERRIER	13.8						$200/300
635		161/35	50335 4		1988 PRICE LIST	YORKSHIRE-TERRIER	13.8						$200/300
636	16014 4			1,000	1994 PRICE LIST	PANDA	5.5	BLK & WHT MOHAIR PLUSH W/RED BOW	NONE	YES	RED	SML RED PL	$80
637	16030 4			1,000	1996 PRICE LIST	PANDA	11.8	BLK & WHT MOHAIR PLUSH W/RED BOW	NONE	YES	RED	MTL HD+ SML RD	$125
638	16114 1		61/14		1988 PRICE LIST	ORIGINAL HERMANN	4.7	CINNAMON COLORED MOHAIR, W/BLUE BOW	NONE	YES	RED	RED PAPER	$45
639	16125 4		61/25		1988 PRICE LIST	ORIGINAL HERMAN	7.8	BUFF					$75
640	16125 7		61/25		1988 PRICE LIST	ORIGINAL HERMAN	11	CINNAMON MOHAIR 53%W 47%C	NONE	YES	BRN	RED PAPER	$125
641	16136 3		61/36		1988 PRICE LIST	ORIGINAL HERMAN	14.2	CINNAMON 100%W MOHAIR	GROWLER	YES	RED	RED PLASTIC	$150
642	16140?		61/40		HERMANN	ORIGINAL HERMANN	15.75	OLD GOLD 53%W & 47%C MOHAIR	GROWLER	YES	BRN	RED PLASTIC	$180
643	16150 9		61/50		1988 PRICE LIST	ORIGINAL HERMAN	19.7	CARAMEL MOHAIR 62%W 38% C	GROWLER	YES	GRN	RED PLASTIC	$225
644		162/40	50040 7		1982 PRICE LIST	YORKSHIRE TERRIER	15.75						$250/350
645	16210 0				1995 FLYER CATALOG	XMAS CHILDREN	4	LT BRN W/RED HOLLY BOW AND SANTA CAP					$100
646	16211 7				1995 FLYER CATALOG	XMAS CHILDREN	4	GRN W/RED HOLLY BOW AND SANTA CAP					$100
647	16214 8		62/14		1990 PRICE LIST	NOSTALGIC TEDDY	4.7	CARAMEL 53%W & 47%C MOHAIR, RED BOW TIE	NONE	YES	BRN	NO	$85
648	16214 8		62/14		HERMANN	NOSTALGIC TEDDY	4.7	CARAMEL 100% WOOL MOHAIR, RED BOW	NONE	YES	RED	SML RED PL	$85
649	16214 8		62/14 OLD		HERMANN 1993	NOSTALGIC TEDDY	5	CARAMEL 53%W & 47%C MOHAIR, LILAC TIE	NONE	NO	GRN	NO	$60
650	16217?		62/17w		ALSO SEE SU 70	NOSTALGIC TEDDY	4.7	WHT, 53%W & 47%C MOHAIR, STRIPED TIE, DBL TAGGED FOR JESCO	NONE	YES	BRN	MISSING	$65
651	16217 9		62/17		HERMANN	NOSTALGIC TEDDY	6.6	CARAMEL 53%W & 47%C MOHAIR, RED BOW TIE	NONE	YES	BRN	RED PAPER	$65
652	16217 9		62/17/1		1988 CATALOG	NOSTALGIC TEDDY	6.6	CHOCOLATE 53%W & 47%C MOHAIR, RED PLAID TIE	NONE	YES	BRN	NONE	$60
653	16220 9		62/20		CATALOG 1989	NOSTALGIC TEDDY	8.1	CARAMEL 53%W 47%C MOHAIR PLUSH W/RED BOW	NONE	YES	BRN	RED PAPER	$99
654	16225 4		62/25		1988 CATALOG	NOSTALGIC TEDDY	10.2	BRN 62% 38%C MOHAIR	NONE	YES	GRN	RED PAPER	$110

REF #	EAN #	HERMANN OLD #	ALSO SEE	LIMITED NUMBER	DATA FROM	NAME	INCHES TALL	DESCRIPTION	VOICE	HANGING BOOKLET	ARM TAG	COMPANY LOGO	CURRENT RETAIL
655	16230 8?		?62/30NSO?		1990 PRICE LIST	NOSTALGIC TEDDY	11.8	CARAMEL					$151
656	16230 8		62/30		HERMANN CIRCA 1982	ORIGINAL TEDDYBEAR	11.8	FADED ORANGE SHORT PILE MOHAIR, W/GLASS EYES, BLUE BOW; WAS MRF# "1"	GROWLER	NO	BRN	GRN PAPER	$135
657	16230 8?		62/30NSO		CATALOG 1994/95	NOSTALGIC TEDDY	11.8	CARAMEL MOHAIR PLUSH W/PLAID BOW, BRN DBL, ACRYLIC, 30% COTTON	GROWLER	YES	BRN	RED PLASTIC	$130
658	16235 3		62/35		1988 CATALOG	NOSTALGIC TEDDY	13.7	CARAMEL MOHAIR PLUSH W/RED BOW	GROWLER	YES	BRN	RED PLASTIC	$150
659	16235?		62/35/1		SEE JESCO CH 140	NOSTALGIC TEDDY	13.7	CHOCOLATE 53%W & 47%C MOHAIR, PLAID TIE, SHEARED PADS & PAWS	GROWLER	YES	BRN	GOLD PLASTIC	$150
660	16240 7		62/40		1990 PRICE LIST	NOSTALGIC TEDDY	15.75	CARAMEL 53%W & 47%C MOHAIR PLUSH W/RED BOW	GROWLER	YES	BRN	RED PLASTIC	$188
661	16250 6		62/50		1990 PRICE LIST	NOSTALGIC TEDDY	19.7	CARAMEL 62%W & 38%C MOHAIR PLUSH W/RED BOW	GROWLER	YES	GRN	RED PLASTIC	$279
662	16250?		62/50 LI		HERMANN 1988	NOSTALGIC TEDDY	19.7	BLK MOHAIR W/RED & WHT STRIPED BOW	GROWLER	YES	GRN	RED PLASTIC	$200
663		163/40	50140 4		1982 PRICE LIST	YORKSHIRE TERRIER	15.75						$250/350
664	16308 4		63/8		1988 PRICE LIST	NOSTALGIC TEDDY	3.15	OLD GOLD MOHAIR PLUSH W/PLAID BOW; 1923 REPLICA	NONE	NO	BRN	RED PAPER	$45
665	16314 5		63/14		1988 PRICE LIST	NOSTALGIC TEDDY	5.5	OLD GOLD MOHAIR PLUSH W/PLAID BOW; 1923 REPLICA	NONE	YES	RED	SML RED PL	$77
666	16317 6		63/17		1988 PRICE LIST	NOSTALGIC TEDDY	7	OLD GOLD 100% MOHAIR RED BOW; 1923 REPLICA	NONE	YES	RED	SML RED PL	$83
667	16320 6		63/20		1988 PRICE LIST	NOSTALGIC TEDDY	7.9	OLD GOLD MOHAIR WITH PLAID BOW; 1923 REPLICA	NONE	YES	RED	HD+SML RD	$95
668	16325 1		63/25		1988 PRICE LIST	NOSTALGIC TEDDY	10.2	OLD GOLD MOHAIR PLUSH W/PLAID BOW; 1923 REPLICA	NONE	YES	RED	SML RED PL	$108
669	16330 5		63/30		1988 PRICE LIST	NOSTALGIC TEDDY	11.8	OLD GOLD; 1923 REPLICA	GROWLER	YES	RED	RED PLASTIC	$144
670	16335 0		63/35		1988 PRICE LIST	NOSTALGIC TEDDY	14.2	OLD GOLD MOHAIR PLUSH W/PLAID BOW; 1923 REPLICA	GROWLER	YES	BRN	RED PLASTIC	$161
671	16340 4		63/40		1988 PRICE LIST	NOSTALGIC TEDDY	15.75	OLD GOLD MOHAIR PLUSH W/PLAID BOW, W/KATHY ANN TAG; 1923 REPLICA	GROWLER	YES	RED	RED PLASTIC	$186
672	16350 3		63/50		1988 PRICE LIST	NOSTALGIC TEDDY	18.1	OLD GOLD; 1923 REPLICA	GROWLER	YES	RED	RED PLASTIC	$279
673	16360 2		63/60		1988 PRICE LIST	NOSTALGIC TEDDY	23.6	OLD GOLD MOHAIR PLUSH W/PLAID BOW; 1923 REPLICA	GROWLER	YES	RED	HD+RED PL	$377
674	16380 0		06380 0 & 63/80	500	BOOK 1989 PG 87	NOSTALGIC BEAR	31.5	OLD GOLD MOHAIR W/RED BOW	GROWLER	YES	RED	RED PLASTIC	$500
675		164/28			1982 PRICE LIST	SKYE TERRIER GREY	11						$200/300
676	16408 1		64/8		1988 CATALOG	TEDDY GREY BENDABLE	3.3	GREY 53%W & 47%C MOHAIR, BENDABLE	NONE	NO	BRN	RED PAPER	$39
677	16414 2		64/14		1988 PRICE LIST	TEDDY BEAR GREY CUB	4.7	GREY	NONE	YES	RED	RED PAPER	$77
678	16420 3		64/20		HERMANN 1986	TEDDY BEAR GREY CUB	7.9	GREY	NONE	YES	BRN	RED PAPER	$75
679	16425 8		64/25		1988 CATALOG	TEDDY BEAR GREY	10.2	GREY	NONE	YES	BRN	RED PAPER	$75
680	16430 2		64/30		1988 CATALOG	TEDDY BEAR GREY	11.8	GREY	GROWLER	YES	BRN	RED PLASTIC	$100
681	16440 1		64/40		HERMANN 1986	TEDDY BEAR PAPA GREY	15.75	GREY	GROWLER	YES	BRN	RED PLASTIC	$150
682		165/28			1982 PRICE LIST	SKYE TERRIER BRN	11						$250/350
683	16514 9		62/14 MAIS		1988 CATALOG	NOSTALGIC CLASSIC	5.6	MAIZE 100% WOOL MOHAIR	NONE	YES	RED	RED PAPER	$50
684	16517 0		62/17MAIS		1988 CATALOG	NOSTALGIC CLASSIC	6.6	MAIZE MOHAIR					$60
685	16530 3		62/30MAIS		HERMANN CIRCA 1986	NOSTALGIC TEDDY	11.8	MAIZE 53%W & 47%C MOHAIR W/BLUE BOW, SHEARED PADS	GROWLER	SHORT BOOKLET	GRN	RED PLASTIC	$200
686		166/18			1982 PRICE LIST	YOUNG BEAR, LYING	7						$200/300
687		166/25			1982 PRICE LIST	YOUNG BEAR, LYING	9.8						$200/300
688		166/28			1982 PRICE LIST	YOUNG BEAR, SLEEPING	11	WITH MUSIC BOX					$250/350
689	16614 6		62/14s		KATHY ANN CAT 1989	NOSTALGIC BLK BEAR	5.6	BLK 100%W MOHAIR W/RED BOW	NONE	YES	RED	RED PAPER	$77
690	16620 7		62/20s		KATHY ANN CAT 1989	NOSTALGIC BLK BEAR	7.9	BLK 53%W & 47%C MOHAIR W/RED BOW - ALSO SEE SU 80LI	NONE	YES	BRN	RED PAPER	$95
691	16625?		62/25s		KATHY ANN #SU 100LI	NOSTALGIC BLK BEAR	10.2	BLK 53%W & 47%C MOHAIR W/RED BOW - LISTED AS SU 100LI	NONE	SHORT BOOKLET	GRN	NONE	$130
692	16630 6		62/30s		KATHY ANN CAT 1989	NOSTALGIC BLK BEAR	11.8	BLK 100%W MOHAIR W/RED BOW	GROWLER	YES	RED	RED PLASTIC	$144
693	16714 3		62/14w		KATHY ANN CAT 1989	NOSTALGIC TEDDY	5.6	WHT 100% WOOL MOHAIR W/RED BOW	NONE	YES	RED	SML RD PL	$82
694	16720 4		62/20w		KATHY ANN CAT 1989	NOSTALGIC TEDDY	7.9	WHT 100% WOOL MOHAIR W/RED BOW	NONE	YES	RED	RED PAPER	$120
695	16730 3		62/30w		KATHY ANN CAT 1989	NOSTALGIC TEDDY	11.8	WHT 53% WOOL & 47% COTTON MOHAIR W/RED BOW	GROWLER	YES	BRN	RED PLASTIC	$144
696		168/32			1984 PRICE LIST	BEAR, SLEEPING W/MUSIC	12.6						$150
697	16830 0				1991 PRICE LIST	RUGGED REGGIE BEAR	11.8	BRN MOHAIR 100% WOOL PLUSH W/PLAID BOW	GROWLER	YES	RED	RED PLASTIC	$170
698	16840 9				1991 PRICE LIST	RUGGED REGGIE BEAR	15.75	BRN MOHAIR 100% WOOL PLUSH W/PLAID BOW	GROWLER	YES	RED	RED PLASTIC	$198
699	16850 8				1991 PRICE LIST	RUGGED REGGIE BEAR	19.7	BRN MOHAIR 100 % WOOL PLUSH W/PLAID BOW	GROWLER	YES	RED	RED PLASTIC	$277
700	16860?				GROVE CATALOG	RUGGED REGGIE BEAR	23.6	BRN MOHAIR PLUSH W/PLAID BOW					$240
701	16880 5			500	BOOK 1991 PG 88	RUGGED REGGIE BEAR	31	BRN MOHAIR PLUSH W/PLAID BOW					$750/1000
702	16880?			500	BOOK 1993 PG 92	RUGGED REGGIE BEAR	31	ANTIQUE BEIGE MOHAIR					$750/1000
703		169/24			1984 PRICE LIST	BEAR, SLEEPING	9.5	BRN					$200/300
704		169/28			1982 PRICE LIST	BEAR, MUSICAL SLEEPING	11						$200/300
705		169/32			1984 PRICE LIST	BEAR, SLEEPING	12.6	EGGSHELL					$250/350
706	16913 0		01632	300	1996 SPECIAL	HUMMEL	12.6	OLD GOLD, WATER CARRIER DRESSED	GROWLER	YES	RED	MTL+RED PL	$600
707	16914 7		69/14AG	5,000	KATHY ANN CAT 1989	NO/NO BEAR	5.5	OLD GOLD 100% WOOL MOHAIR ON DISPLAY BOX, RED RIBBON	NONE	YES	RED	RED PAPER/PL	$75
708	16915 4		69/14s	5,000	KATHY ANN CAT 1989	NO/NO BEAR	5.5	BLK 100% WOOL MOHAIR ON DISPLAY BOX, RED RIBBON	NONE	YES	RED	RED PLASTIC	$105
709	16915 7			5,000	BOOK 1989 PG 87	NO-NO BEAR	5.5	BLK W/RED RIBBON					$105
710	16916 1			5,000	1994 PRICE LIST	NO-NO-BEAR, NOSTALGIC	5.5	CINNAMON MOHAIR PLUSH W/GRN PRTD BOW	NONE	YES	RED	RED PLASTIC	$105
711	16920 8			1,500	1998 PRICE LIST	NO-NO BEAR	7.9	OLD GOLD MOHAIR W/YELLOW BOW	NONE	YES	RED	RED PLASTIC	$123

REF #	EAN #	HERMANN OLD #	ALSO SEE	LIMITED NUMBER	DATA FROM	NAME	INCHES TALL	DESCRIPTION	VOICE	HANGING BOOKLET	ARM TAG	COMPANY LOGO	CURRENT RETAIL
712	16930 7			4,000	1990 PRICE LIST	NO-NO BEAR	11.8	SAND COLOR 100% WOOL MOHAIR W/ RED BOW; 1922 REPLICA	NONE	YES	RED	RED PLASTIC	$190
713	16931 4			2,000	1996 PRICE LIST	NO-NO BEAR	11.8	CARAMEL MOHAIR PLUSH	NONE	YES	RED	RED PLASTIC	$190
714	16935 2		69/35		HERMANN	NO-NO BEAR	14.1	SILVER MINK 100% WOOL MOHAIR W/RED BOW; 1922 REPLICA	NONE	YES	RED	RED PLASTIC	$190
715	16935 2		69/35		BOOK 1986 PG 87	NO-NO BEAR	14.1	NOUGAT 100% MOHAIR, W/RED BOW, SIGNED BOOKLET; 1922 REPLICA	NONE	YES	RED	RED PLASTIC	$190
716	16935 2		69/35		BOOK 1986 PG 87	NO-NO BEAR	14.1	NUTMEG 53%W & 47%C MOHAIR, W/RED BOW; 1922 REPLICA	NONE	YES	BRN	RED PLASTIC	$190
717		170/30	50530 3		1986 PRICE LIST	FOX TERRIER	11.8						$200/300
718		170/35	50535 8		1989 PRICE LIST	FOX TERRIER	13.8						$200/300
719		170/40			1986 PRICE LIST	FOX TERRIER	15.75						$250/350
720	17040 2		70/40	3,000	BOOK 1986 PG 87	JUBILEE BEAR	15.75	BRN TIPPED CREAM LONG FIBER MOHAIR W/SHAVED MUZZLE; 1925 REPLICA	GROWLER	YES	GRN	RED PLASTIC	$175
721	17145 4		71/45	2,000	KATHY ANN CAT 1989	LILLY	18.1	LILAC TIPPED LONG MOHAIR W/LAVENDER BOW	GROWLER	YES	RED	RED PLASTIC	$185
722	17220 6			2,000	1993 PRICE LIST	BEAR, STANDING	7.9	WHT MOHAIR	NONE	YES	RED	HD+SML PL	$157
723	17221 3			2,000	1993 PRICE LIST	BEAR, STANDING	7.9	FASHION MOHAIR					$121
724	17222 0			2,000	BOOK 1993 PG 91	LOU, STANDING BEAR	7.9	BRN W/RED VEST WHT SHIRT BOW TIE					$157
725	17225 3		72/25	2,000	1990 PRICE LIST	CIRKUS BEAR	10.1	CARAMEL 100% WOOL MOHAIR W/CHAIN IN NOSE TO COLLAR; 1929 REPLICA	NONE	YES	RED	RED PLASTIC	$120
726	17320 5			1,000	1996 PRICE LIST	SKIER	10.2	BRN MOHAIR PLUSH ON SKIES, FULLY JTD	NONE	YES	RED	SML RED PL	$150
727	17321 2			1,000	1996 PRICE LIST	CHIMNEY CLEANER	7.9	OLD GOLD MOHAIR FULLY JTD WITH TOOLS	NONE	YES	RED	HD+SML PL	$145
728	17326 7			2,000	1991 PRICE LIST	BERLIN WALL BEAR	10.2	HONEY DISTRESSED CURLY MOHAIR, SOFT, W/BRN SUEDE BAG; PIECE OF BERLIN WALL IN BAG	NONE	YES	RED	RED	$250
729	17328 1			2,000	BOOK 1988 PG 81	ICH BIN EIN BERLINER	11	BRN MOHAIR W/CROWN & "ICH BIN EIN BERLINER" SASH	NONE	YES	RED	RED PLASTIC	$120
730		174/30			1982 PRICE LIST	FOX TERRIER	11.8						$200/300
731	17420 2			300	HERMANN 1998 DATA	ALPINE HORN PLAYER	7.9	ANTIQUE MOHAIR, STANDING W/ALPINE HORN, BLK HAT/ JACKET		YES	RED	RED PLASTIC	$150
732	17425 7		74/25	2,000	KATHY ANN CAT 1989	STANDING BEAR	10.2	DARK BRN MOHAIR PLUSH, TAN MUZZLE, 5 JOINTS; 1929 REPLICA				RED PLASTIC	$250
733	17550 6			2,000	1991 PRICE LIST	DESIGNER BEAR	18.1	OLD GOLD MOHAIR W/PLAID BOW, EMBROIDERED PAW PAD	GROWLER	YES	RED	RED PLASTIC	$350
734		176/30			1982 PRICE LIST	AIREDALE	11.8						$250/350
735	17630 5		76/30		1990 PRICE LIST	TEDDY BEAR	11.8	BRN MINK 30%C & 70% ACRYLIC PLUSH W/RED BOW	NONE	YES	RED	RED PLASTIC	$203
736	17640 4		76/40		1990 PRICE LIST	TEDDY BEAR	15.75	BRN MINK 30%C & 70% ACRYLIC PLUSH W/RED BOW	GROWLER	YES	BRN	RED PLASTIC	$162
737	17650 3		76/50		1990 PRICE LIST	TEDDY BEAR	19.7	BRN MINK 30%C & 70% ACRYLIC PLUSH W/RED BOW	GROWLER	YES	BRN	RED PLASTIC	$183
738	17680 0		76/80		1990 PRICE LIST	TEDDY BEAR	31	BRN MINK PLUSH W/RED BOW, TAN SHAVED MUZZLE					$426
739	17698 5		76/120		1990 PRICE LIST	TEDDY BEAR	47	BRN MINK PLUSH W/RED BOW, TAN SHAVED MUZZLE					$1,538
740	17699 2		76/150		1990 PRICE LIST	TEDDY BEAR	60	BRN MINK PLUSH W/RED BOW, TAN SHAVED MUZZLE	GROWLER	YES	RED	LG RED PL	$2,118
741	17730 2		77/30		1988 CATALOG	TEDDY BEAR	11.8	BEIGE, BIBER IMITATION, RED PLASTIC LOGO, ALL LIMBS MOVEABLE					$114
742	17731 9				1996 PRICE LIST	TEDDY BEAR	11.8	BRN, BIBER IMITATION, ALL LIMBS AND HEAD MOVEABLE	SQUEAKER	YES	RED	RED PLASTIC	$114
743	17740 1		77/40		1988 CATALOG	TEDDY BEAR	15.75	BEIGE, BIBER IMITATION, RED PLASTIC LOGO, ALL LIMBS MOVEABLE					$300/400
744	17750 0		77/50		1988 CATALOG	TEDDY BEAR	19.7	BEIGE MINK PLUSH, RED PLASTIC LOGO, ALL LIMBS MOVEABLE					$400/500
745	17780 7		77/80		1988 CATALOG	TEDDY BEAR	31	BEIGE MINK PLUSH, RED PLASTIC LOGO, ALL LIMBS MOVEABLE					$550/750
746	17830 9				1991 PRICE LIST	TEDDY BEAR	11.8	LIGHT BRN					$250/350
747	17840 8				1991 PRICE LIST	TEDDY BEAR	15.75	LIGHT BRN; DUPL #					$300/400
748	17840 8			2,000	1997 PRICE LIST	BENJAMIN (DUPL. #)	15.75	LT BEIGE WOVEN FUR "BENJAMIN" W/BLUE STRIPED DENIM JUMPER; ARTIST SCHAFER-SIGMUND	NONE	YES	RED	HD+RD PL	$174
749	17841 5			2,000	1998 PRICE LIST	BRAUNI	15.75	BRN MINK PLUSH, "BRNI"; ARTIST SCHAFER-SIGMUND	NONE	YES	RED	HD+RD PL	$174
750	17843 9			1,500	1998 PRICE LIST	LARS, POLAR BEAR	15.75	WHT MOHAIR, W/BLUE-WHT SCARF, TAN PAWS	NONE	YES	RED	HD+RD PL	$215
751	17850 7				1991 PRICE LIST	TEDDY BEAR	19.7	LIGHT BRN					$250/350
752		180/15	54515 6		1987 PRICE LIST	MOLLY, SITTING DOG	5.5	LIGHT BRN TIPPED W/WHT BELLY AND FRONT PAWS				RED PAPER	$100/150
753		180/25	54525 5		1987 PRICE LIST	MOLLY, SITTING DOG	10.2	LIGHT BRN TIPPED W/WHT BELLY AND FRONT PAWS				RED PAPER	$125/175
754	18025 8				1992 PRICE LIST	YOUNG BEAR	10.2	LT BRN MINK PLUSH W/LT PLAID BOW					$110
755	18030 2				1992 PRICE LIST	YOUNG BEAR	11.8	LT BRN MINK PLUSH W/LT PLAID BOW					$129
756	18040 1		80/40		1992 PRICE LIST	YOUNG BEAR	15.75	LT BEIGE 30%C 70% ACRYLIC PLUSH, RED BOW, ALL LIMBS MOVEABLE	NONE	YES	RED PAPER	RED PLASTIC	$195
757	18121 7				1993 PRICE LIST	COATI BEAR	7.9	WHT LLAMA PLUSH					$150/200
758	18122 4				1993 PRICE LIST	COATI BEAR	7.9	EGGPLANT (CREAM WHT) LAMA PLUSH					$150/200
759	18123 1				1993 PRICE LIST	COATI BEAR	7.9	BRN MINK PLUSH					$150/200
760	18135 4				1995 CATALOG	TEDDY BEAR	14.2	BRN TIPPED WOVEN FUR W/PLAID BOW W/OPEN MOUTH & TAN MUZZLE					$170
761	18140 8		81/40		1995 CATALOG	TEDDY BEAR	15.75	BRN BIBER IMITATION, RED BOW, ALL LIMBS MOVEABLE				RED PLASTIC	$201
762	18418 8		84/18		1985 PRICE LIST	YOUNG BEAR	8.5	MINK PLUSH W/RED BOW, 70% ACRYLIC, 30% COTTON, SET IN MUZZLE, TAN SHAVED	NONE	YES	RED	RED PAPER	$96
763	18425 6		84/25		1984 PRICE LIST	YOUNG BEAR	10.2	MINK PLUSH W/RED BOW, 70% ACRYLIC 30% COTTON, SET IN MUZZLE, TAN SHAVED	NONE	YES	RED	RED PAPER	$108

REF #	EAN #	HERMANN OLD #	ALSO SEE	LIMITED NUMBER	DATA FROM	NAME	INCHES TALL	DESCRIPTION	VOICE	HANGING BOOKLET	ARM TAG	COMPANY LOGO	CURRENT RETAIL
764	18430 0	84/30			1984 PRICE LIST	YOUNG BEAR	11.8	MINK PLUSH W/RED BOW, 70% ACRYLIC 30% COTTON, SET IN MUZZLE, TAN SHAVED	NONE	YES	RED	RED PLASTIC	$127
765	18435 5	84/35			1982 PRICE LIST	YOUNG BEAR	14.2	MINK PLUSH W/RED BOW, 70% ACRYLIC 30% COTTON, SET IN MUZZLE, TAN SHAVED	GROWLER	YES	RED	RED PLASTIC	$153
766	18440 9	84/40			1982 PRICE LIST	YOUNG BEAR	15.75	MINK PLUSH W/RED BOW, 70% ACRYLIC 30% COTTON, SET IN MUZZLE, TAN SHAVED	GROWLER	YES	BRN	RED PLASTIC	$170
767	18450 8	84/50			1982 PRICE LIST	YOUNG BEAR	19.7	MINK PLUSH W/RED BOW, 70% ACRYLIC 30% COTTON, SET IN MUZZLE, TAN SHAVED					$246
768	18528 4			500	1998 PRICE LIST	YOUNG BEAR	11	BRN TIPPED MOHAIR PLUSH W/RED BOW, SET IN MUZZLE, TAN SHAVED	GROWLER	YES	RED	HD+RED PL	$141
769	18535 2			2,000	1995 CATALOG	YOUNG BEAR REPLICA	14.2	BRN TIPPED MOHAIR PLUSH W/RED BOW					$214
770	18618 2	86/18		4,000	KATHY ANN CAT 1989	PANDA	7	BLK & WHT 30%C & 70% ACRYLIC W/RED BOW, 5 JOINTS	NONE	YES	RED	RED PAPER	$70
771	18625 0	86/25		3,000	KATHY ANN CAT 1989	PANDA	10.2	BLK & WHT 30%C & 70% ACRYLIC W/RED BOW, 5 JOINTS; ALSO JESCO (FROM HERMANN FAMILY)	NONE	YES	RED	RED PAPER	$200
772	18630 4	86/30		2,000	KATHY ANN CAT 1989	PANDA	11.8	BLK & WHT 30%C & 70% ACRYLIC W/RED BOW, 5 JOINTS; ALSO JESCO					$200/300
773	19040 0	80081/40			1988 CATALOG	SITTING TEDDY BEAR	15.75	SITTING BRN MINK PLUSH, ARMS MOVEABLE				RED PLASTIC	$250/350
774	19047 9			800	1997 PRICE LIST	FROSTY	18.1	GREY-WHT TIPPED WOVEN MOHAIR, NAME & # EMBROIDERED ON PAW	GROWLER	YES	RED	HD+RED PL	$209
775	19055 4			2,000	1992 PRICE LIST	AMANDA	21.7	WHT MINK PLUSH ARTIST BEAR BY JOYCE ANN HAUGHEY	NONE	YES	RED	RED PLASTIC	$250
776	19155 1			1,000	1994 PRICE LIST	TEDDY BEAR, FLEXIBLE	21.7	BEIGE MOHAIR PLUSH W/PLAID DRESS, FLEXIBLE FRAME	NONE	YES	RED	HD+RED PL	$710
777	19156 8			1	1994 PRICE LIST	TEDDY BEAR, FLEXIBLE	21.7	BEIGE MOHAIR PLUSH W/FLOWERED DRESS	NONE	NO	RED	RED PLASTIC	$710
778		192/45			1982 PRICE LIST	PARROT	17.7						$250/350
779	19328 9			2,000	KATHY ANN CAT 1989	HONEY BEAR	11	ORANGE-BRN BODY W/WHT FACE, DRESSED IN RAINBOW OVERALLS W/HAT					$200/300
780	19445 3				1994 PRICE LIST	NOSTALGIC TEDDY	16.5	CREAM WHT 70% ACRYLIC 30% COTTON PLUSH, LAV PADS	NONE	YES	RED	RED PLASTIC	$175
781	19540 5				1992 PRICE LIST	TOM	15.75	BLK MINK PLUSH W/BRN NOSE BLUE & GRN BOW, DARK GRN PADS	GROWLER	YES	RED	RED PLASTIC	$167
782		196/16	42016 3		1982 PRICE LIST	OWL	6.3						$125/175
783		196/16K	42017 0		1982 PRICE LIST	OWL	6.3						$125/175
784		196/18	42018 7		1982 PRICE LIST	OWL	7						$125/175
785		196/18K	42019 4		1982 PRICE LIST	OWL	7						$125/175
786		196/25	42025 5		1982 PRICE LIST	OWL	9.8						$150/200
787		1960/35	56035 7		1988 PRICE LIST	MALTESE CAT	13.8						$150/200
788		1961/35	56135 4		1988 PRICE LIST	MALTESE CAT	13.8						$150/200
789		1962/30			1982 PRICE LIST	BOBTAIL	11.8						$125/175
790		1962/48	55048 8		1987 PRICE LIST	BOBTAIL NEWFIE	18.9	WHT FOREPAWS AND FACE, LONG PILE, DARK GREY HINDQUARTERS				RED PLASTIC	$200/300
791		1962/60	55060 0		1987 PRICE LIST	BOBTAIL NEWFIE	23.6	WHT FOREPAWS AND FACE, LONG PILE, DARK GREY REAR AND EARS				RED PLASTIC	$200/300
792	19645 7			1,000	1992 PRICE LIST	BILL	18.1	CREAM UNCOMBED WOOL PLUSH					$300/400
793		197/18			1982 PRICE LIST	OWL, MUSICAL	7						$150/200
794	19745 4			1,000	1993 PRICE LIST	"OLIVER"	18.1	BRN TIPPED MINK 70% ACRYLIC & 30%C PLUSH W/PINK NOSE	NONE	YES	RED	RED PLASTIC	$192
795	19845 1			1,000	1996 PRICE LIST	PETER	18.1	BLK TIPPED HONEY 70% ACRYLIC, 30% COTTON PLUSH					$175
796		198/25	42125 2		1984 PRICE LIST	PARROT, GRN	9.84						$125/175
797		199/25	42225 9		1984 PRICE LIST	PARROT, BLUE	9.84						$125/175
798		20/16			BEHA 1927 CATALOG	DOG, YELLOW	6.3	YELLOW WOOL PLUSH W/BRN EARS					$150/200
799		20/20?			BEHA 1927 CATALOG	DOG, YELLOW	7.9	YELLOW WOOL PLUSH W/BRN EARS					$150/200
800		20/23?			BEHA 1927 CATALOG	DOG, YELLOW	9	YELLOW WOOL PLUSH W/BRN EARS					$150/200
801		20/27?			BEHA 1927 CATALOG	DOG, YELLOW	10.6	YELLOW WOOL PLUSH W/BRN EARS					$200/300
802		20/28			BEHA 1927 CATALOG	DOG, YELLOW	11.8	YELLOW WOOL PLUSH W/BRN EARS					$200/300
803		20/28			1982 PRICE LIST	PINGO	11.8						$200/300
804		20/32			BEHA 1927 CATALOG	DOG, YELLOW	12.6	YELLOW WOOL PLUSH W/BRN EARS					$200/300
805		200/35			BEHA 1927 CATALOG	PARROT	13.8	1a LONG PILE PLUSH, COLORED, SOFT STUFFED					$250/350
806		200/40			BEHA 1927 CATALOG	PARROT	15.75	1a LONG PILE PLUSH, COLORED, SOFT STUFFED					$250/350
807		200/50			BEHA 1927 CATALOG	PARROT	19.8	1a LONG PILE PLUSH, COLORED, SOFT STUFFED					$300/400
808		200/60			BEHA 1927 CATALOG	PARROT	23.75	1a LONG PILE PLUSH, COLORED, SOFT STUFFED					$500/600
809		2000/33	37033 8		1982 PRICE LIST	PANTHER, BLK	12.6						$75/125
810		2000/58			1982 PRICE LIST	PANTHER, BLK	22.8						$75/125
811		2001/58			1982 PRICE LIST	LION	22.8						$75/125
812		2002/50			1982 PRICE LIST	LION	19.7						$75/125
813	20025 3		4/25		1988 CATALOG	TEDDY BEAR WASHABLE	10.2	HONEY MINK PLUSH, RED BOW, GRN PAPER TAG					$150/200
814	20026 0		4/25K		1988 CATALOG	TEDDY BEAR WASHABLE	10.2	HONEY MINK PLUSH, RED BOW, GRN PAPER TAG					$150/200
815		2003/33			1983 PRICE LIST	LEOPARD, LYING	12.6						$75/125
816		2003/40			1982 PRICE LIST	LEOPARD	15.75						$75/125

REF #	EAN #	HERMANN OLD #	ALSO SEE	LIMITED NUMBER	DATA FROM	NAME	INCHES TALL	DESCRIPTION	VOICE	HANGING BOOKLET	ARM TAG	COMPANY LOGO	CURRENT RETAIL
817		2003/58			1982 PRICE LIST	LEOPARD	22.8						$100/150
818	20030 7		4/30		1988 CATALOG	TEDDY BEAR WASHABLE	11.8	HONEY MINK PLUSH, RED BOW, GRN PAPER TAG					$200/300
819	20035 2		4/35		1988 CATALOG	TEDDY BEAR WASHABLE	14.2	HONEY MINK PLUSH, RED BOW, GRN PAPER TAG					$200/300
820		2005/25	43025 4		1988 PRICE LIST	FOX	9.8						$75/125
821		2005/35	43035 3		1988 PRICE LIST	FOX	13.8						$75/125
822		2010/55			KALINKE CIRCA 1980	BEAR, LAYING DOWN	22	LINK CHAIN COLLAR, DATA FROM BLK/ WHT PHOTOCOPY OF CATALOG SEGMENT				MTL W/PAPER	$100/150
823		2014/35			1982 PRICE LIST	LION	13.8						$100/150
824		2014/45			1982 PRICE LIST	LION	17.7						$100/150
825		2014/60			1982 PRICE LIST	LION	23.6						$125/175
826		2016/35	36135 0		1982 PRICE LIST	LEOPARD	13.8						$100/150
827		2016/45			1982 PRICE LIST	LEOPARD	17.7						$100/150
828		2016/60	36160 2		1982 PRICE LIST	LEOPARD	23.6						$125/175
829		2016/80			1982 PRICE LIST	LEOPARD	31.5						$150/200
830		2017/45			1982 PRICE LIST	LEOPARD	17.72						$125/175
831		2017/60			1982 PRICE LIST	LEOPARD	17.7						$125/175
832		2017/80			1982 PRICE LIST	LEOPARD	31.5						$150/200
833		2018/35	37135 9		1982 PRICE LIST	PANTHER	13.8						$100/150
834	20185 4				1994 PRICE LIST	BEAR, SPECTACLED	33	DARK BRN MINK PLUSH 30% C & 70% ACRYLIC W/COLOR AROUND EYES	NONE	YES	RED	RED PLASTIC	$400
835		2019/42	37542 5		1988 PRICE LIST	PANTHER	16.5						$125/175
836		2019/60	37560 9		1989 PRICE LIST	PANTHER	23.6						$150/200
837		2021/30			1982 PRICE LIST	CAT, LYING DOWN	11.8						$100/150
838		2022/25			1982 PRICE LIST	CAT, STANDING	9.8						$100/150
839		2023/25			1982 PRICE LIST	CAT, STANDING	9.8						$75/125
840		2024/20			1982 PRICE LIST	CAT, STANDING	7.9						$75/125
841		2024/25			1982 PRICE LIST	CAT, STANDING	9.8						$75/125
842		2025/20			1986 PRICE LIST	CAT	7.9						$75/125
843		2025/25			1986 PRICE LIST	CAR	9.8						$100/150
844	20250 9		80002/50		1988 CATALOG	POLAR BEAR	19.7						$250/350
845		2026/20			1984 PRICE LIST	CAT	7.9						$100/150
846		2026/20F			1984 PRICE LIST	CAT ON WHEELS	7.9	TAWNY W/WHT MUZZLE & INNER EAR, RED BOW & NOSE, RED WOOD WHEELS	NONE	YES	RED	RED PLASTIC	$100/150
847		2026/25			1982 PRICE LIST	CAT, STANDING	9.8						$100/150
848		2028/20	62120 1		1987 PRICE LIST	CAT, STANDING	7.9	TAWNY W/WHT MUZZLE & INNER EAR, GRN BOW				RED PAPER	$100/150
849		2028/25	62125 6		1987 PRICE LIST	CAT, STANDING	9.8	TAWNY W/WHT MUZZLE & INNER EAR, GRN BOW				RD PAPER+PL?	$100/150
850	20285 1		80002/85		1988 CATALOG	POLAR BEAR	33	WHT MINK PLUSH, RED PLASTIC LOGO					$300/400
851		2029/20	62220 8		1988 PRICE LIST	CATS	7.9						$100/150
852		203		1,000	D.H. HILL	BEAR ON WHEELS		WHT BEAR ON RED WHEELS; SHE HAS #79 OF 1000					$300/400
853		2030/22	61222 3		1988 PRICE LIST	CAT	8.7						$100/150
854		2040/25			1986 PRICE LIST	CAT	9.8						$100/150
855	20425 1		80004/25		1988 CATALOG	TEDDY BEAR	10.2	LT BRN BIBER IMITATION, RED BOW				RED PLASTIC	$79
856	20430 5		80004/30		1988 CATALOG	TEDDY BEAR	11.8	LT BRN BIBER IMITATION, RED BOW				RED PLASTIC	$96
857		2045/30	64130 8		1986 PRICE LIST	CAT	11.8						$75/125
858	20548 7		80005/48		1988 CATALOG	TEDDY BEAR	18.9	BRN 70% ACRYLIC & 30% C MINK PLUSH, RED BOW	NONE	YES	BRN	GOLD PLASTIC	$160
859	20551 7				1994 PRICE LIST	TEDDY BEAR	19.7	BRN MINK PLUSH, RED BOW					$169
860	20560 9		80005/60		1988 CATALOG	TEDDY BEAR	23.6	BRN 70% ACRYLIC & 30% C MINK PLUSH, RED BOW	NONE	YES	BRN	GOLD PLASTIC	$200
861	20561 6				1994 PRICE LIST	TEDDY BEAR	23.6	BRN MINK PLUSH, RED BOW					$222
862	20570 8		80005/70B		1988 CATALOG	TEDDY BEAR	27.5	BRN 70% ACRYLIC & 30%C MINK PLUSH, GRN BOW	NONE	YES	BRN	GOLD PLASTIC	$250
863	20571 5				1994 PRICE LIST	TEDDY BEAR	27.5	BRN MINK PLUSH, RED BOW				RED PLASTIC	$268
864	20590 6		80005/90		1988 CATALOG	TEDDY BEAR	35	BRN MINK PLUSH, RED BOW				RED PLASTIC	$300
865	20650 7		80006/50		1988 CATALOG	TEDDY BEAR, SOFT	19.7	BRN TIPPED BEIGE MINK PLUSH W/RED (LT PLAID?) BOW				RED PLASTIC	$171
866	20660 6				1993 PRICE LIST	TEDDY BEAR, SOFT	23.6	BRN TIPPED MINK PLUSH W/LT PLAID BOW					$227
867	20662 0		80006/62		1988 CATALOG	TEDDY BEAR, SOFT	23.6	LT BEIGE MINK PLUSH W/RED BOW; ALSO KATHY ANN CAT 1989				RED PLASTIC	$200/300
868	20672 9		80006/72		1988 CATALOG	TEDDY BEAR, SOFT	27.6	BRN TIPPED BEIGE MINK PLUSH W/RED BOW				RED PLASTIC	$200/300
869	20750 4		80007/50		1988 CATALOG	TEDDY BEAR, SITTING	19.7	BRN MINK PLUSH W?RED BOW					$150/200
870	20751 1				1994 PRICE LIST	TEDDY BEAR, SITTING	19.7	BRN MINK PLUSH 30%C & 70% ACRYLIC W/RED BOW	NONE	YES	RED	RED PLASTIC	$211
871	20785 6		80007/85		1988 CATALOG	TEDDY BEAR, SITTING	33.5	BRN MINK PLUSH W/RED BOW; ALSO KATHY ANN CAT 1989					$200/300
872	20786 3				1994 PRICE LIST	TEDDY BEAR, SITTING	33.5	BRN MINK PLUSH W?RED BOW					$389
873	20798 6		80007/120		1988 CATALOG	TEDDY BEAR, SITTING	47	BRN MINK PLUSH W?RED BOW					$400/500
874	20799 3				1994 PRICE LIST	TEDDY BEAR, SITTING	47	BRN MINK PLUSH W?RED BOW					$1,014
875	20850 1				1993 PRICE LIST	TEDDY BEAR, SITTING	19.7	BRN TIPPPED MINK PLUSH					$211
876	20850 4				1991 PRICE LIST	TEDDY BEAR	19.7	LIGHT BRN					$215
877	20860 3				1991 PRICE LIST	TEDDY BEAR	23.6	LIGHT BRN					$250

REF #	EAN #	HERMANN OLD #	ALSO SEE	LIMITED NUMBER	DATA FROM	NAME	INCHES TALL	DESCRIPTION	VOICE	HANGING BOOKLET	ARM TAG	COMPANY LOGO	CURRENT RETAIL
878	20870 2				1991 PRICE LIST	TEDDY BEAR	28.3	LIGHT BRN					$325
879	20885 3				1993 PRICE LIST	TEDDY BEAR, SITTING	33	BRN TIPPED MINK PLUSH					$390
880	20950 1				1992 PRICE LIST	TEDDY BEAR	19.7	LIGHT BRN					$215
881	20960 0				1992 PRICE LIST	TEDDY BEAR	23.6	LIGHT BRN					$250
882		210/18			1982 PRICE LIST	MONKEY	7						$150/200
883		210/24			1982 PRICE LIST	MONKEY	9.5						$200/300
884		210/30			1982 PRICE LIST	MONKEY	11.8						$200/300
885		210/38			1982 PRICE LIST	MONKEY	15						$250/350
886		210/50			1982 PRICE LIST	MONKEY	19.7						$400/500
887	21026 9		80010/26		1988 CATALOG	TEDDY BEAR, WASHABLE	10.2	WHT BIBER 130% C & 70% ACRYLIC IMITATION MOHAIR, ORANGE BOW	NONE	YES	GRN	GOLD PLASTIC	$90
888	21126 6		80011/26		1988 CATALOG	TEDDY BEAR, WASHABLE	10.2	LT BRN BIBER IMITATION, GRN BOW				RED PLASTIC	$75/125
889		214/50			1983 PRICE LIST	CHIMPANZEE	19.7						$400/500
890		215/40			1982 PRICE LIST	CHIMPANZEE	15.75						$300/400
891		215/50			1982 PRICE LIST	CHIMPANZEE	19.7						$400/500
892		218/35			1982 PRICE LIST	MONKEY	13.8						$250/350
893		218/45			1982 PRICE LIST	MONKEY	17.7						$300/400
894		220/35	38035 1		1983 PRICE LIST	MONKEY	13.8						$300/400
895		2200/25			1982 PRICE LIST	RAVEN	9.8						$100/150
896	22031 0				TB&PLUSCH FLIER	TEDDY BEAR	11.8	SOLD OUT 6/1996					$150
897	22032 7				TB&PLUSCH FLIER	TEDDY BEAR	11.8	SOLD OUT 6/1996					$150
898	22035 0		80020/35		1988 CATALOG	TEDDY BEAR, WASHABLE	14.2	BEIGE BIBER IMITATION, WASHABLE, CORD TIE				RED PLASTIC	$125/175
899	22128 9				1996 PRICE LIST	BABY BEAR	11	LT BEIGE WOVEN FUR, COTTON LIKE					$72
900	22133 3				1996 PRICE LIST	BABY BEAR	13.8	LT BEIGE WOVEN FUR, COTTON LIKE					$87
901	22135 7		80021/35		1988 CATALOG	TEDDY BEAR, WASHABLE	13.8	BRN BIBER IMITATION, WASHABLE, CORD TIE				RED PLASTIC	$75/125
902	22235 4		80023/35		CIRCA 1986	TEDDY BEAR, WASHABLE	13.8	LT BLUE ROSE SOFT 70% ACRYLIC & 30% COTTON PLUSH W/WHT MUZZLE	NONE	NO	GRN	GOLD PLASTIC	$75/125
903	22235 1		80022/35		1988 CATALOG	TEDDY BEAR, WASHABLE	13.8	ROSE BIBER IMITATION, WASHABLE, CORD TIE				RED PLASTIC	$75/125
904	22740 3		80029/41		1988 CATALOG	TEDDY BEAR, WASHABLE	16.5	RED BIBER IMITATION, PLAID BOW				RED PLASTIC	$100/150
905	22840 0		80029/42		1988 CATALOG	TEDDY BEAR, WASHABLE	16.5	BLUE BIBER IMITATION, PLAID BOW				RED PLASTIC	$100/150
906	22940 7		80029/43		1988 CATALOG	TEDDY BEAR, WASHABLE	16.5	YELLOW BIBER IMITATION, PLAID BOW				RED PLASTIC	$100/150
907		2300/24			1982 CATALOG	SITTING BEAR	9.5	DARK BRN BODY, TAN SNOUT & INSIDE EARS					$75/125
908	23028 1		80030/28		1988 CATALOG	TEDDY BEAR, WASHABLE	11	BEIGE BIBER IMITATION, RED BOW				RED PLASTIC	$100/150
909	23033 5		80030/33		1988 CATALOG	TEDDY BEAR, WASHABLE	12.6	BEIGE BIBER IMITATION, RED BOW				RED PLASTIC	$100/150
910	23042 7		80030/42		1988 CATALOG	TEDDY BEAR, WASHABLE	16.5	BEIGE BIBER IMITATION, RED BOW				RED PLASTIC	$125/175
911	23128 8		80031/28		1994/5 CATALOG	TEDDY BEAR	11	BRN WOVEN FUR W/RED BOW					$82
912	23133 2		80031/33		1994/5 CATALOG	TEDDY BEAR	12.6	BRN WOVEN FUR W/RED BOW					$99
913	23142 4		80031/42		1994/5 CATALOG	TEDDY BEAR	16.5	BRN WOVEN FUR W/RED BOW					$131
914		232/20	38120 4		1982 PRICE LIST	SITTING MONKEY	7.9						$75/125
915		232/28			1982 PRICE LIST	SITTING MONKEY	11						$75/125
916	23228 5		80032/28		1989 CATALOG	TEDDY BEAR	11	DARK BRN BIBER IMITATION FUR, SURFACE WASHABLE, RED BOW				RED PAPER	$82
917	23233 9		80032/33		1994/5 CATALOG	TEDDY BEAR	12.6	CREAM WHT SOFT 70% ACRYLIC & 30% COTTON PLUSH BLUE BOW	NONE	YES	BRN	RED PAPER	$99
918	23242 1		80032/42		1988 PRICE LIST	TEDDY BEAR	16.5	CREAM WHT SOFT 70% ACRYLIC & 30% COTTON PLUSH RED BOW	NONE	YES	BRN	RED PLASTIC	$131
919	23328 2		80033/28		1989 PRICE LIST	TEDDY BEAR	11						$100/150
920	23333 6		80033/33		1989 PRICE LIST	TEDDY BEAR	12.6	DARK BRN BIBER IMITATION FUR, SURFACE WASHABLE, RED BOW				RED PLASTIC	$100/150
921	23342 8		80033/42		1989 PRICE LIST	TEDDY BEAR	16.5	DARK BRN BIBER IMITATION FUR, SURFACE WASHABLE, RED BOW				RED PLASTIC	$125/175
922	23350 9				1996 PRICE LIST	TEDDY BEAR	19.7	BEIGE					$125/175
923	23430 2				1994 PRICE LIST	ADAC TEDDY BEAR	11.8	GOLD 30% ACRYLIC & 30% COTTON SOFT PLUSH FUR, YELLOW OVERALLS W/ADAC	NONE	YES	RED	SML RD PL	$142
924	23440 2		80034/30		1988 CATALOG	TEDDY BEAR	11.8	PURPLE BIBER IMITATION, PINK STRIPED BOW				RED PLASTIC	$125/175
925	23442 5		80034/42		1988 CATALOG	TEDDY BEAR	16.5	PURPLE BIBER IMITATION, PINK STRIPED BOW				RED PLASTIC	$125/175
926	23530 9				1994 PRICE LIST	TEDDY BEAR	11.8	BEIGE WOVEN FUR W/PLAID BOW					$90
927	23540 8				1994 PRICE LIST	TEDDY BEAR	15.75	BEIGE WOVEN FUR W/PLAID BOW					$127
928	23639 9				1995 PRICE LIST	TEDDY BEAR	15.7	BRN TIPPED WOVEN FUR W/WHT MUZZLE W/PLAID BOW					$114
929	24540 4		80046/40		1988 CATALOG	TEDDY BEAR	15.75	BRN BIBER IMITATION, W/JUMPER, EARS WHT INSIDE				RED PLASTIC	$150/200
930	24640 4		80046/40		1988 PRICE LIST	TEDDY BEAR	15.75						$150/200
931	24740 1		80047/40		1988 CATALOG	TEDDY BEAR	15.75	LT BRN BIBER IMITATION, W/JUMPER, EARS WHT INSIDE				RED PLASTIC	$150/200
932		250/20			BEHA 1927 CATALOG	PUG DOG ON WHEELS	7.9	BEST FINISH, 1a WOOL PLUSH, LEATHER COLLAR, RED VARN WHEELS					$200/300

149

REF #	EAN #	HERMANN OLD #	ALSO SEE	LIMITED NUMBER	DATA FROM	NAME	INCHES TALL	DESCRIPTION	VOICE	HANGING BOOKLET	ARM TAG	COMPANY LOGO	CURRENT RETAIL
933		250/25			BEHA 1927 CATALOG	PUG DOG ON WHEELS	9.8	BEST FINISH, 1a WOOL PLUSH, LEATHER COLLAR, RED VARNISHED WHEELS					$200/300
934		250/30			BEHA 1927 CATALOG	PUG DOG ON WHEELS	11.8	BEST FINISH, 1a WOOL PLUSH, LEATHER COLLAR, RED VARNISHED WHEELS					$200/300
935		2500/15	33515 3		1982 PRICE LIST	RACCOON	5.9	TAN W/WHT FACE & BELLY, BLK NOSE & EYES				RED PAPER	$75/125
936		2500/25			1982 PRICE LIST	RACCOON	9.8	TAN W/WHT FACE & BELLY, BLK NOSE & EYES, W/STRIPED TAIL				RED PLASTIC	$125/175
937		2500/35			1982 PRICE LIST	RACCOON	13.8						$150/200
938a		2550/15			1982 PRICE LIST	RACCOON	5.9						$50/100
938		2550/25	33625 9		1982 PRICE LIST	RACCOON	9.8						$75/125
939	25535 2		55/35/1		1988 CATALOG	DIRNDL	14.2	LT BRN ACRYLIC, NOT JTD, DRESSED	NONE	YES	BRN	RED PAPER	$90
940	25635 9		55/35/2		1988 CATALOG	SEPPL	14.2	LT BRN ACRYLIC, NOT JTD, DRESSED	NONE	YES	BRN	RED PAPER	$90
941	25735 3		56/35/3		1988 CATALOG	JEANSROCK	14.2	LT BRN ACRYLIC, NOT JTD, DRESSED					$90
942	25835 3		56/35/4		1988 CATALOG	JEANSHOSE	14.2	LT BRN ACRYLIC, NOT JTD, DRESSED IN OVERALLS	NONE	YES	BRN	RED PAPER	$50
943		260/14			BEHA 1927 CATALOG	DOG, PLUSH	5.5	WHT LONG PILE WITH LONG PILE PLUSH EARS, RED VARNISHED WHEELS					$75/125
944		260/17?			BEHA 1927 CATALOG	DOG, PLUSH	6.7	WHT LONG PILE WITH LONG PILE PLUSH EARS, RED VARNISHED WHEELS					$75/125
945		260/20			BEHA 1927 CATALOG	DOG, PLUSH	7.9	WHT LONG PILE WITH LONG PILE PLUSH EARS, RED VARNISHED WHEELS					$75/125
946		260/23?			BEHA 1927 CATALOG	DOG, PLUSH	7.5	WHT LONG PILE WITH LONG PILE PLUSH EARS, RED VARNISHED WHEELS					$100/150
947		260/27?			BEHA 1927 CATALOG	DOG, PLUSH	10.6	WHT LONG PILE WITH LONG PILE PLUSH EARS, RED VARNISHED WHEELS					$100/150
948		260/30			BEHA 1927 CATALOG	DOG, PLUSH	11.8	WHT LONG PILE WITH LONG PILE PLUSH EARS, RED VARNISHED WHEELS					$125/175
949		261/14			BEHA 1927 CATALOG	DOG, PLUSH	5.5	WHT WOOL LONG PILE PLUSH WITH LONG PILE PLUSH EARS, RED VARNISHED WHEELS					$75/125
950		261/17?			BEHA 1927 CATALOG	DOG, PLUSH	6.7	WHT WOOL LONG PILE PLUSH WITH LONG PILE PLUSH EARS, RED VARNISHED WHEELS					$75/125
951		261/20			BEHA 1927 CATALOG	DOG, PLUSH	7.9	WHT WOOL LONG PILE PLUSH WITH LONG PILE PLUSH EARS, RED VARNISHED WHEELS					$75/125
952		261/23?			BEHA 1927 CATALOG	DOG, PLUSH	9.5	WHT WOOL LONG PILE PLUSH WITH LONG PILE PLUSH EARS, RED VARNISHED WHEELS					$75/125
953		261/27?			BEHA 1927 CATALOG	DOG, PLUSH	10.6	WHT WOOL LONG PILE PLUSH WITH LONG PILE PLUSH EARS, RED VARNISHED WHEELS					$100/150
954		261/30			BEHA 1927 CATALOG	DOG, PLUSH	11.8	WHT WOOL LONG PILE PLUSH WITH LONG PILE PLUSH EARS, RED VARNISHED WHEELS					$100/150
955		274/100		10001 0	1986 CATALOG	SCHOOL ROOM	47 X 21 X 12	8" TEACHER AND 6 PUPILS + DESKS AND 1 BLACKBOARD; NO SCHOOLROOM SUPPLIED	GROWLER	NO	BRN	RD PL& RD PAPER	$750
956		30/16			BEHA 1927 CATALOG	DOG	6.3	LONG PILE PLUSH DOG, POINTS OF PLUSH GREY AND WHT, ARTIFICIAL SILK RIBBON					$100/150
957		30/18?			BEHA 1927 CATALOG	DOG	7	LONG PILE PLUSH DOG, POINTS OF PLUSH GREY AND WHT, ARTIFICIAL SILK RIBBON					$100/150
958		30/20?			BEHA 1927 CATALOG	DOG	7.9	LONG PILE PLUSH DOG, POINTS OF PLUSH GREY AND WHT, ARTIFICIAL SILK RIBBON					$125/175
959		30/23?			BEHA 1927 CATALOG	DOG	9.5	LONG PILE PLUSH DOG, POINTS OF PLUSH GREY AND WHT, ARTIFICIAL SILK RIBBON					$125/175
960		30/28?			BEHA 1927 CATALOG	DOG	11	LONG PILE PLUSH DOG, POINTS OF PLUSH GREY AND WHT, ARTIFICIAL SILK RIBBON					$150/200
961		30/32			BEHA 1927 CATALOG	DOG	12.6	LONG PILE PLUSH DOG, POINTS OF PLUSH GREY AND WHT, ARTIFICIAL SILK RIBBON					$150/200
962		300/16	LI 75			BEAR, RED WHEELED	5.5H X 6L	DARK BLK 53% WOOL & 47% COTTON MOHAIR.	NONE	YES	BRN	RED PAPER	$100
963		300/16/3	CI 75			BEAR, RED WHEELED	5.5H X 6L	CINNAMON 53% WOOL & 47% COTTON MOHAIR.	NONE	YES	BRN	RED PAPER	$100
964		300/16	SU 75			BEAR, RED WHEELED	5.5H X 6L	WHT 53% WOOL & 47% COTTON MOHAIR.	NONE	YES	BRN	RED PAPER	$100
965		300/16/4F			HERMAN JESCO 1980S	BEAR, RED WHEELED	5.5H X 6L	NOUGAT 53% WOOL & 47% COTTON MOHAIR.	NONE	YES	BRN	RED PAPER	$100
966		300/20			HERMAN 1980S	BEAR, 4 LEGGED	5H X 6L	DARK BRN MOHAIR, 62% W/38% C, NO FRAME, NO WHEELS	NONE	YES	GRN	NONE	$90
967		300/20			HERMANN (1985-89)	BEAR, RED WHEELED	6H X 7L	DARK BRN MOHAIR, 62% W/38% C, ON RED WHEELS	NONE	YES	GRN	RED PAPER	$90
968		300/20 F			KATHY ANN CATALOG	BEAR, RED WHEELED	7.9	DARK BRN PURE LLAMA ON RED WHEELS					$90
969		300/28			BEHA 1927 CATALOG	WIRE HAIR TERRIER	11	MADE OF MOHAIR PLUSH, W/LEATHER COLLAR, W/ VOICE	GROWLER				$100
970		3001/42			KALINKE CIRCA 1980	KOALA BEAR	16.5	KOALA WITH LINK CHAIN COLLAR, DATA FROM PHOTOCOPY OF CATALOG SEGMENT					$200/300
971		3002/20			1982 PRICE LIST	KOALA BEAR	7.9						$150/200
972		3002/30			1982 PRICE LIST	KOALA BEAR	11.8						$150/200
973	30040 3		80166/40		1988 CATALOG	BEAR LYING	15.75	BRN-GREY MINK PLUSH				RED PLASTIC	$150/200

REF #	EAN #	HERMANN OLD #	ALSO SEE	LIMITED NUMBER	DATA FROM	NAME	INCHES TALL	DESCRIPTION	VOICE	HANGING BOOKLET	ARM TAG	COMPANY LOGO	CURRENT RETAIL
974	30050 2		80166/50		1988 CATALOG	BEAR LYING	19.7	BRN-GREY MINK PLUSH				RED PLASTIC	$150/200
975	30065 6		80166/65		1988 CATALOG	BEAR LYING	26	BRN-GREY MINK PLUSH	NONE	YES	BRN	GOLD PLASTIC	$195
976		3008/45			1982 PRICE LIST	MINK	17.7						$125/175
977	30095 3		80166/95		1988 CATALOG	BEAR LYING	37	GREY MINK PLUSH					$200/300
978	30130 I		80168/30		1988 CATALOG	BEAR LYING	11.8	BRN MINK PLUSH				RED PLASTIC	$150/200
979	30130 I				1997 PRICE LIST	BEAR LYING	11.8	WOVEN FUR WASHABLE , BEIGE				RED PLASTIC	$150/200
980	30131 8				1997 PRICE LIST	BABY BEAR LYING	11.8	WOVEN FUR WASHABLE , BRN					$150/200
981	30140 0		80168/40		1988 CATALOG	BEAR LYING, WASHABLE	15.75	BRN MINK PLUSH				RED PLASTIC	$125/175
982	30141 7				1994 PRICE LIST	BEAR LYING	15.75	BRN MINK PLUSH				RED PLASTIC	$150
983	30142 4				1996 PRICE LIST	BEAR LYING	15.75	BRN MINK PLUSH				RED PLASTIC	$125/175
984	30150 9		80168/50		1988 CATALOG	BEAR LYING	19.7	BRN MINK PLUSH, WASHABLE				RED PLASTIC	$200/300
985	30151 6				1994 PRICE LIST	BEAR LYING	19.7	BRN MINK PLUSH				RED PLASTIC	$207
986	30152 3				1996 PRICE LIST	BEAR LYING	19.7	BRN MINK PLUSH				RED PLASTIC	$184
987	30165 3		80168/65		1988 CATALOG	BEAR LYING	25.5	BRN MINK PLUSH, WASHABLE				RED PLASTIC	$200/300
988	30166 0				1994 PRICE LIST	BEAR LYING	25.5	BRN MINK PLUSH				RED PLASTIC	$312
989	30167 7				1996 PRICE LIST	BEAR LYING	25.5	BRN MINK PLUSH				RED PLASTIC	$279
990	30195 0		80168/95		1988 CATALOG	BEAR LYING	37.5	BRN MINK PLUSH, WASHABLE; 1996 PRICE LIST				RED PLASTIC	$522
991	30240 7				1990 PRICE LIST	BEAR LYING	15.75	TIGER STRIPED MINK PLUSH, WASHABLE					$125/175
992	30241 4				1994 PRICE LIST	BEAR, LYING SOFT	15.75	LT BRN MINK PLUSH MOHAIR W/SHAVED NOSE					$154
993	30250 6				1990 PRICE LIST	BEAR LYING	23.6	TIGER STRIPED MINK PLUSH, WASHABLE					$125/175
994	30251 3				1994 PRICE LIST	BEAR LYING	19.7	LT BRN MINK PLUSH MOHAIR W/SHAVED NOSE					$154
995	30265 0				1990 PRICE LIST	BEAR LYING	25.6	TIGER STRIPED MINK PLUSH, WASHABLE					$250/350
996	30266 7				1994 PRICE LIST	BEAR LYING	25.5	LT BRN MINK PLUSH MOHAIR W/SHAVED NOSE					$321
997	30275 9		82012/75		1988 CATALOG	BEAR LYING	30	BEIGE MINK PLUSH, RED PLASTIC LOGO					$300/400
998	30350 3				1994 PRICE LIST	BEAR LYING	19.7	DARK BRN MINK PLUSH MOHAIR W/SHAVED NOSE	NONE	YES	YES	RED PLASTIC	$207
999	30360 2				1994 PRICE LIST	BEAR LYING	23.6	DARK BRN MINK PLUSH MOHAIR W/SHAVED NOSE;					$266
1000	30380 0				1994 PRICE LIST	BEAR LYING	31.5	DARK BRN MINK PLUSH MOHAIR W/SHAVED NOSE;					$337
1001		3045/40			1982 PRICE LIST	COCKER SPANIEL	15.75						$125/175
1002		305/22			BEHA 1927 CATALOG	DOG	8.7	SPOTTED LONG PILE PLUSH					$100/150
1003		310/12			1982 PRICE LIST	ELEPHANT	4.7						$75/125
1004		310/22			BEHA 1927 CATALOG	ST. BERNARD	8.7	WOOL PLUSH, NATURAL FINISH, WITH VOICE	YES				$100/150
1005	31020 4		80300/20		1989 PRICE LIST	BRN BEAR	7.9	BRN BIBER IMITATION FUR, TAN MUZZLE, SURFACE WASHABLE				RED PAPER	$100/150
1006	31030 3		80300/30		1989 PRICE LIST	BRN BEAR	11.8	BRN BIBER IMITATION FUR, TAN MUZZLE, SURFACE WASHABLE				RED PLASTIC	$100/150
1007	31040 2			2,000	1992 PRICE LIST	BEAR- 4 LEGS W/VOICE	14LX10H	DARK BRN 100% WOOL MOHAIR W/PULL VOICE	PULL STRING	YES	RED	RED PLASTIC	$224
1008	31130 0		80009/30		1989 PRICE LIST	BRN BEAR, SITTING	11.8	BRN BIBER IMITATION FUR, WHT INSET FACE				RED PLASTIC	$125/175
1009	31145 4			800	1997 PRICE LIST	ALASKA BEAR CLUMSY CUB	18.1	MINK PLUSH, SURFACE WASHABLE	NONE	YES	RED	RED PLASTIC	$256
1010	31150 8			800	1997 PRICE LIST	ALASKA BEAR NOSY CUB	19.7	MINK PLUSH, SURFACE WASHABLE	NONE	YES	RED	RED PLASTIC	$256
1011	31170 6			500	1997 PRICE LIST	ALASKA BEAR MOTHER DICK	28.3	MINK PLUSH, SURFACE WASHABLE	NONE	YES	RED	RED PLASTIC	$305
1012	31175 I			500	1997 PRICE LIST	ALASKA BEAR DIVER	30	MINK PLUSH, SURFACE WASHABLE	NONE	YES	RED	RED PLASTIC	$366
1013		312/20			1982 PRICE LIST	ELEPHANT	10.2						$125/175
1014		312/25			1982 PRICE LIST	ELEPHANT	9.8						$150/200
1015		315/20			BEHA 1927 CATALOG	DOG, BOLOGNA	7.9	WHT MOHAIR PLUSH, W/LEATHER COLLAR, PAINTED & SPRAYED					$200/300
1016	31540 7		82000/40		1988 CATALOG	PANDABEAR	15.75	BLK & WHT MINK PLUSH				RED PAPER	$200/300
1017	31628 2		82006/28		1988 CATALOG	PANDABEAR "PIEPE"	11	BLK & WHT MINK PLUSH				RED PAPER	$150/200
1018	31660 2		82006/60		1988 CATALOG	PANDABEAR	23.6	BLK & WHT MINK PLUSH				RED PLASTIC	$300/400
1019	31725 8		82007/25		1988 CATALOG	PANDABEAR "SCHNURZ"	10.2	BLK & WHT MINK PLUSH				RED PAPER	$150/200
1020	31755 5		82007/55		1988 CATALOG	PANDABEAR CROUCHING	19LX12H	BLK & WHT MINK PLUSH, WASHABLE, LISTED AS 55cm;	NONE	YES	RED	RED PLASTIC	$181
1021	31855 2		84090/55		1988 CATALOG	PANDABEAR SITTING	22	BLK & WHT BIBER IMITATION				RED PLASTIC	$150/200
1022	31875 0		84090/75		1988 CATALOG	PANDABEAR SITTING	29.5	BLK & WHT MINK PLUSH				RED PLASTIC	$200/300
1023	31897 2		84090/110		1988 CATALOG	PANDABEAR SITTING	43	BLK & WHT MINK PLUSH				RED PLASTIC	$250/350
1024		320/33			BEHA 1927 CATALOG	SKYE TERRIER, STANDING	12.6	WOOL PLUSH, BLK & WHT, WITH BROAD RIBBON AROUND NECK, TURNING HEAD					$200/300
1025		321/24			BEHA 1927 CATALOG	SKYE TERRIER, SITTING	9.5	WOOL PLUSH, BLK & WHT, WITH BROAD RIBBON AROUND NECK, TURNING HEAD					$150/200
1026		321/32			1982 PRICE LIST	ELEPHANT	12.6						$200/300
1027		3200/30			1982 PRICE LIST	BOAR	11.8						$100/150
1028		3200/44	44644 6		1982 PRICE LIST	BOAR	17.3						$125/175
1029		3200/52	44652 I		1982 PRICE LIST	BOAR	20.5						$150/200
1030		3250/28			1982 PRICE LIST	BOAR, CUB	11						$100/150
1031		3260/28	44728 3		1984 PRICE LIST	BOAR, CUB	11						$100/150
1032	32532 I		3701/32		1988 CATALOG	POLAR BEAR SITTING	12.6	WHT MINK PLUSH				RED PLASTIC	$125/175

REF #	EAN #	HERMANN OLD #	ALSO SEE	LIMITED NUMBER	DATA FROM	NAME	INCHES TALL	DESCRIPTION	VOICE	HANGING BOOKLET	ARM TAG	COMPANY LOGO	CURRENT RETAIL
1033	32635 9		3705/35		1988 CATALOG	POLAR BEAR LYING	14.2	WHT MINK PLUSH				RED PLASTIC	$125/175
1034	32728 8		590/28	2,000	KATHY ANN CAT 1989	POLAR BEAR	8HX11L	WHT MOHAIR ON 4 FEET, WOOL PLUSH, SURFACE WASHABLE;	NONE	YES	RED	RED PLASTIC	$95
1035	32845 2		80001/45		1989 PRICE LIST	POLAR BEAR, LYING DOWN	17.7	WHT MINK PLUSH LYING DOWN, WASHABLE				RED PLASTIC	$100/150
1036	32860 5		80001/60		KATHY ANN CAT 1989	POLAR BEAR, LYING DOWN	23.6	WHT MINK PLUSH LYING DOWN, WASHABLE				RED PLASTIC	$125/175
1037	32875 9		80001/75		1989 PRICE LIST	POLAR BEAR, LYING DOWN	29.5	WHT MINK PLUSH LYING DOWN, WASHABLE				RED PLASTIC	$150/200
1038		330/40		1,000	HERMANN JESCO 1985	BEAR, RED WHEELED	11HX13L	HONEY 62% WOOL & 38% COTTON MOHAIR	NONE	YES	GRN	RED PLASTIC	$250
1039		330/45			BEHA 1927 CATALOG	BEAR ON WHEELS	12H X 17.7L	COLORED LONG PILE PLUSH, LEATHER COLLAR, SOLID IRON FRAME, RED VARNISHED WHEELS					$200/300
1040		33040FW			1990? JESCO	BEAR, WHEELED	11HX13L	WHT W /RED WHEELS					$200/300
1041	33515 3		2500/15		1988 PRICE LIST	RACCOON	5.9	TAN W/WHT BELLY & FACE, MINK PLUSH, WASHABLE			RED	RED PAPER	$75/125
1042		335/40			KATHY ANN CAT 1986	BEAR, WHEELED	15.75	DARK BRN W/RED WHEELS, RED COLLAR					$250/350
1043	33625 9		2550/25		1988 PRICE LIST	RACCOON	9.8						$75/125
1044		340/40		1,000	1986 JESCO	BEAR, WHEELED	11HX13L	WHT 53% WOOL & 47% C MOHAIR, W/RD STRIPED BOW, RED WHEELS	NONE	YES	BRN	RED PLASTIC	$160
1045		340/40		1,000	1986 JESCO	BEAR, WHEELED	11HX13L	WHT 53% WOOL & 47% C MOHAIR, W/RD STRIPED BOW, RED WHEELS	NONE	YES	BRN	RED PLASTIC	$160
1046		340/40			HERMANN	BEAR, WHEELED	11HX13L	DARK BRN 30% COTTON, 70% ACRYLIC, W/RED COLLAR, RED WHEELS	NONE	NO	BRN	RED PLASTIC	$125/175
1047		3400/26	43526 6		1988 PRICE LIST	CAMEL	10.2						$75/125
1048		3400/58	43558 7		1988 PRICE LIST	CAMEL	22.8						$250/350
1049	34030 0		80770/30		1988 PRICE LIST	ELEPHANT, LYING	11.8	DARK GREY W/WHT EARS, BIBER IMITATION, WASHABLE				RED PLASTIC	$75/125
1050	34031 7				1994 PRICE LIST	ELEPHANT, LYING	11.8						$110
1051	34050 8		80770/50		1988 PRICE LIST	ELEPHANT, LYING	19.7	DARK GREY W/WHT EARS, BIBER IMITATION, WASHABLE				RED PLASTIC	$100/150
1052	34051 5				1994 PRICE LIST	ELEPHANT, LYING	19.7						$190
1053	34061 4				1994 PRICE LIST	ELEPHANT, LYING	23.6						$264
1054	34075 1		80770/75		1988 PRICE LIST	ELEPHANT, LYING	29.5	DARK GREY W/WHT EARS, BIBER IMITATION, WASHABLE				RED PLASTIC	$125/175
1055	34115 4		80312/15		1988 PRICE LIST	ELEPHANT, STANDING	5.9	GREY MINK PLUSH, WASHABLE				RED PLASTIC	$75/125
1056	34116 1				1992 PRICE LIST	ELEPHANT, STANDING	5.9	GREY WOVEN FUR, WASHABLE				RED PAPER	$75
1057	34120 8		80312/20		1988 PRICE LIST	ELEPHANT, STANDING	10.2	GREY MINK PLUSH, WASHABLE					$100/150
1058	34121 5				1992 PRICE LIST	ELEPHANT, STANDING	10.2	GREY WOVEN FUR, WASHABLE				RED PAPER	$98
1059	34125 3		80312/25		1988 PRICE LIST	ELEPHANT	9.8						$100/150
1060	34236 6		80321/36		1988 PRICE LIST	ELEPHANT	14.2						$125/175
1061	34330 1		80771/30		1988 PRICE LIST	ELEPHANT	11.8						$100/150
1062	34350 9		80771/50		1988 PRICE LIST	ELEPHANT	19.7						$125/175
1063	34425 4		80316/25		1989 PRICE LIST	ELEPHANT, STANDING	9.8	GREY WOVEN BIBER IMITATION FUR, WASHABLE				RED PLASTIC	$124
1064	34465 0		80316/65		1989 PRICE LIST	ELEPHANT, STANDING	25.6	GREY WOVEN BIBER IMITATION FUR, WASHABLE				RED PLASTIC	$200/300
1065		3450/26	43826 7		1989 PRICE LIST	DROMEDARY	10.2						$125/175
1066		3450/58	43858 8		1989 PRICE LIST	DROMEDARY	22.8						$200/300
1067		3450/120	43898 4		1989 PRICE LIST	DROMEDARY	47.2						$300/400
1068	35030 9		80442/30		1988 PRICE LIST	LION, SITTING	11.8	BIBER IMITATION, WASHABLE DARK TAN				RED PLASTIC	$100/150
1069	35138 2		80443/38		1988 PRICE LIST	LION	15						$100/150
1070	34145 0				1992 PRICE LIST	LION, LYING	17.7						$125/175
1071	35230 3		82014/30		1988 PRICE LIST	LION, LYING	11.8	BIBER IMITATION, WASHABLE DARK TAN				RED PLASTIC	$127
1072	35232 7				1992 PRICE LIST	LION, LYING	13	TAN WOVEN FUR, WASHABLE				RED PLASTIC	$125/175
1073	35265 5		82014/65		1988 PRICE LIST	LION, LYING	25.6	BIBER IMITATION, WASHABLE DARK TAN				RED PLASTIC	$125/175
1074	35335 5				1992 PRICE LIST	LION CUB, LYING	13.8	TAN WOVEN FUR, WASHABLE				RED PLASTIC	$125/175
1075	36030 8		499/30		1988 PRICE LIST	LEOPARD, SITTING	11.8	MINK PLUSH, SURFACE WASHABLE				RED PLASTIC	$100/150
1076	36042 1				1992 PRICE LIST	LEOPARD	16.5						$100/150
1077	36060 5				1992 PRICE LIST	LEOPARD, SITTING	23.6	MINK PLUSH, WASHABLE				RED PLASTIC	$125/175
1078	36062 9		499/62		1988 PRICE LIST	LEOPARD, SITTING	24.4	MINK PLUSH, SURFACE WASHABLE				RED PLASTIC	$125/175
1079		3601/15	70115 6		1982 PRICE LIST	CAT, STANDING	5.9						$100/150
1080		3602/15	70215 3		1982 PRICE LIST	CAT, SITTING	5.9						$100/150
1081		3603/24	70324 2		1982 PRICE LIST	CAT, LYING	9.5						$100/150
1082		3604/15	70415 7		1982 PRICE LIST	ST. BERNARD DOG	5.9						$100/150
1083		3605/15	70515 4		1982 PRICE LIST	MOLLY SITTING	5.9						$100/150
1084		3606/15	70615 1		1982 PRICE LIST	FOX TERRIER	5.9						$100/150
1085		3608/15	70815 5		1982 PRICE LIST	BEAR, LAUGHING	5.9						$100/150
1086	36135 0		2016/35		1988 PRICE LIST	LEOPARD, LYING	13.8	MINK PLUSH, WASHABLE				RED PLASTIC	$125/175
1087	36160 2		2016/60		1988 PRICE LIST	LEOPARD, LYING	23.6	MINK PLUSH, WASHABLE				RED PLASTIC	$200/300
1088	36235 7				1992 PRICE LIST	LEOPARD, LYING	15	MINK PLUSH, WASHABLE				RED PLASTIC	$124
1089	36260 9				1992 PRICE LIST	LEOPARD, LYING	23.6	MINK PLUSH, WASHABLE				RED PLASTIC	$262
1090		3650/25			1982 PRICE LIST	PEKINGESE	9.8						$100/150
1091		3660/25	54025 0		1984 PRICE LIST	PEKINGESE	9.8						$100/150
1092	36570 9				1994 PRICE LIST	TIGER, GOLD	27.6						$315

REF #	EAN #	HERMANN OLD #	ALSO SEE	LIMITED NUMBER	DATA FROM	NAME	INCHES TALL	DESCRIPTION	VOICE	HANGING BOOKLET	ARM TAG	COMPANY LOGO	CURRENT RETAIL
1093	36571 6				1994 PRICE LIST	TIGER, WHT	27.6						$315
1094	36840 3		490/40		1989 PRICE LIST	LYNX, STANDING	15.75	TAWNY SPOTTED MINK PLUSH, SURFACE WASHABLE				RED PLASTIC	$150/200
1095	36860 1		490/60		1989 PRICE LIST	LYNX, STANDING	23.6	TAWNY SPOTTED MINK PLUSH, SURFACE WASHABLE				RED PLASTIC	$200/300
1096	37033 8		2000/33		1988 PRICE LIST	PANTHER, BLK	13						$200/300
1097		3700/30			HERMANN CAT 1982	POLAR BEAR	11.8	12" WHT IMITATION BEAVER PLUSH, WHT PADS, SNOUT & INSIDE EARS, PAINTED OUTLINES OF SNOUT & CLAWS				RED PAPER	$125/175
1098		3701/32	32532 1		1984 PRICE LIST	POLAR BEAR	13	SEE 32532 1, 12" WHT IMITATION BEAVER PLUSH, DARK WHT PADS, SNOUT & INSIDE EARS, PAINTED OUTLINES OF SNOUT & CLAWS					$150/200
1099		3705/35	32635 9		1982 PRICE LIST	POLAR BEAR	14.2	SEE 32635 9, WHT IMITATION BEAVER PLUSH, DARK WHT PADS, SNOUT & INSIDE EARS, PAINTED OUTLINES OF SNOUT & CLAWS					$200/300
1100		3708/35			1982 PRICE LIST	BRN BEAR	13.8						$200/300
1101	37135 9		2018/35		1996 PRICE LIST	PANTHER, LYING	13.8	MINK PLUSH WASHABLE, BLK					$111
1102	37160 1		2018/60		1988 PRICE LIST	PANTHER, LYING	23.6	MINK PLUSH WASHABLE, BLK				RED PLASTIC	$249
1103	37542 5		2019/42		1988 PRICE LIST	PANTHER, SITTING	16.5	MINK PLUSH WASHABLE, BLK				RED PLASTIC	$125/175
1104	37543 5		2019/42		1988 PRICE LIST	PANTHER	16.5						$125/175
1105	37560 9		2019/60		1989 PRICE LIST	PANTHER, SITTING	23.6	MINK PLUSH WASHABLE, BLK				RED PLASTIC	$200/300
1106	38035 1		220/35		1988 PRICE LIST	MONKEY	13.8	MINK PLUSH, SURFACE WASHABLE, BLK W/WHT AROUND FACE					$140
1107	38036 8				1992 PRICE LIST	MONKEY	14.2	WOVEN FUR, WASHABLE. DARK BRN W/WHT BEARD				RED PLASTIC	$125
1108	38120 4		232/20		1990 CATALOG	MONKEY, SITTING	7.9	LLAMA PLUSH, WASHABLE, BLK W/WHT AROUND FACE					$75/125
1109	38240 9		80215/40		1996 PRICE LIST	CHIMPANZEE	15.75	WOVEN BIBER IMITATION FUR, WASHABLE. BEIGE W/WHT BEARD				RED PLASTIC	$151
1110	38340 6				1990 CATALOG	CHIMPANZEE	15.75	WOVEN BIBER IMITATION FUR, WASHABLE. BRN W/WHT BEARD					$125/175
1111	38458 8		80217/58		1988 PRICE LIST	CHIMPANZEE	22.8						$200/300
1112	39020 6		890/20		1988 PRICE LIST	TORTOISE	7.9	GRN WOVEN FUR, WASHABLE				RED PAPER	$50/100
1113	39120 3		892/20		1988 PRICE LIST	TORTOISE	7.9	GRN BIBER IMITATION FUR, WASHABLE					$46
1114	39240 8		84095/40		1988 PRICE LIST	TORTOISE	15.75						$75/125
1115	39255 2		84095/55		1988 PRICE LIST	TORTOISE	21.7						$100/150
1116	39275 0		84095/75		1988 PRICE LIST	TORTOISE	29.5						$150/200
1117	39320 7		894/20		1988 PRICE LIST	TORTOISE	7.9	MAUVE BIBER IMITATION FUR, WASHABLE					$50/100
1118	39420 4		802416/40		1992 PRICE LIST	TORTOISE	15.75	BRN WOVEN FUR, WASHABLE				RED PAPER	$46
1119	39525 6				1991 PRICE LIST	SNAIL	9.8	WOVEN FUR, BRN, WASHABLE					$96
1120		4/25	20025 3		1988 PRICE LIST	TEDDY BEAR	9.8						$100/150
1121		4/30	20030 7		1988 PRICE LIST	TEDDY BEAR	11.8						$125/175
1122		4/35	20035 2		1988 PRICE LIST	TEDDY BEAR	13.78						$125/175
1123		40S/20			BEHA 1927 CATALOG	DOG, PLASTIC	7.9	LONG PILE WOOL PLUSH, PAINTED & SPRAYED, BROAD ARTIFICIAL SILK RIBBON AROUND NECK					$75/125
1124		40W/20			BEHA 1927 CATALOG	DOG, PLASTIC	7.9	LONG PILE WOOL PLUSH, PAINTED & SPRAYED					$75/125
1125		40S/23			BEHA 1927 CATALOG	DOG, PLASTIC	9.5	LONG PILE WOOL PLUSH, PAINTED & SPRAYED, BROAD ARTIFICIAL SILK RIBBON AROUND NECK					$75/125
1126		40W/23			BEHA 1927 CATALOG	DOG, PLASTIC	9.5	LONG PILE WOOL PLUSH, PAINTED & SPRAYED					$75/125
1127		40S/27?			BEHA 1927 CATALOG	DOG, PLASTIC	10.6	LONG PILE WOOL PLUSH, PAINTED & SPRAYED, BROAD ARTIFICIAL SILK RIBBON AROUND NECK					$100/150
1128		40W/27?			BEHA 1927 CATALOG	DOG, PLASTIC	10.6	LONG PILE WOOL PLUSH, PAINTED & SPRAYED					$100/150
1129		40S/30			BEHA 1927 CATALOG	DOG, PLASTIC	11.8	LONG PILE WOOL PLUSH, PAINTED & SPRAYED, BROAD ARTIFICIAL SILK RIBBON AROUND NECK					$100/150
1130		40W/30			BEHA 1927 CATALOG	DOG, PLASTIC	11.8	LONG PILE WOOL PLUSH, PAINTED & SPRAYED					$100/150
1131	40030 1		83714/30		1988 PRICE LIST	HIPPOPOTAMUS	11.8	GREY WOVEN BIBER IMITATION FUR, STANDING				RED PLASTIC	$75/125
1132	40031 8				1994 PRICE LIST	HIPPOPOTAMUS	11.8						$90
1133	40043 1		83714/43		1988 PRICE LIST	HIPPOPOTAMUS	16.9	GREY WOVEN BIBER IMITATION FUR, STANDING				RED PLASTIC	$100/150
1134	40045 5				1994 PRICE LIST	HIPPOPOTAMUS	17.7						$135
1135	40062 2		83714/62		1988 PRICE LIST	HIPPOPOTAMUS	24.4	GREY WOVEN BIBER IMITATION FUR, STANDING				RED PLASTIC	$200/300
1136	40063 9				1994 PRICE LIST	HIPPOPOTAMUS	24.8						$250
1137	40096 7		83714/100		1988 PRICE LIST	HIPPOPOTAMUS	39.4	GREY WOVEN BIBER IMITATION FUR, STANDING				RED PLASTIC	$250/350
1138		4001/30			1982 PRICE LIST	AQUARIUS	11.8						$75/125
1139	40130 8		83717/30		1988 PRICE LIST	HIPPOPOTAMUS	11.8						$79
1140	40144 5				1996 PRICE LIST	HIPPOPOTAMUS	17.3						$120
1141	40162 9				1996 PRICE LIST	HIPPOPOTAMUS	24.4						$215
1142		4010/30	48030 3		1982 PRICE LIST	HORSE	11.8						$75/125
1143		4010/30F			1984 PRICE LIST	HORSE ON WHEELS	11.8						$100/150
1144		4020/30	48530 8		1982 PRICE LIST	DONKEY	11.8						$75/125
1145		4020/30F			1984 PRICE LIST	DONKEY ON WHEELS	11.8						$100/150
1146		4030/35			1982 PRICE LIST	DONKEY	13.8						$75/125
1147		403/40			1982 PRICE LIST	RABBIT	15.75						$100/150
1148		403/55			1982 PRICE LIST	RABBIT	21.7						$125/175
1149		404/33			1982 PRICE LIST	RABBIT	13						$100/150

153

REF #	EAN #	HERMANN OLD #	ALSO SEE	LIMITED NUMBER	DATA FROM	NAME	INCHES TALL	DESCRIPTION	VOICE	HANGING BOOKLET	ARM TAG	COMPANY LOGO	CURRENT RETAIL
1150	40630 3		83719/30		1988 PRICE LIST	HIPPOPOTAMUS	11.8	BLUE					$75/125
1151		410/13	78525 5		1982 PRICE LIST	BEAR, HAND PUPPET	9.8						$75/125
1152		410/14	78625 2		1982 PRICE LIST	RABBIT, HAND PUPPET	9.8						$75/125
1153		410/15	78725 9		1982 PRICE LIST	CAT, HAND PUPPET	9.8						$75/125
1154		410/16	78825 6		1982 PRICE LIST	DONKEY, HAND PUPPET	9.8						$75/125
1155		410/18	78925 3		1982 PRICE LIST	DOG, HAND PUPPET	9.8						$75/125
1156		410/19	79025 9		1982 PRICE LIST	FOX, HAND PUPPET	9.8						$75/125
1157	41022 5		1399/22		1984 PRICE LIST	FROG	8.7	WOVEN BIBER IMITATION FUR, GRN W/YELLOW UNDERBELLY				RED PAPER	$75/125
1158	41030 0		1399/30		1984 PRICE LIST	FROG	11.8	WOVEN BIBER IMITATION FUR, GRN W/YELLOW UNDERBELLY				RED PAPER	$100/150
1159	41040 9		1399/40		1984 PRICE LIST	FROG	15.75	WOVEN BIBER IMITATION FUR, GRN W/YELLOW UNDERBELLY				RED PAPER	$125/175
1160	41060 7		1399/60		1984 PRICE LIST	FROG	23.6	WOVEN BIBER IMITATION FUR, GRN W/YELLOW UNDERBELLY				RED PAPER	$150/200
1161	41122 2				1994 PRICE LIST	FROG	8.7						$67
1162	41130 7				1994 PRICE LIST	FROG	11.8						$92
1163	41140 6				1994 PRICE LIST	FROG	15.75						$160
1164	41160 4				1994 PRICE LIST	FROG	23.6						$262
1165	41230 4		81398/30		1988 PRICE LIST	FROG	11.8						$50/100
1166		420/8	86012 9		1982 PRICE LIST	LAMB	4.72						$50/100
1167		420/8/1			INCLUDED W/ #62/35/5	LAMB, BRN	4.72						$50/100
1168		420/9	86020 4		1982 PRICE LIST	LAMB	7.9						$50/100
1169		420/9			INCLUDED W/ #62/35/5	LAMB, WHT	7.9		NONE	NO	GRN	RED PAPER	$50/100
1170		420/10	86024 2		1982 PRICE LIST	LAMB	9.5						$50/100
1171		420/40	86040 2		1985 PRICE LIST	LAMB, MERNO	15.75						$100/150
1172		420/50			1984 PRICE LIST	LAMB	19.7						$100/150
1173		420/60	86160 7		1989 PRICE LIST	SHEEP	23.6						$125/175
1174	42016 3		196/16		1988 PRICE LIST	OWL	6.3						$75/125
1175	42017 0		196/16K		1988 PRICE LIST	OWL	6.3						$75/125
1176	42018 7		196/18		1988 PRICE LIST	OWL	7						$75/125
1177	42019 4		196/18K		1988 PRICE LIST	OWL	7						$75/125
1178	42022 4				1990 PRICE LIST	OWL	8.7	BRN W/WHT EYE AREA, MINK PLUSH, WASHABLE				RED PAPER	$91
1179	42025 5		196/25		1988 PRICE LIST	OWL	9.8						$75/125
1180	42035 4				1990 PRICE LIST	EAGLE-OWL	13.8	BRN W/WHT EYE AREA, MINK PLUSH, WASHABLE					$150/200
1181	42036 1				1993 PRICE LIST	OWL	13.8	MINK PLUSH, SURFACE WASHABLE					$203
1182	42125 2		198/25		1984 PRICE LIST	PARROT, GRN	9.8	BIBER IMITATION FUR, WASHABLE				RED PLASTIC	$75/125
1183		421/50			1982 PRICE LIST	LAMB, STANDING	19.7						$125/175
1184		422/30	86530 8		1982 PRICE LIST	LAMB	11.8						$100/150
1185		422/55			1982 PRICE LIST	LAMB	21.7						$125/175
1186		422/60	86560 5		1984 PRICE LIST	LAMB	23.6						$125/175
1187	42225 9		199/25		1984 PRICE LIST	PARROT, BLUE	9.8	BIBER IMITATION FUR, WASHABLE				RED PLASTIC	$100/150
1188	42330 0		81350/30		1988 PRICE LIST	RAVEN	11.8						$100/150
1189	42530		43530 3		1998 PRICE LIST (USA)	ERROR- PRICE LIST ENTRY SHOULD BE 43530 5							$138
1190	42560 1		84110/60		1988 PRICE LIST	DUCK, FLYING	23.6	GREY HEAD, PURPLE BACK, WHT BELLY, WOVEN BIBER IMITATION FUR, WASHABLE				RED PLASTIC	$100/150
1191	42580 9		84110/80		1988 PRICE LIST	DUCK, FLYING	31.5						$125/175
1192	43025 4		2005/25		1988 PRICE LIST	FOX, ROUND LYING	10.2	CINNAMON W/WHT MUZZLE ALSO IN JESCO CATALOG, MINK PLUSH, WASHABLE				RED PLASTIC	$113
1193	43035 3		2005/35		1988 PRICE LIST	FOX, ROUND LYING	13.8	CINNAMON W/WHT MUZZLE ALSO IN JESCO CATALOG, MINK PLUSH, WASHABLE					$100/150
1194	43165 7		83020/65		1988 PRICE LIST	FOX, LYING	25.6	MINK PLUSH, WASHABLE, CINNAMON W/WHT MUZZLE					$150/200
1195		434/16			1982 PRICE LIST	DACHSHUND	6.3						$75/125
1196		434/22			1982 PRICE LIST	DACHSHUND	8.7						$75/125
1197	43460 9				1993 PRICE LIST	MINK	23.6	MINK PLUSH, STANDING, WASHABLE					$126
1198	43526 6		3400/26		1988 PRICE LIST	CAMEL	10.2	TAN ACRYLIC, WASHABLE					$104
1199	43530 3				1996 PRICE LIST	CAMEL	11.8						$138
1200	43558 7		3400/58		1988 PRICE LIST	CAMEL	22.8	TAN ACRYLIC, WASHABLE					$290
1201	43560 0				1996 PRICE LIST	CAMEL	23.62						$269
1202	43826 7			3450/26	1989 PRICE LIST	DROMEDARY, STANDING	10.2	TAN ACRYLIC, SURFACE WASHABLE				RED PLASTIC	$100/150
1203	43858 8		3450/58		1989 PRICE LIST	DROMEDARY, STANDING	22.8	TAN ACRYLIC, SURFACE WASHABLE				RED PLASTIC	$150/200
1204	43898 4		3450/120		1989 PRICE LIST	DROMEDARY, STANDING	47.2	TAN ACRYLIC, SURFACE WASHABLE				RED PLASTIC	$250/350
1205	44030 7		550/30		1988 PRICE LIST	GIRAFFE	11.8	DRALON PLUSH, WASHABLE					$100/150
1206	44080 2		550/80		1988 PRICE LIST	GIRAFFE	31.5	DRALON PLUSH, WASHABLE					$200/300
1207		442/20			1982 PRICE LIST	LION, SITTING	7.9						$100/150
1208		442/30			1982 PRICE LIST	LION, SITTING	11.8						$125/175
1209		442/42			1982 PRICE LIST	LION, SITTING	16.5						$150/200

REF #	EAN #	HERMANN OLD #	ALSO SEE	LIMITED NUMBER	DATA FROM	NAME	INCHES TALL	DESCRIPTION	VOICE	HANGING BOOKLET	ARM TAG	COMPANY LOGO	CURRENT RETAIL
1210		444/30			1982 PRICE LIST	LION, SITTING	11.8						$100/150
1211		444/40			1982 PRICE LIST	LION, SITTING	15.75						$150/200
1212	44530 2		80742/30		1985 PRICE LIST	PIGLET, CROUCHING	11.8	PINK WOVEN BIBER IMITATION FUR, WASHABLE				RED PLASTIC	$100/150
1213	44540 1		80742/40		1985 PRICE LIST	PIGLET, CROUCHING	15.75	PINK WOVEN BIBER IMITATION FUR, WASHABLE				RED PLASTIC	$125/175
1214	44550 0		80742/50		1985 PRICE LIST	PIGLET, CROUCHING	19.7	PINK WOVEN BIBER IMITATION FUR, WASHABLE				RED PLASTIC	$150/200
1215	44630 9				1994 PRICE LIST	BOAR	11.8						$96
1216	44644 6		3200/44		1982 PRICE LIST	BOAR	17.3						$100/150
1217	44650 5/7?				1990 PRICE LIST	BOAR	19.7	ACRYLIC, WASHABLE				RED PLASTIC	$168
1218	44652 1		3200/52		1982 PRICE LIST	BOAR	20.5						$150/200
1219	44660 4				1990 PRICE LIST	BOAR	23.6	ACRYLIC, WASHABLE				RED PLASTIC	$150/200
1220	44728 3		3260/28		1984 PRICE LIST	BOAR, CUB	11						$100/150
1221	44732 0				1990 PRICE LIST	BOAR, CUB	12.6	ACRYLIC, WASHABLE				RED PLASTIC	$95
1222		450/30			1987 PRICE LIST	JERRY, THE TV DOG	11.8						$125/175
1223		450/35			1986 PRICE LIST	JERRY, THE TV DOG	13.8	SITTING					$150/200
1224	45035 1				1994 PRICE LIST	MAMMOTH	13.8						$240
1225		451/35			1987 PRICE LIST	JERRY, THE TV DOG	13.8						$125/175
1226		451/40			1986 PRICE LIST	JERRY, THE TV DOG	15.75	STANDING					$200/300
1227		452/28			1986 PRICE LIST	JERRY, THE TV DOG	11	SPRINGING					$125/175
1228		453/1			1986 PRICE LIST	JERRY, THE TV DOG		WITH MUSIC CASSETTE					$200/300
1229	45526 4		830/26		1985 PRICE LIST	COW	10.2	DRALON PLUSH, BEIGE W/BROAD WHT STRIPE , SURFACE WASHABLE				RED PAPER	$112
1230	45665 0		830/27		1983 PRICE LIST	COW	10.6						$100/150
1231		457/25			1982 PRICE LIST	POODLE	9.8						$75/125
1232		459/30			1982 PRICE LIST	POODLE	11.8						$100/150
1233		460/18	73518 2		1982 PRICE LIST	DEER, YOUNG	7						$50/100
1234	46023 7		571/23		1982 PRICE LIST	PENGUIN	9.5						$100/150
1235	46030 5		571/30		1982 PRICE LIST	PENGUIN	11.8						$100/150
1236	46123 4		572/23		1989 PRICE LIST	PENGUIN	9.5	MINK PLUSH, WASHABLE				RED PAPER	$66
1237	46130 2		572/30		1989 PRICE LIST	PENGUIN	11.8	MINK PLUSH, WASHABLE				RED PAPER	$90
1238	46148 7		572/48		1989 PRICE LIST	PENGUIN	18.9	MINK PLUSH, WASHABLE				RED PLASTIC	$153
1239	46170 8		572/70		1989 PRICE LIST	PENGUIN	27.6	MINK PLUSH, WASHABLE				RED PLASTIC	$150/200
1240	46230 9				1996 PRICE LIST	PENGUIN	11.8						$91
1241	46240 8				1996 PRICE LIST	PENGUIN	15.75						$122
1242	46250 7				1996 PRICE LIST	PENGUIN	19.7						$159
1243	46524 9		736/24		1982 PRICE LIST	SEAL	9.5	GREY MINK PLUSH, WASHABLE				RED PAPER	$50/100
1244	46532 4		736/32		1982 PRICE LIST	SEAL	12.6	GREY MINK PLUSH, WASHABLE				RED PAPER	$47
1245	46542 3		736/42		1982 PRICE LIST	SEAL	16.5	GREY MINK PLUSH, WASHABLE				RED PLASTIC	$75/125
1246	46624 6		739/24		1982 PRICE LIST	SEA LION, BABY	9.5	WHT MINK PLUSH, WASHABLE				RED PAPER	$54
1247	46632 1		739/32		1982 PRICE LIST	SEA LION, BABY	12.6	WHT MINK PLUSH, WASHABLE				RED PAPER	$52
1248	46642 0		739/42		1984 PRICE LIST	SEA LION, BABY	16.5	WHT MINK PLUSH, WASHABLE				RED PAPER	$61
1249	46665 9		739/65		1986 PRICE LIST	SEA LION, BABY	25.6	WHT MINK PLUSH, WASHABLE				RED PLASTIC	$75/125
1250		4700/30			1982 PRICE LIST	OCELOT	11.8						$75/125
1251	47560 6		83690/60		1987 PRICE LIST	CROCODILE	23.6	GRN BIBER IMITATION FUR, WASHABLE					$125/175
1252	47580 4		83690/80		1987 PRICE LIST	CROCODILE	31.5						$125/175
1253		476/18			1982 PRICE LIST	CHOW	7						$50/100
1254		476/30	53030 5		1982 PRICE LIST	CHOW	11.8						$50/100
1255		476/40	53040 4		1982 PRICE LIST	CHOW	15.75						$75/125
1256		476/50	53050 3		1982 PRICE LIST	CHOW	19.7						$100/150
1257	47660 3				1994 PRICE LIST	ALLIGATOR	23.6						$158
1258	47675 7				1994 PRICE LIST	ALLIGATOR	29.5						$205
1259	47825 6				1994 PRICE LIST	ALLIGATOR	9.8						$86
1260	47840 9				1994 PRICE LIST	ALLIGATOR	15.75						$102
1261	47850 8				1990 PRICE LIST	ALLIGATOR	19.7						$75/125
1262	47865 2				1990 PRICE LIST	ALLIGATOR	25.6						$100/150
1263	48030 3		4010/30		1989 PRICE LIST	HORSE	11.8	BRN W/BLK MANE, WHT NOSE, MINK PLUSH, WASHABLE				MTL W/PAPER INSERT	$93
1264	48130 0		560/30		1982 PRICE LIST	ZEBRA	11.8	DRALON PLUSH, SURFACE WASHABLE, WHT W/BLK STRIPES				MTL W/PAPER INSERT	$50/100
1265	48460 8				1995 PRICE LIST	FOAL, LYING	23.6	TAN W/WHT MANE & TAIL, WOVEN FUR, WASHABLE				RED PLASTIC	$124
1266	48530 8		4020/30		1982 PRICE LIST	DONKEY, STANDING	11.8	GREY W/WHT NOSE, BLK MANE, MINK PLUSH, WASHABLE				MTL W/PAPER INSERT	$102
1267	48660 2				1991 PRICE LIST	DONKEY, LYING	23.6	GREY W/WHT NOSE, BLK MANE, WOVEN FUR, WASHABLE				RED PLASTIC	$234
1268	48730 2				1995 PRICE LIST	DONKEY	11.8	GREY WOVEN FUR, WHT FACE, WASHABLE				RED PLASTIC	$91
1269		490/32			BEHA 1927 CATALOG	DOG ON WHEELS	12.6	LONG PILE SPOTTED PLUSH. SOLID IRON FRAME, LEATHER COLLAR, RED VARNISHED WHEELS					$75/125

REF #	EAN #	HERMANN OLD #	ALSO SEE	LIMITED NUMBER	DATA FROM	NAME	INCHES TALL	DESCRIPTION	VOICE	HANGING BOOKLET	ARM TAG	COMPANY LOGO	CURRENT RETAIL
1270		490/40	36840 3		1989 PRICE LIST	LYNX	15.75						$75/125
1271		490/60	36860 1		1989 PRICE LIST	LYNX	23.6						$100/150
1272	49035 7		84100/35		1988 PRICE LIST	WHALE	13.8						$50/100
1273	49045 6		84100/45		1988 PRICE LIST	WHALE	17.7						$75/125
1274	49065 4		84100/65		1988 PRICE LIST	WHALE	25.6						$100/150
1275	49565 9		84120/65		1988 PRICE LIST	ALLIGATOR	25.6						$125/175
1276	49590 1		84120/90		1988 PRICE LIST	ALLIGATOR	35.4						$150/200
1277	49598 7		84120/120		1988 PRICE LIST	ALLIGATOR	47.2						$200/300
1278		495/30			1982 PRICE LIST	LEOPARD	11.8						$75/125
1279		495/45			1982 PRICE LIST	LEOPARD	17.7						$100/150
1280		496/30			1982 PRICE LIST	LEOPARD, SNOW	11.8						$75/125
1281		496/35			1984 PRICE LIST	LEOPARD, SNOW	13.8						$75/125
1282		499/30	36030 8		1982 PRICE LIST	LEOPARD, SITTING	11.8						$75/125
1283		499/42			1982 PRICE LIST	LEOPARD, SITTING	16.5						$100/150
1284		499/62	36062 9		1982 PRICE LIST	LEOPARD, SITTING	24.4						$125/175
1285		5/10			1985 PRICE LIST	MINITEDDY	4	BEIGE AND BRN					$50/100
1286		5/23			BEHA 1927 CATALOG	BEAR, YOUNG	9.5	COMIC SHAPE W/PACIFIER, 1a WOOL PLUSH, WOOD WOOL & WADDING STUFFED, LIMBS W/WIRE-FLEXIBLE THROUGHOUT	GROWLER				$125/175
1287		5/26			BEHA 1927 CATALOG	BEAR, YOUNG	10.2	COMIC SHAPE W/PACIFIER, 1a WOOL PLUSH, WOOD WOOL & WADDING STUFFED, LIMBS W/WIRE-FLEXIBLE THROUGHOUT	GROWLER				$125/175
1288		5/30			BEHA 1927 CATALOG	BEAR, YOUNG	11.8	COMIC SHAPE W/PACIFIER, 1a WOOL PLUSH, WOOD WOOL & WADDING STUFFED, LIMBS W/WIRE-FLEXIBLE THROUGHOUT	GROWLER				$125/175
1289		5/40			BEHA 1927 CATALOG	BEAR, YOUNG	12.6	COMIC SHAPE W/PACIFIER, 1a WOOL PLUSH, WOOD WOOL & WADDING STUFFED, LIMBS W/WIRE-FLEXIBLE THROUGHOUT	GROWLER				$150/200
1290		5/50			HERMANN CAT 1982	TEDDY, SOFT	19.7	HONEY 30%C & 70% ACRYLIC W/TAN SHORT PILE MUZZLE, RED BOW	NONE	YES	BRN	GRN PAPER	$150
1291		5/60			HERMANN CAT 1982	TEDDY, SOFT	23.6	HONEY 30%C & 70% ACRYLIC W/TAN SHORT PILE MUZZLE, RED BOW					$200/300
1292		5/70			HERMANN CAT 1982	TEDDY, SOFT	28.3	HONEY 30%C & 70% ACRYLIC W/TAN SHORT PILE MUZZLE, RED BOW					$200/300
1293		5/90			HERMANN CAT 1986	TEDDY, SOFT	35	HONEY 30%C & 70% ACRYLIC W/TAN SHORT PILE MUZZLE, RED BOW					$250/350
1294		5/90/2			HERMANN CAT 1982	TEDDY, SOFT	35	SAME AS ABOVE EXCEPT LONG PILE MOHAIR PLUSH					$250/350
1295		50/15			BEHA 1927 CATALOG	FOX, GROTESQUE JOLLY	5.5	W/FLY ON NOSE, COMIC TURNING HEAD, MOHAIR PLUSH					$100/150
1296		50/42			HERMANN CAT 1982	TEDDY, SOFT	16.5	BRN WITH WHT TUMMY					$50/100
1297		500/1			BEHA 1927 CATALOG	PINCUSHION, BULLDOG		CUSHION OF COLORED LONG PILE PLUSH, CUSHION AND ANIMAL HEAD STUFFED	YES				$100/150
1298		500/2			BEHA 1927 CATALOG	PINCUSHION, PEKINGESE		CUSHION OF COLORED LONG PILE PLUSH, CUSHION AND ANIMAL HEAD STUFFED	YES				$100/150
1299		500/3			BEHA 1927 CATALOG	PINCUSHION, TERRIER		CUSHION OF COLORED LONG PILE PLUSH, CUSHION AND ANIMAL HEAD STUFFED	YES				$100/150
1300		500/4			BEHA 1927 CATALOG	PINCUSHION, SPORTING DOG		CUSHION OF COLORED LONG PILE PLUSH, CUSHION AND ANIMAL HEAD STUFFED	YES				$100/150
1301		5000/38			1982 PRICE LIST	LLAMA	15						$50/100
1302		5000/48			1982 PRICE LIST	LLAMA	18.9						$50/100
1303	50040 7		162/40		1989 PRICE LIST	YORKSHIRE TERRIER	15.75	STANDING, LONG PILE BRN ACRYLIC PLUSH				RED PLASTIC	$96
1304	50041 4		162/40K		1982 PRICE LIST	YORKSHIRE TERRIER	15.75	SITTING, LONG PILE BRN ACRYLIC PLUSH				RED PLASTIC	$96
1305	50140 4		163/40		1989 PRICE LIST	YORKSHIRE TERRIER	15.75						$96
1306	50235 7		160/35		1989 PRICE LIST	YORKSHIRE TERRIER	13.8						$96
1307	50245 6				1995 PRICE LIST	WEST HIGHLAND TERRIER	17.7	SITTING, WHT LONG PILE MOHAIR PLUSH, WASHABLE, W/RED COLLAR				RED PLASTIC	$158
1308	50335 4		161/35		1989 PRICE LIST	YORKSHIRE TERRIER	13.8						$75/125
1309	50345 3				1996 PRICE LIST	SCOTTISH TERRIER	17.7	BLK					$100/150
1310	50346 0				1996 PRICE LIST	SCOTTISH TERRIER	17.7	WHT					$100/150
1311	50530 3		170/30		1989 PRICE LIST	FOX TERRIER	11.8	WHT W/BRN EARS, BLK SPOT ON BACK AROUND BASE OF TAIL, MINK PLUSH				RED PLASTIC	$124
1312	50535 8		170/35		1989 PRICE LIST	FOX TERRIER	13.8						$100/150
1313	50630 0			1,000	1997 PRICE LIST	JACK RUSSELL TERRIER	11.8	MOHAIR PLUSH					$157
1314	50635 5		80174/35		1989 PRICE LIST	FOX TERRIER	13.8						$100/150
1315	50730 7				1990 PRICE LIST	KROMFOHRLANDER, PUPPY	11.8	SITTING, WHT BIBER IMITATION FUR, WASHABLE, BRN BEARD-EARS AND TAIL				RED PLASTIC	$100/150
1316		510/1			BEHA 1927 CATALOG	PINCUSHION, BULLDOG		CUSHION OF COLORED LONG PILE PLUSH. CUSHION AND ANIMAL HEAD STUFFED, SIMILAR TO 510/1	YES				$125/175

REF #	EAN #	HERMANN OLD #	ALSO SEE	LIMITED NUMBER	DATA FROM	NAME	INCHES TALL	DESCRIPTION	VOICE	HANGING BOOKLET	ARM TAG	COMPANY LOGO	CURRENT RETAIL
1317		510/2			BEHA 1927 CATALOG	PINCUSHION, PEKINGESE		CUSHION OF COLORED LONG PILE PLUSH. CUSHION AND ANIMAL HEAD STUFFED, SIMILAR TO 510/2	YES				$125/175
1318		510/3			BEHA 1927 CATALOG	PINCUSHION, TERRIER		CUSHION OF COLORED LONG PILE PLUSH. CUSHION AND ANIMAL HEAD STUFFED, SIMILAR TO 510/3	YES				$125/175
1319		510/4			BEHA 1927 CATALOG	PINCUSHION, SPORTING DOG		CUSHION OF COLORED LONG PILE PLUSH. CUSHION AND ANIMAL HEAD STUFFED, SIMILAR TO 510/4	YES				$125/175
1320	51035 2		80176/35		1988 PRICE LIST	AIREDALE	13.8						$75/125
1321		512/10	71010 3		1988 PRICE LIST	SQUIRREL	4						$50/100
1322		512/17	71017 2		1988 PRICE LIST	SQUIRREL	6.7						$75/125
1323		512/24	71024 0		1988 PRICE LIST	SQUIRREL	9.5						$75/125
1324	51545 6		801745/45		1988 PRICE LIST	COLLIE, LYING	17.7	MINK PLUSH				RED PLASTIC	$100/150
1325	51550 0				1994 PRICE LIST	COLLIE	19.7						$198
1326		51/42			HERMANN CAT 1982	TEDDY, SOFT	16.5	BLUE WITH WHT TUMMY					$50/100
1327	52040 5		80438/40		1988 PRICE LIST	DACHSHUND "WALDI"	15.75						$75/125
1328		52/42			HERMANN CAT 1982	TEDDY, SOFT	16.5	ROSE WITH WHT TUMMY					$50/100
1329	52145 7				1990 PRICE LIST	DACHSHUND, LYING	17.7	BRN MINK PLUSH				RED PLASTIC	$156
1330		525/9	71509 2		1982 PRICE LIST	MOUSE, WHT	3.5						$50/100
1331		525/9	71609 9		1982 PRICE LIST	MOUSE, GRAY	3.5						$50/100
1332		525/9	71709 6		1988 PRICE LIST	MOUSE, OLD ROSE	3.5						$50/100
1333		525/20			1982 PRICE LIST	MOUSE, BLUE	7.9						$50/100
1334		525/21			1982 PRICE LIST	MOUSE, REDDISH BRN	8.3						$50/100
1335		525/22			1982 PRICE LIST	MOUSE, GRN	8.7						$50/100
1336		525/23			1983 PRICE LIST	MOUSE W MUSIC BOX	9.5						$100/150
1337	52540 0		83100/40		1985 PRICE LIST	BOXER	15.75						$125/175
1338	52552 3		83100/52		1985 PRICE LIST	BOXER	20.5						$150/200
1339		526/20	71720 1		1987 CATALOG	MOUSE, WHT	7.9	WHT W/BEIGE INNER EAR, BLK NOSE & EYES, SOFT				RED PAPER	$75/125
1340	52635 3				1990 PRICE LIST	BOXER, LYING	13.8	BRN BIBER IMITATION FUR, WASHABLE				RED PLASTIC	$100/150
1341		527/20	7118208		1987 CATALOG	MOUSE, RED	7.9	RED BODY W/WHT INNER EAR, SOFT, W/BLK NOSE & EYES				RED PAPER	$75/125
1342		527/25	71825 3		1987 CATALOG	MOUSE, RED	9.8	RED BODY W/WHT INNER EAR, SOFT, W/BLK NOSE & EYES				RED PAPER	$75/125
1343	52735 0				1992 PRICE LIST	BOXER, LYING	13.8	BRN W/BLK SNOUT, WOVEN FUR, WASHABLE				RED PLASTIC	$177
1344	52760 2				1992 PRICE LIST	BOXER, LYING	23.6	BRN W/BLK SNOUT, WOVEN FUR, WASHABLE				RED PLASTIC	$150/200
1345		528/20	71920 5		1987 CATALOG	MOUSE	7.9	BLUE W/WHT INNER EAR, BLK NOSE & EYES				RED PAPER	$50/100
1346		528/25	71925 0		1987 CATALOG	MOUSE	9.8	BLUE W/WHT INNER EAR, BLK NOSE & EYES				RED PAPER	$50/100
1347		529/20	72020 1		1987 CATALOG	MOUSE	7.9	YELLOW W/WHT INNER EAR, BLK NOSE & EYES				RED PAPER	$50/100
1348		530/15	72515 2		1982 PRICE LIST	HAMSTER	5.9						$50/100
1349		530/25			BEHA 1927 CATALOG	HARE	9.8	GREY & YELLOW WOOL PLUSH W/VOICE, ARTIFICIAL SILK RIBBON	GROWLER				$75/125
1350	53030 5		476/30		1988 PRICE LIST	CHOW	11.8	BRN MINK PLUSH, WASHABLE				RED PLASTIC	$149
1351	53040 4		476/40		1988 PRICE LIST	CHOW	15.75	BRN MINK PLUSH, WASHABLE				RED PLASTIC	$223
1352	53050 3		476/50		1988 PRICE LIST	CHOW	19.7	BRN MINK PLUSH, WASHABLE				RED PLASTIC	$279
1353		535/16	72616 6		1982 PRICE LIST	HAMSTER	6.3						$75/125
1354		535/25	72625 8		1982 PRICE LIST	HAMSTER	9.8						$75/125
1355	53530 0		80458/30		1988 PRICE LIST	POODLE, GRAY	11.8						$100/150
1356	53630 7		80458/31		1988 PRICE LIST	POODLE, BRN	11.8	MINK PLUSH, WASHABLE				RED PLASTIC	$100/150
1357	53730 4		80460/30		1988 PRICE LIST	POODLE, STANDING	11.8	BLK WOVEN FUR, WASHABLE, W/RED LEATHER COLLAR				RED PLASTIC	$131
1358	53830 1				1993 PRICE LIST	POODLE, APRICOT	11.8	STANDING, WASHABLE WOVEN FUR					$147
1359	53930 8				1993 PRICE LIST	POODLE, COGNAC	11.8	STANDING, WASHABLE WOVEN FUR					$147
1360		540/20	73020 0		1982 PRICE LIST	GUINEA PIG	7.9						$50/100
1361		540/21			BEHA 1927 CATALOG	CHICKEN	8.3	YORK YELLOW WOOL PLUSH					$50/100
1362		540/20K	73021 7		1988 PRICE LIST	GUINEA PIG	7.9						$50/100
1363	54025 0		3660/25		1988 PRICE LIST	PEKINGESE	9.8						$75/125
1364	54515 6		180/15		1988 PRICE LIST	"MOLLY" DOG	5.9						$50/100
1365	54525 5		180/25		1988 PRICE LIST	"MOLLY" DOG	9.8						$50/100
1366		550/24			1986 CATALOG	RHINOCEROS	9.5	MOSS GRN				RED PAPER	$50/100
1367		550/30	44030 7		1988 PRICE LIST	GIRAFFE	11.8						$50/100
1368		550/80	44080 2		1988 PRICE LIST	GIRAFFE	31.5						$125/175
1369		551/20			BEHA 1927 CATALOG	DUCK	7.9	ARTIFICIAL SILK PLUSH, SEVERAL COLORS, RED VARNISHED WHEELS					$100/150
1370		55/35/1	25535 2		1988 PRICE LIST	TEDDY BEAR	14.2	GIRL IN RED SKIRT, "DIRNDL"					$150/200
1371		55/35/2	25635 9		1988 PRICE LIST	TEDDY BEAR	14.2	BOY IN GRN SHORT PANTS, "SEPPL"					$150/200
1372		55/35/3	25735 6		1988 PRICE LIST	TEDDY BEAR	14.2	GIRL IN DENIM SKIRT, "JEANSROCK"					$150/200
1373		55/35/4	25835 3		1988 PRICE LIST	TEDDY BEAR	12.6	BOY CINNAMON W/BLUE OVERALLS, RED POCKET WITH HEARTS, NO TAG, "JEANSHOSE"	YES			RED PAPER	$50/100
1374	55048 8		1962/48		1987 PRICE LIST	BOBTAIL, SITTING	18.9	WHT FOREQUARTER, GREY HINDQUARTER, LONG PILE ACRYLIC				RED PLASTIC	$195
1375	55060 0		1962/60		1987 PRICE LIST	BOBTAIL, SITTING	23.6	WHT FOREQUARTER, GREY HINDQUARTER, LONG PILE ACRYLIC				RED PLASTIC	$290

REF #	EAN #	HERMANN OLD #	ALSO SEE	LIMITED NUMBER	DATA FROM	NAME	INCHES TALL	DESCRIPTION	VOICE	HANGING BOOKLET	ARM TAG	COMPANY LOGO	CURRENT RETAIL
1376		552/25			BEHA 1927 CATALOG	DUCK	9.8	WHT WOOL PLUSH					$75/125
1377		555/24			1984 PRICE LIST	HIPPOPOTAMUS, DWARF	9.5						$50/100
1378		555/32			1984 PRICE LIST	HIPPOPOTAMUS, DWARF	12.6						$75/125
1379		555/55			1984 PRICE LIST	HIPPOPOTAMUS, DWARF	21.7						$100/150
1380	55550 6	84070/50			1988 CATALOG	JOESEF THE TV DOG	19.7	ACRYLIC PLUSH, WASHABLE; FROM "HEIDI" PROGRAM		YES		RED PLASTIC	$125/175
1381	55655 8	84072/55			1988 CATALOG	JOESEF THE TV DOG	21.7	ACRYLIC PLUSH, WASHABLE; FROM "HEIDI" PROGRAM		YES		RED PLASTIC	$125/175
1382	55760 9		84060/60		1988 PRICE LIST	DOG, ST. BERNARD, LYING	23.6	WHT FOREQUARTERS & PAWS, BRN HINDQUARTERS, MINK PLUSH				RED PLASTIC	$125/175
1383		56/35/3			HERMANN CAT 1986	"LATZHOSE"	14.2	SOFT HONEY MINK PLUSH DRESSED IN STRIPED OVERALLS				RED PAPER	$75/125
1384		56/35/4			HERMANN CAT 1986	"KLEID"	14.2	SOFT HONEY MINK PLUSH DRESSED IN PINK STRIPED APRON DRESS				RED PAPER	$75/125
1385		560/30	48130 0		1982 PRICE LIST	ZEBRA	11.8						$75/125
1386	56035 7		1960/35		1988 PRICE LIST	CAT, MALTESE	13.8						$75/125
1387	56080 7				1993 CATALOG	LABRADOR	31.8	WOVEN FUR, WASHABLE, BEIGE					$100/150
1388	56081 4				1993 PRICE LIST	LABRADOR	31.8	WOVEN FUR, WASHABLE, BRN					$100/150
1389	56089 7				1993 PRICE LIST	LABRADOR	35						$100/150
1390	56135 4		1961/35		1988 PRICE LIST	CAT, MALTESE	13.8						$75/125
1391	56555 0		84085/55		1988 PRICE LIST	BEAGLE	21.7						$125/175
1392	57040 0		83110/40		1989 PRICE LIST	HUSKY, LYING	15.75						$100/150
1393	57050 9				1990 PRICE LIST	HUSKY, LYING	19.7	GREY BODY, WHT PAWS & FACE, MINK PLUSH, WASHABLE				RED PLASTIC	$100/150
1394		571/23	46023 7		1982 PRICE LIST	PENGUIN	9						$50/100
1395		571/30	46030 5		1982 PRICE LIST	PENGUIN	11.8						$50/100
1396		572/23	46123 4		1989 PRICE LIST	PENGUIN	9						$50/100
1397		572/30	46130 2		1989 PRICE LIST	PENGUIN	11.8						$50/100
1398		572/48	46148 7		1989 PRICE LIST	PENGUIN	18.9						$75/125
1399		572/70	46170 8		1989 PRICE LIST	PENGUIN	27.6						$125/175
1400		58/30/1			GROVE	TEDDY BEAR	11.8	CARAMEL 53% W & 47% C MOHAIR, W/GRN SWISS DRESS, RED APRON	GROWLER	YES	BRN	RED PAPER	$150
1401		58/30/2			HIXSON	TEDDY BEAR	11.8	CARAMEL 53%W & 47% C MOHAIR, W/ GRN FELT LEDERHOSEN, RED FELT TIE	GROWLER	YES	BRN	RED PLASTIC	$150
1402		590/28	32728 8	2,000	KATHY ANN CAT 1989	POLAR BEAR	8HX11L	WHT MOHAIR STANDING ON 4 FEET; ALSO JESCO	NONE	YES	RED	RED PLASTIC	$95
1403		6/23			BEHA 1927 CATALOG	YOUNG BEAR	9	COMIC SHAPE W/APRON OR PANTALOON, 1a WOOL PLUSH, WOOD WOOL & WADDING STUFFED, LIMBS W/WIRE- FLEXIBLE THROUGHOUT	GROWLER				$75/125
1404		6/26			BEHA 1927 CATALOG	YOUNG BEAR	10.3	COMIC SHAPE W/APRON OR PANTALOON, 1a WOOL PLUSH, WOOD WOOL & WADDING STUFFED, LIMBS W/WIRE- FLEXIBLE THROUGHOUT	GROWLER				$75/125
1405		6/30			BEHA 1927 CATALOG	YOUNG BEAR	11.8	COMIC SHAPE W/APRON OR PANTALOON, 1a WOOL PLUSH, WOOD WOOL & WADDING STUFFED, LIMBS W/WIRE- FLEXIBLE THROUGHOUT	GROWLER				$100/150
1406		6/40			BEHA 1927 CATALOG	YOUNG BEAR	12.6	COMIC SHAPE W/APRON OR PANTALOON, 1a WOOL PLUSH, WOOD WOOL & WADDING STUFFED, LIMBS W/WIRE- FLEXIBLE THROUGHOUT	GROWLER				$125/175
1407		60/30/1			1985 PRICE LIST	TEDDYBEAR, DRESSED	11.8	"DIRNDL"					$150/200
1408		60/30/2			1985 PRICE LIST	TEDDYBEAR, DRESSED	11.8	"SEPPL"					$150/200
1409		60/33	060/33	3,000		HELEN SIEVERLING BEAR	13	MULTIPLE NUMBERS FOR SAME BEAR					$150/200
1410		600/1			BEHA 1927 CATALOG	HARE, GROTESQUE	8.7	22 CM HIGH					$75/125
1411		600/2			BEHA 1927 CATALOG	FORESTER, GROTESQUE	8.7	22 CM HIGH					$75/125
1412		600/3			BEHA 1927 CATALOG	BRIDEGROOM, GROTESQUE	8.7	22 CM HIGH					$75/125
1413		600/4			BEHA 1927 CATALOG	BRIDE, GROTESQUE	8.7	22 CM HIGH					$75/125
1414		600/5			BEHA 1927 CATALOG	TREFF, GROTESQUE	8.7	22 CM HIGH					$75/125
1415		600/6			BEHA 1927 CATALOG	GRANDFATHER, GROTESQUE	8.7	22 CM HIGH					$75/125
1416		600/14			1982 PRICE LIST	RABBIT POUNCING, SMALL	5.5						$75/125
1417		600/17			1982 PRICE LIST	RABBIT POUNCING, SMALL	6.7						$75/125
1418	60015 2		153/15		1982 PRICE LIST	CAT, BLK	5.9						$75/125
1419	60020 6		153/20		1982 PRICE LIST	CAT, BLK	7.9						$75/125
1420		604/23	85023 6	2,000	1987 PRICE LIST	RABBIT, WALKING UPRIGHT	9.5	TAN W/CLOTH INNER EARS				RED PLASTIC	$100/150
1421		607/21			1982 PRICE LIST	RABBIT, CROUCHING	8.3						$75/125
1422		607/28			1982 PRICE LIST	RABBIT, CROUCHING	11						$75/125
1423		607/42			1982 PRICE LIST	RABBIT, CROUCHING	16.5						$100/150
1424		61/14	16114 1		1982 PRICE LIST	TEDDY BEAR	5.5	CINNAMON W/BLUE BOW				RED PLASTIC	$50/100
1425		61/25	16125 7		SEE 16125 7	TEDDY BEAR	10.2	CINNAMON W/RED BOW					$65
1426		61/36	16136 3		SEE 16136 3	TEDDY BEAR	14.2	CINNAMON W/RED BOW					$75/125
1427		61/36/1		300	TOLEDO TOY STORE	TEDDY BEAR	14.2	PEACH MOHAIR W/WHT SHAVED MOHAIR PADS, WHT BOW; SPECIAL FOR TOLEDO TOY STORE	GROWLER	YES	RED	RED PLASTIC	$99
1428		61/40				TEDDY BEAR	15.75	OLD GOLD MOHAIR	GROWLER	YES	BRN	RED PLASTIC	$100/150

REF #	EAN #	HERMANN OLD #	ALSO SEE	LIMITED NUMBER	DATA FROM	NAME	INCHES TALL	DESCRIPTION	VOICE	HANGING BOOKLET	ARM TAG	COMPANY LOGO	CURRENT RETAIL
1429		61/50	16150 9		1987 CATALOG	TEDDY BEAR	19.7	CINNAMON W/RED BOW				RED PLASTIC	$125/175
1430		61/60 OLD			BOOK 1930 PG 51/54	TEDDY BEAR CIRCA 1930	23.6	CARAMEL SHORT PILE MOHAIR, SONNEBERG TYPE; METAL LOGO W/PAPER INSERT					$200/300
1431		610/35			1982 PRICE LIST	RABBIT	13.8						$75/125
1432	61022 9		155/22		1988 PRICE LIST	CAT	8.7						$50/100
1433	61122 6		156/22		1988 PRICE LIST	CAT	8.7						$50/100
1434	61222 3		2030/22		1988 PRICE LIST	CAT, WHT	8.7	MINK PLUSH, WASHABLE				RED PAPER	$75/125
1435		615/21			1982 PRICE LIST	RABBIT	8.7						$75/125
1436		616/26			1982 PRICE LIST	RABBIT	10.2						$75/125
1437		616/33			1982 PRICE LIST			GRN INK FED REPUBLIC OF GERM TAG					
1439		62/14	16214 8?		ACTUAL BEAR	TEDDY BEAR	5.6	CARAMEL FULLY JTD	NONE	YES	BRN	NONE	$50/100
1440		62/14 MAIS	16514 9		SEE 16214 9	TEDDY BEAR	5.6	MAISE 100% WOOL MOHAIR	NONE	YES	RED	RED PAPER	$50/100
1441		62/14s	16614 6		SEE 16614 6 OR LI 55	TEDDY BEAR	5.6	BLK					$50/100
1442		62/14w	16714 3		SEE 16714 3	TEDDY BEAR	5.6	WHT					$50/100
1443		62/17	16217 9			TEDDY BEAR	6.5	CARAMEL MOHAIR EXCELSIOR STUFFING					$50/100
1444		62/17 MAIS	16517 0		SEE 16217 0	TEDDY BEAR	6.5	MAISE, BRN INK TAG, RED PAPER LOGO	NONE	NO	BRN	RED PAPER	$50/100
1445		62/17w	16217 & SU70			TEDDY BEAR	6.5	WHT 53%W & 47%C MOHAIR, STRIPED TIE, DBL TAGGED FOR JESCO	NONE	YES	BRN	MISSING	$50/100
1446		62/17/1				TEDDY BEAR	6.5	CHOCOLATE, PLAID TIE, BRN INK, NO LOGO; JESCO #CH40					$50/100
1447		62/20	16220 9			TEDDY BEAR	7.9	CARAMEL BEIGE MOHAIR					$50/100
1448		62/20/?				TEDDY BEAR	7.9	HONEY MOHAIR	NONE	YES	BRN	NONE	$50/100
1449		62/20s	16620 7			TEDDY BEAR	7.9	BLK					$50/100
1450		62/20w	16720 4			TEDDY BEAR	7.9	WHT					$50/100
1451		62/20/4	PART OF S0003			TEDDY BEAR	7.9	NOUGAT					$50/100
1452		62/25	16225 4			TEDDY BEAR	11	CARAMEL MOHAIR PLUSH, W/RED BOW; ALSO CALLED "RUST BROWN COLOR"	NONE	NO	GRN	RED PAPER	$50/100
1453		62/25LA			1980 TEDDY BEAR	TEDDY BEAR	11	GREY MOHAIR PLUSH 62%W & 38%C, BLUE BOW	NONE	YES	GRN	RED PAPER	$50/100
1454		62/30 OLD				TEDDY BEAR	11.8	HONEY MOHAIR DRESSED IN TYROLEAN LEDERHOSEN					$100/150
1455		62/30	16230 8		HERMANN CAT 1986	TEDDY BEAR	11.8	CARAMEL, SHEARED PADS, SHORT PILE MOHAIR, PLASTIC EYES, GRN BOW	GROWLER	YES	BRN	RED PLASTIC	$100/150
1456		62/30			HERMANN CIRCA 1982	TEDDY BEAR	11.8	FADED ORANGE SHORT PILE MOHAIR, W/GLASS EYES, BLUE BOW	GROWLER	NO	BRN	GRN PAPER	$100/150
1457		62/30MAIS	16530? MAIS			TEDDY BEAR	11.8	MAIZE MOHAIR, SHEARED PADS	NONE	NO #	GRN	RED PLASTIC	$100/150
1458		62/30/1	16630?		HERMANN CIRCA 1980	TEDDY BEAR	11.8	BRN, PLAID BOW	GROWLER	YES	GRN	RED PLASTIC	$100/150
1459		62/30s	16630 7			TEDDY BEAR	11.8	BLK					$100/150
1460		62/30w	16730 3			TEDDY BEAR	11.8	WHT					$100/150
1461		62/30/5		400	TBEAR&F DEC '89 PG 21	DIANE	14.2	MAUVE ENGLISH MOHAIR W/MAUVE RUFFLE AROUND NECK	GROWLER	YES	RED	GOLD PLASTIC	$100/150
1462		62/30NSO	16230 8			TEDDY BEAR	11.8	CARAMEL W/PLAID BOW, FULLY JTD, DBL TAGGED 70% ACRYLIC, 30% C	GROWLER	YES	BRN	RED PLASTIC	$100/150
1463		62/30/4TSP			TBEAR&F 11/89 PG 21	MELODY, W/MUSIC BOX	11.8	NOUGAT ENGLISH MOHAIR, PLAYS "TB PICNIC", W/STRAW HAT	MUSIC	YES	BRN	RED PLASTIC	$100/150
1464		62/31/3??			KATHY ANN CAT	MELODY, MUSIC BEAR	11.8	OLD GOLD MOHAIR, NO RUFFLE, PLAYS "TB PICNIC"	MUSIC	YES	BRN	RED PLASTIC	$100/150
1465		62/31/3TP		500	KATHY ANN CAT	MELODY, MUSIC BEAR	11.8	CINNAMON W/LACE NECK RUFFLE, PLAYS "TB PICNIC"	MUSIC	YES	RED	RED PLASTIC	$100/150
1466		62/35/5	12035 3			SHEPHERD SET	14.2	CONTAINS 62/35/6 + 420/8/1 BRN LAMB PLUS 420/9 WHT LAMB	GROWLER	YES	BRN	RED PLASTIC	$150/200
1467		62/36/6			INCLUDED IN 62/35/5	SHEPHERD BEAR	14.2	ANT GOLD DRESSED IN VELVET COAT WITH TAM, 53%W & 47%C	GROWLER	YES	BRN	RED PLASTIC	$150/200
1468		62/35 SU140			HERMANN JESCO RUBIN	PICNIC, MUSICAL SET	11.8	WHT MOHAIR, ALSO LACE RUFFLE NECK PIECE	MUSIC	YES	BRN	RED PLASTIC	$150/200
1469		62/35	16235 3		HERMANN CAT 1986	TEDDY BEAR	14.2	CARAMEL, RED BOW TIE, RED PLASTIC LOGO	GROWLER	YES	BRN	RED PLASTIC	$150/200
1470		62/35??	16235 3			TEDDY BEAR	14.2	CARAMEL 53%W & 47%C MOHAIR, GRN BOW TIE, 1954 REPLICA?	GROWLER	YES	BRN	RED PLASTIC	$150/200
1471		62/35/NWR			HERMANN	KARI	14.2	WHT 53% W & 47% C PLUSH W/BRN PAWS, TAN TIE W/POLKA DOTS	GROWLER	SHORT BKLT	BRN	RED PLASTIC	$150/200
1472		62/35/1			SEE CH 140 JESCO	TEDDY BEAR	14.2	CHOCOLATE 53%W & 47%C MOHAIR, PLAID BOW TIE	GROWLER	YES	BRN	GOLD PLASTIC	$150/200
1473		62/40 MAIS			SEE 16240 7	TEDDY BEAR	15.75	MAIS SHORT PILE 53% W & 47% C MOHAIR	GROWLER	YES	BRN	RED PLASTIC	$150/200
1474		62/40	16240 7			TEDDY BEAR	15.75	CARAMEL 62%W & 38%C MOHAIR W/RED BOW	GROWLER	YES	BRN	RED PLASTIC	$150/200
1475		62/40 OLD			WAS MRF# "C"	TEDDY	15.75	OFF-WHT MOHAIR; BLK FLOSS NOSE/MOUTH; PLASTIC EYES; FULLY JTD; SHORT SHEARED PADS	GROWLER	NONE	GRN	GOLD PLASTIC	$150/200
1476		62/40/3/O		300	HERMANN	TEDDY BEAR	16.5	ORANGE 70% ACRYLIC & 30% COTTON PLUSH W/BLUE BOW	GROWLER	YES	BRN	RED PLASTIC	$150/200
1477		62/45			KALINKE, WAS "AK"	TEDDY BEAR	18.1	CINNAMON, FULLY JTD, W/ "AMHERST TEDDY BEAR RALLY 1985", 62% W & 38% C; AMHERST, MA SPECIAL	GROWLER	SGD BY 2	GRN	RED PLASTIC	$200/300
1478		62/50	16250 6		1984 PRICE LIST	TEDDY BEAR	19.6	CARAMEL 62%W & 38%C MOHAIR W/RED BOW	GROWLER	YES	GRN	RED PLASTIC	$200/300
1479		62/50 LI	16250 LI			TEDDY BEAR	19.6	BLK MOHAIR W/RED & WHT STRIPED BOW	GROWLER	YES	GRN	RED PLASTIC	$200/300
1480		62/50NSB			1988 JESCO CATALOG	TEDDY BEAR	19.6	BLK 70% ACRYLIC & 30 %C PLUSH, TAN SHORT PILE PADS, W/TAN POLKA DOT TIE	GROWLER	SHORT BKLT	BRN	RED PLASTIC	$200/300

REF #	EAN #	HERMANN OLD #	ALSO SEE	LIMITED NUMBER	DATA FROM	NAME	INCHES TALL	DESCRIPTION	VOICE	HANGING BOOKLET	ARM TAG	COMPANY LOGO	CURRENT RETAIL
1481		62/50NWB			1988 JESCO CATALOG	SWEET TEDDY	16.5	WHT 70% ACRYLIC & 30% C PLUSH W/TAN POLKA DOT BOW	GROWLER	YES	BRN	RED PLASTIC	$200/300
1482		62/60	CA 240			ROBIN HOOD, ORIGINAL	23.6	CARAMEL MOHAIR, 53%W,47% C, GRN VEST, PEAKED HAT, PLAID PANTS, PLASTIC EYES, FULLY JTD	GROWLER	YES	GRN	RED PLASTIC	$200/300
1483		62/85	CA 330			TEDDY BEAR	33	RUBIN VERSION ON STD SERIES IN COCOA, PLASTIC EYES, FULLY JTD	GROWLER	NO	GRN	RED PLASTIC	$550/750
1484		62/90		10?	1990? RUBEN STORE SAMPLE	TEDDY BEAR	35.5	EXTRA LONG PILE TAN MOHAIR, BRN TIPPED, RED BOW	GROWLER	YES	GRN	RED PLASTIC	$550/750
1485	62120 1		2028/20		1987 PRICE LIST	CAT, STANDING	7.87	BRN, MINK PLUSH, WASHABLE, GRN BOW				RED PLASTIC	$50/100
1486	62125 6		2028/25		1987 PRICE LIST	CAT	9.84						$75/125
1487	62220 8		2029/20		1988 PRICE LIST	CAT, STANDING	7.87	GREY, MINK PLUSH, WASHABLE, RED BOW				RED PLASTIC	$50/100
1488		620/35			1982 PRICE LIST	RABBIT, FIELD	13.78						$100/150
1489		6225HW	S0003		VERNA MAE COLLECTIBLES	TEDDY BEAR SANDBOX	8 &10	SEE JESCO S0003 FOR FULL DESCRIPTION					$150/200
1490		6225NSO			1988 JESCO CATALOG	TEDDY BEAR	10	OLD GOLD W/RED PLAID BOW; SEE 62/25NSO					$150/200
1491		6230			1990? JESCO CATALOG	TEDDY BEAR	12	DARK BRN W PLAID BOW (LT BACKGROUND); SEE 62/30					$150/200
1492		6230NSO			1990? JESCO CATALOG	TEDDY BEAR	12	OLD GOLD W/RED BOW; SEE 62/30NSO					$150/200
1493	62320 5				1994 PRICE LIST	CAT, REDDISH BRN	7.87						$92
1494		6235NSB			1990? JESCO CATALOG	TEDDY BEAR	14	BLK W/TAN POLKA DOT TIE; SEE 62/30NSB					$150/200
1495		6235NWB			1990? JESCO CATALOG	TEDDY BEAR	14	WHT W/TAN POLKA DOT TIE; SEE 62/35NWB					$150/200
1496	62420 2				1994 PRICE LIST	CAT, GREY	7.87						$91
1497		6240			1990? JESCO CATALOG	TEDDY BEAR	16	DARK BRN W PLAID BOW (LT BACKGROUND); SEE 62/40					$125/175
1498		6240MW			1990? JESCO CATALOG	TEDDY BEAR	16	WHT W/RED BOW; SEE 62/40MW					$125/175
1499		625/25/1			1982 PRICE LIST	RABBIT, FIELD, BLK & WHT	9.84						$125/175
1500		625/25/2			1982 PRICE LIST	RABBIT, FIELD, BRN & WHT	9.84						$125/175
1501		6280C			1990? JESCO CATALOG	TEDDY BEAR	32	CINNAMON; SEE 62/80C					$200/300
1502		63/01	10001 0		1986 PRICE LIST	SCHOOL SET COMPLETE	47X22 X13	TEACHER W/6 PUPILS AND SCHOOLROOM, 2 SCHOOL BAGS, WITH SCHOOLROOM SUPPLIED					$650
1503		63/8	16308 4		1986 PRICE LIST	TEDDY BEAR, BEND (3)	3.2	OLD GOLD, W/RED BOW, HAVE TWO - ONE W/RED TAG	NONE	NO	BRN	RED PAPER	$39
1504		63/14	16314 5		1985 PRICE LIST	TEDDY BEAR	5.6	OLD GOLD, W/RED BOW	NONE	NO	BRN	NO	$50/100
1505		63/17	16317 6		1984 PRICE LIST	TEDDY BEAR, MOVEABLE	6.6	OLD GOLD, W/RED BOW	NONE	NO	GRN	NO	$50/100
1506		63/20	16320 6		1984 PRICE LIST	TEDDY BEAR, MOVEABLE	8	OLD GOLD, W/RED BOW				RED	$75/125
1507		63/20/2 K	10220 5		1986 PRICE LIST	SCHOOL GIRL, 1986 KA	8	SCHOOL GIRL	NONE	YES	BRN	RED PAPER	$75/125
1508		63/20/3 K	10320 2		1986 PRICE LIST	SCHOOL BOY 1986 KA	8	SCHOOL BOY					$75/125
1509		63/20/4 K	10420 9		1986 PRICE LIST	SCHOOL BABY 1986	8	GOLD 53%W & 47%C MOHAIR	NONE	YES	BRN	RED PAPER	$75/125
1510		63/20/5K	10520 6		1986 PRICE LIST	SCHOOL BABY 1986	8	GOLD 53%W & 47%C MOHAIR	?	YES	BRN	RED PLASTIC	$100/150
1511		63/20/6K	10620 3		1986 PRICE LIST	HIKING GIRL 1986 KA	8	GOLD MOHAIR DRESSED W/BACK PACK	NONE	YES	BRN	RED PAPER	$100/150
1512		63/20/7K	10720 0		1986 PRICE LIST	HIKING BOY 1986 KA	8	GOLD MOHAIR DRESSED W/BACK PACK	NONE	YES	BRN	RED PAPER	$100/150
1513		63/25	16325 1		1984 PRICE LIST	NOSTALGIC TEDDY	10	OLD GOLD MOHAIR	NONE	YES	RED	SML RD PL	$125/175
1514		63/30/1			1986 PRICE LIST	BEAR W/ BIB	11.8	OLD GOLD MOHAIR W/RED PANTS & WHT BIB APRON					$125/175
1515		63/30/2 K	10220 5			TEACHER	11.8	TEACHER; K=TRANSPARENT GIFT BOX					$125/175
1516		63/30/3	10930 3			MUSICAL BEAR	11.8	OLD GOLD W/RED RIBBON IN HERMANN CATALOG 1986; PLAYS TEDDYBEAR PICNIC	MUSIC	YES	BRN	RED PLASTIC	$125/175
1517		63/30/4			HERMANN CAT 1986	BEAR IN SWEAT SUIT	11.8	OLD GOLD MOHAIR IN RED SWEAT SUIT W/ HEAD BAND, 5 JOINTS, (FOR OLYMPICS?)	GROWLER	YES	RED	RED PAPER	$125/175
1518		63/30	16330 5		1984 PRICE LIST	NOSTALGIC MOVEABLE	11.8	OLD GOLD ALL JOINTS MOVEABLE	GROWLER	YES	RED	RED PLASTIC	$125/175
1519		63/35 OLD			HERMAN CIRCA 1940	NOSTALGIC MOVEABLE	13.8	OLD GOLD ALL JOINTS MOVEABLE, REPLACED PADS	GROWLER	NO	NO	NO	$400
1520		63/35	16335 0		1984 PRICE LIST	NOSTALGIC MOVEABLE	13.8	OLD GOLD ALL JOINTS MOVEABLE	GROWLER	YES	BRN	RED PLASTIC	$125
1521		63/35TBP			KATHY ANN 1986 CAT	BEAR, MUSICAL	13.8	MUSICAL BEAR PLAYS TEDDY BEAR PICNIC, OLD GOLD, RED BOW	MUSIC			RED PLASTIC	$125/175
1522		63/40	16340 4		1984 PRICE LIST	NOSTALGIC MOVEABLE	15.8	OLD GOLD ALL JOINTS MOVEABLE	GROWLER	YES	RED	RED PLASTIC	$150/200
1523		63/50	16350 3		1984 PRICE LIST	NOSTALGIC MOVEABLE	19.7	OLD GOLD ALL JOINTS MOVEABLE	GROWLER	YES	RED	RED PLASTIC	$200/300
1524		63/60	16360 2		1984 PRICE LIST	NOSTALGIC MOVEABLE	23.6	OLD GOLD ALL JOINTS MOVEABLE	GROWLER	YES	RED	HD+RED PL	$250/350
1525		630/28			1982 PRICE LIST	RABBIT, STANDING	11						$75/125
1526		630/33			1982 PRICE LIST	RABBIT, STANDING	13						$75/125
1527		630/40			1982 PRICE LIST	RABBIT, STANDING	15.75						$100/150
1528	63030 2		83605/30		1983 PRICE LIST	CAT, LYING	11.8	TAN MINK PLUSH, WASHABLE, WHT MUZZLE, BLUE BOW				RED PLASTIC	$75/125
1529	63130 9		83606/30		1987 PRICE LIST	CAT, LYING	11.8	BRN MINK PLUSH, WASHABLE, WHT MUZZLE, GRN BOW				RED PLASTIC	$110
1530		63205K			1990? JESCO 1988 JESCO CAT	STUDENT	8	SEE 63/20/5K					$100/150
1531	63230 6		82021/30		1988 PRICE LIST	CAT, SIAMESE	11.8						$110
1532	63231 3				1998 PRICE LIST	CAT, LYING	11.8	RED BRN MINK PLUSH, WASHABLE		YES	RED	RED PLASTIC	$109
1533	63330 3		83607/30		1988 PRICE LIST	CAT, LYING	11.8	GREY MINK PLUSH, WASHABLE, WHT MUZZLE, RED BOW				RED PLASTIC	$100/150
1534		635/50			1984 PRICE LIST	RABBIT WITH APRON	19.69						$125/175
1535		635/60			1983 PRICE LIST	RABBIT WITH APRON	23.6						$125/175
1536	63540 6				1992 PRICE LIST	CAT, LYING	15.75	MOTTLED GREY, WHT MUZZLE, WOVEN FUR, WASHABLE				RED PLASTIC	$154
1537		64/8	16408 1			TEDDY BEAR, BENDABLE	3.2	GREY, W/RED BOW	NONE	NO	BRN	RED PAPER	$39
1538		64/14	16414 2			TEDDY BEAR, GREY CUB	5.6	GREY FULLY JTD	NONE	YES	RED	RED PAPER	$50
1539		64/20	16420 3			TEDDY BEAR, GREY CUB	8	GREY	NONE	YES	BRN	RED PAPER	$50/100

REF #	EAN #	HERMANN OLD #	ALSO SEE	LIMITED NUMBER	DATA FROM	NAME	INCHES TALL	DESCRIPTION	VOICE	HANGING BOOKLET	ARM TAG	COMPANY LOGO	CURRENT RETAIL
1540		64/25	16425 8			TEDDY BEAR, GREY CUB	10	GREY	NONE	YES	BRN	RED PAPER	$50/100
1541		64/30	16430 2			TEDDY BEAR, GREY CUB	12	GREY	GROWLER	YES	BRN	RED PLASTIC	$75/125
1542		64/40	16440 1			TEDDY BEAR, GREY CUB	16	GREY	GROWLER	YES	BRN	RED PLASTIC	$100/150
1543	64022 6		759/22		1988 PRICE LIST	CAT, SIAMESE	8.66						$50/100
1544		640/38	85138 7		1986 PRICE LIST	RABBIT	15						$75/125
1545	64130 8		2045/30		1988 PRICE LIST	CAT	11.8						$50/100
1546	64230 5				1990 PRICE LIST	CAT, GREY	11.8	MINK PLUSH, WASHABLE				RED PLASTIC	$148
1547	64231 2				1996 PRICE LIST	CAT, GREY	11.8						$131
1548	64325 8				1990 PRICE LIST	CAT, REDDISH BRN	9.84	MINK PLUSH, WASHABLE				RED PLASTIC	$121
1549	64326 5				1996 PRICE LIST	CAT, REDDISH BRN	9.84						$114
1550		645/30			1984 PRICE LIST	RABBIT, CROUCHING	11.8						$75/125
1551		645/60			1983 PRICE LIST	RABBIT, CROUCHING	23.6						$125/175
1552		645/40			1983 PRICE LIST	RABBIT, CROUCHING	15.75						$100/150
1553		646/30	80630 1		1985 PRICE LIST	RABBIT, CROUCHING	11.8						$75/125
1554		647/40	80740 7		1987 PRICE LIST	RABBIT, STANDING	15.75	TAN DRESSED IN BLUE PLAID SHORTS AND EYE SHADE				RED PAPER	$100/150
1555		647/45			1987 PRICE LIST	RABBIT, STANDING	17.72	TAN DRESSED IN BLUE PLAID OVERALLS AND EYE SHADE				RED PLASTIC	$100/150
1556		650/13			BEHA 1927 CATALOG	APACHE-BULLY, GROTESQUE	5.12	BULL DOG, SOFT STUFFED, W/HAT & PIPE, RED FELT NECK CLOTH, MADE OF BEST OF FELT					$100/150
1557		650/18			BEHA 1927 CATALOG	APACHE-BULLY, GROTESQUE	7	BULL DOG, SOFT STUFFED, W/HAT & PIPE, RED FELT NECK CLOTH, MADE OF BEST OF FELT					$125/175
1558	65040 9		83615/40		1985 PRICE LIST	TOMCAT	15.75	BLK					$100/150
1559	65130 7		83620/30		1987 PRICE LIST	CAT	11						$75/125
1560		655/13			BEHA 1927 CATALOG	BULLY, GROTESQUE	5.17	DOG HAS TOOTHACHE, ARTISTIC FACE W/GLASSES & BANDAGE. LEATHER COLLAR. MADE OF 1a FELT					$100/150
1561		655/18			BEHA 1927 CATALOG	BULLY, GROTESQUE	7	DOG HAS TOOTHACHE, ARTISTIC FACE W/GLASSES & BANDAGE. LEATHER COLLAR. MADE OF 1a FELT					$125/175
1562		655/35			1983 PRICE LIST	RABBIT	13.78						$150/200
1563		66/35			HERMANN CAT 1982	TEDDY BEAR	14	WHT WOOLY LAMB PLUSH W/BRN SNOUT, PADS & EAR LININGS					$150/200
1564		66/42			HERMANN CAT 1982	TEDDY BEAR	17	WHT WOOLY LAMB PLUSH W\BRN SNOUT, PADS & EAR LININGS					$200/300
1565		660/13			BEHA 1927 CATALOG	BULLDOG	5.12	BULL DOG, COMIC FACE, W/RUFFLE, MOLTON CLOTH; MOLTON-BULLY					$100/150
1566		660/20			BEHA 1927 CATALOG	BULLDOG	7.87	BULL DOG, COMIC FACE, W/RUFFLE, MOLTON CLOTH; MOLTON-BULLY					$125/175
1567		660/48			1983 PRICE LIST	RABBIT	18.9						$125/175
1568		665/50			1983 PRICE LIST	RABBIT	19.7						$150/200
1569		67/55	11555 7	2,000		PROFESSOR BERNHARD	22	OLD GOLD MOHAIR EXCELSIOR FILLING, STRIPED VEST W/RED BOW	GROWLER	YES	RED	RED PLASTIC	$390
1570		670/40			BEHA 1927 CATALOG	HARE, STANDING	15.75	W/BASKET. 1a LONG PILE PLUSH, MOVEABLE LIMBS					$150/200
1571		675/40			BEHA 1927 CATALOG	HARE, STANDING	15.75	W/BASKET. 1a LONG PILE WOOL PLUSH, W/COLORED POINTS. MOVEABLE LIMBS					$150/200
1572	67017 9		80512/17		1989 PRICE LIST	SQUIRREL	6.7	TAN MINK PLUSH, WASHABLE				RED PAPER	$74
1573	67115 2		80524/15		1989 PRICE LIST	MOUSE, STANDING	5.9	GREY WOVEN BIBER IMITATION FUR				RED PAPER	$63
1574	67212 8		80725/12		1989 PRICE LIST	MARMOT, STANDING	4.7	BEIGE MINK PLUSH				RED PAPER	$53
1575	67316 3		80535/16		1989 PRICE LIST	HAMSTER, STANDING	6.3	TAN WOVEN BIBER IMITATION FUR				RED PAPER	$57
1576	67413 9		80538/13		1989 PRICE LIST	MOLE, STANDING	5.1	DARK GREY W/WHT BELLY, WOVEN BIBER IMITATION FUR				RED PAPER	$59
1577	67527 3		83020/27		1989 PRICE LIST	FOX, LYING	10.6	REDDISH-BRN WOVEN BIBER IMITATION FUR				RED PAPER	$60
1578	67613 3		80886/13		1989 PRICE LIST	HEDGEHOG, STANDING	5.1	MINK PLUSH, WASHABLE				RED PAPER	$53
1579		69/14ag	16914 7		1989 PRICE LIST	NO-NO BEAR	5.5	OLD GOLD					$50/100
1580		69/14s	16915 4		1989 PRICE LIST	NO-NO BEAR	5.5	BLK					$50/100
1581		6935			1986 PRICE LIST	NO-NO BEAR	13.75	COCOA W/RED TIE					$75/125
1582		69/35	16935 2			NO-NO-BEAR	13.75	NUTMEG PER KATHY ANN 1986 CATALOG "1986 PRODUCTION"; IN HERMANN CATALOG 1986	NONE	YES	BRN	RED PLASTIC	$75/125
1583	69015 3			3,000	1992 PRICE LIST	BLK TOMCAT	5.9	REPLICA, MOHAIR PLUSH					$64
1584	69020 7			3,000	1992 PRICE LIST	BLK TOMCAT	7.9	REPLICA, MOHAIR PLUSH					$76
1585	70001 2			3,000	1990 PRICE LIST	AIREDALE	4	MOHAIR PLUSH, BRN W/BLK			RED	RED PAPER	$63
1586	70002 9			3,000	1990 PRICE LIST	SCHNAUZER	4	MOHAIR PLUSH, GREY W/BLK			RED	RED PAPER	$63
1587	70003 6			5,000	1990 PRICE LIST	ELEPHANT	4.7	MOHAIR PLUSH, GREY W/RED SADDLE			RED	RED PAPER	$88
1588	70004 3			5,000	1990 PRICE LIST	MONKEY	5.9	MOHAIR PLUSH			RED	RED PAPER	$95
1589		70004/31		300	1988 DISNEY CONV	HIKING BOY	11.8	SOFT HONEY MOHAIR W/TYROLEAN HAT & BACKPACK, RED BOW	NONE	YES	RED	RED PAPER	$200
1590	70005 0			4,000	1996 PRICE LIST	STANDING PANDA	6H	BLK & WHT MOHAIR PLUSH	NONE	YES	RED	RED PLASTIC	$125/175
1591		70007/45	7007/45	500	DISNEY 1989 CONV	DISNEY 1989 CONV	15.75	LEMON MOHAIR, TARTAN BOW (ALSO SEE ERROR #7007/45)	GROWLER	YES	RED	RED PLASTIC	$250/350
1592	70016 6			3,000	1994 PRICE LIST	WHEELED BRN BEAR	5HX6.5L	BRN MOHAIR PLUSH W/RED WOOD WHEELS	NONE	YES	RED	SML RED PL	$121
1593	70017 3			3,000	1994 PRICE LIST	WHEELED POLAR BEAR	5HX6.5L	WHT MOHAIR PLUSH W/RED WOOD WHEELS	NONE	YES	RED	SML RED PL	$121
1594	70020				BOOK 1991 PG 88	RUNNING BEAR	7.9	MOHAIR; REPLICA 1956					$100/150
1595	70020 3			3,000	HERMANN 1989	RED WHEELED BEAR	6H X 8L	HONEY BRN MOHAIR ON 4 WHEELED FRAME; REPLICA 1950	NONE	YES	RED	SML RD PL	$100/150
1596	70021 0			3,000	1991 PRICE LIST	HORSE 1950 REPLICA	7.9	WHT W/BLK MANE ON 4 WHEELED FRAME, REPLICA				SML RD PL	$176

REF #	EAN #	HERMANN OLD #	ALSO SEE	LIMITED NUMBER	DATA FROM	NAME	INCHES TALL	DESCRIPTION	VOICE	HANGING BOOKLET	ARM TAG	COMPANY LOGO	CURRENT RETAIL
1597		70022 7			1994 PRICE LIST	DONKEY							$189
1598		70061/36		100	HERMANN	TEDDY BEAR	14.2	CURLY ACRYLIC BEIGE W/RED BOW; NOTE: RED INK TAG IS PAPER	GROWLER	YES	RD PAPER	RED PLASTIC	$75
1599		70062/20		500	HERMANN KATHY ANN	SWEETHEART	7.9	RED 53%W & 47%C MOHAIR, FULLY JTD, HEART BOW	NONE	NO	SPECIAL	RED PAPER	$100
1600		70062/25		140	KATHY ANN CATALOG	TEDDY BEAR	9.5	RUST W/ORANGE BOW	NONE	YES	RD PAPER	RED PAPER	$125
1601		70062/35W		500	KATHY ANN CATALOG	ANGELICA	14.2	WHT W/PINK LACE NECK RUFFLE & EAR BOW, PINK PAW PADS	GROWLER	YES	BRN	RED PLASTIC	$130
1602		70062/40		90	KATHY ANN CATALOG	TEDDY BEAR	15.75	HONEY WITH ORANGE BOW	GROWLER	YES	RD PAPER	RED PLASTIC	$150
1603		70062/40/3		90	KATHY ANN CATALOG	TEDDY BEAR	15.75	CINNAMON W/YELLOW BOW					$150/200
1604	70076 8				1990? JESCO CATALOG	TEDDY BEAR	?	BRN LONG MOHAIR W/RED BOW					$150/200
1605		7007/45 3	70007/45	500	1989 DISNEY CONV	TEDDY BEAR	16.5	LEMON MOHAIR, TARTAN BOW (ALSO SEE 70007/45)	GROWLER	YES	RED	RED PLASTIC	$250/350
1606		70084/18		500	HERMANN	TEDDY BEAR	7.5	NOUGAT MOHAIR SPECIAL FOR USA HERMANN CLUB 1988	NONE	LTD ONLY	RED	RED PAPER	$125/175
1607		70084/35		500	KATHY ANN CATALOG	TEDDY BEAR	14.2	BRN TIPPED LONG MOHAIR W/RED BOW, SEE 04035 4 FOR SIMILAR; DIFFERENT MOHAIR	GROWLER	YES	RED	RED PLASTIC	$150
1608	70115 6		3601/15		1982 PRICE LIST	CAT, STANDING	5.9	GREY MINK PLUSH, WASHABLE				RED PAPER	$75/125
1609	70215 3		3602/15		1982 PRICE LIST	CAT, SITTING	5.9	WHT W/BLK TAIL AND OUTER EARS, MINK PLUSH, WASHABLE				RED PAPER	$75/125
1610	70324 2		3603/24		1982 PRICE LIST	CAT, LYING	9.5	GREY MINK PLUSH				RED PAPER	$75/125
1611		70330/60	73360F/ 03060 7	500		BEAR, RIDING	17HX25L	DARK BRN BEAR ON WHEELS	NONE	YES	RED	RED PLASTIC	$225
1612		7040			1988 JESCO CATALOG	TEDDY BEAR	15.75	BRN TIPPED LONG MOHAIR W/RED BOW					$75/125
1613		70/28 OLD			HERMANN CIRCA 1960	TEDDY BEAR	11	CARAMEL MOHAIR, SHAVED NOSE, ORANGE FELT PADS, PLASTIC EYES, MAROON RIBBON	SQUEAKER	NONE	NONE	NONE	$145
1614		70/38			HERMANN CIRCA 1950	TEDDY BEAR	15	BRN TIPPED LONG MOHAIR	YES	NO	NO	NO	$375
1615		70/40	17040 2	3,000	1986 PRICE LIST	ZOTTEL, 75TH ANNIV.	15.75	BRN TIPPED LONG MOHAIR	GROWLER	YES	GRN	RED PLASTIC	$125
1616		70/50?			BOOK MID 1930s	TEDDY BEAR	19.6	BRN TIPPED MOHAIR W/YELLOW BOW				MTL+PAPER	$100/150
1617		70/50?			BOOK 1930s PG 51	TEDDY BEAR	19.6	BEIGE SHORT PILE MOHAIR					$100/150
1618		70/50 OLD			CIRCA 1930	TEDDY BEAR	19.6	BRN TIPPED HONEY LONG PILE MOHAIR, EXCELSIOR STUFFED, GLASS EYES, WORN PADS	GROWLER	NO	NO	NO	$475
1619		70/60 OLD			1950 BOOK PG 51	TEDDY BEAR	23.5	POINTED SNOUT					$400/500
1620	70415 7		3604/15		1988 PRICE LIST	DOG, ST. BERNARD	5.9	BRN W/WHT STRIPE, MINK PLUSH, WASHABLE				RED PAPER	$75/125
1621	70515 4		3605/15		1988 PRICE LIST	DOG MOLLY, SITTING	5.9	TAN W/WHT STRIPE, MINK PLUSH, WASHABLE				RED PAPER	$75/125
1622		705/20			1982 PRICE LIST	DOG, ST. BERNARD	1.9						$75/125
1623	70615 1		3606/15		1988 PRICE LIST	FOX TERRIER	5.9	STANDING, WHT MINK PLUSH, WASHABLE				RED PAPER	$75/125
1624		708/28			1982 PRICE LIST	RABBIT, SITTING	11						$75/125
1625	70815 5		3608/15		1988 PRICE LIST	BEAR, RUNNING	5.9	BRN MINK PLUSH, WASHABLE				RED PAPER	$75/125
1626		709/28			1984 PRICE LIST	RABBIT, SITTING	11						$75/125
1627		71 SERIES			BOOK	TEDDY BEARS		VARIOUS; 3 1/2 cm LONG PILE SHAGGY MOHAIR PLUSH					
1628		71/45	17145 4		1989 PRICE LIST	"LILLY"	17.7						$100/150
1629		710/21			1982 PRICE LIST	RABBIT	8.3						$50/100
1630	71010 3		512/10		1988 PRICE LIST	SQUIRREL	4						$50/100
1631	71017 2		512/17		1988 PRICE LIST	SQUIRREL	6.7						$50/100
1632	71024 0		512/24		1988 PRICE LIST	SQUIRREL	9.5						$50/100
1633		711/20			1982 PRICE LIST	RABBIT	7.9						$50/100
1634	711100				1988 KATHY ANN CAT	DOG	4	AIREDALE				RED PAPER	$50/100
1635		712/21	83221 8		1988 PRICE LIST	RABBIT ASST'D COLORS	8.3						$75/125
1636	712100					DOG	4	TERRIER				RED PAPER	$50/100
1637		714/18			1982 PRICE LIST	RABBIT, POUNCING	6.7						$50/100
1638		715/25			1982 PRICE LIST	RABBIT	9.8						$75/125
1639	71509 2		525/9		1982 PRICE LIST	MOUSE, WHT	3.5	MINK PLUSH, WASHABLE			RED	RED PAPER	$20
1640	71609 9		525/9		1982 PRICE LIST	MOUSE, GRAY	3.5	MINK PLUSH, WASHABLE			RED	RED PAPER	$20
1641	71709 6		525/9		1988 PRICE LIST	MOUSE, OLD ROSE	3.5	MINK PLUSH, WASHABLE					$20
1642	71720 1		526/20		1987 PRICE LIST	MOUSE, WHT	7.9						$50/100
1643		718/35			1983 PRICE LIST	RABBIT, LYING	13.8						$75/125
1644	718208		527/20		1987 PRICE LIST	MOUSE, RED	1.9						$50/100
1645	71825 3		527/25		1987 PRICE LIST	MOUSE, RED	9.8						$75/125
1646		719/35			1982 PRICE LIST	RABBIT	13.8						$75/125
1647	71920 5		528/20		1987 PRICE LIST	MOUSE, LILAC	7.9	LILAC					$50/100
1648	71925 0		528/25		1987 PRICE LIST	MOUSE, LILAC	9.8	LILAC					$75/125
1649		720/52			1982 PRICE LIST	RABBIT, DANGLING	20.5						$100/150
1650	72020 1		529/20		1987 PRICE LIST	MOUSE, GOLD	7.9	GOLD					$50/100
1651		72/25	17225 3		1989 PRICE LIST	CIRKUS BEAR	9.8						$150/200
1652		722/35			1982 PRICE LIST	HARE	13.8						$75/125
1653		725/16	73316 4		1982 PRICE LIST	MARMOT	6.3						$50/100

REF #	EAN #	HERMANN OLD #	ALSO SEE	LIMITED NUMBER	DATA FROM	NAME	INCHES TALL	DESCRIPTION	VOICE	HANGING BOOKLET	ARM TAG	COMPANY LOGO	CURRENT RETAIL
1654	72515 2		530/15		1982 PRICE LIST	HAMSTER, LYING	5.9	BRN MINK PLUSH, WHT EARS, WASHABLE			RED	RED PAPER	$50/100
1655	72518 3				1993 PRICE LIST	TEDDY HAMSTER	7	MINK PLUSH, WASHABLE					$49
1656	72616 6		535/16		1982 PRICE LIST	HAMSTER, STANDING	6.3	BRN MINK PLUSH, WHT EARS, WASHABLE			RED	RED PAPER	$50/100
1657	72625 8		535/25		1982 PRICE LIST	HAMSTER, STANDING	9.8	MIXED BRNS W/WHT BELLY MINK PLUSH, WASHABLE			RED	RED PAPER	$75/125
1658	73020 0		540/20		1982 PRICE LIST	GUINEA PIG	7.9	MOTTLED GREY, BRN AND WHT, MINK PLUSH				RED PAPER	$50/100
1659	73021 7		540/20K		1988 PRICE LIST	GUINEA PIG	7.9						$50/100
1660	73022 4				1993 PRICE LIST	GUINEA PIG, SPECKLED	7.9	MINK PLUSH, WASHABLE					$52
1661	73023 1				1993 PRICE LIST	GUINEA PIG, BEIGE	7.9	MINK PLUSH, WASHABLE					$52
1662	73024 8				1993 PRICE LIST	GUINEA PIG, DARK BRN	7.9	MINK PLUSH, WASHABLE					$52
1663	73040 8				1993 PRICE LIST	GUINEA PIG, SPOTTED	7.9	MINK PLUSH, WASHABLE					$75/125
1664	73316 4		725/16		1982 PRICE LIST	MARMOT	6.3						$50/100
1665		73360F	03060 7	500		RIDING BEAR	17HX25L	DARK BRN BEAR, WOODEN WHEELS	NONE	YES	RED	RED PLASTIC	$225
1666		735/28			1982 PRICE LIST	SEA LION, BABY	11						$75/125
1667	73518 2		460/18		1982 PRICE LIST	DEER, YOUNG	7						$50/100
1668		736/24	46524 9		1982 PRICE LIST	SEA LION	9.5						$50/100
1669		736/32	46532 4		1982 PRICE LIST	SEA LION	12.6						$75/125
1670		736/42	46542 3		1982 PRICE LIST	SEA LION	16.5						$75/125
1671		736/65			1982 PRICE LIST	SEA LION	25.6						$100/150
1672		737/32			1982 PRICE LIST	SEA LION	12.6						$75/125
1673		739/24	46624 6		1982 PRICE LIST	SEA LION, BABY	9.5						$75/125
1674		739/32	46632 1		1982 PRICE LIST	SEA LION, BABY	12.6						$75/125
1675		739/42	46642 0		1984 PRICE LIST	SEA LION, BABY	16.5						$100/150
1676		739/65	46665 9		1986 PRICE LIST	SEA LION, BABY	25.6						$125/175
1677		74/25	17425 7		1989 PRICE LIST	BEAR, STANDING	9.8						$75/125
1678	74010 0		880/10		1982 PRICE LIST	HEDGEHOG	4						$50/100
1679	74016 2		880/16		1982 PRICE LIST	HEDGEHOG	6.3						$50/100
1680	74022 3		880/22		1982 PRICE LIST	HEDGEHOG	8.7						$75/125
1681	74112 1		885/12		1982 PRICE LIST	HEDGEHOG	4.7	BRN WHT TIPPED MOHAIR PLUSH, SURFACE WASHABLE			RED	RED PAPER	$24
1682	74116 9		882/16		1982 PRICE LIST	HEDGEHOG	6.3	BRN WHT TIPPED MOHAIR PLUSH, SURFACE WASHABLE			RED	RED PAPER	$37
1683	74117 6		882/16K		1988 PRICE LIST	HEDGEHOG	6.3						$37
1684	74122 0		885/22		1982 PRICE LIST	HEDGEHOG	8.7	BRN WHT TIPPED MOHAIR PLUSH, SURFACE WASHABLE			RED	RED PAPER	$51
1685	74218 0		886/18		1984 PRICE LIST	HEDGEHOG	7						$50/100
1686	74313 2		881/13		1989 PRICE LIST	HEDGEHOG	5.1	BRN WHT TIPPED MINK PLUSH, WASHABLE				RED PAPER	$24
1687	74316 3		881/16		1989 PRICE LIST	HEDGEHOG	6.3	BRN WHT TIPPED MINK PLUSH, WASHABLE				RED PAPER	$33
1688	74322 4				1989 CATALOG	HEDGEHOG	8.7	BRN WHT TIPPED ACRYLIC PLUSH, WASHABLE				RED PAPER	$50/100
1689	74324 4		881/22		1989 PRICE LIST	HEDGEHOG	8.7	PRICE LIST ERROR?					$50/100
1690	74330 9				1993 PRICE LIST	HEDGEHOG	11.8	MINK PLUSH, WASHABLE					$91
1691	74335 4				1993 PRICE LIST	HEDGEHOG	13.8	MINK PLUSH, WASHABLE					$140
1692	74528 0		870/28		1988 PRICE LIST	RAVEN	11						$75/125
1693	74628 7		871/28		1988 PRICE LIST	MOUSE	11						$75/125
1694	74728 4		872/28		1988 PRICE LIST	MONKEY	11						$75/125
1695	74828 1		874/28		1989 PRICE LIST	MOUSE, RED	11	W/KNAPSACK, RED BODY TROUSERS, GREY BODY, MINK PLUSH				RED PAPER	$75/125
1696	74829 8		874/29		1989 PRICE LIST	MOUSE, GOLD	11	W/KNAPSACK, YELLOW BODY TROUSERS, GREY BODY, MINK PLUSH				RED PAPER	$75/125
1697		750/22			1982 PRICE LIST	CAT, HOUSE	8.7						$50/100
1698	75120 5		1200/1		1982 PRICE LIST	ELEPHANT, BABY'S	9.8	SOFT, CUDDLY, WASHABLE					$50/100
1699	75122 9					ELEPHANT, NIKKI	9.8	SOFT, CUDDLY, WASHABLE					$33
1700	75220 2					DONKEY, NIKKI	9.8	SOFT, CUDDLY, WASHABLE					$32
1701	75317 9		1200/3		1982 PRICE LIST	FISH, BABY'S	6.7	SOFT, CUDDLY, WASHABLE					$50/100
1702	75328 5					RABBIT	11	SOFT, CUDDLY, WASHABLE					$45
1703	75418 3		1200/4		1982 PRICE LIST	DOG, BABY'S	7	SOFT, CUDDLY, WASHABLE					$50/100
1704	75420 6					DOG	7.9	SOFT, CUDDLY, WASHABLE					$36
1705	75525 8		1200/5		1982 PRICE LIST	TEDDY BEAR, BABY'S	9.8	RED SOFT TOY W\WHT PADS, SNOUT, EARS					$50/100
1706	75526 5					TEDDY BEAR	10.2	SOFT, CUDDLY, WASHABLE					$45
1707	75607 1		1200/6		1982 PRICE LIST	BALL, BABY'S	2.8	SOFT, CUDDLY, WASHABLE					$28
1708	75614 9					BALL	5.5	SOFT, CUDDLY, WASHABLE					$30
1709	75618 7					BALL W/MUSIC	7	SOFT, CUDDLY, WASHABLE					$42
1710		757/22			1982 PRICE LIST	CAT, ANGORA	8.7	SOFT, CUDDLY, WASHABLE					$50/100
1711	75712 2		1200/7		1982 PRICE LIST	MOUSE, BABY'S	4.7	SOFT, CUDDLY, WASHABLE					$50/100
1712	75724 5				1990 PRICE LIST	MOUSE, MULTICOLORED	9.5	SOFT, CUDDLY, WASHABLE					$45
1713		758/22			1982 PRICE LIST	CAT, HOUSE	8.7	SOFT, CUDDLY, WASHABLE					$50/100
1714	75818 1					DUCK	7	SOFT, CUDDLY, WASHABLE					$33
1715		759/22	64022 6		1982 PRICE LIST	CAT, SIAMESE	8.7	SOFT, CUDDLY, WASHABLE					$50/100
1716	76020 7		1200/10		1982 PRICE LIST	SEA LION, BABY'S	7.9	SOFT, CUDDLY, WASHABLE					$50/100
1717	76120 4		1200/11		1982 PRICE LIST	SEA LION, BABY'S	7.9	SOFT, CUDDLY, WASHABLE					$50/100

REF #	EAN #	HERMANN OLD #	ALSO SEE	LIMITED NUMBER	DATA FROM	NAME	INCHES TALL	DESCRIPTION	VOICE	HANGING BOOKLET	ARM TAG	COMPANY LOGO	CURRENT RETAIL
1718	76226 3		1200/12		1984 PRICE LIST	PUNCH	10.2	SOFT, CUDDLY, WASHABLE					$50/100
1719	76314 7		1200/13		1983 PRICE LIST	DUCK, RED-GOLD	5.5	SOFT, CUDDLY, WASHABLE					$50/100
1720	76414 4		1200/14		1983 PRICE LIST	DUCK, GOLD-WHT	5.5	SOFT, CUDDLY, WASHABLE					$50/100
1721		76235W			1988 JESCO CATALOG	TEDDY BEAR	13.75	WHT W/PINK RUFFLE ON NECK & PINK EAR BOW					$100/150
1722		7630W			1990? JESCO CATALOG	TEDDY BEAR	11.8	WHT W/RED BOW					$100/150
1723		76/30	17630 5		1984 PRICE LIST	TEDDY BEAR	11.8	BRN MINK PLUSH	NONE	YES	RED	RED PLASTIC	$75/125
1724		76/30W			1990? JESCO CATALOG	TEDDY BEAR	11.8	WHT W/RED BOW					$75/125
1725		76/40	17640 4		1984 PRICE LIST	TEDDY BEAR	15.75	BRN MINK PLUSH	GROWLER	YES	BRN	RED PLASTIC	$75/125
1726		76/40B			1990? JESCO CATALOG	TEDDY BEAR	15.75	BRN W/RED BOW					$75/125
1727		7650B			1988 JESCO CATALOG	TEDDY BEAR	19.6	BRN W CINNAMON MUZZLE					$125/175
1728		76/50	17650 3		1984 PRICE LIST	TEDDY BEAR	19.6	BRN FULLY JTD 70% ACRYLIC & 30%C PLUSH	GROWLER	YES	BRN	RED PLASTIC	$164
1729		76/50W			1990? JESCO CATALOG	TEDDY BEAR	19.6	WHT W/ STRIPED RED BOW					$125/175
1730		76/80	17880 0		1982 PRICE LIST	TEDDY BEAR	31	BRN	GROWLER				$106
1731		76/80W			1990? JESCO CATALOG	TEDDY BEAR	32	WHT W/RED PLAID BOW					$125/175
1732		76/120	17698 5		1984 PRICE LIST	TEDDY BEAR	47	BRN	GROWLER				$150/200
1733		76/150	17699 2		1984 PRICE LIST	TEDDY BEAR	59	BRN	GROWLER				$200/300
1734		76/150W			1990? JESCO CATALOG	TEDDY BEAR	59	WHT DRESSED					$200/300
1735	76516 5		1250/14		1982 PRICE LIST	BALL, PLUSH	5.5						$50/100
1736	76620 9		1255/16		1988 PRICE LIST	BALL PLUSH W/MUSIC	6.3						$50/100
1737		77/30	17730 2		1984 PRICE LIST	TEDDY BEAR	11.8						$75/125
1738		77/40	17740 1		1984 PRICE LIST	TEDDY BEAR	15.75						$75/125
1739		77/50	17750 0		1984 PRICE LIST	TEDDY BEAR	19.6						$100/150
1740		7750H			1988 JESCO CATALOG	TEDDY BEAR	19.6	HONEY W/TAN MUZZLE, BLUE BOW					$100/150
1741		77/80	17780 7		1984 PRICE LIST	TEDDY BEAR	31						$125/175
1742	77031 2				1990 PRICE LIST	LAMB, YOUNG	12.2	W/MUSIC BOX, WHT WOOL PLUSH, SURFACE WASHABLE				RED PAPER	$104
1743	77030 5		1422/30		1982 PRICE LIST	LAMB W/MUSIC	11.8						$75/125
1744	77114 9		1481/14		1982 PRICE LIST	MOONFISH W/MUSIC	5.5	ACRYLIC, SURFACE WASHABLE				RED PAPER	$75/125
1745	77115 9				1992 PRICE LIST	MOONFISH W/MUSIC	5.9	COLOR STRIPED WOVEN FUR				RED PAPER	$70
1746	77214 9		1483/14		1983 PRICE LIST	LADYBUG W/MUSIC	5.5	WOVEN BIBER IMITATION FUR, RED AND BLK					$62
1747	77325 2		1484/25		1985 PRICE LIST	SUN W/MUSIC	9.8	WOVEN BIBER IMITATION FUR, BRIGHT YELLOW					$83
1748	77422 8		1485/22		1982 PRICE LIST	HEDGEHOG W/MUSIC	8.7						$50/100
1749	77522 5		1488/22		1985 PRICE LIST	TURTLE W/MUSIC	8.7	WOVEN BIBER IMITATION FUR, GRN + VARIED COLORS				RED PAPER	$63
1750	77628 4				1990 PRICE LIST	FLOWER	11	WOVEN BIBER IMITATION FUR, RED PETALS, YELLOW CENTER				SML RD PL	$83
1751	77725 0				1991 PRICE LIST	SNAIL	9.8	WOVEN BIBER IMITATION FUR, YELLOW					$106
1752	77825 7				1991 PRICE LIST	SNAIL	9.8						$75/125
1753		78/30			1985 PRICE LIST	TEDDY BEAR	11.8	GREY W/WHT NOSE AND PAW PADS, SOFT	NONE				$75/125
1754		78/40			1985 PRICE LIST	TEDDY BEAR	15.75	GREY W/WHT NOSE AND PAW PADS, SOFT	YES				$100/150
1755		780/10	81010 0		1982 PRICE LIST	RABBIT, DWARF	3.9						$50/100
1756		780/10K	81011 7		1988 PRICE LIST	RABBIT, DWARF	3.9						$50/100
1757		780/20			1982 PRICE LIST	RABBIT, DWARF	7.9						$50/100
1758		781/15	81115 2		1985 PRICE LIST	RABBIT, DWARF	5.9	BEIGE					$50/100
1759		781/20	81120 6		1986 PRICE LIST	RABBIT, DWARF	7.9	BEIGE					$50/100
1760		782/15	81215 9		1985 PRICE LIST	RABBIT, DWARF	5.9	BRN					$50/100
1761		782/20	81220 3		1986 PRICE LIST	RABBIT, DWARF	7.9	BRN					$50/100
1762		783/20	81320 0		1986 PRICE LIST	RABBIT, DWARF	7.9	WHT					$50/100
1763		784/20	81420 7		1986 PRICE LIST	RABBIT, DWARF	7.9	DARK BRN					$50/100
1764	78504 3		02002 8	250	HERMANN 1996	DISNEY 1996 CONV.	11.8	WINNIE THE POOH W/ "HUNNY" JAR , RED SWEATER; INCLS. CONVENTION PIN	NONE	YES	2 RED	RED+HD MTL	$385
1765	78525 5		410/13		1982 PRICE LIST	HAND PUPPETS, BEAR	9.8	DRALON PLUSH, SURFACE WASHABLE, BRN BODY				MTL W/PAPER INSERT	$61
1766	78625 2		410/14		1982 PRICE LIST	HAND PUPPETS, RABBIT	9.8	DRALON PLUSH, SURFACE WASHABLE, WHT BODY					$61
1767	78725 9		410/15		1982 PRICE LIST	HAND PUPPETS, CAT	9.8	DRALON PLUSH, SURFACE WASHABLE, WHT BODY					$61
1768	78825 6		410/16		1982 PRICE LIST	HAND PUPPETS, DONKEY	9.8	DRALON PLUSH, SURFACE WASHABLE, BRN BODY					$61
1769	78925 3		410/18		1982 PRICE LIST	HAND PUPPETS, DOG	9.8	DRALON PLUSH, SURFACE WASHABLE, WHT BODY					$61
1770	79025 9		410/19		1982 PRICE LIST	HAND PUPPETS, FOX	9.8	DRALON PLUSH, SURFACE WASHABLE, WHT BODY					$61
1771		796/32			1982 PRICE LIST	RABBIT, SITTING	12.6	DRALON PLUSH, SURFACE WASHABLE, WHT BODY					$50/100
1772		79/25			HERMANN CAT 1982	SOFT TEDDY BEAR	9.6	CARAMEL /SHAVED SNOUT, OPEN MOUTH, SOFT FILLING, FULLY JTD, CHAIN COLLAR				RED PLASTIC	$24
1773		79/30			HERMANN CAT 1982	SOFT TEDDY BEAR	11.8	CARAMEL /SHAVED SNOUT, OPEN MOUTH, SOFT FILLING, FULLY JTD, CHAIN COLLAR				RED PLASTIC	$27
1774		79/36			HERMANN CAT 1982	SOFT TEDDY BEAR	14.2	CARAMEL /SHAVED SNOUT, OPEN MOUTH, SOFT FILLING, FULLY JTD, CHAIN COLLAR				GOLD PLASTIC	$36
1775		79/45			HERMANN CAT 1982	SOFT TEDDY BEAR	18.1	CARAMEL /SHAVED SNOUT, OPEN MOUTH, SOFT FILLING, FULLY JTD, CHAIN COLLAR				GOLD PLASTIC	$41

REF #	EAN #	HERMANN OLD #	ALSO SEE	LIMITED NUMBER	DATA FROM	NAME	INCHES TALL	DESCRIPTION	VOICE	HANGING BOOKLET	ARM TAG	COMPANY LOGO	CURRENT RETAIL
1776		79/55			HERMANN CAT 1982	SOFT TEDDY BEAR	21.7	CARAMEL /SHAVED SNOUT, OPEN MOUTH, SOFT FILLING, FULLY JTD, CHAIN COLLAR				GOLD PLASTIC	$56
1777		80/23			BEHA 1927 CATALOG	KING CHARLES DOG	9.5	MADE OF BEST WHT MOHAIR PLUSH, PAINTED & SPRAYED					$150/200
1778		80/40	18040 1		1987 CATALOG	TEDDY BEAR	15.75	BRN BIBER IMITATION, ALL LIMBS MOVEABLE, RED BOW	NONE	YES	RED	RED PLASTIC	$100/150
1779		80001/45	32845 2		1989 PRICE LIST	POLAR BEAR, LYING DOWN	17.7						$125/175
1780		80001/60	32860 5		KATHY ANN CAT 1989	POLAR BEAR, LYING DOWN	23.6	WHT MINK PLUSH LYING DOWN				RED PLASTIC	$150/200
1781		80001/75	32875 9		1989 PRICE LIST	POLAR BEAR, LYING DOWN	29.5						$150/200
1782		80002/20			1990? JESCO CATALOG	POLAR BEAR	7.9	BRN W/ TAN MUZZLE, RED BOW					$50/100
1783		80002/30			1990? JESCO CATALOG	POLAR BEAR	11.8	BRN W/TAN MUZZLE					$50/100
1784		80002/50	20250 9		1988 PRICE LIST	POLAR BEAR	19.6	WHT MINK PLUSH				RED PLASTIC	$100/150
1785		80002/85	20285 1		1988 PRICE LIST	POLAR BEAR	33	WHT MINK PLUSH				RED PLASTIC	$125/175
1786		80003/21			1983 PRICE LIST	TEDDY BEAR, SUPER SOFT	8.3						$50/100
1787		80003/30			1983 PRICE LIST	TEDDY BEAR, SUPER SOFT	11.8						$50/100
1788		80004/25	20425 1		1988 PRICE LIST	TEDDY BEAR	14.2	SEE 1986 CATALOG					$100/150
1789		80004/30	20430 5		1988 PRICE LIST	TEDDY BEAR	11.8	SEE 1986 CATALOG					$100/150
1790		80005/48	20548 7		HERMANN CAT 1982	TEDDY BEAR	18.9	SOFT STUFFED, BRN	NONE	YES	BRN	GOLD PLASTIC	$125/175
1791		80005/60	20560 9		1988 PRICE LIST	TEDDY BEAR	23.6	SOFT STUFFED, BRN	NONE	YES	BRN	GOLD PLASTIC	$125/175
1792		80005/60B			1990? JESCO CATALOG	TEDDY BEAR	23.6	BRN LONG MOHAIR W/RED BOW					$125/175
1793		80005/70	20570 8		1988 PRICE LIST	TEDDY BEAR	27.5	BRN					$125/175
1794		80005/70B	20570 8		1988 PRICE LIST	TEDDY BEAR	27.5	SOFT STUFFED	NONE	YES	BRN	GOLD PLASTIC	$150
1795		80005/90	20590 6		1988 PRICE LIST	TEDDY BEAR	35	BRN					$150/200
1796		80005/90B			1990? JESCO CATALOG	TEDDY BEAR	35	BRN W/RED BOW					$150/200
1797		80006/50	20650 7		HERMANN CAT 1982	TEDDY BEAR	19.6	BEIGE					$100/150
1798		80006/62	20662 0		HERMANN CAT 1982	TEDDY BEAR	23.6	BEIGE					$125/175
1799		80006/62H			1990? JESCO CATALOG	TEDDY BEAR	23.6	HONEY W/WHT MUZZLE RED BOW					$125/175
1800		80006/72	20672 9		1988 PRICE LIST	TEDDY BEAR	28.3	BEIGE					$150/200
1801		80006/72H			1990? JESCO CATALOG	TEDDY BEAR	28.3	HONEY W/WHT MUZZLE RED BOW					$150/200
1802		80007/50	20750 4		1988 PRICE LIST	TEDDY BEAR	19.6						$100/150
1803		80007/85	20785 6		1988 PRICE LIST	TEDDY BEAR	33						$125/175
1804		80007/120	20798 6		1988 PRICE LIST	TEDDY BEAR	47						$150/200
1805		80008/45			HERMANN CAT 1982	SOFT TEDDY	18.1	HONEY BEIGE W/ SHAVED BEIGE NOSE & PADS					$100/150
1806		80008/48			HERMANN CAT 1986	SOFT TEDDY	18.9	HONEY BEIGE W/ SHAVED BEIGE NOSE & PADS					$100/150
1807		80008/50			TB&F V2#3 FALL 1984	SOFT TEDDY	19.6	WHT				GOLD PLASTIC	$100/150
1808		80008/61			TB&F V2#3 FALL 1984	SOFT TEDDY	23.6	WHT				GOLD PLASTIC	$125/175
1809		80008/62			HERMANN CAT 1986	SOFT TEDDY	24.5						$125/175
1810		80008/72			TB&F V2#3 FALL 1984	SOFT TEDDY	28.3	WHT				GOLD PLASTIC	$125/175
1811		80009/30			1989 PRICE LIST	BRNBEAR	11.8						$75/125
1812		80009/40			HERMANN CAT 1986	SOFT TEDDY	15.75	LT BEIGE W RED BOW, FELT PADS				RED PLASTIC	$100/150
1813		80010/26	21026 9		1988 PRICE LIST	TEDDY BEAR WASHABLE	9.6	WHT 30%C & 70% ACRYLIC BIBER IMITATION, ORANGE BOW, HERMANN CAT, 1986	NONE	YES	GRN	GOLD PLASTIC	$90
1814		80011/26	21126 6		1988 PRICE LIST	TEDDY BEAR WASHABLE	9.6	LT BRN BIBER IMITATION, GRN BOW, HERMANN CAT 1986				RED PLASTIC	$75/125
1815		80012/26			1983 PRICE LIST	TEDDY BEAR WASHABLE	9.6	ROSE, HERMANN CAT 1986					$75/125
1816		80013/26			1983 PRICE LIST	TEDDY BEAR WASHABLE	9.6	LIGHT BLUE					$75/125
1817		80020/35	22035 0		1988 PRICE LIST	TEDDY BEAR WASHABLE	14.1	BEIGE SOFT, 70% ACRYLIC, 30% COTTON, HERMANN CAT 1986			BRN	GOLD PLASTIC	$50/100
1818		80021/35	22135 7		1988 PRICE LIST	TEDDY BEAR WASHABLE	14.1	BRN SOFT, 70% ACRYLIC, 30% COTTON, HERMANN CAT 1986			GRN	GOLD PLASTIC	$50/100
1819		80022/35	22235 4		1988 PRICE LIST	TEDDY BEAR WASHABLE	14.1	PINK SOFT, 70% ACRYLIC, 30% COTTON, HERMANN CAT 1986			BRN	GOLD PLASTIC	$50/100
1820	80022 4	101/22			1985 PRICE LIST	RABBIT, BABY	8.7	RED OVERALLS, BODY, BRN ARMS AND HEAD, BIBERE IMITATION FUR, WASHABL				RED PAPER	$50/100
1821		80023/35	22335 1		1988 PRICE LIST	TEDDY BEAR WASHABLE	14.2	BLUE SOFT 70% ACRYLIC & 30% C PLUSH W/WHT MUZZLE	NONE	NO	GRN	GOLD PLASTIC	$50/100
1822		80028/28			KATHY ANN 1968 CAT	TEDDY BEAR	11	GREY TIPPED SOFT W/LT TAN MUZZLE-INSIDE EARS-PADS				RED PLASTIC	$50/100
1823		80028/33			KATHY ANN 1968 CAT	TEDDY BEAR	12.6	GREY TIPPED SOFT W/LT TAN MUZZLE-INSIDE EARS-PADS				RED PLASTIC	$50/100
1824		80029/33			KATHY ANN 1968 CAT	TEDDY BEAR	12.6	WHT SOFT W/LT TAN MUZZLE-INSIDE EARS-PADS				RED PLASTIC	$50/100
1825		80029/41	22740 3		1988 PRICE LIST	TEDDY BEAR WASHABLE	15.75	RED, SOFT, PLAID TIE				RED PLASTIC	$75/125
1826		80029/42	22840 0		1988 PRICE LIST	TEDDY BEAR WASHABLE	15.75	BLUE, SOFT, PLAID TIE				RED PLASTIC	$75/125
1827		80029/43	22940 7		1988 PRICE LIST	TEDDY BEAR WASHABLE	15.75	YELLOW, SOFT, PLAID TIE				RED PLASTIC	$75/125
1828		80030/28H			1990? JESCO CATALOG	SOFT TEDDY	11	HONEY W GRN BOW					$75/125
1829		80030/28	23028 1		1988 PRICE LIST	SOFT TEDDY, BEIGE	11	HONEY W/RED BOW				RED PAPER	$75/125
1830		80030/33	23033 5		1988 PRICE LIST	SOFT TEDDY, BEIGE	12.6	HONEY W/RED BOW				RED PAPER	$100/150
1831		80030/42	23042 7		1988 PRICE LIST	SOFT TEDDY, BEIGE	16.5	HONEY W/RED BOW				RED PAPER	$100/150
1832		80031/28	23128 8		1988 PRICE LIST	SOFT TEDDY	11	1986 PRICE LIST					$75/125
1833		80031/33	23133 2		1988 PRICE LIST	SOFT TEDDY	12.6	1986 PRICE LIST					$100/150
1834		80031/42	23142 4		1988 PRICE LIST	SOFT TEDDY	16.5	1983 PRICE LIST					$100/150
1835		80032/28	23228 5		1984 PRICE LIST	TEDDY BEAR, SUPER SOFT	11	EGGSHELL LONG PLUSH, RED BOW				RED PAPER	$75/125
1836		80032/33	23233 9		1984 PRICE LIST	TEDDY BEAR, SUPER SOFT	12.6	EGGSHELL LONG PLUSH, BLUE BOW (CATALOG SHOWS RED BOW)	NONE	YES	BRN	RED PAPER	$75/125

REF #	EAN #	HERMANN OLD #	ALSO SEE	LIMITED NUMBER	DATA FROM	NAME	INCHES TALL	DESCRIPTION	VOICE	HANGING BOOKLET	ARM TAG	COMPANY LOGO	CURRENT RETAIL
1837		80032/42	23242 1		1988 PRICE LIST	TEDDY BEAR, SUPER SOFT	16.5	EGGSHELL LONG PLUSH, RED BOW, IN HERMANN 1986 CATALOG	NONE	YES	BRN	RED PLASTIC	$100/150
1838	80032 3		100/32		1985 PRICE LIST	RABBIT, MOTHER	12.6						$50/100
1839		80033/28	23328 2		1989 PRICE LIST	TEDDY BEAR	11	DARK BRN					$100/150
1840		80033/33	23333 6		1989 PRICE LIST	TEDDY BEAR	12.6	DARK BRN					$100/150
1841		80033/42	23334 8		1989 PRICE LIST	TEDDY BEAR	16.5	DARK BRN					$100/150
1842		80034/30	23430 2		1988 PRICE LIST	TEDDY BEAR	11.8						$100/150
1843		80034/42	23442 5		1988 PRICE LIST	TEDDY BEAR	16.5						$100/150
1844		80035/28			1985 PRICE LIST	SOFT TEDDY	11	TAN MINK PLUSH W/WHT NOSE & INSIDE EARS & PAWS, W/RED BOW				RED PLASTIC	$100/150
1845		80035/33			1985 PRICE LIST	SOFT TEDDY	12.6	TAN MINK PLUSH W/WHT NOSE & INSIDE EARS & PAWS, W/RED BOW				RED PLASTIC	$100/150
1846		80035/42			1985 PRICE LIST	SOFT TEDDY	16.5	TAN MINK PLUSH W/WHT NOSE & INSIDE EARS & PAWS, W/RED BOW				RED PLASTIC	$100/150
1847		80036/35			1985 PRICE LIST	SOFT TEDDY	14.2	BRN MINK PLUSH W/WHT NOSE & INSIDE EARS & PAWS, W/RED BOW				RED PLASTIC	$100/150
1848		80036/45			1985 PRICE LIST	SOFT TEDDY	16.5	BRN MINK PLUSH W/WHT NOSE & INSIDE EARS & PAWS, W/RED BOW				RED PLASTIC	$100/150
1849		80040/42			1983 PRICE LIST	SOFT TEDDY	16.5						$100/150
1850		80041/42			HERMANN CAT 1986	SOFT TEDDY	16.5	ALL WHT MINK PLUSH, SHAVED PADS, RED BOW				RED PLASTIC	$100/150
1851		80045/40	63/30/4		1987 PRICE LIST	SOFT TEDDY	15.75	ALL WHT WEARING RED EXERCISE JUMPER				RED PAPER	$100/150
1852		80045/42			1983 PRICE LIST	SOFT TEDDY	16.5						$100/150
1853		80046/40	24640 4		1987 PRICE LIST	SOFT TEDDY	15.75	TAN SOFT TEDDY IN BLUE CHECKED OVERALLS, WHT MUZZLE & INNER EARS & PADS				RED PLASTIC	$100/150
1854		80047/40	24740 1		1987 PRICE LIST	SOFT TEDDY	15.75	BRN SOFT TEDDY IN BLUE CHECKED OVERALLS, WHT MUZZLE & INNER EARS & PADS				RED PLASTIC	$100/150
1855		80081/40	19040 0		1988 PRICE LIST	SOFT TEDDY	15.75	BRN MINK PLUSH, ARMS MOVEABLE; 1987 PRICE LIST				RED PLASTIC	$100/150
1856		80083/40			HERMANN CAT 1982	SOFT TEDDY	15.75	LT BRN WITH WHT CHEST AREA				RED PLASTIC	$100/150
1857	80122 1		102/22		1985 PRICE LIST	RABBIT, BABY	8.7	YELLOW BODY W/BRN EARS, HEAD, ARMS, LEGS, BIBER IMITATION FUR, WASHABLE					$50/100
1858		80164/35			1983 PRICE LIST	SOFT TEDDY	13.8						$50/100
1859		80166/40	30040 3		HERMANN CAT 1982	BEAR, LYING DOWN	15.75	DARK BRN FUR W/LIGHTER STRIPS, TAN SHAVED MUZZLE, OPEN MOUTH				GOLD PLASTIC	$75/125
1860		80166/50	30050 2		HERMANN CAT 1982	BEAR, LYING DOWN	19.6	DARK BRN FUR W/LIGHTER STRIPS, TAN SHAVED MUZZLE, OPEN MOUTH				GOLD PLASTIC	$75/125
1861		80166/65	30065 6		HERMANN CAT 1982	BEAR, LYING DOWN	25.6	DARK BRN FUR W/LIGHTER STRIPS, TAN SHAVED MUZZLE, OPEN MOUTH	NONE	YES	BRN	GOLD PLASTIC	$75/125
1862		80166/95	30095 3		HERMANN CAT 1982	BEAR, LYING DOWN	37	DARK BRN FUR W/LIGHTER STRIPS, TAN SHAVED MUZZLE, OPEN MOUTH				GOLD PLASTIC	$100/150
1863		0167/50			1982 PRICE LIST	BEAR, LYING DOWN	19.7						$75/125
1864		80167/65			1982 PRICE LIST	BEAR, LYING DOWN	23.6						$75/125
1865		80168/22			HERMANN CAT 1982	BEAR, LYING DOWN	9.5	LT BRN WITH LIGHT SNOUT, SOFT BODY				RED PLASTIC	$50/100
1866		80168/30	30130 1		HERMANN CAT 1982	BEAR, LYING DOWN	11.8	LT BRN WITH LIGHT SNOUT, SOFT BODY				RED PLASTIC	$50/100
1867		80168/40	30140 0		HERMANN CAT 1982	BEAR, LYING DOWN	15.75	LT BRN WITH LIGHT SNOUT, SOFT BODY					$75/125
1868		80168/50	30150 9		HERMANN CAT 1982	BEAR, LYING DOWN	19.6	LT BRN WITH LIGHT SNOUT, SOFT BODY					$100/150
1869		80168/65	30165 9		HERMANN CAT 1982	BEAR, LYING DOWN	26	LT BRN WITH LIGHT SNOUT, SOFT BODY					$100/150
1870		80168/95	30195 0		HERMANN CAT 1982	BEAR, LYING DOWN	37	LT BRN WITH LIGHT SNOUT, SOFT BODY					$125/175
1871		80169/22			1983 PRICE LIST	GERMAN SHEPHERD	8.7						$75/125
1872		80170/42			1982 PRICE LIST	GERMAN SHEPHERD	16.5						$75/125
1873		80170/70			1982 PRICE LIST	GERMAN SHEPHERD	27.6						$100/150
1874		80171/42			1982 PRICE LIST	GERMAN SHEPHERD	16.5						$75/125
1875		80171/70			1982 PRICE LIST	GERMAN SHEPHERD	27.6						$100/150
1876		80170/80			1983 PRICE LIST	GERMAN SHEPHERD	31.5						$125/175
1877		80174/35	50635 5		1986 PRICE LIST	FOX TERRIER	13.8						$75/125
1878		80175/45	51545 6		1985 PRICE LIST	COLLIE, LYING	17.7						$75/125
1879		80176/35	51035 2		1986 PRICE LIST	AIREDALE	13.8						$75/125
1880		80180/22			1983 PRICE LIST	"MOLLI" DOG	8.7						$75/125
1881		80215/40			1988 PRICE LIST	CHIMPANZEE	15.75	BEIGE					$75/125
1882		80216/40			1988 PRICE LIST	CHIMPANZEE	15.75	BRN					$100/150
1883		80217/58			1988 PRICE LIST	CHIMPANZEE	22.8	BEIGE					$100/150
1884		80219/40			1982 PRICE LIST	CHIMPANZEE	15.75						$125/175
1885		80219/52			1982 PRICE LIST	CHIMPANZEE	20.5						$125/175
1886		80219/58			1982 PRICE LIST	CHIMPANZEE	22.8						$150/200
1887		80219/75			1982 PRICE LIST	CHIMPANZEE	29.5						

REF #	EAN #	HERMANN OLD #	ALSO SEE	LIMITED NUMBER	DATA FROM	NAME	INCHES TALL	DESCRIPTION	VOICE	HANGING BOOKLET	ARM TAG	COMPANY LOGO	CURRENT RETAIL
1888		80300/20	31020 4		1989 PRICE LIST	BRN BEAR	7.9						$75/125
1889		80300/30	31030 3		1989 PRICE LIST	BRN BEAR	11.8						$100/150
1890		80312/15	34115 4		1982 PRICE LIST	ELEPHANT, STANDING	5.9						$50/100
1891		80312/20	34120 8		1983 PRICE LIST	ELEPHANT, STANDING	7.9						$75/125
1892		80312/25			1983 PRICE LIST	ELEPHANT, STANDING	9.8						$75/125
1893		80316/25	34425 4		1989 PRICE LIST	ELEPHANT	9.8						$75/125
1894		80316/65	34465 0		1989 PRICE LIST	ELEPHANT	25.6						$100/150
1895		80321/25	34125 3		1982 PRICE LIST	ELEPHANT, SITTING	9.8						$75/125
1896		80321/32			1982 PRICE LIST	ELEPHANT, SITTING	12.6						$75/125
1897		80321/36	34236 6		1988 PRICE LIST	ELEPHANT, SITTING	14.2						$100/150
1898		80322/45			1982 PRICE LIST	ELEPHANT, SITTING	17.7						$100/150
1899		80331/30			1982 PRICE LIST	ELEPHANT, LYING	11.8						$75/125
1900		80331/50			1982 PRICE LIST	ELEPHANT, LYING	19.7						$100/150
1901		80331/60			1982 PRICE LIST	ELEPHANT, LYING	23.6						$125/175
1902		80420/30			1982 PRICE LIST	LAMB, SITTING	11.8						$75/125
1903		80423/45			1987 PRICE LIST	LAMB, LAYING	17.7	EGGSHELL W/RED BOW				RED PLASTIC	$100/150
1904		80425/40			1982 PRICE LIST	LAMB, LYING	15.75						$100/150
1905		80425/45			1986 PRICE LIST	LAMB, CARACUL	17.7						$100/150
1906		80436/38			1982 PRICE LIST	DACHSHUND "WALDI"	15						$100/150
1907		80438/40	52040 5		1985 PRICE LIST	DACHSHUND "WALDI"	15.75						$100/150
1908		80440/50			1984 PRICE LIST	DALMATIAN	19.7						$100/150
1909		80442/30	35030 9		1985 PRICE LIST	LION, SITTING	11.8						$75/125
1910		80443/38	35138 2		1985 PRICE LIST	LION, LYING	15						$100/150
1911		80443/85			1986 PRICE LIST	LION. LYING	33.5						$125/175
1912		80445/42			1982 PRICE LIST	SHEEPDOG	16.5						$100/150
1913		80448/50			1984 PRICE LIST	SHEEPDOG	19.7						$100/150
1914		80450/35			1982 PRICE LIST	VAGABOND, HOBO, SCAMP?	13.8						$75/125
1915		80458/30	53530 0		1988 PRICE LIST	POODLE, GRAY	11.8	GRAY					$75/125
1916		80458/31	53630 7		1988 PRICE LIST	POODLE, BRN	11.8	BRN					$75/125
1917		80460/30	53730 4		1988 PRICE LIST	POODLE, BLK	11.8	BLK					$75/125
1918		80492/42			1982 PRICE LIST	LEOPARD, LYING	16.5						$100/150
1919		80492/52			1982 PRICE LIST	LEOPARD, LYING	20.5						$100/150
1920		80510/35			1982 PRICE LIST	SQUIRREL	13.8						$75/125
1921		80510/50			1982 PRICE LIST	SQUIRREL	19.7						$100/150
1922		80512/17	67017 9		1989 PRICE LIST	SQUIRREL	6.7						$50/100
1923		80512/24			1985 PRICE LIST	SQUIRREL	9.5						$75/125
1924		80524/15	67115 2		1989 PRICE LIST	MOUSE	5.9						$50/100
1925		80535/16	67316 3		1989 PRICE LIST	HAMSTER	6.3						$50/100
1926	80535 9		80660/35		1989 PRICE LIST	DANGLING BUNNY, GRAY	13.8	BIBER IMITATION FUR, WHT BELLY & FACE, WASHABLE, GREY				RED PAPER	$75/125
1927	80536 6		80660/35/1		1989 PRICE LIST	RABBIT, DANGLING	13.8	BIBER IMITATION FUR, WHT BELLY & FACE, WASHABLE BRN				RED PAPER	$75/125
1928		80538/13	67413 9		1989 PRICE LIST	RABBIT, DANGLING	5.1						$50/100
1929	80550 2		80660/50		1986 PRICE LIST	RABBIT, STANDING	19.7	GREY AND WHT BIBER IMITATION FUR, WASHABLE				RED PLASTIC	$129
1930		80560B			1990? JESCO CATALOG	TEDDY BEAR	23.6	LT BRN LONG MOHAIR W/RED BOW					$150/200
1931		80600/28	84028 2		1984 PRICE LIST	RABBIT, LYING	11	BEIGE					$75/125
1932		80601/28	84128 9		1984 PRICE LIST	RABBIT, LYING	11	EGGSHELL					$75/125
1933		80607/21			1984 PRICE LIST	RABBIT, LYING	8.3	ROSE					$75/125
1934		80607/28			1982 PRICE LIST	RABBIT, LYING	11						$75/125
1935		80607/42			RABBIT, LYING		16.5						$100/150
1936		80608/21			1984 PRICE LIST	RABBIT, LYING	8.3	LT BLUE					$75/125
1937		80608/42	84242 2		1988 PRICE LIST	RABBIT	16.5						$100/150
1938		80609/21	84321 4		1986 PRICE LIST	RABBIT, LYING	8.3						$75/125
1941		80620/25			1982 PRICE LIST	RABBIT, ANGORA	9.8						$75/125
1942		80620/35			1982 PRICE LIST	RABBIT, ANGORA	13.8						$75/125
1943		80621/35			1985 PRICE LIST	RABBIT, ANGORA	13.8						$75/125
1944		80622/25	82025 3		1988 PRICE LIST	RABBIT, ANGORA	9.8						$75/125
1945		80622/35	82035 2		1988 PRICE LIST	RABBIT, ANGORA	13.8						$75/125
1946		80625/35			1987 PRICE LIST	RABBIT	13.8	BRN W/ WHT FACE & INNER EARS, RED BOW				RED PLASTIC	$75/125
1947		80626/35	82135 9		1988 PRICE LIST	RABBIT	13.8						$75/125
1948	80630 1		646/30		1985 PRICE LIST	RABBIT, CROUCHING	11.8	BRN & WHT BIBER IMITATION FUR, WASHABLE				RED PAPER/PL	$80
1949		80640/35			1982 PRICE LIST	RABBIT	13.8						$75/125
1950		80640/40			1982 PRICE LIST	RABBIT	15.75						$100/150
1951		80642/35			1984 PRICE LIST	RABBIT	13.8						$75/125
1952		80650/30			1982 PRICE LIST	RABBIT, CROUCHING	11.8						$75/125
1953		80650/35			1987 PRICE LIST	RABBIT, GRAY	13.8	GRAY WITH WHT FACE, BELLY, INNER EARS, SITTING ON HINDQRTRS				RED PAPER	$75/125

REF #	EAN #	HERMANN OLD #	ALSO SEE	LIMITED NUMBER	DATA FROM	NAME	INCHES TALL	DESCRIPTION	VOICE	HANGING BOOKLET	ARM TAG	COMPANY LOGO	CURRENT RETAIL
1954		80651/35			1987 PRICE LIST	RABBIT, BRN	13.8	BRN WITH TAN FACE, BELLY, INNER EARS, SITTING ON HINDQRTRS				RED PAPER	$75/125
1955		80650/50			1982 PRICE LIST	RABBIT, CROUCHING	19.7						$100/150
1956		80652/30			1984 PRICE LIST	RABBIT, CROUCHING	11.8	BRN					$75/125
1957		80660/35	80535 9		1989 PRICE LIST	RABBIT, GRAY	13.8						$75/125
1958		80660/35/1	80536 6		1989 PRICE LIST	RABBIT, BRN	13.8						$75/125
1959		80660/50	80550 2		1986 PRICE LIST	RABBIT	19.7						$100/150
1960		80672H			1990? JESCO CATALOG	TEDDY BEAR	28.3	HONEY W/BLUE BOW					$150/200
1961		80704/25			1983 PRICE LIST	BEAR, RUNNING	9.8						$100/150
1962		80705/20			1983 PRICE LIST	DOG, ST. BERNARD	7.9						$75/125
1963		80709/28			1986 PRICE LIST	RABBIT, SITTING	11						$75/125
1964		80714/20	82420 6		1988 PRICE LIST	RABBIT	7.9						$75/125
1965		80715/20	82520 3		1988 PRICE LIST	RABBIT	7.9						$75/125
1966		80716/20	82620 0		1988 PRICE LIST	RABBIT	7.9						$75/125
1967		80725/12	67212 8		1989 PRICE LIST	MARMOT, STANDING	4.7						$50/100
1968		80709/28	83028 3		1989 PRICE LIST	RABBIT, BEIGE	11						$75/125
1969	80740 7		647/40		1987 PRICE LIST	RABBIT, CROUCHING	15.75						$100/150
1970		80740/30			1983 PRICE LIST	PIGLET	11.8						$75/125
1971		80742/30	44530 2		1985 PRICE LIST	PIGLET	11.8						$75/125
1972		80742/40	44540 1		1985 PRICE LIST	PIGLET	15.75						$100/150
1973		80742/50	44550 0		1985 PRICE LIST	PIGLET	19.7						$100/150
1974		80745/18			1985 PRICE LIST	PIGLET, SITTING	7						$50/100
1975		80761/28			1983 PRICE LIST	ELEPHANT, GOLD	11						$75/125
1976		80762/28			1983 PRICE LIST	ELEPHANT, GRAY	11						$75/125
1977		80763/28			1983 PRICE LIST	ELEPHANT, ROSE	11						$75/125
1978		80764/28			1983 PRICE LIST	ELEPHANT, LT BLUE	11						$75/125
1979		80765/30			1983 PRICE LIST	ELEPHANT, GRAY	11.8						$75/125
1980		80765/50			1983 PRICE LIST	ELEPHANT, GRAY	19.7						$100/150
1981		80766/30			1983 PRICE LIST	ELEPHANT, ROSE	11.8						$75/125
1982		80767/30			1983 PRICE LIST	ELEPHANT, LT BLUE	11.8						$75/125
1983		80768/30			1983 PRICE LIST	ELEPHANT, GOLD	11.8						$75/125
1984		80770/30	34030 0		1986 PRICE LIST	ELEPHANT, GRAY	11.8						$75/125
1985		80770/50	34050 8		1986 PRICE LIST	ELEPHANT, GRAY	19.7						$100/150
1986		80770/75	34075 1		1986 PRICE LIST	ELEPHANT, GRAY	29.5						$150/200
1987		80771/30	34330 1		1988 PRICE LIST	ELEPHANT	11.8						$75/125
1988		80771/50	34350 9		1988 PRICE LIST	ELEPHANT	19.7						$100/150
1989		80785C			1988 JESCO CATALOG	TEDDY BEAR	33	CINNAMON W/TAN MUZZLE					$200/300
1990		80850B			1988 JESCO CATALOG	TEDDY BEAR	19.7	DARK BRN W/TAN MUZZLE					$150/200
1991		80885B			1988 JESCO CATALOG	TEDDY BEAR	33	DARK BRN W/TAN MUZZLE & EARS					$200/300
1992		80886/13	67613 3		1989 PRICE LIST	HEDGEHOG	5.1						$50/100
1993		81/40	18140 8		1987 PRICE LIST	TEDDY BEAR	15.75	EGGSHELL BIBER IMITATION, ALL LIMBS MOVEABLE, RED BOW,				RED PLASTIC	$75/125
1994		81/50			1982 PRICE LIST	TEDDY BEAR	19.7						$75/125
1995	81010 0		780/10		1982 PRICE LIST	BUNNY	4	MINK PLUSH, WASHABLE, BEIGE, BRN, GREY, WHT, ASSORTED				RED PAPER	$43
1996	81011 7		780/10K		1988 PRICE LIST	BUNNY	4						$43
1997	81115 2		781/15		1985 PRICE LIST	BUNNY	5.9	BEIGE BIBER IMITATION FUR, WASHABLE				RED PAPER	$50/100
1998	81120 6		781/20		1986 PRICE LIST	BUNNY	7.9	BEIGE BIBER IMITATION FUR, WASHABLE				RED PAPER	$50/100
1999	81215 9		782/15		1985 PRICE LIST	BUNNY	5.9	BRN BIBER IMITATION FUR, WASHABLE				RED PAPER	$50/100
2000	81220 3		782/20		1986 PRICE LIST	BUNNY	7.9	BRN BIBER IMITATION FUR, WASHABLE				RED PAPER	$50/100
2001	81320 0		783/20		1986 PRICE LIST	BUNNY, ASST'D COLORS	7.9	WHT, BIBER IMITATION FUR, WASHABLE				RED PAPER	$39/$52
2002		81350/30	42330 0		1988 PRICE LIST	RAVEN	11.8	BLK BODY W/YELLOW BEAK & LEGS				RED PAPER	$75/125
2003		81357/30	87630 4		1987 CATALOG	DUCKLING	11.8	YELLOW W/BLK EYES, SOFT STUFFED				RED PLASTIC	$75/125
2004		81358/30			1987 CATALOG	DUCKLING	11.8	REDDISH-PURPLE W/WHT LEGS, UNDER WINGS & BEAK, SOFT STUFFED				RED PLASTIC	$75/125
2005		81398/30	41230 4		1988 PRICE LIST	FROG	11.8						$75/125
2006		81399/30			1987 CATALOG	FROG	11.8	GRN BODY, YELLOW BODY, CROWN ON HEAD				RED PLASTIC	$75/125
2007	81420 7		784/20		1986 PRICE LIST	BUNNY, DARK BRN	7.9	DARK BRN, BIBER IMITATION FUR, WASHABLE				RED PAPER	$58
2008	81683 0				1988 JESCO CATALOG	BEAR, LYING DOWN	33L X??	BRN LYING DOWN					$150/200
2009	81685 0				1990? JESCO	BEAR, LYING DOWN	33L X??	BRN LYING DOWN					$150/200
2010		82/26 MW			PART OF S0003	TEDDY BEAR	10.2	WHT 53% WOOL & 47% COTTON MOHAIR, SHAVED PAWS	NONE	YES	BRN	RED PAPER	$100/150
2011		82000/40	31540 7		1983 PRICE LIST	PANDA BEAR	15.75						$100/150
2012		82006/28	31628 2		1988 PRICE LIST	PANDA BEAR	11	"PIEPE"					$50/100
2013		82006/60	31660 2		1988 PRICE LIST	PANDA BEAR	23.6						$75/125
2014		82007/25	31725 8		1988 PRICE LIST	PANDA BEAR	10.2	"SCHNURZE"					$50/100

REF #	EAN #	HERMANN OLD #	ALSO SEE	LIMITED NUMBER	DATA FROM	NAME	INCHES TALL	DESCRIPTION	VOICE	HANGING BOOKLET	ARM TAG	COMPANY LOGO	CURRENT RETAIL
2015		82007/55	31755 5		1988 PRICE LIST	PANDA BEAR	19LX12H	BLK & WHT PLUSH; 1996 PRICE LIST	NONE	YES	RED	RED PLASTIC	$150/200
2016		82008/60			1982 PRICE LIST	BEAR, WASHABLE	23.6						$150/200
2017		82009/30			HERMANN CAT 1982	BEAR ON 4 LEGS	11.8	DARK BRN PLUSH W/TAN MUZZLE & PADS, PLAYFUL 4 LEGGED POSITION				GOLD PLASTIC	$100/150
2018		82009/40			HERMANN CAT 1982	BEAR ON 4 LEGS	15.75	DARK BRN PLUSH W/TAN MUZZLE & PADS, PLAYFUL 4 LEGGED POSITION				GOLD PLASTIC	$100/150
2019		82009/60			HERMANN CAT 1982	BEAR ON 4 LEGS	23.6	DARK BRN PLUSH W/TAN MUZZLE & PADS, PLAYFUL 4 LEGGED POSITION				GOLD PLASTIC	$125/175
2020		82010/35			HERMANN CAT 1982	BEAR, LYING DOWN	14.2	DARK BRN PLUSH W/TAN MUZZLE & PADS, PLAYFUL 4 LEGGED POSITION				GOLD PLASTIC	$75/125
2021		82010/55			HERMANN CAT 1982	BEAR, LYING DOWN	22	DARK BRN PLUSH W/TAN MUZZLE & PADS, PLAYFUL 4 LEGGED POSITION				GOLD PLASTIC	$125/175
2022		82010/75			HERMANN CAT 1982	BEAR, LYING DOWN	28LX4H	BRN W/TAN MUZZLE	NONE	YES	BRN	GOLD	$175
2023		82010/100			HERMANN CAT 1982	BEAR, LYING DOWN	39	DARK BRN PLUSH W/TAN MUZZLE & PADS, PLAYFUL 4 LEGGED POSITION				GOLD PLASTIC	$150/200
2024		82012/75	30275 9		SEE 30275 9	BEAR, LYING DOWN	28LX14H	CREAM BEIGE; HERMANN CATALOG 1986					$125/175
2025		82014/30	35230 3		1985 PRICE LIST	LION	11.8						$75/125
2026		82014/65	35265 5		1988 PRICE LIST	LION	25.6						$125/175
2027		82015/30			1985 PRICE LIST	LIONESS	11.8						$75/125
2028		82017/60			1982 PRICE LIST	LION, LYING DOWN	23.6						$100/150
2029		82017/80			1982 PRICE LIST	LION, LYING DOWN	31.5						$100/150
2030		82018/30			1985 KATHY ANN CAT	LION, LYING DOWN	12					RED PLASTIC	$75/125
2031		82021/30	63230 6		1985 PRICE LIST	CAT, SIAMESE	11.8						$75/125
2032		82024/20			1983 PRICE LIST	CAT, STANDING	10.2						$50/100
2033	82025 3		80622/25		1988 PRICE LIST	RABBIT, ANGORA	9.8	SITTING, TAN BIBER IMITATION FUR, WASHABLE				RED PLASTIC	$108
2034	82035 2		80622/35		1988 PRICE LIST	RABBIT, ANGORA	13.8						$125/175
2035	82135 9		80626/35		1988 PRICE LIST	RABBIT	13.8						$125/175
2036	82420 6		80714/20		1988 PRICE LIST	RABBIT, LYING	10.2	BEIGE BIBER IMITATION FUR, WASHABLE				RED PAPER	$75/125
2037	82520 3		80715/20		1988 PRICE LIST	RABBIT	10.2						$75/125
2038	82620 0		80716/20		1988 PRICE LIST	RABBIT	10.2						$75/125
2039		83020/27	67527 3		1989 PRICE LIST	FOX	10.6						$75/125
2040		83020/65	43165 7		1988 PRICE LIST	FOX	25.6						$100/150
2041		83020/85			1982 PRICE LIST	FOX	33.5						$125/175
2042		830/23			1982 PRICE LIST	COW	9.5						$75/125
2043		830/26	45526 4		1985 PRICE LIST	COW	10.2						$75/125
2044		830/27	45665 0		1983 PRICE LIST	COW	10.6						$75/125
2045		830/65			1985 PRICE LIST	COW	25.6						$100/150
2046		83025/85			1982 PRICE LIST	SILVER FOX	33.5						$125/175
2047	83028 3		80709/28		1989 PRICE LIST	RABBIT, SITTING	11	BRN MINK PLUSH, WASHABLE				RED PLASTIC	$75/125
2048	83221 8		712/21		1988 PRICE LIST	RABBIT, ASST'D COLORS	8.3						$75/125
2049		83041/40			1982 PRICE LIST	COCKER SPANIEL	15.75						$100/150
2050		83042H			1990? JESCO	TEDDY BEAR	16.5	HONEY W/RED BOW					$100/150
2051		83045/40			1983 PRICE LIST	COCKER SPANIEL	15.75						$100/150
2052		83100/40	52540 0		1985 PRICE LIST	BOXER	15.75						$100/150
2053		83100/52	52552 3		1985 PRICE LIST	BOXER	20.5						$100/150
2054		83110/40	57040 0		1989 PRICE LIST	HUSKY, LYING	15.75						$100/150
2055		83133			1988 JESCO CATALOG	TEDDY BEAR	12.6	HONEY W/RED BOW					$125/175
2056		83233			1988 JESCO CATALOG	TEDDY BEAR	13.5	WHT W/BLUE BOW					$125/175
2057		83242			1988 JESCO CATALOG	TEDDY BEAR	16.5	WHT W/RED BOW					$125/175
2058		83603/35			1982 PRICE LIST	CAT	13.8						$100/150
2059		83605/30	63030 2		1983 PRICE LIST	CAT, LYING	11.8						$100/150
2060		83606/30	63130 9		1987 PRICE LIST	CAT, LYING	11.8	TAWNY W/DARKER SHORT STRIPES, WHT MUZZLE, LONG PILE				RED PAPER	$100/150
2061		83607/30	63330 3		1988 PRICE LIST	CAT, LYING	11.8						$100/150
2062		83610/40			1985 PRICE LIST	TOMCAT	15.75	GRAY					$100/150
2063		83615/40	65040 9		1985 PRICE LIST	TOMCAT	15.75	BLK					$100/150
2064		83620/30	65130 7		1987 PRICE LIST	CAT, STANDING	11.8	MAUVE W/WHT MUZZLE. DRESSED IN LAV STRIPED DRESS				RED PLASTIC	$100/150
2065	83663 0				1988 JESCO CATALOG	BEAR, LYING DOWN	24.8	BRN TIPPED MOHAIR W/GRN BOW					$150/200
2066		83690/60	47560 6		1987 PRICE LIST	CROCODILE	23.6	GRN W/OPEN EGGSHELL JAWS & PAWS				RED PLASTIC	$100/150
2067		83690/80	47580 4		1987 PRICE LIST	CROCODILE	31.5	GRN W/OPEN EGGSHELL JAWS & PAWS				RED PLASTIC	$125/175
2068		83710/30			1982 PRICE LIST	HIPPOPOTAMUS	11.8						$75/125
2069		83710/43			1982 PRICE LIST	HIPPOPOTAMUS	16.9						$75/125
2070		83710/62			1982 PRICE LIST	HIPPOPOTAMUS	24.4						$100/150
2071		83710/100			1982 PRICE LIST	HIPPOPOTAMUS	39.4						$150/200
2072		83714/30	40030 1		1988 PRICE LIST	HIPPOPOTAMUS	11.8						$75/125

REF #	EAN #	HERMANN OLD #	ALSO SEE	LIMITED NUMBER	DATA FROM	NAME	INCHES TALL	DESCRIPTION	VOICE	HANGING BOOKLET	ARM TAG	COMPANY LOGO	CURRENT RETAIL
2073		83714/43	40043 1		1988 PRICE LIST	HIPPOPOTAMUS	16.9						$100/150
2074		83714/62	40062 2		1988 PRICE LIST	HIPPOPOTAMUS	24.4						$125/175
2075		83714/100	40096 7		1988 PRICE LIST	HIPPOPOTAMUS	39.4						$150/200
2076		83715/30			1982 PRICE LIST	HIPPOPOTAMUS	11.8						$75/125
2077		83715/43			1982 PRICE LIST	HIPPOPOTAMUS	16.9						$100/150
2078		83715/62			1982 PRICE LIST	HIPPOPOTAMUS	23.6						$125/175
2079		83715/100			1982 PRICE LIST	HIPPOPOTAMUS	39.4						$150/200
2080		83716/30			1983 PRICE LIST	HIPPOPOTAMUS	11.8						$75/125
2081		83716/43			1983 PRICE LIST	HIPPOPOTAMUS	16.9						$100/150
2082		83716/62			1983 PRICE LIST	HIPPOPOTAMUS	23.6						$125/175
2083		83716/100			1983 PRICE LIST	HIPPOPOTAMUS	39.4						$150/200
2084		83717/30	40130 8		1988 PRICE LIST	HIPPOPOTAMUS	11.8						$75/125
2085		83718/30			1983 PRICE LIST	HIPPOPOTAMUS, SITTING	11.8						$75/125
2086		83719/30	40603 03		1983 PRICE LIST	HIPPOPOTAMUS, SITTING	11.8	BLUE					$75/125
2087		83720/42			HERMANN CAT 1982	BEAR, SITTING	16.5	SEATED BEAR W/WHT PATCH AT NECK				GOLD PLASTIC	$50/100
2088		83725/42			1984 PRICE LIST	BEAR, 4 LEGGED	14.2L	SEATED BEAR W/WHT PATCH AT NECK				RED PLASTIC	$50/100
2089		83730/40			HERMANN CAT 1982	BEAR, 4 LEGGED	15.75	DARK BRN 4-LEGGED STANDING BEAR WITH TAN MUZZLE				GOLD PLASTIC	$50/100
2090		83731/40			HERMANN CAT 1982	BEAR, 4 LEGGED	13LX10H	LIGHT BRN W/TAN MUZZLE	NONE	YES	GRN	GOLD PLASTIC	$60
2091		83735/36			1984 PRICE LIST	BEAR, 4 LEGGED	14.2L	DARK BRN WITH WHT RING AROUND NECK, TAN MUZZLE/PADS					$50/100
2092	84028 2		80600/28		1984 PRICE LIST	RABBIT, LYING	11	BEIGE BIBER IMITATION FUR, WASHABLE				RED PAPER	$50/100
2093		84030/40			1984 PRICE LIST	FOAL	15.75						$75/125
2094		84050/40			1982 PRICE LIST	FOAL	15.75						$75/125
2095		84050/60			1982 PRICE LIST	FOAL	23.6						$100/150
2096		84055/40			1982 PRICE LIST	FOAL	15.75						$75/125
2097		84060/45			1982 PRICE LIST	DOG, ST. BERNARD	17.7						$75/125
2098		84060/55			1982 PRICE LIST	DOG, ST. BERNARD	21.7						$100/150
2099		84060/60	55760 9		1988 PRICE LIST	DOG, ST. BERNARD	23.6						$100/150
2100		84070/50	55550 6		1987 PRICE LIST	JOSEF THE TV DOG	19.7	ACRYLIC PLUSH, WASHABLE; FROM "HEIDI" TV PROGRAM					$100/150
2101		84072/55	56655 8		1988 CATALOG	JOSEF THE TV DOG	21.7	ACRYLIC PLUSH, WASHABLE; FROM "HEIDI" TV PROGRAM		YES		RED PLASTIC	$100/150
2102		84080/40			1984 PRICE LIST	DOG, ST. BERNARD	15.75						$100/150
2103		84085/55	56555 0		1988 PRICE LIST	BEAGLE	21.7	BRN BACK REAR LEGS & OVER EYES, BLK TAIL SPOT + PAWS, WHT ELSEWHERE				RED PLASTIC	$100/150
2104		84090/55	31855 2		1987 PRICE LIST	PANDA BEAR	21.7	BLK UPPER HALF BODY, WHT LOWER, BLK LEGS, SOFT STUFFED				RED PLASTIC	$125/175
2105		84090/75	31875 0		1987 PRICE LIST	PANDA BEAR	29.5	BLK UPPER HALF BODY, WHT LOWER, BLK LEGS, SOFT STUFFED				RED PLASTIC	$150/200
2106		84090/110	31897 2		1987 PRICE LIST	PANDA BEAR	43.3	BLK UPPER HALF BODY, WHT LOWER, BLK LEGS, SOFT STUFFED				RED PLASTIC	$200/300
2107		84095/40	39240 8		1987 PRICE LIST	TURTLE ON 4 LEGS	15.75	GRN SHELL, REST YELLOW, WHT UNDER NECK, SOFT STUFFED				RED PLASTIC	$75/125
2108		84095/55	39255 2		1987 PRICE LIST	TURTLE ON 4 LEGS	21.7	GRN SHELL, REST YELLOW, WHT UNDER NECK, SOFT STUFFED				RED PLASTIC	$100/150
2109		84095/75	39275 0		1987 PRICE LIST	TURTLE ON 4 LEGS	29.5	GRN SHELL, REST YELLOW, WHT UNDER NECK, SOFT STUFFED				RED PLASTIC	$125/175
2110		84/18	18418 8		1985 PRICE LIST	TEDDY BEAR	7	MINK PLUSH, 70% ACRYLIC 30% COTTON, FULLY JTD	NONE	YES	RED	RED PAPER	$50/100
2111		84/24			HERMANN CAT 1982	TEDDY BEAR	9.5	MINK PLUSH, 70% ACRYLIC 30% COTTON, FULLY JTD				RED PAPER	$75/125
2112		84/25	18425 6		1984 PRICE LIST	TEDDY BEAR	10.2	MINK PLUSH, 70% ACRYLIC 30% COTTON, ALL LIMBS MOVEABLE	NONE	YES	RED	RED PAPER	$75/125
2113		84/28			HERMANN CAT 1982	TEDDY BEAR	11	MINK PLUSH, 70% ACRYLIC 30% COTTON, FULLY JTD				RED PAPER	$75/125
2114		84/30	18430 0		HERMANN CAT 1986	TEDDY BEAR	11.8	MINK PLUSH, 70% ACRYLIC 30% COTTON, FULLY JTD	SQUEAKER	YES	GRN	RED PLASTIC	$150/200
2115		84/35	18435 5		HERMANN CAT 1982	TEDDY BEAR	14.2	BRN MINK PLUSH, 70 % ACRYLIC 30% COTTON, ALL LIMBS MOVEABLE	GROWLER	YES	RED	RED PLASTIC	$200/300
2116		84/40	18440 9		1983 PRICE LIST	TEDDY BEAR	15.75	MINK PLUSH, 70% ACRYLIC 30% COTTON, FULLY JTD	GROWLER	YES	BRN	RED PLASTIC	$100
2117		84/42			HERMANN CAT 1982	TEDDY BEAR	16.5	MINK PLUSH, 70% ACRYLIC 30% COTTON, FULLY JTD				GRN PAPER	$75/125
2118		84/50	18450 8		1982 PRICE LIST	TEDDY BEAR	19.7	SILVER MINK PLUSH, 70% ACRYLIC 30% COTTON,					$165
2119		84100/35	49035 7		1988 PRICE LIST	WHALE	13.8						$50/100
2120		84100/45	49045 6		1988 PRICE LIST	WHALE	17.7						$50/100
2121		84100/65	49065 4		1988 PRICE LIST	WHALE	25.6						$100/150
2122		84110/60	42560 1		1988 PRICE LIST	DUCK, FLYING	23.6						$100/150
2123		84110/80	42580 9		1988 PRICE LIST	DUCK, FLYING	31.5						$125/175
2124		84120/55	49565 9		1988 PRICE LIST	ALLIGATOR	25.6						$100/150
2125		84120/90	49590 1		1988 PRICE LIST	ALLIGATOR	35.4						$125/175
2126		84120/120	49598 7		1988 PRICE LIST	ALLIGATOR	47.2						$150/200
2127	84128 9		80601/28		1984 PRICE LIST	RABBIT, LYING	11	EGGSHELL, BIBER IMITATION FUR, WASHABLE				RED PAPER	$81
2128	84242 2		80608/42		1988 PRICE LIST	RABBIT, LYING	16.5	TAN BIBER IMITATION FUR, WASHABLE				RED PLASTIC	$127
2129	84321 4		80609/21		1986 PRICE LIST	RABBIT, LYING	8.3	BIBER IMITATION FUR WASHABLE, LT BEIGE, FOXY, BEIGE ASSTD				RED PAPER	$54
2130	84442 6				1996 PRICE LIST	RABBIT	16.5						$116
2131		85/18			1982 PRICE LIST	YOUNG BEAR FAMILY	7	CARAMEL SILVER TIPPED LONG MOHAIR W/BOW	NONE	NO	NO	NO	$200/300
2132	85/23				HERMANN 1983	TEDDY BEAR, ZOTTY	9.5	CARAMEL SILVER TIPPED LONG 53%W & 47%C MOHAIR, W/RED BOW	NONE	SHORT BKLT	GRN	NONE	$150/200
2133		85/24			HERMANN CAT 1982	TEDDY BEAR, ZOTTY	9.5	COCOA BEIGE TIPPED LONG 53%W & 47%C MOHAIR W/RED BOW					$150/200

REF #	EAN #	HERMANN OLD #	ALSO SEE	LIMITED NUMBER	DATA FROM	NAME	INCHES TALL	DESCRIPTION	VOICE	HANGING BOOKLET	ARM TAG	COMPANY LOGO	CURRENT RETAIL
2134		85/28 ('60)			HERMANN 1960	YOUNG BEAR FAMILY	11	COCOA BEIGE TIPPED LONG 53%W & 47%C MOHAIR W/RED BOW	SQUEAKER	NO	NO	NO	$250
2135		85/28 ('70)			BOOK 1950 PRODUCT	YOUNG BEAR FAMILY	11	COCOA BEIGE TIPPED LONG 53%W & 47%C MOHAIR W/RED OR GRN BOW	SQUEAKER	SHORT BKLT	GRN	RED PLASTIC	$100/150
2136		85/28			BOOK 1950 PRODUCT	YOUNG BEAR FAMILY	11	CARAMEL SILVER TIPPED LONG 53%W & 47%C MOHAIR W/RED BOW	SQUEAKER	NO	GRN	RED PLASTIC	$100/150
2137		85/35			BOOK 1950 PRODUCT	YOUNG BEAR FAMILY	14.2	CARAMEL SILVER TIPPED LONG MOHAIR W/RED OR GRN BOW					$125/175
2138		85/42			1983 PRICE LIST	YOUNG BEAR FAMILY	15.75	CARAMEL SILVER TIPPED LONG 53%W & 47%C MOHAIR W/RED BOW	GROWLER	YES	GRN	RED PLASTIC	$125/175
2139		85/50			HERMANN CAT 1982	YOUNG BEAR FAMILY	19.7	COCOA BEIGE TIPPED LONG 53%W & 47%C MOHAIR W/RED BOW					$150/200
2140	85023 6		604/23	2,000	1987 PRICE LIST	RABBIT, STANDING	9.5	MOHAIR PLUSH, 5 JOINTS				RED PLASTIC	$98
2141	85025 0				1990 PRICE LIST	RABBIT W/PACK BACK	9.8	BRN MINK PLUSH, FULLY JTD, SURFACE WASHABLE				RED PAPER	$102
2142	85138 7		640/38		1986 PRICE LIST	HARE, STANDING	15	DARK MUSTARD MINK PLUSH, FULLY JTD, WHT INSIDE EARS				RED PLASTIC	$100/150
2143		85/55			BOOK, HERMANN 1960	YOUNG BEAR	19.7	CARAMEL SILVER TIPPED LONG 53%W & 47%C MOHAIR W/RED BOW; THIS WAS FIRST BEAR WITH SOFT KAPOK FILLING					$125/175
2144		855/25			1982 PRICE LIST	COCKER SPANIEL	9.8						$75/125
2145		855/30			1982 PRICE LIST	COCKER SPANIEL	11.8						$75/125
2146		860/7			1982 PRICE LIST	LADYBUG	2.8						$50/100
2147		860/9			1982 PRICE LIST	LADYBUG	3.5						$50/100
2148		86/18	18618 2		1989 PRICE LIST	PANDA	7						$50/100
2149		86/25	18625 0		HERMANN 1985(?)	PANDA W/SQUEAKER	11.5	BLK & WHT 62%W & 38%C MOHAIR	SQUEAKER	YES	GRN	RED PLASTIC	$150
2150		86/30	18630 4		BOOK 1956 PG 58	PANDA	11.8	BLK & WHT MOHAIR, WOOL STUFFING W/RED BOW				RED PLASTIC	$125/175
2151		86/35			BOOK 1956 PG 58	PANDA W/GROWLER	14.2	BLK & WHT 62%W & 38%C MOHAIR, WOOL STUFFING W/RED BOW	GROWLER	YES	GRN	RED PLASTIC	$200
2152	86012 9		420/8		1982 PRICE LIST	LAMB, MERINO	4.7	MERINO WOOL, SURFACE WASHABLE, WHT				RED PAPER	$33
2153	86020 4		420/9		1982 PRICE LIST	LAMB, MERINO	7.9	MERINO WOOL, SURFACE WASHABLE, WHT				RED PAPER	$59
2154	86024 2		420/10		1982 PRICE LIST	LAMB, MERINO	9.5	MERINO WOOL, SURFACE WASHABLE, WHT				RED PAPER	$69
2155	86040 2		420/40		1985 PRICE LIST	LAMB, MERINO	15.75	MERINO WOOL, SURFACE WASHABLE, WHT				RED PLASTIC	$155
2156		861/30	060/33		KATHY ANN 1986 CAT	HELEN SIEVERLING,	13	ALTHOUGH PART # INDICATES A 30CM BEAR, IT IS ACTUALLY A 33CM BEAR					$150
2157	86123 2				1995 PRICE LIST	LAMB	9.5	WHT WOVEN FUR, WASHABLE, PLAID BOW				RED PLASTIC	$96
2158	86160 7		420/60		1989 PRICE LIST	SHEEP, GRAZING	23.6	WOOL PLUSH, SURFACE WASHABLE, WHT				RED PLASTIC	$213
2159	86228 4				1993 PRICE LIST	LAMB	11	WOOL PLUSH, SURFACE WASHABLE					$75/125
2160	86530 8		422/30		1982 PRICE LIST	LAMB	11.8						$75/125
2161	86560 5		422/60		1984 PRICE LIST	LAMB	23.6						$100/150
2162	86630 5				1990 PRICE LIST	LAMB, MERINO, SLEEPING	11.8	MERINO WOOL, WASHABLE, WHT				RED PAPER	$79
2163	86732 6				1995 PRICE LIST	LAMB, SLEEPING	12.6	WOVEN FUR, WASHABLE, CLOTH FACE				RED PLASTIC	$192
2164	86745 6				1995 PRICE LIST	LAMB, SLEEPING	17.7	WOVEN FUR, WASHABLE, CLOTH FACE				RED PLASTIC	$122
2165	86842 6				1996 PRICE LIST	LAMB	16.5						$75/125
2166		87/24			BOOK 1963 PG 58	YOUNG BEAR	9.5	CINNAMON DRALON, WOOL STUFFING				MTL W/PAPER	$75/125
2167		87/28			BOOK 1963 PG 58	YOUNG BEAR	11	WHT DRALON, WOOL STUFFING					$75/125
2168	87012 8				1991 PRICE LIST	SMALL DUCK	4.7	BEIGE OR BRN OR WHT OR BRN TIPPED ASSORTED				SML RED PL	$43
2169	87015 9		1356/15		1988 PRICE LIST	WILD DUCK	5.9	BIBER IMITATION WOVEN FUR, WASHABLE, BLUE HEAD, YELLOW BODY, BRN WINGS					$49
2170	87020 3		1356/20		1983 PRICE LIST	WILD DUCK	10.2						$75/125
2171	87025 8				1990 PRICE LIST	WILD DUCK	9.8	BIBER IMITATION WOVEN FUR, WASHABLE, DARK BRN W/WHT BACK				RED PAPER	$93
2172	87026 5				1990 PRICE LIST	WILD DUCK	9.8	BIBER IMITATION WOVEN FUR, WASHABLE, BRN W/BEIGE TAIL FEATHERS				RED PLASTIC	$105
2173		870/28	74528 0		1988 PRICE LIST	RAVEN	11						$75/125
2174		871/28	74628 7		1988 PRICE LIST	MOUSE	11						$75/125
2175	87116 3		1357/16/1		1998 PRICE LIST	DUCK, RED	6.3	BIBER IMITATION FUR, WASHABLE				RED PAPER	$50/100
2176		872/28	74728 4		1988 PRICE LIST	MONKEY	11						$75/125
2177	87216 0		1357/16/2		1998 PRICE LIST	DUCK, LT BLUE	6.3	BIBER IMITATION FUR, WASHABLE				RED PAPER	$50/100
2178	87316 7		1357/16/3		1998 PRICE LIST	DUCK, GRN	6.3	BIBER IMITATION FUR, WASHABLE				RED PAPER	$50/100
2179	87416 4		1357/16/4		1998 PRICE LIST	DUCK, BLUE	6.3	BIBER IMITATION FUR, WASHABLE				RED PAPER	$50/100
2180		874/28	74828 1		1989 PRICE LIST	MOUSE, RED	11						$75/125
2181		874/29	74829 8		1989 PRICE LIST	MOUSE, GOLD	11						$75/125
2182	87515 4		1353/15		1984 PRICE LIST	DUCK, GOLD	5.9	BIBER IMITATION FUR, WASHABLE				RED PAPER	$45
2183	87630 4		81357/30		1988 PRICE LIST	SCHLENKERENTE	11.8						$75/125
2184	87717 2				1990 PRICE LIST	DUCKLING, ORANGE-WHT	6.7						$50/100
2185	87722 6				1990 PRICE LIST	DUCKLING, ORANGE-WHT	8.7						$50/100
2186	87817 9				1990 PRICE LIST	DUCKLING, WHT-GOLD	6.7						$50/100

REF #	EAN #	HERMANN OLD #	ALSO SEE	LIMITED NUMBER	DATA FROM	NAME	INCHES TALL	DESCRIPTION	VOICE	HANGING BOOKLET	ARM TAG	COMPANY LOGO	CURRENT RETAIL
2187	87822 3				1990 PRICE LIST	DUCKLING, WHT-GOLD	8.7						$50/100
2188		88/30			BOOK 1973 PG 58	YOUNG BEAR	11.8	NOUGAT WOVEN MINK PLUSH, WOOL STUFFING				MTL W/PAPER	$75/125
2189		88/38			HERMANN CAT 1982	YOUNG BEAR	14.9	LONG PILE CARAMEL W/WHT CHEST, CHAIN COLLAR WHT PADS, OPEN MOUTH				GRN PAPER	$100/150
2190		88/42			HERMANN CAT 1982	YOUNG BEAR	16.5	LONG PILE CARAMEL W/WHT CHEST, CHAIN COLLAR WHT PADS, OPEN MOUTH				RED PLASTIC	$100/150
2191		880/10	74010 0		1982 PRICE LIST	HEDGEHOG FAMILY	3.9						$50/100
2192		880/16	74016 2		1982 PRICE LIST	HEDGEHOG FAMILY	6.3						$50/100
2193		880/22	74022 3		1982 PRICE LIST	HEDGEHOG FAMILY	8.7						$75/125
2194	88022 6		1310/22		1982 PRICE LIST	HEN	8.7	BRN SPOTTED MINK PLUSH, SURFACE WASHABLE				RED PAPER	$75/125
2195	88035 6				1991 PRICE LIST	HEN	13.8	MULTI COLORED WOVEN FUR				RED PLASTIC	$164
2196		881/13	74313 2		1989 PRICE LIST	HEDGEHOG	5.12						$50/100
2197		881/16	74316 3		1989 PRICE LIST	HEDGEHOG	6.3						$50/100
2198		881/22	74324 4		1989 PRICE LIST	HEDGEHOG	8.7						$75/125
2199	88135 3				1991 PRICE LIST	HEN	13.8	WHT WOVEN FUR				RED PLASTIC	$164
2200		885/12	74112 1		1982 PRICE LIST	HEDGEHOG FAMILY	4.7						$50/100
2201		885/16	74116 9		1982 PRICE LIST	HEDGEHOG FAMILY	6.3						$50/100
2202		885/16K	74117 6		1988 PRICE LIST	HEDGEHOG FAMILY	6.3						$50/100
2203	88225 1		1452/25		1982 PRICE LIST	STANDING GOAT	9.8	BLK & WHT ACRYLIC, SURFACE WASHABLE				RED PAPER	$75/125
2204	88325 8				1992 PRICE LIST	GOAT	9.8	MINK PLUSH, SURFACE WASHABLE, BRN					$120
2205	88326 5				1992 PRICE LIST	GOAT	9.8	MINK PLUSH, SURFACE WASHABLE, WHT					$120
2206	88350 0				1992 PRICE LIST	GOAT	19.7	MINK PLUSH, SURFACE WASHABLE, BRN					$267
2207		885/22	74122 0		1982 PRICE LIST	HEDGEHOG FAMILY	8.7						$75/125
2208	88503 0		1316/10/3		1986 PRICE LIST	CHICKS (3) IN A BASKET	6.3	YELLOW DRALON PLUSH, SURFACE WASHABLE				RED PAPER	$50/100
2209	88510 8		1316/10		1988 PRICE LIST	CHICK	6.3	YELLOW DRALON PLUSH, SURFACE WASHABLE			RED	RED PAPER	$50/100
2210		886/18	74218 0		1984 PRICE LIST	HEDGEHOG	7						$50/100
2211		890/20	39020 6		1982 PRICE LIST	TURTLE	7.9						$75/125
2212		890/30			1982 PRICE LIST	TURTLE	11.8						$75/125
2213	89024 9		1330/24		1982 PRICE LIST	SWAN, WHT	9.5	MINK PLUSH, WASHABLE, WHT W/BACK BAND AT EYES				RED PAPER	$83
2214	89055 3				1992 PRICE LIST	SWAN	21.6	MINK PLUSH, WASHABLE, WHT W/BACK BAND AT EYES					$267
2215	89124 6		1331/24		1988 PRICE LIST	SWAN, OLD ROSE	9.5						$75/125
2216		892/20	39120 3		1986 PRICE LIST	TURTLE	7.9						$75/125
2217		894/20	39320 7		1988 PRICE LIST	TURTLE	7.9						$75/125
2218	89530 5		1370/30		1989 PRICE LIST	GOOSE	11.8	WHT WOVEN BIBER IMITATION FUR, WASHABLE				RED PLASTIC	$74
2219	89540 4		1370/40		1989 PRICE LIST	GOOSE	15.75	WHT WOVEN BIBER IMITATION FUR, WASHABLE				RED PLASTIC	$74
2220		90/30			HERMANN CAT 1982	BEAR, WHT NECK	11.8	LONG PILE CARAMEL W/WHT CHEST, CHAIN COLLAR WHT PADS, OPEN MOUTH	GROWLER			RED PLASTIC	$100/150
2221		90/38			HERMANN CAT 1982	BEAR, WHT NECK	14.5	LONG PILE, OPEN MOUTH, CHAIN COLLAR, WHT NECK AREA, PLASTIC EYES, SHAVED NOSE	SQUEAKER	NO	GRN	RED PLASTIC	$150/200
2222		90/42			HERMANN CAT 1982	BEAR, WHT NECK	16.5	LONG PILE, OPEN MOUTH, SHAVED TAN MUZZLE, RED BOW, WHT NECK AREA, BRN, PLASTIC EYES	GROWLER			RED PLASTIC	$125/175
2223		900/10			BEHA CATALOG 1927	TEDDY-BEARS	3.9	SHORT HAIRED SILK PLUSH, GOLDEN YELLOW OR BRN, ARTIFICIAL SILK BOW	NONE				$400/500
2224		900/20			BEHA CATALOG 1927	TEDDY-BEARS	7.9	SHORT HAIRED SILK PLUSH, GOLDEN YELLOW OR BRN, ARTIFICIAL SILK BOW	NONE				$500/600
2225		900/25			BEHA CATALOG 1927	TEDDY-BEARS	9.8	SHORT HAIRED SILK PLUSH, GOLDEN YELLOW OR BRN, ARTIFICIAL SILK BOW, DISC JOINTS	GROWLER				$750/1000
2226		900/30			BEHA CATALOG 1927	TEDDY-BEARS	11.8	SHORT HAIRED SILK PLUSH, GOLDEN YELLOW OR BRN, ARTIFICIAL SILK BOW, DISC JOINTS	GROWLER				$1,000+
2227		900/35			BEHA CATALOG 1927	TEDDY-BEARS	13.8	SHORT HAIRED SILK PLUSH, GOLDEN YELLOW OR BRN, ARTIFICIAL SILK BOW, DISC JOINTS	GROWLER				$1,000+
2228		900/40			BEHA CATALOG 1927	TEDDY-BEARS	15.8	SHORT HAIRED SILK PLUSH, GOLDEN YELLOW OR BRN, ARTIFICIAL SILK BOW, DISC JOINTS	GROWLER	NO	NO	NO	$1,500
2229		900/50			BEHA CATALOG 1927	TEDDY-BEARS	19.7	SHORT HAIRED SILK PLUSH, GOLDEN YELLOW OR BRN, ARTIFICIAL SILK BOW, DISC JOINTS	GROWLER				$1,000+
2230		900/60			BEHA CATALOG 1927	TEDDY-BEARS	23.6	SHORT HAIRED SILK PLUSH, GOLDEN YELLOW OR BRN, ARTIFICIAL SILK BOW, DISC JOINTS	GROWLER				$1,000+
2231		900/70			BEHA CATALOG 1927	TEDDY-BEARS	27.6	SHORT HAIRED SILK PLUSH, GOLDEN YELLOW OR BRN, ARTIFICIAL SILK BOW, DISC JOINTS	GROWLER				$1,000+
2232		900/80			BEHA CATALOG 1927	TEDDY-BEARS	31.8	SHORT HAIRED SILK PLUSH, GOLDEN YELLOW OR BRN, ARTIFICIAL SILK BOW, DISC JOINTS	GROWLER				$1,000+
2233	90028 3				1991 PRICE LIST	TEDDY 2000	11						$1/50
2234	90050 4				1991 PRICE LIST	TEDDY 2000	19.7						$1/50
2235	90065 8				1991 PRICE LIST	TEDDY 2000	25.6						$1/50

REF #	EAN #	HERMANN OLD #	ALSO SEE	LIMITED NUMBER	DATA FROM	NAME	INCHES TALL	DESCRIPTION	VOICE	HANGING BOOKLET	ARM TAG	COMPANY LOGO	CURRENT RETAIL
2236	90085 6				1991 PRICE LIST	TEDDY 2000	33.5						$1/50
2237	90115 0				1991 PRICE LIST	TEDDY 2000	5.9						$1/50
2238	90122 8				1991 PRICE LIST	TEDDY 2000	8.7						$1/50
2239	90155 6				1991 PRICE LIST	TEDDY 2000	21.7						$1/50
2240	90230 0				1991 PRICE LIST	TEDDY 2000, FOAL	11.8						$1/50
2241	90250 8				1991 PRICE LIST	TEDDY 2000	19.7						$1/50
2242	90320 8				1991 PRICE LIST	TEDDY 2000	7.87						$1/50
2243	90350 0				1991 PRICE LIST	TEDDY 2000	19.7						$1/50
2244	90460 1				1991 PRICE LIST	TEDDY 2000	23.6						$1/50
2245	90520 2				1991 PRICE LIST	TEDDY 2000	7.87						$1/50
2246	90522 6				1991 PRICE LIST	TEDDY 2000	8.66						$1/50
2247	90624 7				1992 PRICE LIST	TEDDY 2000	9.45						$1/50
2248	90635 3				1992 PRICE LIST	TEDDY 2000	13.8						$1/50
2249	90730 7				1992 PRICE LIST	TEDDY 2000	11.8						$1/50
2250	90825 8				1992 PRICE LIST	TEDDY 2000	9.84						$1/50
2251	91022 0				1992 PRICE LIST	TEDDY 2000	8.66						$1/50
2252	91030 5				1991 PRICE LIST	TEDDY 2000	11.8						$1/50
2253	91022 0				1991 PRICE LIST	TEDDY 2000	5HX7L	SOFT BEAR LYING, POLYESTER FIBERS	NONE	NO	YES	TEDDY 2000	$17
2254	91025 1				1992 PRICE LIST	TEDDY 2000, XMAS	9.84						$1/50
2255	91030 5				1992 PRICE LIST	TEDDY 2000, XMAS	11.8						$1/50
2256	91108 1				1997 SPECIAL	TEDDY 2000, XMAS	3.9	WHT WITH RED XMAS HAT, MADE IN CHINA; XMAS TREE ORNAMENT	NONE	NO	RED	TEDDY 2000	$1/50
2257	91130 2				1991 PRICE LIST	TEDDY 2000	11.8						$1/50
2258	91240 8				1991 PRICE LIST	TEDDY 2000	15.75						$1/50
2259	91250 7				1992 PRICE LIST	TEDDY 2000	19.7						$1/50
2260	91270 5				1991 PRICE LIST	TEDDY 2000	27.6						$1/50
2261	91325 2				1991 PRICE LIST	TEDDY 2000	9.8						$1/50
2262	91328 3				1991 PRICE LIST	TEDDY 2000	11						$1/50
2263		91/30			1982 PRICE LIST	TEDDY 2000	11.8	BRIGHT BRN					$75/125
2264	91330 6				1991 PRICE LIST	TEDDY 2000	11.8						$1/50
2265	91335 1				1991 PRICE LIST	TEDDY 2000	13.8						$1/50
2266		91/38			1982 PRICE LIST	TEDDY 2000	15	BRIGHT BRN					$75/125
2267		91/42			1982 PRICE LIST	TEDDY 2000	16.5	BRIGHT BRN					$75/125
2268	91425 9				1991 PRICE LIST	TEDDY 2000	9.84						$1/50
2269	91430 3				1991 PRICE LIST	TEDDY 2000	11.8						$1/50
2270	91523 2				1992 PRICE LIST	TEDDY 2000	9						$1/50
2271	91536 2				1992 PRICE LIST	TEDDY 2000	14.2						$1/50
2272	91556 0				1992 PRICE LIST	TEDDY 2000	22						$1/50
2273	91640 6				1991 PRICE LIST	TEDDY 2000	15.75						$1/50
2274	91720 5				1991 PRICE LIST	TEDDY 2000	7.9						$1/50
2275	91735 9				1991 PRICE LIST	TEDDY 2000	13.8						$1/50
2276	91820 2				1991 PRICE LIST	TEDDY 2000	1.9						$1/50
2277	92114 1				1991 PRICE LIST	TEDDY 2000	5.5						$1/50
2278	92120 2				1991 PRICE LIST	TEDDY 2000	7.9						$1/50
2279	92225 4				1991 PRICE LIST	TEDDY 2000	9.8						$1/50
2280	92320 6				1991 PRICE LIST	TEDDY 2000	7.9						$1/50
2281	92320 6				1992 PRICE LIST	TEDDY 2000	7.9						$1/50
2282	92321 3				1996 FLYER	BUSSI	7.9	SOFT STUFFED W/"BUSSI" FEATURES + YELLOW HEART LOCKET	NONE	YES	RED	2000 LOGO	$50/100
2283	92322 0				1992 PRICE LIST	TEDDY 2000	8.7						$1/50
2284	92345 9				1996 FLYER	BUSSI	17.7	45 CM					$1/50
2285	92430 2				1992 PRICE LIST	TEDDY 2000	11.8						$1/50
2286		925/30			BEHA CATALOG 1927	TEDDY-BEAR	11.8	LONG HAIRED SILK PLUSH, GOLDEN YELLOW OR BRN ARTIFICIAL SILK BOW,	SQUEAKER				$300/400
2287		925/30B			BEHA CATALOG 1927	TEDDY-BEAR, NO-NO	11.8	LONG HAIRED SILK PLUSH, GOLDEN YELLOW OR BRN, ARTIFICIAL SILK BOW, NO-NO MECHANISM	SQUEAKER				$400/500
2288		925/35			BEHA CATALOG 1927	TEDDY-BEAR	14.2	LONG HAIRED SILK PLUSH, GOLDEN YELLOW OR BRN, ARTIFICIAL SILK BOW	SQUEAKER				$400/500
2289		925/35B			BEHA CATALOG 1927	TEDDY-BEAR, NO-NO	14.2	LONG HAIRED SILK PLUSH, GOLDEN YELLOW OR BRN, ARTIFICIAL SILK BOW, NO-NO MECHANISM	SQUEAKER				$400/500
2290		925/40			BEHA CATALOG 1927	TEDDY-BEAR	15.75	LONG HAIRED SILK PLUSH, GOLDEN YELLOW OR BRN, ARTIFICIAL SILK BOW, DISC JOINTS	GROWLER				$400/500
2291		925/40B			BEHA CATALOG 1927	TEDDY-BEAR, NO-NO	15.75	LONG HAIRED SILK PLUSH, GOLDEN YELLOW OR BRN, ARTIFICIAL SILK BOW, DISC JOINTS, NO-NO	GROWLER				$500/600

REF #	EAN #	HERMANN OLD #	ALSO SEE	LIMITED NUMBER	DATA FROM	NAME	INCHES TALL	DESCRIPTION	VOICE	HANGING BOOKLET	ARM TAG	COMPANY LOGO	CURRENT RETAIL
2292		925/50			BEHA CATALOG 1927	TEDDY-BEAR	19.6	LONG HAIRED SILK PLUSH, GOLDEN YELLOW OR BRN, ARTIFICIAL SILK BOW, DISC JOINTS	GROWLER				$500/600
2293		925/50B			BEHA CATALOG 1927	TEDDY-BEAR, NO-NO	19.6	LONG HAIRED SILK PLUSH, GOLDEN YELLOW OR BRN, ARTIFICIAL SILK BOW, DISC JOINTS, NO-NO	GROWLER				$550/750
2294		925/60			BEHA CATALOG 1927	TEDDY-BEAR	23.6	LONG HAIRED SILK PLUSH, GOLDEN YELLOW, ARTIFICIAL SILK BOW, DISC JOINTS	GROWLER	NO	NO	NO	$550/750
2295		925/60B			BEHA CATALOG 1927	TEDDY-BEAR, NO-NO	23.6	LONG HAIRED SILK PLUSH, GOLDEN YELLOW OR BRN, ARTIFICIAL SILK BOW, DISC JOINTS, NO-NO	GROWLER				$750/1000
2296		925/70			BEHA CATALOG 1927	TEDDY-BEAR	28.3	LONG HAIRED SILK PLUSH, GOLDEN YELLOW OR BRN, ARTIFICIAL SILK BOW, DISC JOINTS	GROWLER				$750/1000
2297		925/80			BEHA CATALOG 1927	TEDDY-BEAR	31	LONG HAIRED SILK PLUSH, GOLDEN YELLOW OR BRN, ARTIFICIAL SILK BOW, DISC JOINTS	GROWLER				$1,000+
2298		925/90			BEHA CATALOG 1927	TEDDY-BEAR	35	LONG HAIRED SILK PLUSH, GOLDEN YELLOW OR BRN, ARTIFICIAL SILK BOW, DISC JOINTS	GROWLER				$1,000+
2299		925/100			BEHA CATALOG 1927	TEDDY-BEAR	39.4	LONG HAIRED SILK PLUSH, GOLDEN YELLOW OR BRN, ARTIFICIAL SILK BOW, DISC JOINTS	GROWLER				$1,000+
2300		925/40			BOOK CIRCA '20 PG 47	TEDDY BEAR	11.8	SHORT PILE, GOLD/YELLOW W/BOWS, STIFF HEAD					$1,000+
2301		925/60B			BOOK CIRCA '20 PG 47	TEDDY BEAR	23.6	LONG PILE, GOLD/YELLOW W/BOWS, HEAD TURNS					$1,000+
2302	92525 5				1991 PRICE LIST	TEDDY 2000	9.8						$1/50
2303	92630 6				1991 PRICE LIST	TEDDY 2000	11.8						$1/50
2304	92635 1				1991 PRICE LIST	TEDDY 2000	13.8						$1/50
2305	92650 4				1991 PRICE LIST	TEDDY 2000	19.7						$1/50
2306	92715 0				1991 PRICE LIST	TEDDY 2000	5.9						$1/50
2307	92840 9				1991 PRICE LIST	TEDDY 2000	15.75						$1/50
2308	92923 9				1992 PRICE LIST	TEDDY 2000	9.5						$1/50
2309	93020 4				1992 PRICE LIST	TEDDY 2000	7.9						$1/50
2310	93035 8				1991 PRICE LIST	TEDDY 2000	13.8						$1/50
2311	93114 0				1991 PRICE LIST	TEDDY 2000	5.5						$1/50
2312	93135 5				1991 PRICE LIST	TEDDY 2000	13.8						$1/50
2313	93226 0				1991 PRICE LIST	TEDDY 2000	10.2						$1/50
2314	93245 1				1992 PRICE LIST	TEDDY 2000	17.7						$1/50
2315	93246 8				1991 PRICE LIST	TEDDY 2000	18.1						$1/50
2316	93245 1				1991 PRICE LIST	TEDDY 2000	17.8						$1/50
2317	93250 5				1991 PRICE LIST	TEDDY 2000	19.7						$1/50
2318	93270 3				1991 PRICE LIST	TEDDY 2000	27.6						$1/50
2319	93317 5				1991 PRICE LIST	TEDDY 2000	6.7						$1/50
2320	93330 4				1991 PRICE LIST	TEDDY 2000	11.8						$1/50
2321	93340 3				1991 PRICE LIST	TEDDY 2000	15.75						$1/50
2322	93417 2				1992 PRICE LIST	TEDDY 2000	6.7						$1/50
2323	93518 8				1992 PRICE LIST	TEDDY 2000	7						$1/50
2324	93540 9				1992 PRICE LIST	TEDDY 2000	15.75						$1/50
2325	93620 6				1992 PRICE LIST	TEDDY 2000	7.9						$1/50
2326	93635 0				1992 PRICE LIST	TEDDY 2000	13.8						$1/50
2327		9000.1	98001 8		1996 CATALOG	POSTER, RIDING A HORSE							$10
2328		9000.2	98002 5		1988 PRICE LIST	POSTER							$10
2329		9000.3	98003 2		1988 PRICE LIST	POSTER							$10
2330		9000.4	95001 1		1996 CATALOG	TEA SET, MINI PORCELAIN		8 PIECES, REPLICA OF 1930					$48
2331		9000.4	98004 9		1989 PRICE LIST	POSTER							$10
2332		9002.4	95001 1		1989 PRICE LIST	TEA SET, MINI PORCELAIN		8 PIECES					$50
2333	95001 1		9000.4		1991 CATALOG	TEA SET, MINI PORCELAIN		8 PIECES, REPLICA OF 1930					$41
2334	95001 1		9002.4		1989 PRICE LIST	TEA SET, MINI PORCELAIN		8 PIECES, REPLICA OF 1930					$50
2335	95003 5				1994 PRICE LIST	CHINA, HERMANN TEDDY NURSERY		15PCS					$73
2336	95005 9				1992 CATALOG	PLATE, BEAR	6.7 DIA	CERAMIC, ROUND					$16
2337	95005 9			3,000	1991 PRICE LIST	BOWL, ROUND		CERAMIC					$16
2338	95006 6				1992 CATALOG	PLATE, BEAR	4 DIA	CERAMIC PLATE					$11
2339	95006 6				1991 PRICE LIST	BOWL, HEART SHAPED	2 X 2 X 2 X 1	CERAMIC					$21
2340	95007 3				1992 CATALOG	MUG, BEAR	1.6	CERAMIC					$20
2341	95007 3				1991 PRICE LIST	PIGGY BANK		CERAMIC					$20
2342	95011 0				1991 PRICE LIST	TEA SET, MINI PORCELAIN		8 PIECES, REPLICA OF 1930					$35
2343	95013 4				1996 PRICE LIST	TEA SET, MINI PORCELAIN		8 PIECES, REPLICA OF 1930					$71
2344	95015 8				1996 PRICE LIST	BOWL, ROUND		CERAMIC, REPLICA OF 1930					$15
2345	95016 5				1996 PRICE LIST	BOWL, HEART SHAPED		CERAMIC, REPLICA OF 1930					$10

REF #	EAN #	HERMANN OLD #	ALSO SEE	LIMITED NUMBER	DATA FROM	NAME	INCHES TALL	DESCRIPTION	VOICE	HANGING BOOKLET	ARM TAG	COMPANY LOGO	CURRENT RETAIL
2346	95017 2				1996 PRICE LIST	PIGGY BANK		CERAMIC, REPLICA OF 1930					$20
2347	95018 9				1996 PRICE LIST	VASE, 1930 REPLICA		CERAMIC					$15
2348	95021 9				1997 PRICE LIST	PICNIC BASKET		PICNIC BASKET W/ PORCELAIN TEA SET W/11 PCS					$53
2349	95023 3				1997 PRICE LIST	CHINA, NURSERY		CHINA SET W/GOLD RIM 15 PCS					$78
2350	95025 7				1997 PRICE LIST	BOWL, ROUND		CERAMIC					$17
2351	95027 1				1997 PRICE LIST	PIGGY BANK		CERAMIC					$20
2352	95029 5				1997 PRICE LIST	MUG		CERAMIC					$17
2353	95030 1			1,000	1996 PRICE LIST	WRIST WATCH		BEARS ON STRAP, CLEAR PLASTIC STRAP				STAMPED	$117
2354	95031 8			1,000	1996 PRICE LIST	WRIST WATCH		FACE IS SIR ARTUR, TAN MOTTLED PLASTIC STRAP				STAMPED	$60
2355	95032 5				1996 PRICE LIST	WRIST WATCH		FACE IS TRADITIONAL BEAR WITH TAN LEATHER STRAP					$65
2356	95033 2			2,000	1997 PRICE LIST	WRIST WATCH							$60
2357	95034 9			2,000	1997 PRICE LIST	WRIST WATCH							$78
2358	95035 6			2,000	1997 PRICE LIST	WRIST WATCH							$93
2359	95037 0				1997 PRICE LIST	ALARM CLOCK		BIRTHDAY CHARLIE					$21
2360	95038 7				1997 PRICE LIST	ALARM CLOCK		FATHER & SON					$26
2361	95040 0				1997 PRICE LIST	KEY RING, TEDDY		SILVER PLATED WITH CASE					$37
2362	95040 8				1993 PRICE LIST	KEY RING, TEDDY							$37
2363	95041 5/7?				1993 PRICE LIST	BROOCH, TEDDY							$60
2364	95042 2/4?				1993 PRICE LIST	BROOCH, TEDDY							$60
2365	95043 1				1995 CATALOG	PIN, BEAR LABEL	0.375	GOLD PLATED METAL BEAR W/EARRING TYPE PIN & CLASP					
2366	95043 9				1993 PRICE LIST	PIN, TEDDY							
2367	95049 5				1992 PRICE LIST	CHAIN, GOLDEN							
2368	95050 9				1991 PRICE LIST	PENDANT	1.57	GOLDEN					
2369	95051 6				1991 PRICE LIST	PENDANT	1.57	GOLDEN					
2370	95052 3				1991 PRICE LIST	PIN, WOODEN							
2371	95053 0				1992 PRICE LIST	PIN	1.57	ENAMEL					
2372	95054 7				1992 PRICE LIST	EARRING	0.6	ENAMEL					
2373	95101 8				1990 PRICE LIST	DESK W/BENCH		SCHOOLDESK & BENCH FOR 7.9" BEARS					$58
2374	95105 6				1994 PRICE LIST	LECTERN		PODIUM (DESK)					$34
2375	95106 3				1997 XMAS FLYER	SLED	7.9	WOOD, NATURAL	NONE	NO	NO	NO	$37
2376	95120 9				1997 PRICE LIST	BENCH	5	WROUGHT IRON AND WOOD					$27
2377	95121 6				1997 PRICE LIST	BENCH	9	WROUGHT IRON AND WOOD					$33
2378	95201 5				1990 PRICE LIST	SATCHEL, LEATHER		FOR 7.9" BEAR					$16
2379	95203 9				1990 PRICE LIST	RUCKSACK		FOR 7.9" BEAR					$8
2380	95204 6				1992 PRICE LIST	GROWLER VOICE							$6
2381	95301 2				1992 PRICE LIST	STAND, BEAR 9-15CM							$9
2382	95302 9				1992 PRICE LIST	STAND, BEAR 18-30 CM							$10
2383	95303 6				1992 PRICE LIST	STAND, BEAR 26-46 CM							$15
2384	95311 1				1998 PRICE LIST	STAND, BEAR 9-15 CM							$7
2385	95500 9				1990 PRICE LIST	CHEST, SML TO HOLD BEARS		UNPAINTED WOOD					$1,102
2386	95501 6				1995 PRICE LIST	DEN FOR TEDDY BEARS		UNPAINTED WOOD FOR TEDDY BEARS UP TO 9.8" TALL					$732
2387	95502 3				1995 PRICE LIST	FURNITURE FOR BEAR DEN		UNPAINTED WOOD-ROCKING CHAIR, CHAIR, TABLE & BED					$122
2388	95503 0				1995 PRICE LIST	SHOP FOR TEDDIES		UNPAINTED WOOD FOR TEDDY BEARS UP TO 11.8" TALL					$453
2389	95505 4				1995 PRICE LIST	CASE ONLY FOR 15705 2							$110
2390	95510 8				1995 PRICE LIST	BENCH, WOODEN		UNPAINTED WOOD				WOOD TEDDY	$74
2391	95521 4				1995 PRICE LIST	TABLE		UNPAINTED WOOD; FOR BEARS UP TO 11.8" TALL					$96
2392	95522 1				1995 PRICE LIST	SETTEE		UNPAINTED WOOD; FOR BEARS UP TO 11.8" TALL					$153
2393	95523 8				1995 PRICE LIST	CHAIR, ROCKING		UNPAINTED WOOD; FOR BEARS UP TO 11.8" TALL					$143
2394	95524 5				1995 PRICE LIST	CHAIR, ARM		UNPAINTED WOOD; FOR BEARS UP TO 11.8" TALL					$122
2395	95525 2				1995 PRICE LIST	CRADLE		UNPAINTED WOOD; FOR BEARS UP TO 11.8" TALL					$169
2396	95601 3				1997 CATALOG	GIFT BOX	7.9	PRINTED BOX					$3
2397	95602 0				1997 CATALOG	GIFT BOX	11.8	PRINTED BOX					$5
2398	95603 7				1997 CATALOG	GIFT BOX	15.6	PRINTED BOX					$8
2399		960/50			BOOK CIRCA 1920	TEDDY BEAR, PG 47	19.6	LONG PILE, GOLD/YELLOW W/BOWS, STIFF HEAD					$200/300
2400		960/60B			BOOK CIRCA 1920	TEDDY BEAR, PG 47	23.6	LONG PILE, GOLD/YELLOW W/BOWS, HEAD TURNS					$250/350
2401	96030 0				1990 PRICE LIST	JACKET & PANTS							
2402	96031 7				1992 PRICE LIST	JACKET & PANTS							
2403	96040 9				1990 PRICE LIST	JACKET & PANTS							
2404	96041 6				1992 PRICE LIST	JACKET & PANTS							
2405	96050 8				1990 PRICE LIST	JACKET & PANTS							
2406	96051 5				1992 PRICE LIST	JACKET & PANTS							
2407	96130 7				1990 PRICE LIST	DIRNDL DRESS & APRON		RED DRESS W/WHT APRON W/RED STRIPES					
2408	96131 4				1992 PRICE LIST	DIRNDL DRESS & APRON	FOR 11.8	RED DRESS W/WHT APRON W/RED STRIPES					
2409	96140 6				1990 PRICE LIST	DIRNDL DRESS & APRON		RED DRESS W/WHT APRON W/RED STRIPES					

REF #	EAN #	HERMANN OLD #	ALSO SEE	LIMITED NUMBER	DATA FROM	NAME	INCHES TALL	DESCRIPTION	VOICE	HANGING BOOKLET	ARM TAG	COMPANY LOGO	CURRENT RETAIL
2410	96141 3				1992 PRICE LIST	DIRNDL DRESS & APRON	FOR 15.8	RED DRESS W/WHT APRON W/RED STRIPES					
2411	96150 5				1990 PRICE LIST	DIRNDL DRESS & APRON		RED DRESS W/WHT APRON W/RED STRIPES					
2412	96151 2				1992 PRICE LIST	DIRNDL DRESS & APRON	FOR 19.7	RED DRESS W/WHT APRON W/RED STRIPES					
2413	96230 4				1990 PRICE LIST	SWEATER & PANTS		KNIT GRN PANTS W/WHT PULLOVER SWEATER					
2414	96231 1				1992 PRICE LIST	SWEATER & PANTS	FOR 11.8	KNIT GRN PANTS W/WHT PULLOVER SWEATER					
2415	96240 3				1990 PRICE LIST	SWEATER & PANTS		KNIT GRN PANTS W/WHT PULLOVER SWEATER					
2416	96241 0				1992 PRICE LIST	SWEATER & PANTS	FOR 15.8	KNIT GRN PANTS W/WHT PULLOVER SWEATER					
2417	96250 2				1990 PRICE LIST	SWEATER & PANTS		KNIT GRN PANTS W/WHT PULLOVER SWEATER					
2418	96251 9				1992 PRICE LIST	SWEATER & PANTS	FOR 19.7	KNIT GRN PANTS W/WHT PULLOVER SWEATER					
2419	96330 1				1990 PRICE LIST	CARDIGAN		BLUE AND WHT KNITTED CARDIGAN W/BLUE KNIT PANTS					
2420	96331 8				1992 PRICE LIST	CARDIGAN	FOR 11.8	BLUE AND WHT KNITTED CARDIGAN W/BLUE KNIT PANTS					
2421	96340 0				1990 PRICE LIST	CARDIGAN		BLUE AND WHT KNITTED CARDIGAN W/BLUE KNIT PANTS					
2422	96341 7				1992 PRICE LIST	CARDIGAN	FOR 15.8	BLUE AND WHT KNITTED CARDIGAN W/BLUE KNIT PANTS					
2423	96350 9				1990 PRICE LIST	CARDIGAN		BLUE AND WHT KNITTED CARDIGAN W/BLUE KNIT PANTS					
2424	96351 6				1992 PRICE LIST	CARDIGAN	FOR 19.7	BLUE AND WHT KNITTED CARDIGAN W/BLUE KNIT PANTS					
2425	96430 8				1990 PRICE LIST	SWEATER + CAP		NAUTICAL OUTFIT, BLUE & WHT ONE PIECE W/WHT CAP					
2426	96431 5				1992 PRICE LIST	SWEATER + CAP	FOR 11.8	NAUTICAL OUTFIT, BLUE & WHT ONE PIECE W/WHT CAP					
2427	96440 7				1990 PRICE LIST	SWEATER + CAP		NAUTICAL OUTFIT, BLUE & WHT ONE PIECE W/WHT CAP					
2428	96441 4				1992 PRICE LIST	SWEATER + CAP	FOR 15.8	NAUTICAL OUTFIT, BLUE & WHT ONE PIECE W/WHT CAP					
2429	96450 6				1990 PRICE LIST	SWEATER + CAP		NAUTICAL OUTFIT, BLUE & WHT ONE PIECE W/WHT CAP					
2430	96451 3				1992 PRICE LIST	SWEATER + CAP	FOR 19.7	NAUTICAL OUTFIT, BLUE & WHT ONE PIECE W/WHT CAP					
2431	96530 5				1994 PRICE LIST	SAILOR OUTFIT		NAUTICAL DRESS W/BLUE BOW					
2432	96531 2				1992 PRICE LIST	SAILOR SUIT	FOR 11.8	NAUTICAL DRESS W/BLUE BOW					
2433	96540 4				1994 PRICE LIST	SAILOR OUTFIT		NAUTICAL DRESS W/BLUE BOW					
2434	96541 1				1992 PRICE LIST	SAILOR SUIT	FOR 15.8	NAUTICAL DRESS W/BLUE BOW					
2435	96550 3				1994 PRICE LIST	SAILOR OUTFIT		NAUTICAL DRESS W/BLUE BOW					
2436	96551 0				1992 PRICE LIST	SAILOR SUIT	FOR 19.7	NAUTICAL DRESS W/BLUE BOW					
2437	96630 2				1996 PRICE LIST	OVERALLS	FOR 11.8						
2438	96640 1				1996 PRICE LIST	OVERALLS	FOR 15.8						
2439	96650 0				1996 PRICE LIST	OVERALLS	FOR 19.7						
2440	96730 9				1996 PRICE LIST	PANTS	FOR 11.8						
2441	96740 8				1996 PRICE LIST	PANTS	FOR 15.8						
2442	96750 7				1996 PRICE LIST	PANTS	FOR 19.7						
2443	96830 6				1996 PRICE LIST	JACKET W/TWEED PANTS	FOR 11.8						
2444	96840 5				1996 PRICE LIST	JACKET W/TWEED PANTS	FOR 15.8						
2445	96050 4				1996 PRICE LIST	JACKET W/TWEED PANTS	FOR 19.7						
2446	97002 0				1994 PRICE LIST	OUTFIT, HIKING BOY	FOR 7.9						$44
2447	97021 7				1996 PRICE LIST	OUTFIT, HIKING BOY							
2448	97120 7				1994 PRICE LIST	OUTFIT, HIKING GIRL							$38
2449	97220 4				1994 PRICE LIST	COUNTRY CLOTHES							$38
2450	97320 1				1994 PRICE LIST	COUNTRY CLOTHES							$44
2451	97420 8				1994 PRICE LIST	SAILOR DRESS							$22
2452	97520 5				1994 PRICE LIST	SAILOR OUTFIT							$34
2453	97620 2				1996 PRICE LIST	OVERALLS							
2454	97720 9				1996 PRICE LIST	DRESS, LINEN							
2455	98001 8		9000.1		1996 CATALOG	POSTER, RIDING A HORSE							$6
2456	98002 5		9000.2		1988 PRICE LIST	POSTER, TEDDYHEAD							$6
2457	98003 2		9000.3		1988 PRICE LIST	POSTER, JUBILEE BEARS							$6
2458	98004 9		9000.4		1989 PRICE LIST	POSTER, STANDING BEARS							$6
2459	98005 6				1992 PRICE LIST	POSTER, SAILOR							$6
2460	98006 3				1996 PRICE LIST	POSTER, "SIR ARTUR"							$6
2461	98007 0				1996 PRICE LIST	POSTER, ROMANCE IN ROTHENBERG							$6
2462	98008 7				1996 PRICE LIST	POSTER, DEN OF BEARS							$6
2463	98009 4				1996 PRICE LIST	POSTER, BIRTHDAY CHARLIE							$6
2464	98010 0				1997 PRICE LIST	POSTER, MINIATURES							$6
2465	98011 7				1997 PRICE LIST	POSTER, BENJAMIN							$6
2466	98012 4				1997 PRICE LIST	POSTER, ALASKA BEARS							$6
2467	98013 1				1998 PRICE LIST	POSTER, BEAR W/CUB							$6
2468	98014 8				1998 PRICE LIST	POSTER, BEARS IN DESERT							$6
2469	98100 8				1990 PRICE LIST	CATALOG, K'90							$10
2470	98104 6				1994 PRICE LIST	CATALOG, K'94/95							$10
2471	98104 6				1996 PRICE LIST	CATALOG, K'96/97							$10
2472	98105 3				1998 PRICE LIST	CATALOG, K'98/99							

REF #	EAN #	HERMANN OLD #	ALSO SEE	LIMITED NUMBER	DATA FROM	NAME	INCHES TALL	DESCRIPTION	VOICE	HANGING BOOKLET	ARM TAG	COMPANY LOGO	CURRENT RETAIL
2473	98150 3				1994 PRICE LIST	BOOK, GERMAN							$60
2474	98151 0				1994 PRICE LIST	BOOK, ENGLISH		HERMANN HISTORY					$60
2475	98210 4				1996 PRICE LIST	TEDDY BEAR 2000 SIGN							
2476	98211 1				1992 PRICE LIST	LOGO, TEDDY SIGN	4.3 DIA	RED PLASTIC					$18
2477	98212 8				1993 PRICE LIST	STICKER, TEDDY SIGN	5" DIA						$4
2478	98230 2				1990 CATALOG	STICKER, TEDDY SIGN	12" DIA						$5
2479		985/25			1982 PRICE LIST	DOG							$75/125
2480	99001 7				1996 CATALOG	BAG, PLASTIC TEDDY	15 X 20	PLASTIC PRINTED					$.05 each
2481	99002 4				1989 PRICE LIST	POSTCARDS, STANDING BEARS							
2482	99003 1				1990 PRICE LIST	POSTCARD, CHEF OTTO							
2483	99004 8				1990 PRICE LIST	POSTCARD, SWEET ROSE							
2484	99005 5				1990 PRICE LIST	POSTCARD, SHEPHERD							
2485	99005 5				1998 PRICE LIST	SHOPPING BAG, 6 PCS		PACKAGE OF 6 VAGABOND SHOPPING BAGS; DUPL #					
2486	99006 2				1992 PRICE LIST	POSTCARD, SAILOR							
2487	99007 9				1993 PRICE LIST	POSTCARD, SIR ARTHUR							
2488	99008 6				1994 PRICE LIST	POSTCARD							
2489	99009 3				1994 PRICE LIST	POSTCARD							
2490	99010 7				1994 PRICE LIST	POSTCARD							
2491	99011 4				1994 PRICE LIST	POSTCARD							
2492	99012 1				1996 PRICE LIST	POSTCARD, GARDEN PARTY							
2493	99013 8				1996 PRICE LIST	POSTCARD, BEAR IN BAMBERG							
2494	99014 5				1996 PRICE LIST	POSTCARD, FOR YOU							
2495	99015 2				1996 PRICE LIST	POSTCARD, FRIENDS							
2496	99016 1				1998 PRICE LIST	POSTCARD, ASS'TD		3 SETS OF 4 DIFFERENT POSTCARDS					

Chapter 8: Jesco/Rubin and Kathy Ann Dolls Teddy Bears

The following are Jesco Division of Rubin Co. products made by Hermann Teddy Original and also produced for "Kathy Ann Dolls." The bears come in various colors: CH = Chocolate; CI = Cinnamon; SU = Sugar (cream/white); CO = Cocoa; CA = Caramel; LI = Licorice (black); GO = Gold; GR = Grey. NO = Nougat. Bear number gives size in tenths of an inch, e.g., CA 40 = 4.0"; CA 55 = 5.5"; CA 100 = 10"; CA 140 = 14".

REF #	EAN #	HERMANN OLD #	ALSO SEE	LIMITED NUMBER	DATA FROM	NAME	INCHES TALL	DESCRIPTION	VOICE	HANGING BOOKLET	ARM TAG	COMPANY LOGO	CURRENT RETAIL
2501		CA 40			1985 JESCO + 1988 CAT	SWEET TEDDYS	4	CARAMEL, AVAILABLE IN 7 SIZES					$50/100
2502		CA 55			1988 JESCO CATALOG	SWEET TEDDYS	5.5	CARAMEL W/RED BOW					$75/125
2503		CA 75			HERMANN JESCO (1985)	TRAINED BEAR, WHEELED	5H X 6L	CARAMEL MOHAIR, NOT JTD, ON RUBBER TIRES W/CHAIN IN NOSE	NONE	NO	BRN	MTL W/PAPER	$100/150
2504		CA 75			HERMANN JESCO (1980)	TRAINED BEAR, WHEELED	5H X 6L	CARAMEL MOHAIR, NOT JTD, ON RUBBER TIRES W/CHAIN IN NOSE	NONE	NO	GRN	RED PAPER	$100/150
2505		CA 140			1990? JESCO	SWEET TEDDYS	14	CARAMEL WITH PICNIC BASKET					$150/200
2506		CA 240			SEE 62/60	ROBIN HOOD, ORIGINAL	24	COCOA MOHAIR DRESSED AS ROBIN HOOD?, PLASTIC EYES, FULLY JTD	GROWLER	YES	GRN	RED PLASTIC	$250/350
2507		CA 330			SEE 62/85	SWEET TEDDY	33	COCOA MOHAIR WITH RED & GRN STRIPED BOW, PLASTIC EYES	GROWLER	NO	GRN	RED PLASTIC	$550/750
2508		CH 40			1985 JESCO	SWEET TEDDYS	4	CHOCOLATE, AVAILABLE IN 7 SIZES					$50/100
2509		CH 80			1988 JESCO CATALOG	SWEET TEDDYS	8	CHOCOLATE W/PLAID BOW					$100/150
2510		CH 140	62/35/1			SWEET TEDDYS	14	CHOCOLATE W/PLAID BOW	GROWLER	SHORT BKLT	BRN	GLD PLASTIC	$150/200
2511		CI 40			1985 JESCO	SWEET TEDDYS	4	CINNAMON, AVAILABLE IN 7 SIZES					$50/100
2512		CI 75			SEE 300/16/3	TRAINED BEAR, WHEELED	5H X 6L	CINNAMON	NONE	NO	BRN	MTL W/PAPER	$100/150
2513		CI 80			1988 JESCO CATALOG	SWEET TEDDYS	8	CINNAMON					$100/150
2514		CI 140			1990? JESCO	SWEET TEDDYS	14	CINNAMON W/GOLD BOW					$150/200
2515		CO 40			1985 JESCO	SWEET TEDDYS	4	COCOA, AVAILABLE IN 7 SIZES					$50/100
2516		CO 180			1980s JESCO	TEDDY BEAR	18	COCOA LONG PILE MOHAIR, PLASTIC EYES, W/DARK PLAID TIE	GROWLER	NO	BRN	RED PLASTIC	$200/300
2517		GO 80			1988 JESCO CATALOG	SWEET TEDDYS	8	OLD GOLD MOHAIR W/RED BOW					$100/150
2518		GR 55			1990? JESCO	TEDDY BEAR, GREY CUB	5.5	GREY W/RED BOW					$75/125
2519		GR 80			1990? JESCO	TEDDY BEAR, GREY CUB	8	GREY W/RED BOW					$100/150
2520		GR 100			1990? JESCO	TEDDY BEAR, GREY CUB	10	GREY W/RED BOW					$125/175
2521		GR 140			1990? JESCO	TEDDY BEAR, GREY CUB	14	GREY W/RED BOW					$150/200
2522		H 0001			1985 JESCO	TO GRNDMOTHER'S HOUSE	4	2 BEARS ON SLED + 3 BEARS IN CHAIRS + XMAS TREE					$250/350
2523		H 0002			1985 JESCO	HOME FOR HOLIDAYS	4	2 BEARS ON SLED + 3 BEARS IN CHAIRS + XMAS TREE					$250/350
2524		LI 40			1985 JESCO	SWEET TEDDYS	4	LICORICE, AVAILABLE IN 7 SIZES					$50/100
2525		LI 55 OR 62/14			BEAR SHOW 1995	SWEET TEDDYS	5.5	LICORICE, FULLY JTD, W/BOOKLET HAVING BOTH #'S					$75/125
2526		LI 75			HERMANN JESCO	TRAINED BEAR, WHEELED	5H X 6L	BLK W/NOSE CHAIN, RUBBER TIRED WHEELS	NONE	NO	BRN	NONE	$100/150
2527		LI 80			HERMANN JESCO RUBIN	BLK BEAR BRN NOSE	8	BLACK W/RED BOW, SIMILAR TO 16620 7	NONE	SHORT BKLT	GRN	NONE	$100/150
2528		LI 100			HERMANN JESCO RUBIN	BLK BEAR BRN NOSE	10	BLACK W/RED BOW, SIMILAR TO 16630 6	NONE	SHORT BKLT	GRN	NONE	$125/175
2529		LI 140			1990? JESCO	SWEET TEDDYS	14	BLACK W RED BOW					$150/200
2530		LI 140N			1990? JESCO	SWEET TEDDYS	14	BLACK W/RED STRIPED BOW					$150/200
2531		LI 200			HERMANN JESCO RUBIN	BLK BEAR BRN NOSE	20	BLK W/RED BOW, W/BOOKLET NO #, IS 62/50 SCHWARZ	GROWLER	YES	GRN	RED PLASTIC	$250/350
2532		NO 70			1988 JESCO CATALOG	SWEET THING	7	NOUGAT W/BOW					$125/175
2532a		NO 75			1988 JESCO CATALOG	SWEET THING	7.5	NOUGAT W/BOW					$125/175
2533		NO 140N			1990? JESCO	SWEET THING	14	NOUGAT W/LAVENDAR BOW					$150/200
2534		S 0002	12035 3			SHEPHERD SET	14	DRESSED WITH TWO LAMBS	GROWLER	YES	BRN	RED PLASTIC	$200/300
2535		S 0003	6225HW	750	1988 JESCO CATALOG	SANDBOX W/2 BEARS	8 & 10	INCLS ONE 8" NOUGAT BEAR (62/20/4), ONE 10" WHT BEAR (82/26 MW)	NONE	YES	BRN	RED PAPER	$200/300
2536		SU 40			1988 JESCO CATALOG	SWEET TEDDYS	4	SUGAR (WHITE), AVAILABLE IN 7 SIZES					$50/100
2537		SU 55			1985 JESCO	SWEET TEDDYS	5.5	AVAILABLE IN 6 COLORS					$75/125
2538		SU 70			1985 SEE 62/17w	SWEET TEDDYS	7	ALSO AVAILABLE IN 6 COLORS	NONE	YES	BRN	MISSING	$100/150
2539		SU 75			SEE 300/16	SWEET TEDDYS	5H X 6L	BEAR ON WHEELS, ALSO AVAILABLE IN 6 COLORS					$100/150
2540		SU 80			1985 JESCO	SWEET TEDDYS	8	AVAILABLE IN 6 COLORS					$100/150
2541		SU 100			1985 JESCO	SWEET TEDDYS	10	AVAILABLE IN 6 COLORS					$125/175
2542		SU120			1985 JESCO	SWEET TEDDYS	12	AVAILABLE IN 6 COLORS	YES	YES	BRN DBL	RED PLASTIC	$125/175
2543		SU140			SEE 62/35	SWEET TEDDYS	14	AVAILABLE IN 6 COLORS					$150/200
2544		SU 190			1985 JESCO	SWEET TEDDYS	19	AVAILABLE IN 6 COLORS					$200/300
2545		SU 240			1985 JESCO	SWEET TEDDYS	24	AVAILABLE IN 6 COLORS					$250/350
2546		TS001				TEA SET							

Chapter 9: Bears with Unidentified Model Numbers

The following bears have been illustrated or listed in publications or are in the author's collection (MRF #), but have not been identified by Hermann's number.

REF #	EAN #	HERMANN OLD #	ALSO SEE	LIMITED NUMBER	DATA FROM	NAME	INCHES TALL	DESCRIPTION	VOICE	HANGING BOOKLET	ARM TAG	COMPANY LOGO	CURRENT RETAIL
2550					HERMANN 1986	SCHOOL SET	7.9 ; 14.2	14" TEACHER + 6 PUPILS, 8" TALL W/DESKS ETC. LISTED AT $750					$750/1000
2551			MRF "M"		HOCKENBERRY, 187	PANDA, 4 LEGGED	8.25L; 7.5H	BLK/WHT MOHAIR, FELT PADS, EXCELSIOR STUFFED, SWIVEL HEAD, NOSE CHAIN, C. 1960 MIRO COLL.	NONE	NO	NO	SML MTL + PAPER	$150/200
2552			MRF "N"		TB ENCY, 97	MINIBEAR C. 1948	4.7	SHORT GOLD MOHAIR PLUSH, GLASS EYES, NO PAW PADS, 3 CLAWS, EX- VOLP COLLECTION # 2200	NONE	NO	NO	NO	$300/400
2553			MRF "AH"		KALINKE VISIT	BEAR, SOFT 1982	4.7	BRN PLUSH (30% C, 70% ACRYLIC), WAS IN DOLL'S COAT POCKET PER ANNA KALINKE	NONE	NO	BRN	RED PAPER	$75/125
2554					2SIEVERLING, 71	TRAINED BEAR, WHEELED	6H X ?L	GOLD MOHAIR, PLASTIC EYES, NOT JTD, SYN STUFFED, ON RUBBER TIRES W/CHAIN IN NOSE					
2555					2SIEVERLING, 69	TEDDY BEAR, C. '79	5.5	WHT MOHAIR, SHEARED PAW PADS, PLASTIC EYES, FULLY JTD, MADE FOR P&E RUBIN		SML		PLASTIC	
2556					2SIEVERLING, 69	TEDDY BEAR, C. '79	7	WHT MOHAIR, SHEARED PAW PADS, PLASTIC EYES, FULLY JTD, MADE FOR P&E RUBIN		SML		PLASTIC	
2557					2SIEVERLING, 69	TEDDY BEAR, C. '79	7.9	WHT MOHAIR, SHEARED PAW PADS, PLASTIC EYES, FULLY JTD, MADE FOR P&E RUBIN		SML		PLASTIC	
2558					2SIEVERLING, 51	TEDDY BEAR, C. '84	7.9	LT BRN SILVER FROSTED 70% ACYRILIC, 30% COTTON, PLASTIC EYES, FULLY JTD			YES	PAPER	
2559					2SIEVERLING, 68	TEDDY BEAR, C. '70	9.5	BLK MOHAIR/WHT FACE & CHEST, PLASTIC EYES, FULLY JTD, STRAW STUFFED				GRN PAPER	
2560					2SIEVERLING, 68	TEDDY BEAR, C. '60	9.5	TAN MOHAIR W/AIR BRUSH ON FEET, FLESH TONE INNER OP/CL/MO, NOSE CHAIN, GLASS EYES, FULLY JTD				MTL W/PAPER	
2561					3SIEVERLING, 80	TEDDY BEAR, C. '55	9.5	TAN MOHAIR, SHORT SHEARED MUZZLE, GLASS EYES, FULLY JTD, STRAW STUFFING					
2562					HOCKENBERRY, 143	TEDDY BEAR, C. '60	9.5	TAN MOHAIR, SHEARED SNOUT-PADS, OPEN MOUTH & PADS, GLASS EYES, EXCELSIOR STUFFED, NO CHAIN	NONE	NO	NO	NO	
2563					TB & FRIENDS	TEDDY BEAR, C. '59	9.5	TAN MOHAIR, GLASS EYES; FULLY JTD; STRAW STUFFED			GRN	MTL W/PAPER	
2564					BIG BEAR BK, 123	TEDDY BEAR, C. '59	9.5	TAN MOHAIR, GLASS EYES, OPEN FELT MOUTH, TEDDY BABY TYPE, PLASTIC COLLAR	NO			SWINGING PAPER TAG	$200
2565					3SIEVERLING, 84	PANDA C. '50	9.5	STRING PLUSH, BLK NOSE , TAN FELT PADS, GLASS EYES, FULLY JTD, KAPOK STUFFING, OPEN MOUTH					
2566			MRF "AQ"		HOCKENBERRY, TBCOMP	BEAR, MUSICAL, MECH.	9.5	BEIGE MOHAIR, OPEN MOUTH, NOSE CHAIN, FULLY JTD, ON MUSIC STAND, SIGNED, YENKE COLL, 1950				MTL W/PAPER	$1500
2567					2SIEVERLING, 71	TEDDY BEAR, C. '82	10.2	GOLD MOHAIR, GOLD FELT PADS, PLASTIC EYES, FULLY JTD				MTL W/PAPER	$200/300
2568					2SIEVERLING, 69	TEDDY BEAR, C. '79	10.2	WHT MOHAIR, SHEARED PAW PADS, PLASTIC EYES, FULLY JTD, MADE FOR P&E RUBIN		SMALL		MTL W/PAPER	$200/300
2569					ULT. TB BOOK, 78	HORST 1953	10.2	BEIGE SHAGGY MOHAIR EXCELSIOR STUFFING, GLASS EYES SET LOW ,OPEN MOUTH, INSET SHAVED MUZZLE	SQKR			MTL W/PAPER	$200/300
2570					TB ENCY, 97	TEDDY BEAR, C. '50	10.2	BEIGE SHAGGY MOHAIR ON DARK WOVEN BACKING, CLIPPED MUZZLE, GLASS EYES, ZOTTY TYPE	SQKR			MTL W/PAPER	$200/300
2571			MRF "AG"		HOCKENBERRY, 140	TEDDY BEAR, C. '50	10.2	TAN MOHAIR, INSET SHEARED SNOUT, GLASS EYES, EXCELSIOR STUFFED, NO ID	SQKR	NONE	NONE	NONE	$200/300
2572					HOCKENBERRY, TBCOMP	TEDDY BEAR, C. '50	10.2	TAN MOHAIR, INSET MOHAIR SNOUT, GLASS EYES, FELT PADS, EXCELSIOR STUFFED, FULLY JTD, NO ID		NONE	NONE	NONE	$200/300
2573					BIG BEAR BK, 141	TEDDY BEAR	10.2	MOHAIR, PLASTIC EYES, LABELS AND TAGS		YES	YES	YES	$200/300
2574					BIG BEAR BK, 133	TEDDY BEAR, C. '60	10.2	TAN MOHAIR W/INSET MUZZLE, GLASS EYES, NO ID					$200/300
2575					2SIEVERLING, 52	TB W/TRICYCLE, C. '70	11	LT BRN HEAD & PAWS, WHT UPPER MUZZLE & INNER EARS W/PINK AIR BRUSHING, SITTING ON TRICYCLE					$250/350
2576			?		2SIEVERLING, 12	TEDDY BEAR, C. '82	11	FROSTED BRN MOHAIR, TAN PADS, FULLY JTD, STRAW STUFFD HD, 62 SERIES FOR RUBIN? #231 OR ?				RED PAPER	$250/350
2577					3SIEVERLING, 80	TEDDY BEAR, C. '70	11	TAN MOHAIR, MATCHING RAYON JERSEY PAW PADS, GLASS EYES, FULLY JTD			CLOTH	PAPER	$250/350
2578					HOCKENBERRY, 140	TEDDY BEAR, C. '50	11	TAN MOHAIR, INSET SHEARED SNOUT, GLASS EYES, EXCELSIOR STUFFED, NO ID		NONE	NONE	NONE	$300/400

REF #	EAN #	HERMANN OLD #	ALSO SEE	LIMITED NUMBER	DATA FROM	NAME	INCHES TALL	DESCRIPTION	VOICE	HANGING BOOKLET	ARM TAG	COMPANY LOGO	CURRENT RETAIL
2579					HOCKENBERRY, 137	TEDDY BEAR, C. '55	11	CARAMEL MOHAIR, SHEARED INSET SNOUT, GLASS EYES, FELT PADS, EXCELSIOR STUFFED, NO ID		NONE	NONE	NONE	$300/400
2580					HOCKENBERRY, 142	TEDDY BEAR, C. '65	11	BEIGE & PALE BEIGE FROSTED MOHAIR, TAN INSET SHEARED SNOUT, OPEN MOUTH, GLASS EYES, NO ID, ZOTTY		NONE	NONE	NONE	$200/300
2581					HOCKENBERRYTBCOMP	TEDDY BEAR, C. '57	11	TIPPPED MOHAIR, GLASS EYES, FELT PADS, EXCELSIOR STUFFED, FULLY JTD, NO ID, BARROWS COLL, ZOTTY		NONE	NONE	NONE	$250/300
2582					TB&FR 10/96, 130	TEDDY BEAR, C. '50	11	MOHAIR, FELT PADS, BRN GLASS EYES, HUMP BACK, NOSE BLK STITCHES HORIZ. SHORT BOXY FEET, LONG ARMS, SHAVED MUZZLE		NONE	NONE	NONE	$250/350
2583					TB ENCY, 97	TEDDY BEAR, C. '60	11.5	BLOND TIPPED SHAGGY DARK BRN MOHAIR, HEAD EXCELSIOR STUFFED REST SOFT STUFFED, BEIGE MUZZLE, ZOTTY					$250/350
2584					2SIEVERLING, 69	TEDDY BEAR, C. '79	11.8	WHT MOHAIR, SHEARED PAW PADS, PLASTIC EYES, FULLY JTD, MADE FOR P&E RUBIN		SMALL		PLASTIC	$250/350
2585					2SIEVERLING, 69	TEDDY BEAR, C. '78	11.8	GREY MINK, TAN PAWS,& MUZZLE, PLASTIC EYES, FULLY JTD, WOOD WOOL STUFFED, W/CHAIN				PAPER	$250/350
2586					2SIEVERLING, 68	TEDDY BEAR, C. '70	11.8	WHT SYN FUR, PLASTIC EYES, NOT JTD, WOOD SHAVINGS STUFFED, MADE FOR P&E RUBIN		YES	YES	YES	$250/350
2587					3SIEVERLING, 84	PANDA C. 1957	11.8	BLK/WHT MOHAIR, BLK FLOSS NOSE & MOUTH, TAN FELT PADS, GLASS EYES, FULLY JTD					$300/400
2588					4MULLINS GUIDE, 56	TEDDY BEAR, C. '50	11.8	GOLD MOHAIR, 3 CLAWS, GLASS EYES, FULLY JTD					$250/350
2589			MRF "AB"		STEVE HOWARD	TEDDY BEAR, C. '40	11.8	TAN MOHAIR, SET IN SHORT PILE MUZZLE, GLASS EYES, FULLY JTD, FELT PAWS, ORIG BOW	GROWLER	NONE	NONE	NONE	$250/350
2590					C. 1959	BEAR, CHAINED	11.8	TAN MOHAIR, OPEN MOUTH; SHEARED MUZZLE, EARS/PAW; BRUSHED CLAWS; GLASS EYES; FULLY JTD				GOLD PLASTIC	$250/350
2591			MRF "AM"		C. 1970	BEAR, CHAINED	11.8	TAN MOHAIR; OPEN MOUTH; SHEARED MUZZLE, FELT PAWS; GLASS EYES; FULLY JTD, MISSING CHAIN	SQKR	MISSING	MISSING	MISSING	$200/300
2592					TB REVIEW 10/97, 118	TEDDY BEAR, C. '59	11.8	LONG HAIRED, 3 PIECE MUZZLE, NO ID			NONE	NONE	$250/350
2593					2SIEVERLING, 70	' PAYNE' TOOTHACHE BEAR	11.8	COCOA MOHAIR, PLASTIC EYES, W/RAG ON SWOLLEN JAW, PLASTIC TOOTH NECKLACE, MADE FOR "BEAR WITH US" (ROHALY'S); LTD 1000, DBL TAGGED 'BEAR WITH US'				RED PLASTIC	$250/350
2594			MRF "AI"		KALINKE VISIT	TEDDY BEAR, C. '85	12.6	LONG DISTRESSED MOHAIR, LARGE EARS, JENNY KRANTZ DESIGN?, LTD TO 30 PIECES PER KALINKE, SHAVED SNOUT, SOFT FILLING	NONE	NO	NO	NO	$250/350
2595					3SIEVERLING, 77	TEDDY BEAR, C. '30	12.6	WHT MOHAIR, MATCHING PAW PADS, FULLY JTD STRAW STUFFED					$400/500
2596					2SIEVERLING, 47	TEDDY BEAR, C. '50	12.6	LONG OFF WHT MOHAIR, TAN PADS, LT BRN FLOSS NOSE, GLASS EYES, FULLY JTD, REISSUED 1985 AS SIEVERLING					$400/500
2597					3SIEVERLING TITLE PG	TEDDY BEAR, C. '30	12.6	ORIGINAL FOR HELEN SIEVERLING BEAR, GLASS EYES, FULLY JTD, STRAW STUFFED, BEIGE MOHAIR					$400/500
2598			MRF "AF"		HERMANN C. '30	BEAR, ORIGINAL	12.6	COCA MULTICOLOR PLUSH, GLASS EYES, FULLY JTD, STRAW STUFFED, INSET SHORT PILE NOSE	GROWLER	NONE	NONE	NONE	$450/550
2599			MRF "B"		HERMANN C. '30	BEAR W/NIGHTSHIRT	12.6	BEIGE, (POSSIBLY HERMANN SPIELWAREN), GLASS EYES, WORN	GROWLER	NONE	NONE	NONE	$450/550
2600			MRF "AL"		HERMANN C. '50	TEDDY BEAR	12.6	LT. BEIGE W/TAN INSET MUZZLE, DRALON (ACRYLIC) MOHAIR, GLASS EYES, FULLY JTD. BLUE BOW	SQKR	NONE	TAG	NONE	$250/300
2601					2SIEVERLING, 66	TEDDY BEAR, C. '60	14.2	COCOA DRALON W/YELLOW CHEST, OPEN MOUTH, GLASS EYES, FULLY JTD, SEE 90/SERIES					$400/500
2602					2SIEVERLING, 64	TEDDY BEAR, C. '72	14.2	WHT SYN MOHAIR, BRN PADS, GLASS EYES, FULLY JTD, MADE FOR P&E RUBIN				PLASTIC	$400/500
2603					HOCKENBERRY, 142	ZOTTY C. '65	14.2	BRN & TAN FROSTED MOHAIR, TAN INSET SHEARED SNOUT, OPEN MOUTH, GLASS EYES, NO ID		NONE	NONE	NONE	$400/500
2604					HOCKENBERRY, TBCOMP	ZOTTY C. '50	14.2	WHT MOHAIR, CLIPPED MUZZLE-EARS-PAWS, FELT PADS & MOUTH, GLASS EYES, WIRED LIMBS, NOSE CHAIN					$300/400
2605					HOCKENBERRY, 138	TEDDY BEAR, C. '55	14.2	BRN & TAN FROSTED MOHAIR, TAN INSET SHEARED SNOUT & INSIDE EARS, FELT PADS, GLASS EYES, NO ID		NONE	NONE	NONE	$400/500
2606					HOCKENBERRY, 139	TEDDY BEAR, C. '57	14.2	CARAMEL MOHAIR, TAN SHEARED SNOUT, GLASS EYES, NO ID		NONE	NONE	NONE	$400/500
2607					HOCKENBERRY, VOL II	TEDDY BEAR, C. '53	14.2	LONG CREAM MOHAIR, BRN TIPPED, INSET MUZZLE, SHORT HAIR, GLASS EYES FELT PADS, EXCELSIOR, NO MARKS, MARION HERMANN MEHLING COLLECTION	GROWLER				$350\400
2608					HOCKENBERRY, VOL II	TEDDY BEAR, C. '55	14.2	BRN MOHAIR, INSET MUZZLE, GLASS EYES, PADS REPLACED, EXCELSIOR FULLY JTD, KNIT SUIT NOT ORIGINAL		NONE	NONE	NONE	$275/300
2609					TBEAR&F JAN 93, 21	TEDDY BEAR, C. '30	14.2	BRN TIPPED MOHAIR SHORT PILE MUZZLE, GLASSS EYES, SHORT ARMS				MTL W/PAPER	$500/600
2610					TB ENCY, 31	TEDDY BEAR, C. '27	14.2	BRN TIPPED BLOND MOHAIR, FULLY JTD, STRAIGHT LEGS, CURVED TAPERING PAWS					$550/750
2611				500	TBEAR&F SEP 91, 51	MAX	14.2	BEIGE DISTRESSED MOHAIR, SUEDE PADS, PAISLEY TIE	GROWLER				$100/150

REF #	EAN #	HERMANN OLD #	ALSO SEE	LIMITED NUMBER	DATA FROM	NAME	INCHES TALL	DESCRIPTION	VOICE	HANGING BOOKLET	ARM TAG	COMPANY LOGO	CURRENT RETAIL
2612			MRF "E"		HERMANN, C. 1950	COSY-ZOTTY W/SQUEALER	15	BEIGE GLASS EYES, COTTON PLUSH		NONE	NONE	NONE	$350/400
2613					HOCKENBERRY, 138	TEDDY BEAR, C. '50	15	CARAMEL MOHAIR W/SHEARED INSET SNOUT, FELT PADS, GLASS EYES, EXCELSIOR STUFFED, NO ID		NONE	NONE	NONE	$300/400
2614					TB ENCY, 154	TEDDY 1983, NO JOINTS	15	RUST SYN PLUSH W/POLYESTER SOFT FILLING, PLASTIC EYES			GRN	GRN PAPER	$300/400
2615					TBEAR & F	TEDDY BEAR, C. '78	15	TAN COTTON PLUSH W/YEL ACROSS CHEST; FULLY JTD; GLASS EYES; STRAW & KAPOK STUFFED					$500/600
2616			MRF "Z"		STEVE HOWARD	TEDDY BEAR, C. '30	15	BEIGE MOHAIR, SHORT BEIGE SET IN SNOUT, GLASS EYES, FELT PAWS, FULLY JTD	GROWLER	NONE	NONE	NONE	$475/550
2617					4MULLINS GUIDE, 57	TEDDY BEAR, C. '40	15	BEIGE MOHAIR, SHORT BEIGE SET IN SNOUT, GLASS EYES					$300/400
2618					HOCKENBERRY VOL II	TEDDY BEAR, C. '57	15	TAN MOHAIR, GLASS EYES, INSET SNOUT, OPEN MOUTH, CLIPPED & AIRBRUSHED FEET, EXCELSIOR, ALL JTD	NONE	NONE	NONE	NONE	$450/500
2619					BIG BEAR BK, 123	TEDDY BEAR, C. '50	15	GOLD MOHAIR, GLASS EYES, NO ID, 350-400 VALUATION					$400/500
2619A			MRF "C"		HERMANN, C. 1960	TEDDY BEAR	15.75	LIGHT BUFF (BEIGE?) MOHAIR, PLASTIC EYES EXCELSIOR STUFFING	GROWLER	NONE	GRN	GLD PLASTIC	$400/500
2620			MRF "AO"		TEDDY BEAR	TEDDY BEAR, C. '50	15.75	LONG BEIGE MOHAIR, SHEARED SNOUT, GLASS EYES, EXCELSIOR STUFFED, NO ID	GROWLER	NONE	NONE	NONE	$400/500
2621					HOCKENBERRY, 139	TEDDY BEAR, C. '50	15.75	CARAMEL MOHAIR, SHEARED SNOUT, GLASS EYES, EXCELSIOR STUFFING, NO ID		NONE	NONE	NONE	$400/500
2622					2SIEVERLING, 14	TEDDY BEAR, C. '30	15.75	GOLD MOHAIR, SHEARED MUZZLE, GLASS EYES, FULLY JTD, STRAW STUFFED					$400/500
2623					2SIEVERLING, 13	TEDDY BEAR, C. '50	15.75	GOLD MOHAIR, GLASS EYES, FULLY JTD, STRAW STUFFED, BLUE VEST, WHT CUMMERBUND RED EDGING					$400/500
2624					3SIEVERLING, 78	TEDDY BEAR, C. '49	15.75	UNKWN FABRIC, GLASS EYES, FULLY JTD, STRAW STUFFING NO ID		NONE	NONE	NONE	$400/500
2625					HOCKENBERRY, 138	TEDDY BEAR, C. '50	15.75	BEIGE MOHAIR, SHEARED SNOUT, GLASS EYES, EXCELSIOR STUFFED, NO ID		NONE	NONE	NONE	$400/500
2625A			MRF "AP"		HERMANN, C. 1950		15.75	BEIGE MOHAIR, SHEARED SNOUT, GLASS EYES, EXCELSIOR STUFFED	SQUEAKER	NONE	NONE	NONE	$400/500
2626					HOCKENBERRY TBCOMP	TEDDY BEAR, C. '80	15.75	LAVENDER TIPPED MOHAIR, LTD EDITION 2000, LABEL IN SEAM, OAKLEY COLLECTION			YES	PLASTIC	$400/500
2627					HOCKENBERRY, 141	TEDDY BEAR, C. '60	15.75	TAN MOHAIR W/INSET SNOUT, FELT PADS, GLASS EYES, EXCELSIOR STUFFED, W/GRAY FELT LEDERHOSEN					$400/500
2628			MRF "T"		TEDDY BEAR	TEDDY BEAR, C. '60	15.75	HONEY PLUSH, FELT PAWS, FULLY JTD. PLASTIC EYES	GROWLER	NONE	NONE	NONE	$400/500
2629					2SIEVERLING, 71	FUDDO 1982 NOT MADE	15.75	BLK MOHAIR, PINK NOSE, WHT PLASTIC CARTOON EYES, RED BOW, SALLY BOWEN BOOK, DBL TAG, SAMPLED ONLY!	GROWLER		GRN	RED PLASTIC	$400/500
2629A			MRF "AJ"		HERMANN, 1980	MONKEY	15.75	REDDISH BROWN MOHAIR, EXCELSIOR STUFFED	NO	NO	NO	MTL W/PAPER	$150/250
2630					3SIEVERLING, 78	TEDDY BEAR, C. '55	16.5	TAN MOHAIR, BLK FLOSS NOSE, RED FELT TONGUE, MOHAIR PADS, GLASS EYES, FULLY JTD, STRAW+KAPOK STUFFING					$500/600
2631					4MULLINS GUIDE, 57	TEDDY BEAR, C. '40	16.5	BEIGE MOHAIR, SHORT BEIGE SET IN SNOUT, GLASS EYES					$500/600
2632					BIALOSKY TB CAT, 195	BALLERINA, PRE-1980	16.5	MOHAIR, JTD LIMBS, GROWLER, BALLET ITEMS NOT ORIGINAL					$500/600
2633					HOCKENBERRY, 139	TEDDY BEAR, C. '50	16.5	LT BRN MOHAIR, SHEARED SNOUT, GLASS EYES, EXC STUFF, NO ID		NONE	NONE	NONE	$500/600
2634			MRF "F"			TEDDY BEAR, C. '30	16.5	OLD GOLD SHORT PILE MOHAIR, INSET CLIPPED MUZZLE, W/EXCELSIOR STUFFING, GLASS EYES, WORN PADS	GROWLER	NONE	NONE	NONE	$500/600
2635					TBEAR BOOK, 46	SANTA CLAUS 1927	16.5	CIN TIPPED BEIGE MOHAIR, SET IN TAN MUZZLE, W/EXCELSIOR STUFFING, GLASS EYES	GROWLER			MTL W/PAPER	$500/600
2636					TB ENCY, 96	TEDDY BEAR, C. '60	16.5	NUTMEG MOHAIR PLUSH, EXCELSIOR STUFFING, GLASS EYES, INSET CLIPPED MUZZLE	GROWLER			GRN PAPER	$500/600
2637			MRF "G"		?? C. 1950'S??	SANTA CLAUS 1927??	17.5	CIN TIPPED BEIGE MOHAIR, INSET TAN MUZZLE, EXCELSIOR STUFFING, GLASS EYES, W/GRN NECK RUFFLE	GROWLER	NONE	NONE	NONE	$550/750
2638					2SIEVERLING, 67	TEDDY BEAR, C. '60	18.1	BRN FROSTED LONG MOHAIR, BLK EMBROIDERED NOSE, GLASS EYES, FULLY JTD, STRAW STUFFED				PAPER	$550/750
2639					2SIEVERLING, 67	TEDDY BEAR, C. '70	18.1	WHT LONG MOHAIR, OP/MO W/FLESH VELVETEEN, GLASS EYES, FULLY JTD, STRAW STUFFED					$550/750
2640					2SIEVERLING, 50	TEDDY BEAR, C. '55	18.1	LONG WHT CURLY MOHAIR, BRN TIPPED, GLASS EYES, FULLY JTD, PAPER LOGO, W/BRN BOW				PAPER	$550/750
2641					4 MULLIN GUIDE, 56	TEDDY BEAR, C. '30	18.1	LONG SILKY GOLD MOHAIR, SHORT MOHAIR SET IN SNOUT, NO SIDE SEAMS, GLASS EYES, FULLY JTD					$550/750
2642					HOCKENBERRY, TBCOMP	TEDDY BEAR, C. '50	18.1	TAN MOHAIR, INSET SNOUT, GLASS EYES, FELT PADS, EXCELSIOR STUFFED, FULLY JTD		NONE	NONE	NONE	$550/750
2643			MRF "S"			TEDDY BEAR, C. '30	18.1	TAN MOHAIR, INSET SHORT PILE SNOUT, GLASS EYES, FELT PADS, EXCELSIOR STUFFED, FULLY JTD, #1905 VOLPP COLL	GROWLER	NONE	NONE	NONE	$550/750
2644						TEDDY BEAR, C. '30	18.1	TAN MOHAIR W/WHT MUZZLE & TAN FELT PAW PADS; GLASS EYES; EXCELSIOR STUFFED					$550/750
2645					2SIEVERLING, 70	PRINCE, C. '80	18.1	WHT MOHAIR, PLASTIC EYES, FULLY JTD, STRAW/FOAM STUFFED		YES	YES	PAPER	$550/750
2646					2SIEVERLING, 70	PRINCESS, C. '80	18.9	LONG WHT CURLY MOHAIR, GLASS EYES, FULLY JTD, STRAW & FOAM STUFFED		YES	YES	PAPER	$550/750
2647					2SIEVERLING, 14	TEDDY BEAR, C. '45	18.9	GOLD MOHAIR, GLASS EYES, FULLY JTD, STRAW STUFFED					$550/750

REF #	EAN #	HERMANN OLD #	ALSO SEE	LIMITED NUMBER	DATA FROM	NAME	INCHES TALL	DESCRIPTION	VOICE	HANGING BOOKLET	ARM TAG	COMPANY LOGO	CURRENT RETAIL
2648					4 MULLIN GUIDE, 56	TEDDY BEAR, C. '50	18.9	BEIGE MOHAIR, SHORT BEIGE SET IN SNOUT, GLASS EYES, FULLY JTD					$550/750
2649					TBEAR&F JAN 93, 23	LOTTE, C. '50	19.6	CARAMEL MOHAIR KNITTED DRESS & SWEATER, FELT PAWS & PADS, GLASS EYES, SHORT PILE SNOUT				MTL W/PAPER	$550/750
2650					TBEAR&F JAN 93, 23	FRANZ, C. '50	19.6	CARAMEL MOHAIR, FELT PAWS & PADS, GLASS EYES, SHORT PILE SNOUT				MTL W/PAPER	$550/750
2651					3 SIEVERING, 77	TEDDY BEAR, C. '24	19.6	GOLD SILK PLUSH, MATCHING COTTON TWILL PADS, GLASS EYES, FULLY JTD, W/LAVENDER BOW					$550/750
2652					3SIEVERLING, TITLE PG	TEDDY BEAR, C. '50	19.6	GLASS EYES, JTD ARMS AND LEGS, SWIVEL HEAD, STRAW STUFFED, BEIGE, NO ID		NONE	NONE	NONE	$550/750
2653					HOCKENBERRY, 140	TEDDY BEAR, C. '55	19.6	TAN MOHAIR, SHORT MOHAIR INSET SNOUT, GLASS EYES, FELT PADS, EXCELSIOR STUFFED					$550/750
2654			MRF "Q"		TEDDY BEAR	TEDDY BEAR, C. '35	19.6	TAN MOHAIR, SHORT MOHAIR INSET SNOUT, GLASS EYES, FELT PADS, EXCELSIOR STUFFED	GROWLER	NONE	NONE	NONE	$550/750
2655					TBEAR&F JAN 93, 23	TEDDY BEAR, C. '40	19.6	LONG PILE PURPLE TIPPED MOHAIR, SHORT PILE MUZZLE, GLASS EYES, FELT PAWS				MTL W/PAPER	$550/750
2656					TB ENCY, 31	TEDDY BEAR, C. '50	19.6	SHORT PILE BEIGE MOHAIR, INSET CLIPPED PALE GOLDEN PLUSH MUZZLE, EXCELSIOR STUFFED					$550/750
2657					??	TEDDY BEAR, C. '25	19.6	GOLD PLUSH; BEIGE TWILL PAWS PADS; GLASS EYES; FULLY JTD; EXCELSIOR STUFFING					$550/750
2658			MRF "R"		THREADBARE TB	ZOTTY, C. '30	21.3	LONG PILE TIPPED MOHAIR, SHORT PILE MUZZLE, GLASS EYES, FELT PAWS, EX VOLPP COLLECTION	GROWLER	NONE	NONE	NONE	$550/750
2659			MRF "H"		HERMANN C. '50	TEDDY BEAR, C. '50	21.3	BEIGE, SHORT PILE MOHAIR, SHAVED MUZZLE, NO ID, GLASS EYES, ADDED TOY BLOCKS	GROWLER	NONE	NONE	NONE	$550/750
2660			MRF "AA"		STEVE HOWARD	TEDDY BEAR, C. '50	21.3	LT BRN, INSET MUZZLE W/SHORT PILE TAN MOHAIR, GLASS EYES, REPLACED PAW PADS, FULLY JTD	GROWLER	NONE	NONE	NONE	$550/750
2661					TB ENCY, 97	TEDDY BEAR, C. '45	22	SHAGGY HONEY MOHAIR W/SHARP MUZZLE, GLASS EYES, CURVED SLENDER PAWS	GROWLER				$550/750
2662					2SIEVERLING, 63/66	TEDDY BEAR, C. '50	22.8	LONG WHT MOHAIR, GLASS EYES, FULLY JTD, REPLACED PADS, 96 HAS GOLD LOGO				GRN PAPER	$550/750
2663					2SIEVERLING, 13	TEDDY BEAR, C. '60	22.8	LONG FROSTED BRN MOHAIR, GLASS EYES, FULLY JTD, TAN MUZZLE-INNER EARS-FELT PAWS,					$550/750
2664					3SIEVERLING, TITLE PG	TEDDY BEAR, C. '48	22.8	GLASS EYES, FULLY JTD, STRAW STUFFED. BEIGE				GOLD MTL?	$550/750
2665						TEDDY BEAR, C. '50	22.8	WHT MOHAIR W/CLIPPED MUZZLE; GLASS EYES; FULLY JTD; STRAW STUFFED					$550/750
2666			MRF "AN"		HERMANN, C. '50	TEDDY BEAR, C. '50	23.6	WHT MOHAIR W/CLIPPED MUZZLE; GLASS EYES; FULLY JTD; STRAW STUFFED	GROWLER	NONE	NONE	NONE	$750/1000
2667					HOCKENBERRY, VOL II	TEDDY BEAR, C. '48	23.6	CARAMEL MOHAIR, CLIPPED MUZZLE, GLASS EYES, EXCELSIOR, FELT PADS, LG TUMMY, ALL JTD, MINT, NO MARKS, MARION HERMANN MEHLING COLLECTION	GROWLER				$750/1000
2668					3SIEVERLING,80	TEDDY BEAR, C. '40	23.6	GOLD MOHAIR GLASS EYES, JTD LEGS & ARMS, STRAW STUFFING					$750/1000
2669			MRF "L"		BOOK, 20	TEDDY BEAR, C. '48	23.6	CREAM MOHAIR W/FLAT FEET, SHOULDER SCARF & FLOWERS, LEIPZIG FAIR	GROWLER	NONE	NONE	NONE	$750/1000
2670					HOCKENBERRY, VOL II	TEDDY BEAR, C. '53	23.6	LONG CREAM MOHAIR, BRN TIPPED, INSET MUZZLE, SHORT HAIR, GLASS EYES, FELT PADS, EXCELSIOR, NO MARKS MARION HERMANN MEHLING COLLECTION	GROWLER				$750/1000
2671					4TH MULIS GUIDE, 56	TEDDY BEAR, C. '40	23.6	LONG SILKY CREAM MOHAIR, SHORT MOHAIR SET IN SNOUT, BRN STITCHED NOSE, GLASS EYES					$750/1000
2672			MRF "P"		VOLPP COLLECTION	TEDDY BEAR, C. '27	25.6	BEIGE MOHAIR, SHAVED INSET SNOUT, FELT PADS, W/SHIRT COLLAR, GLASS EYES, FULLY JTD	GROWLER	NONE	NONE	NONE	$750/1000
2673			MRF "D"		BOOK, 49 1953	TEDDY BEAR, C. '53	26.8	COTTON YELLOW MOHAIR, FULLY JTD, STRAW STUFFING, GLASS EYES, WORN	GROWLER	NONE	NONE	NONE	$750/1000
2674					3SIEVERLING, 80	TEDDY BEAR, C. '49	26.8	DARK BRN MOHAIR, CREAM SHEARED MUZZLE, TAN FELT PADS, GLASS EYES, FULLY JTD					$750/1000
2675					2SIEVERLING, 51	TEDDY BEAR, C. '18	29.1	GOLD MOHAIR W/SHEARED MUZZLE, GLASS EYES, FULLY JTD, STRAW STUFFED, HEAVY CARDBOARD FEET					$750/1000
2676					BIALOSKY TB CAT, 177	TEDDY BEAR, C. '70	5 X ?	CARAMEL MOHAIR, SWIVEL HEAD, RED COLLAR W/CHAIN TO NOSE				MTLW/PAPER	$250/350
2677					3SIEVERLING, 78	BEAR, RIDING	10 X ?	TAN MOHAIR, UNUSUAL SEAMS ON HEAD, GLASS EYES, NOT JTD, STRAW STUFFING					$250/350
2678			MRF "J"		HERMANN C. '55	POLAR BEAR, ACRYLIC	4H X 7L	WHT, STANDING ON 4 FEET	NONE	NONE	GRN W/ GER	MTLW/PAPER	$75/125
2679			MRF "AE"		HERMANN, 1952	SHEEP DOG	9H X 12L	BUFF WITH COLOR ADDED, NOT JTD, FEDERAL REPUBLIC ARM TAG	NO	NO	NO	MTL W/PAPER	$200/300

Alphabetical Index of Animal and Bear Names

NAME	EAN/OLD#	ALSO SEE	INCHES TALL
ADAC TEDDY BEAR	23430 2		11.8
AGATHE	15635 2		13.8
AGNES	11320 1		7
AIRPLANE & PILOT	10075 1		
ALARM CLOCK	95037 0		
ALARM CLOCK	95038 7		
ALASKA BEAR CLUMSY CUB	31145 4		18.1
ALASKA BEAR DIVER	31175 1		30
ALASKA BEAR MOTHER DICK	31170 6		28.3
ALASKA BEAR NOSY CUB	31150 8		19.7
ALBERT	12640 9		15.75
ALLIGATOR	47660 3		23.6
ALLIGATOR	47675 7		29.5
ALLIGATOR	47825 6		9.8
ALLIGATOR	47840 9		15.75
ALLIGATOR	47850 8		19.7
ALLIGATOR	47865 2		25.6
ALLIGATOR	49590 1	84120/90	35.4
ALLIGATOR	49598 7	84120/120	47.2
ALOIS	13629 3		11
ALPINE HORN PLAYER	17420 2		7.9
AMANDA	19055 4		21.7
AMBER, NO-NO	15747 2		3.3
AMEILIA W/TEDDY	15760 1		2.8
ANDREW	12830 4		11.8
ANGELICA	70062/35W		14.2
ANNABELL	14140 2		15.75
ANNIV BEAR, 90 YEAR	14525 7		10.2
ANNIV BEAR, 90 YEAR	14532 5		12.6
ANNIV BEAR, 90 YEAR	14540 0		15.75
ANTHONY	12530 3		11.8
APACHE-BULLY, GROTESQUE	650/13		5.12
APACHE-BULLY, GROTESQUE	650/18		7
AQUARIUS	4001/30		11.8
ARTIST BEAR BONNIE	11843 5		15.75
ARTIST BEAR CANDY	11842 8		15.75
AUGUST	14531 8		11
AUTO RACER	10082 9		1.5
AUTO RACER	10083 6		1.5
AUTUMN WIND	05229 3		11.8
BAG, PLASTIC TEDDY	99001 7		15 X 20
BALLERINA	15431 5		11.8
BALLERINA PRE-1980	16.5		
BALL,	75614 9		5.5
BALL, BABY'S	75607 1	1200/6	2.8
BALL, PLUSH	1250/16		6.3
BALL, PLUSH	1255/14		5.5
BALL, PLUSH	75516 5	1250/14	5.5
BALL, PLUSH W/MUSIC	76620 9	1255/16	6.3
BALL, W/MUSIC BOX	1251/14		5.5
BALL, W/MUSIC BOX	75618 7		7
BARNABY	12520 4		7.9
BAVARIAN BOY	11331 7		11.8
BAVARIAN BOY	11333 1		11.8
BAVARIAN GIRL	11330 0		11.8
BAVARIAN GIRL	11332 4		11.8
BEAR	103/40/1		15.75
BEAR- 4 LEGS W/VOICE	31040 2		14L X 10H
BEAR IN SWEAT SUIT	63/30/4		11.8
BEAR ON 4 LEGS	82009/30		11.8
BEAR ON 4 LEGS	82009/40		15.75
BEAR ON 4 LEGS	82009/60		23.6
BEAR ON RED WHEELS	70020 3		6H X 8L
BEAR ON WHEELS	203		
BEAR ON WHEELS	330/45		12H X 17.7L
BEAR ON WHEELS	70016 6		5H X 6.5L
BEAR W/ BIB	63/30/1		11.8
BEAR W/APE	15761 8		2.8
BEAR W/DUCK	15763 2		2.8
BEAR W/NIGHTSHIRT		MRF "B"	12.6
BEAR W/PANDA	15762 5		2.8
BEAR W/SHAVED SNOUT	11735 3		14.2
BEAR W/SHAVED SNOUT	11750 6		19.7
BEARFOOT & PREGNANT	15930 8		2.4
BEARY-GO-ROUND	10060 7		4
BEAR, 4 LEGGED	300/20		5H X 6L
BEAR, 4 LEGGED	83725/42		14.2L
BEAR, 4 LEGGED	83730/40		15.75
BEAR, 4 LEGGED	83731/40		13L X 10H
BEAR, 4 LEGGED	83735/36		14.2L
BEAR, BABY	22128 9		11
BEAR, BABY	22133 3		13.8
BEAR, BABY IN CRADLE W/MUSIC	11520 5		6.69
BEAR, BABY ON CUSHION	11414 7		5.9
BEAR, BABY ON CUSHION	11415 4		5.9
BEAR, BABY, LYING	30131 8		11.8
BEAR, BLACK BROWN NOSE	LI 100		10
BEAR, BLACK BROWN NOSE	LI 200		20
BEAR, BLACK BROWN NOSE	LI 80		8
BEAR, BROWN	08417 4		7.5
BEAR, BROWN	31020 4	80300/20	7.9
BEAR, BROWN	31030 3	80300/30	11.8
BEAR, BROWN	3708/35		13.8
BEAR, BROWN, SITTING	31130 0	80009/30	11.8
BEAR, CHAINED			11.8
BEAR, CHAINED		MRF "AM"	11.8
BEAR, COSY-ZOTTY		MRF "E"	15
BEAR, DESIGNER	17550 6		18.1
BEAR, DESIGNER	14935 4		13.78
BEAR, DESIGNER	14936 1		13.78
BEAR, DESIGNER	14945 3		17.72
BEAR, DESIGNER	14946 0		17.72
BEAR, LYING DOWN	2010/55		22
BEAR, LYING DOWN	30040 3	80166/40	15.75
BEAR, LYING DOWN	30050 2	80166/50	19.7
BEAR, LYING DOWN	30065 6	80166/65	26
BEAR, LYING DOWN	30095 3	80166/95	37
BEAR, LYING DOWN	30130 1		11.8
BEAR, LYING DOWN	30130 1	80168/30	11.8
BEAR, LYING DOWN	30140 0	80168/40	15.75
BEAR, LYING DOWN	30141 7		15.75
BEAR, LYING DOWN	30142 4		15.75
BEAR, LYING DOWN	30150 9	80168/50	19.7
BEAR, LYING DOWN	30151 6		19.7
BEAR, LYING DOWN	30152 3		19.7
BEAR, LYING DOWN	30165 3	80168/65	25.5
BEAR, LYING DOWN	30166 0		25.5
BEAR, LYING DOWN	30167 7		25.5
BEAR, LYING DOWN	30195 0	80168/95	37.5
BEAR, LYING DOWN	30240 7		15.75
BEAR, LYING DOWN	30250 6		23.6
BEAR, LYING DOWN	30251 3		19.7
BEAR, LYING DOWN	30265 0		25.6
BEAR, LYING DOWN	30266 7		25.5
BEAR, LYING DOWN	30275 9	82012/75	30
BEAR, LYING DOWN	30350 3		19.7
BEAR, LYING DOWN	30360 2		23.6
BEAR, LYING DOWN	30380 0		31.5
BEAR, LYING DOWN	80167/50		19.7
BEAR, LYING DOWN	80167/65		23.6
BEAR, LYING DOWN	80168/22		9.5
BEAR, LYING DOWN	81683 0		33L X ??
BEAR, LYING DOWN	81685 0		33L X ??
BEAR, LYING DOWN	82010/100		39
BEAR, LYING DOWN	82010/35		14.2
BEAR, LYING DOWN	82010/55		22
BEAR, LYING DOWN	82010/75		28L X14H
BEAR, LYING DOWN	83663 0		24.8
BEAR, LYING SOFT	30241 4		15.75
BEAR, MUSICAL	63/30/3	10930 3	11.8
BEAR, MUSICAL	63/35TBP		13.8
BEAR, MUSICAL SLEEPING	169/28		11
BEAR, MUSICAL, MECH.			9.5
BEAR, MUSICAL, TURN. HEAD	11028 6		11.4
BEAR, MUSICAL, TURN. HEAD	11033 0		11.8
BEAR, MUSICAL, TURN. HEAD	11040 8		15.75
BEAR, ORIGINAL		MRF "AF"	12.6
BEAR, RED WHEELED	300/16	SU 75	5.5H X 6L
BEAR, RED WHEELED	300/16	LI 75	5.5H X 6L
BEAR, RED WHEELED	300/16/3	CI 75	5.5H X 6L
BEAR, RED WHEELED	300/16/4F		5.5H X 6L
BEAR, RED WHEELED	300/20		6H X 7L
BEAR, RED WHEELED	300/20 F		7.9
BEAR, RED WHEELED	330/40		11H X 13L
BEAR, RIDING			10 X?
BEAR, RIDING	03060 7	73360F	17H X 25L
BEAR, RUNNING	70815 5	3608/15	5.9
BEAR, RUNNING	80704/25		9.8
BEAR,SHEPHERD	62/36/6		14.2
BEAR, SITTING	19040 0	80081/40	15.75
BEAR, SITTING	2300/24		9.5
BEAR, SLEEPING	169/24		9.5
BEAR, SLEEPING	169/32		12.6
BEAR, SLEEPING W/MUSIC	168/32		12.6
BEAR, SOFT 1982		MRF "AH"	4.7
BEAR, SPECTACLED	20185 4		33
BEAR, STANDING	17220 6		7.9
BEAR, STANDING	17425 7	74/25	10.2
BEAR, STANDING, NOS.	17221 3		7.9
BEAR, TEACHER	10831 3		11.8
BEAR, TEACHER	10833 7		12
BEAR, TRADITIONAL	14325 3		9.84
BEAR, TRADITIONAL	14330 7		14.2
BEAR, TRADITIONAL	14340 6		15.75
BEAR, TRADITIONAL	14350 5		19.7
BEAR, TRADITIONAL	14360 4		23.6
BEAR, TRADITIONAL	14380 2		31.5
BEAR, TRAINED ON WHEELS			6H X ?L
BEAR, TRAINED ON WHEELS	CA 75		5H X 6L
BEAR, TRAINED ON WHEELS	CA 75		5H X 6L
BEAR, TRAINED ON WHEELS	CI 75		5H X 6L
BEAR, TRAINED ON WHEELS	LI 75		5H X 6L
BEAR, WASHABLE	82008/60		23.6
BEAR, WHEELED	330/40/FW		11H X 13L
BEAR, WHEELED	335/40		15.75
BEAR, WHEELED	340/40		11H X 13L
BEAR, WHEELED	340/40		11H X 13L
BEAR, WHEELED	340/40		11H X 13L
BEAR, WHITE NECK	90/30		11.8
BEAR, WHITE NECK	90/38		14.5
BEAR, WHITE NECK	90/42		16.5
BEAR, YOUNG	5/23		9.5
BEAR, YOUNG	5/26		10.2
BEAR, YOUNG	5/30		11.8
BEAR, YOUNG	5/40		12.6
BEAR. SITTING	83720/42		16.5
BEAUTY	13630 0		12.6
BENCH	95120 9		5
BENCH	95121 6		9
BENCH, WOODEN	95510 8		
BENJAMIN (DUPL. #)	17840 8		15.75
BERLIN "4-SECTIONS BEAR"	01634-1		15
BERLIN WALL BEAR	17326 7		10.2
BIEDERMEIER MAN	11129 0		11
BIEDERMEIER WOMEN	11128 3		11
BILL	19645 7		18.1
BILLY	15219 4		7.9
BIMBO "ERICA"	01633 3		11.8
BIRD, LADY	860/7		2.8
BIRD, LADY	860/9		3.5
BIRTHDAY CHARLIE	14214 0	01421 4	5.5
BIRTHDAY CHARLIE	14230 0		11.8
BIRTHDAY CHARLIE	14280 5		31.5
BISON	015/30		
BLUEBEARY	14950 7		15.75

NAME	EAN/OLD#	ALSO SEE	INCHES TALL
DOG, CHOW	53050 3	476/50	19.7
DOG, COCKER SPANIEL	3045/40		15.75
DOG, COCKER SPANIEL	83041/40		15.75
DOG, COCKER SPANIEL	83045/40		15.75
DOG, COCKER SPANIEL	855/25		9.8
DOG, COCKER SPANIEL	855/30		11.8
DOG, COLLIE	51550 0		19.7
DOG, COLLIE, LYING	51545 6	801745/45	17.7
DOG, DALMATIAN	80440/50		19.7
DOG, DACHSHUND	434/16		6.3
DOG, DACHSHUND	434/22		8.7
DOG, DACHSHUND "WALDI"	80436/38		15
DOG, DACHSHUND "WALDI"	52040 5	80438/40	15.75
DOG, DACHSHUND, LYING	52145 7		17.7
DOG, FOX TERRIER	170/40		15.75
DOG, FOX TERRIER	50530 3	170/30	11.8
DOG, FOX TERRIER	50535 8	170/35	13.8
DOG, FOX TERRIER	50635 5	80174/35	13.8
DOG, FOX TERRIER	70615 1	3606/15	5.9
DOG, FOX-TERRIER	174/30		11.8
DOG, GERMAN SHEPHERD	80169/22		8.7
DOG, GERMAN SHEPHERD	80170/42		16.5
DOG, GERMAN SHEPHERD	80170/70		27.6
DOG, GERMAN SHEPHERD	80170/80		31.5
DOG, GERMAN SHEPHERD	80171/42		16.5
DOG, GERMAN SHEPHERD	80171/70		27.6
DOG, HUSKY, LYING	57040 0	83110/40	15.75
DOG, HUSKY, LYING	57050 9		19.7
DOG, JACK RUSSELL TERRIER	50630 0		11.8
DOG, JERRY THE TV	450/30		11.8
DOG, JERRY THE TV	450/35		13.8
DOG, JERRY THE TV	451/35		13.8
DOG, JERRY THE TV	451/40		15.75
DOG, JERRY THE TV	452/28		11
DOG, JERRY THE TV	453/1		
DOG, JOSEF THE TV	55550 6	84070/50	19.7
DOG, JOSEF THE TV	55655 8	84072/55	21.7
DOG, KROMFOHRLANDER, PUP	50730 7		11.8
DOG, LABRADOR	56080 7		31.8
DOG, LABRADOR	56081 4		31.8
DOG, LABRADOR	56089 7		35
DOG, MOLLI	80180/22		8.7
DOG, MOLLY	54515 6	180/15	5.9
DOG, MOLLY	54525 5	180/25	9.8
DOG, MOLLY, SITTING	70515 4	3605/15	5.9
DOG, PEKINGESE	3650/25		9.8
DOG, PEKINGESE	54025 0	3660/25	9.8
DOG, PLASTIC	40S/20		7.9
DOG, PLASTIC	40S/23		9.5
DOG, PLASTIC	40S/27?		10.6
DOG, PLASTIC	40S/30		11.8
DOG, PLASTIC	40W/20		7.9
DOG, PLASTIC	40W/23		9.5
DOG, PLASTIC	40W/27?		10.6
DOG, PLASTIC	40W/30		11.8
DOG, PLUSH	260/14		5.5
DOG, PLUSH	260/17?		6.7
DOG, PLUSH	260/20		7.9
DOG, PLUSH	260/23?		7.5
DOG, PLUSH	260/27?		10.6
DOG, PLUSH	260/30		11.8
DOG, PLUSH	261/14		5.5
DOG, PLUSH	261/17?		6.7
DOG, PLUSH	261/20		7.9
DOG, PLUSH	261/23?		9.5
DOG, PLUSH	261/27?		10.6
DOG, PLUSH	261/30		11.8
DOG, POODLE	457/25		9.8
DOG, POODLE	459/30		11.8
DOG, POODLE, APRICOT	53830 1		11.8
DOG, POODLE, BROWN	53630 7	80458/31	11.8
DOG, POODLE, GRAY	53530 0	80458/30	11.8
DOG, POODLE, STANDING	53730 4	80460/30	11.8
DOG, POODLE, COGNAC	53930 8		11.8
DOG, PUG ON WHEELS	250/20		7.9
DOG, PUG ON WHEELS	250/25		9.8
DOG, PUG ON WHEELS	250/30		11.8
DOG, SCOTTISHTERRIER	50345 3		17.7
DOG, SCOTTISHTERRIER	50346 0		17.7
DOG, SHEEP	80445/42		16.5
DOG, SHEEP	80448/50		19.7
DOG, SKYE TER. SITTING	321/24		9.5
DOG, SKYE TER. STANDING	320/33		12.6
DOG, SKYE TERRIER	164/28		11
DOG, SKYE TERRIER	165/28		11
DOG, ST. BERNARD	310/22		8.7
DOG, ST. BERNARD	70415 7	3604/15	5.9
DOG, ST. BERNARD	705/20		1.9
DOG, ST. BERNARD	80705/20		7.9
DOG, ST. BERNARD	84060/45		17.7
DOG, ST. BERNARD	84060/55		21.7
DOG, ST. BERNARD	84080/40		15.75
DOG, ST. BERNARD, LYING	55760 9	84060/60	23.6
DOG, TERRIER	71210 0		4
DOG, TERRIER, W. HIGHLAND	50245 6		17.7
DOG, WIRE HAIR TERRIER	300/28		11
DOG, YELLOW	20/16		6.3
DOG, YELLOW	20/20?		7.9
DOG, YELLOW	20/23?		9
DOG, YELLOW	20/27?		10.6
DOG, YELLOW	20/28		11.8
DOG, YELLOW	20/32		12.6
DOG, YORKSHIRE TERRIER	50040 7	162/40	15.75
DOG, YORKSHIRE TERRIER	50041 4	162/40K	15.75
DOG, YORKSHIRE TERRIER	50140 4	163/40	15.75
DOG, YORKSHIRE TERRIER	50235 7	160/35	13.8
DOG, YORKSHIRE TERRIER	50335 4	161/35	13.8
DONKEY	02/60		23.62
DONKEY	4030/35		13.8
DONKEY	48730 2		11.8
DONKEY	70022 7		
DONKEY ON WHEELS	4020/30F		11.8
DONKEY, LYING	48660 2		23.6
DONKEY, NIKKI	75220 2		9.8
DONKEY, STANDING	48530 8	4020/30	11.8
DRESSED GIRL	101200		8
DRESSED GIRL	101215		8
DRESS, LINEN	97720 9		
DROMEDARY, STANDING	43826 7	3450/26	10.2
DROMEDARY, STANDING	43858 8	3450/58	22.8
DROMEDARY, STANDING	43898 4	3450/120	47.2
DUCK	1354/20		7.9
DUCK	551/20		7.9
DUCK	552/25		9.8
DUCK	75818 1		7
DUCK WITH MUSIC BOX	1491/15		5.9
DUCK WITH MUSIC BOX	1492/15		5.9
DUCKLING	1350/15		5.9
DUCKLING	1350/25		9.8
DUCKLING	1350/25		9.8
DUCKLING	1351/15		5.9
DUCKLING	1352/12		4.7
DUCKLING	1355/18		7
DUCKLING	81358/30		11.8
DUCKLING	87630 4	81357/30	11.8
DUCKLING, BABYS	1200/2		?
DUCKLING, WHITE-GOLD	87817 9		6.7
DUCKLING, WHITE-GOLD	87822 3		8.7
DUCKLING, ORANGE-WHITE	87717 2		6.7
DUCKLING, ORANGE-WHITE	87722 6		8.7
DUCK, BLUE	87416 4	1357/16/4	6.3
DUCK, FLYING	42560 1	84110/60	23.6
DUCK, FLYING	42580 9	84110/80	31.5
DUCK, GOLD	87515 4	1353/15	5.9
DUCK, GOLD-WHITE	76414 4	1200/14	5.5
DUCK, GREEN	87316 7	1357/16/3	6.3
DUCK, LIGHT BLUE	87216 0	1357/16/2	6.3
DUCK, RED	87116 3	1357/16/1	6.3
DUCK, RED-GOLD	76314 7	1200/13	5.5
DUCK, SMALL	87012 8		4.7
DUCK, WILD	1356/25		9.8
DUCK, WILD	87015 9	1356/15	5.9
DUCK, WILD	87020 3	1356/20	10.2
DUCK, WILD	87025 8		9.8
DUCK, WILD	87026 5		9.8
EAGLE-OWL	42035 4		13.8
EARRING	95054 7		0.6
EDWIN	15550 8		19.7
ELECTION MTG, RATSKELLAR	10051 5		7.75 X 8 X 10
ELEPHANT	02/65		25.6
ELEPHANT	310/12		4.7
ELEPHANT	312/20		10.2
ELEPHANT	312/25		9.8
ELEPHANT	321/32		12.6
ELEPHANT	34125 3	80312/25	9.8
ELEPHANT	34236 6	80321/36	14.2
ELEPHANT	34330 1	80771/30	11.8
ELEPHANT	34350 9	80771/50	19.7
ELEPHANT	70003 6		4.7
ELEPHANT W/MUSIC	1482/20		7.9
ELEPHANT, BABY'S	75120 5	1200/1	9.8
ELEPHANT, GOLD	80761/28		11
ELEPHANT, GOLD	80768/30		11.8
ELEPHANT, GRAY	80762/28		11
ELEPHANT, GRAY	80765/30		11.8
ELEPHANT, GRAY	80765/50		19.7
ELEPHANT, LIGHT BLUE	80764/28		11
ELEPHANT, LIGHT BLUE	80767/30		11.8
ELEPHANT, LYING	80331/30		11.8
ELEPHANT, LYING	80331/60		23.6
ELEPHANT, LYING	34030 0	80770/30	11.8
ELEPHANT, LYING	34031 7		11.8
ELEPHANT, LYING	34050 8	80770/50	19.7
ELEPHANT, LYING	34051 5		19.7
ELEPHANT, LYING	34061 4		23.6
ELEPHANT, LYING	34075 1	80770/75	29.5
ELEPHANT, NIKKI	75122 9		9.8
ELEPHANT, ROSE	80763/28		11
ELEPHANT, ROSE	80766/30		11.8
ELEPHANT, SITTING	80321/32		12.6
ELEPHANT, SITTING	80322/45		17.7
ELEPHANT, STANDING	34115 4	80312/15	5.9
ELEPHANT, STANDING	34116 1		5.9
ELEPHANT, STANDING	34120 8	80312/20	10.2
ELEPHANT, STANDING	34121 5		10.2
ELEPHANT, STANDING	34425 4	80316/25	9.8
ELEPHANT, STANDING	34465 0	80316/65	25.6
ELEPHANT, STANDING	80312/25		9.8
ELIZABETH	15545 4		18.1
EMIL OF TWINS	11825 1A	11825 1	10.2
EMIL & EMILY TWINS	11825 1 (A + B)		10.2
EMILY OF TWINS	11825 1B	11825 1	10.2
ERNEST	12540 2		15.75
ERROR- PRICE LIST ENTRY, SHOULD BE 43530 5	42530	43530 3	
ETERNITY BEAR	01623 0		11.8
FAMILY, BOY	10322 6		7.9
FAMILY, GIRL	10224 3		7.9
FAMILY, GIRL	10422 3		7.9
FAMILY, GIRL	10832 0		7.9
FATHER BEAR PLASTIC BOX	10830 6	63/30/2K	11.8
FELDHAUS	06017 2		6.69
FELIX	15775 5		3.1
FERRIS WHEEL	10070 6		14.5H
FIBBER	15934 6		3.5
FIPPS	11617 2		7.9
FIRE BEAR	01303 2		11.8
FIRE DEP'T AUTO W/DRIVER	10076 8		
FISHERMAN	11741 4		15.75
FISH, BABY'S	75317 9	1200/3	6.7
FLEA MARKET BEAR	11321 8		7.6
FLOH	11615 8		5.5
FLORI	11616 5		5.5
FLOWER	77628 4		11
FOAL	84030/40		15.75
FOAL	84050/40		15.75
FOAL	84050/60		23.6
FOAL	84055/40		15.75
FOAL, LYING	48460 8		23.6
FONDUE HALL	10026 3		15.7 X 8.5 X 9.5
FORESTER, GROTESQUE	600/2		8.7
FOX	83020/85		33.5
FOX, GROTESQUE JOLLY	50/15		5.5
FOX, LYING	43165 7	83020/65	25.6
FOX, LYING	67527 3	83020/27	10.6
FOX, ROUND LYING	43025 4	2005/25	10.2
FOX, ROUND LYING	43035 3	2005/35	13.8
FRANZ, CIRCA 1950			19.6
FRANZ, FATHER	13030 7		11.8
FREDDY	11618 9		7.9
FRITZ, SON	13025 3		8.7
FROG	1398/20		7.9
FROG	1398/35		13.8
FROG	1398/45		17.7
FROG	1399/75		29.5
FROG	41022 5	1399/22	8.7
FROG	41030 0	1399/30	11.8
FROG	41040 9	1399/40	15.75
FROG	41060 7	1399/60	23.6
FROG	41122 2		8.7
FROG	41130 7		11.8

NAME	EAN/OLD#	ALSO SEE	INCHES TALL
FROG	411406		15.75
FROG	411604		23.6
FROG	412304	81398/30	11.8
FROG	81399/30		11.8
FROSTY	190479		18.1
FUDDO 1982 NOT MADE			15.75
FURNITURE FOR BEAR DEN	955023		
GARTNERBEAR	013029		11.8
GEORGE	118411		15.75
GERTIE	158318		4.7
GIFT BOX	956013		7.9
GIFT BOX	956020		11.8
GIFT BOX	956037		15.6
GIRAFFE	440307	550/30	11.8
GIRAFFE	440802	550/80	31.5
GLOBETROTTER	156307	DUPL. #	11.8
GOAT	883258		9.8
GOAT	883265		9.8
GOAT	883500		19.7
GOAT, STANDING	882251	1452/25	9.8
GOLD-WORKER	016330		11.8
GOLFER	134305		11.8
GOLFER	134558		22
GOLFER	140382		15
GOOSE	895305	1370/30	11.8
GOOSE	895404	1370/40	15.75
GOOSE W/RIDER	159414		4
GOOSEBERRY	148319		11.8
GRANDFATHER, GROTESQUE	600/6		8.7
GRANDMA	012043		15.75
GRANDPA	012042		15.75
GROWLER VOICE	952046		
GUINEA PIG	730200	540/20	7.9
GUINEA PIG	730217	540/20K	7.9
GUINEA PIG W/MUSIC	1486/20		7.9
GUINEA PIG, SPECKLED	730224		7.9
GUINEA PIG, BEIGE	730231		7.9
GUINEA PIG, DARK BROWN	730248		7.9
GUINEA PIG, SPOTTED	730408		7.9
GUSTAV	156451		17.7
HALLOWEEN CAT	159421		3.1
HALLOWEEN WITCH	014836	148364	11.8
HALLOWEEN WITCH	148364	014836	11.8
HAMSTER, LYING	725152	530/15	5.9
HAMSTER, STANDING	673163	80535/16	6.3
HAMSTER, STANDING	726166	535/16	6.3
HAMSTER, STANDING	726258	535/25	9.8
HAND PUPPETS, BEAR	785255	410/13	9.8
HAND PUPPETS, CAT	787259	410/15	9.8
HAND PUPPETS, DOG	789253	410/18	9.8
HAND PUPPETS, DONKEY	788256	410/16	9.8
HAND PUPPETS, FOX	790259	410/19	9.8
HAND PUPPETS, RABBIT	786252	410/14	9.8
HANS	120407		15.75
HANS IM GLUCK	013030		11.8
HANSEL + RUDY W/BASE	157748		3.1
HARE	104/80		31.5
HARE	106/60		23.6
HARE	108/30		11.8
HARE	108/40		15.75
HARE	108/45		17.7
HARE	530/25		9.8
HARE	722/35		13.8

NAME	EAN/OLD#	ALSO SEE	INCHES TALL
HARE, GREEN	109/30/1		11.8
HARE, GROTESQUE	600/1		8.7
HARE, RED	109/30		11.8
HARE, STANDING	670/40		15.7
HARE, STANDING	675/40		15.7
HARE, STANDING	851387	640/38	15
HARE, VARIEGATED GREEN	109/30/3		11.8
HARLEQUIN	132301		11.8
HARLEQUIN	132608		23.6
HARLEQUIN LADY	132318		11.8
HARLEQUIN LADY	132616		23.6
HARRY	012040		15.75
HATTIE	158400		3
HEART TO HEART	013630		11.8
HEART TO HEART	013631		11.8
HEDGEHOG	742180	886/18	7
HEDGEHOG	743132	881/13	5.1
HEDGEHOG	743163	881/16	6.3
HEDGEHOG	743224		8.7
HEDGEHOG	743244	881/22	8.7
HEDGEHOG	743309		11.8
HEDGEHOG	743354		13.8
HEDGEHOG	740100	880/10	4
HEDGEHOG	740163	880/16	6.3
HEDGEHOG	740223	880/22	8.7
HEDGEHOG	741121	885/12	4.7
HEDGEHOG	741169	882/16	6.3
HEDGEHOG	741176	882/16K	6.3
HEDGEHOG	741220	885/22	8.7
HEDGEHOG W/MUSIC	774228	1485/22	8.7
HEDGEHOG, STANDING	676133	80886/13	5.1
HELEN SIEVERLING	060/33	60/33	13
HELEN SIEVERLING	861/30	060/33	13
HEN	1300/22	8.7	
HEN	880226	1310/22	8.7
HEN	880356		13.8
HEN	881353		13.8
HEN W/ BASKET	1305/17		6.7
HEN W/ BASKET	1305/22		8.7
HENNEF (TOTAL SHOW)	011932		11.8
HERMANN & MICKEY	012432		17?
HERMANNCHEN	115151		6.69
HERMANNCHEN	115168		6.69
HERMANNCHEN	115175		6.69
HERSCHEL	158417		3
HIKING BOY	101222		8.5
HIKING BOY	107200	63/20/7K	7.9
HIKING BOY	107217		7.9
HIKING BOY	107224		7.9
HIKING BOY	70004/31		11.8
HIKING GIRL	106203	63/20/6K	7.9
HIKING GIRL	106210		7.9
HIKING GIRL	106227		7.9
HIPPOPOTAMUS	400301	83714/30	11.8
HIPPOPOTAMUS	400318		11.8
HIPPOPOTAMUS	400431	83714/43	16.9
HIPPOPOTAMUS	400455		17.7
HIPPOPOTAMUS	400622	83714/62	24.4
HIPPOPOTAMUS	400639		24.8
HIPPOPOTAMUS	400967	83714/100	39.4
HIPPOPOTAMUS	406303	83719/30	11.8
HIPPOPOTAMUS	83710/100		39.4
HIPPOPOTAMUS	83710/30		11.8

NAME	EAN/OLD#	ALSO SEE	INCHES TALL
HIPPOPOTAMUS	83710/43		16.9
HIPPOPOTAMUS	83710/62		24.4
HIPPOPOTAMUS	83715/100		39.4
HIPPOPOTAMUS	83715/30		11.8
HIPPOPOTAMUS	83715/43		16.9
HIPPOPOTAMUS	83715/62		23.6
HIPPOPOTAMUS	83716/100		39.4
HIPPOPOTAMUS	83716/30		11.8
HIPPOPOTAMUS	83716/43		16.9
HIPPOPOTAMUS	83716/62		23.6
HIPPOPOTAMUS, SITTING	83718/30		11.8
HIPPOPOTAMUS	401308	83717/30	11.8
HIPPOPOTAMUS	401445		17.3
HIPPOPOTAMUS	401629		24.4
HOCHZEITSLADER	114000		39.4
HOFNAR (JESTER)	113249		7
HOLLY	157700		3.1
HOME FOR HOLIDAYS	H 0002		4
HONEY	131304		11.8
HONEY	159117		3.5
HONEY BEAR	193289		11
HORSE	480303	4010/30	11.8
HORSE 1950 REPLICA	700210		7.9
HORSE ON WHEELS	4010/30F		11.8
HORST 1953			10.2
HUGGIE	159223		2.8
HUMMEL + BEAR	169130	01632	12.6
HUMMEL-HUMMEL	01632?	169130	13.4
ICH BIN EIN BERLINER	173281		11
INT'L PLAYMATES	012455		???
IVY	157717		3.1
JACK	154457		18.1
JACKET W/TWEED PANTS	960504		FOR 19.7
JACKET W/TWEED PANTS	968306		FOR 11.8
JACKET W/TWEED PANTS	968405		FOR 15.8
JACKET & PANTS	960300		
JACKET & PANTS	960317		
JACKET & PANTS	960409		
JACKET & PANTS	960416		
JACKET & PANTS	960508		
JACKET & PANTS	960515		
JACK+PUFF	159254		2.8
JADE	116219		6.3
JEANSHOSE	258353	56/35/4	14.2
JEANSROCK	257353	56/35/3	14.2
JENNIE+DELIA	159247		2.8
JENNY	154280		11
JEREMY	126201		7.9
JOHANN	120506		18.1
JOINER'S WORKSHOP	100430		11 X 7.8 X 8
JOLLY JESTER	159209		2.8
JUBILEE BEAR	170402	70/40	
KARI	62/35/NWR		14.2
KATHLEEN	010929		13
KEY RING, TEDDY	950400		
KEY RING, TEDDY	950408		
KIKI W/BASE	157304		2.8
KING CHARLES DOG	80/23		9.5
KIWI BIRD	021/30		11.8
KIWI BIRD	021/30/3		11.8
KLEID	56/35/4		14.2
KLINGENBERG MUSEUM	018037		15.75
KOALA BEAR	3001/42		16.5

NAME	EAN/OLD#	ALSO SEE	INCHES TALL
KOALA BEAR	3002/20		7.9
KOALA BEAR	3002/30		11.8
KOLNER-DOMBAU-BEAR	016335		11.8
KRIS + KRINGLE W/BASE	157731		3.1
KUNIBERT	113225		7
KUSCHWEBEL "OLLI"	015225		7.9
LADY BLUE	141273		10.8
LADYBUG W/MUSIC	1480/14		5.5
LADYBUG W/MUSIC	772149	1483/14	5.5
LAMA	5000/38		15
LAMA	5000/48		18.9
LAMB	420/10	86024 2	9.5
LAMB	420/50		19.7
LAMB	422/55		21.7
LAMB	86123 2		9.5
LAMB	86228 4		11
LAMB	865308	422/30	11.8
LAMB	865605	422/60	23.6
LAMB	868426		16.5
LAMB W/MUSIC	770305	1422/30	11.8
LAMB, BROWN	420/8/1		4.72
LAMB, CARACUL	80425/45		17.7
LAMB, LAYING	420/23/45		17.7
LAMB, LYING	80425/40		15.75
LAMB, MERINO	860129	420/8	4.7
LAMB, MERINO	860204	420/9	7.9
LAMB, MERINO	860242	420/10	9.5
LAMB, MERINO	860402	420/40	15.75
LAMB, MERINO, SLEEPING	866305		11.8
LAMB, SLEEPING	867326		12.6
LAMB, SLEEPING	867456		17.7
LAMB, STANDING	421/50		19.7
LAMB, WHITE	420/9		7.9
LAMB, YOUNG	770312		12.2
LAMB, SITTING	80420/30		11.8
LARS, POLAR BEAR	178439		15.75
LATZHOSE	56/35/3		14.2
LECTERN	951056		
LEO BEAR	062400		15.8
LEOPARD	2003/40		15.75
LEOPARD	2003/58		22.8
LEOPARD	2016/45		17.7
LEOPARD	2016/80		31.5
LEOPARD	2017/45		17.72
LEOPARD	2017/60		17.7
LEOPARD	2017/80		31.5
LEOPARD	36042 1		16.5
LEOPARD	495/30		11.8
LEOPARD	495/45		17.7
LEOPARD, LYING	2003/33		12.6
LEOPARD, LYING	361354	2016/35	13.8
LEOPARD, LYING	361602	2016/60	23.6
LEOPARD, LYING	36235 7		15
LEOPARD, LYING	362609		13
LEOPARD, LYING	80492/42		16.5
LEOPARD, LYING	80492/52	20.5	
LEOPARD, SITTING	360308	499/30	11.8
LEOPARD, SITTING	360605		23.6
LEOPARD, SITTING	360629	499/62	24.4
LEOPARD, SITTING	499/42	16.5	
LEOPARD, SNOW	496/30	11.8	
LEOPARD, SNOW	496/35	13.8	
LILLY	171454	71/45	18.1

NAME	EAN/OLD#	ALSO SEE	INCHES TALL
LINA	01623 8		11.8
LION	2001/58		22.8
LION	2002/50		19.7
LION	2014/35		13.8
LION	2014/45		17.7
LION	2014/60		23.6
LION	35138 2	80443/38	15
LION CUB, LYING	35335 5		13.8
LIONESS	82015/30		11.8
LION, LYING	35230 3	82014/30	11.8
LION, LYING	35232 7		13
LION, LYING	35265 5	82014/65	25.6
LION, LYING DOWN	82016/30		12
LION, LYING DOWN	82017/60		23.6
LION, LYING DOWN	82017/80		31.5
LION, SITTING	35030 9	80442/30	11.8
LION, SITTING	442/20		7.9
LION, SITTING	442/30		11.8
LION, SITTING	442/42		16.5
LION, SITTING	444/30		11.8
LION, SITTING	444/40		15.75
LION. LYING	80443/85		33.5
LOGO, TEDDY SIGN	98211 1		4.3 DIA
LOTTE, CIRCA 1950			19.6
LOU, NOS. STANDING BEAR	17222 0		7.9
LUCKY BEATLE BEAR	15638 3		13.8
LYNX, STANDING	36840 3	490/40	15.75
LYNX, STANDING	36860 1	490/60	23.6
MAGIC	15935 3		3.2
MALCOM W/BASE	15732 8		3.2
MAMMOTH	45035 1		13.8
MARIONETTE PLAYER	12941 7		15.75
MARMELADE	15916 2		2.8
MARMOT	73316 4	725/16	6.3
MARMOT, STANDING	67212 8	80725/12	4.7
MARIONETTE	12940 0		15.75
MAX			14.2
MEIN TEDDYBAR	10002 7 10003 4		5.5
MELODY, MUSIC BEAR	62/31/3 ??		11.8
MELODY, MUSIC BEAR	62/31/3TP		11.8
MELODY, W/MUSIC BOX	62/30/4TSP		11.8
MILLICENT	12726 0		10.6
MINI FROM TAIWAN	15701 4		2.4
MINI FROM TAIWAN	15702 1		2.4
MINI FROM TAIWAN	15703 8		2.4
MINI FROM TAIWAN	15704 5		3.15
MINI FROM TAIWAN	15705 2		2.75
MINI FROM TAIWAN	15706 9		3.15
MINI FROM TAIWAN	15707 6		3.15
MINI FROM TAIWAN	15708 3		4.3
MINI RR "ADLER"	10071 3		NA
MINI TEDDY	15712 0		1.5
MINI TEDDY	15713 7		1.5
MINI TEDDY	15714 4		1.5
MINI TEDDY	15715 1		1.5
MINI TEDDY	15716 8		1.5
MINI TEDDY	15719 9		1.5
MINI TEDDY	15720 5		3
MINI TEDDY	15721 2		3.5
MINI TEDDY	15722 9		3.5
MINI TEDDY	15723 6		2.4
MINI TEDDY	15724 3		3.15
MINI TEDDY	15725 3		3.15
MINI TEDDY	15726 7		4
MINI TEDDY	15727 4		4
MINI TEDDY	15728 1		2.4
MINI TEDDY	15764 9		1.5
MINI TEDDY	15765 6		1.5
MINI TEDDY	15766 3		1.5
MINI TEDDY	15767 0		1.5
MINI TEDDY	15769 4		1.5
MINI TEDDY	15783 0		1.5
MINI TEDDY	15784 7		1.5
MINI TEDDY	15785 4		1.5
MINI TEDDY	15786 1		1.5
MINI TEDDY	15787 8		1.5
MINI TEDDY	15788 5		1.5
MINI TEDDY	15811 0		1.5
MINI TEDDY	15812 7		1.5
MINI TEDDY	15813 4		1.5
MINI TEDDY	15814 1		1.5
MINI TEDDY	15820 2		1.5
MINI TEDDY	15821 9		1.5
MINI TEDDY	15822 6		1.5
MINI TEDDY	15823 3		1.5
MINI TEDDY	15824 0		1.5
MINI TEDDY	15825 7		1.5
MINI TEDDY	5/10		4
MINI TEDDY SCHOOL	10021 8		24 X 12 X 11
MINI TEDDY SCHOOL	10025 6		8 X 5 X 5
MINI TEDDY SCHOOL	10025 8		7.8L X 6W X 5.1H
MINI TEDDY SCHOOL	10041 6		24 X 12 X 11
MINI TEDDY WORKSHOP	10031 7		24 X 12 X 11
MINI TEDDY XMAS SCENE	10040 9		234 X 10 X 11
MINIBEAR CIRCA 1948		MRF "N"	4.7
MINK	3008/45		17.7
MINK	43460 9		23.6
MONKEY	103/40/3		15.75
MONKEY	210/18		7
MONKEY	210/24		9.5
MONKEY	210/30		11.8
MONKEY	210/38		15
MONKEY	210/50		19.7
MONKEY	218/35		13.8
MONKEY	218/45		17.7
MONKEY	38035 1	220/35	13.8
MONKEY	38036 8		14.2
MONKEY	70004 3		5.9
MONKEY	74728 4	872/28	11
MONKEY, SITTING	232/28		11
MONKEY, SITTING	38120 4	232/20	7.9
MOONFISH W/MUSIC	77114 9	1481/14	5.5
MOONFISH W/MUSIC	77115 9		5.9
MOONLIGHT	13632 3		12.6
MOON, BABY'S	1200/8		3.2
MOTHER & BABY	11535 9		13
MOUSE	74628 7	871/28	11
MOUSE W MUSIC BOX	525/23		9.5
MOUSE, BABY'S	75712 2	1200/7	4.7
MOUSE, BLUE	525/20		7.9
MOUSE, GOLD	72020 1	529/20	7.9
MOUSE, GOLD	74829 8	874/29	11
MOUSE, GRAY	71609 9	525/9	3.5
MOUSE, GREEN	525/22		8.7
MOUSE, LILAC	71920 5	528/20	7.9
MOUSE, LILAC	71925 0	528/25	9.8
MOUSE, MULTICOLORED	75724 5		9.5
MOUSE, OLD ROSE	71709 6	525/9	3.5
MOUSE, RED	71820 8	527/20	1.9
MOUSE, RED	71825 3	527/25	9.8
MOUSE, RED	74828 1	874/28	11
MOUSE, REDDISH BROWN	525/21		8.3
MOUSE, STANDING	67115 2	80524/15	5.9
MOUSE, WHITE	71509 2	525/9	3.5
MOUSE, WHITE	71720 1	526/20	7.9
MUG	95029 5		
MUG, BEAR	95007 3		1.6
MÜNCHNER KINDL	01632 0		7.87
NEUSTADT BEAR	01563 0		11.8
NICHOLAS W/BASE	15772 4		3.1
NICOLAUS	15430 8		11.8
NIEDIEK	01432 5		9.8
NO SEE, NO HEAR, NO TELL	15932 2		2.4
NO-NO BEAR	16914 7	69/14ag	5.5
NO-NO BEAR	16915 4	69/14s	5.5
NO-NO BEAR	16915 7		5.5
NO-NO BEAR	16920 8		7.9
NO-NO BEAR	16931 4		11.8
NO-NO BEAR	6935		13.75
NO-NO BEAR	16930 7		11.8
NO-NO BEAR	16935 2		14.1
NO-NO BEAR	16935 2	69/35	14.1
NO-NO BEAR	16935 2	69/35	14.1
NO-NO BEAR	16935 2	69/35	14.1
NO-NO-BEAR, NOSTALGIC	16916 1		5.5
OCELOT	4700/30		11.8
OLD FASHIONED	15915 5		3
OLD SALIGHT	15/28		11
OLIVER	19745 4		18.1
OMA (GRANDMOTHER)	11550 2		20
ONE-OF-A-KIND	NO#		19.69
ORIGINAL HERMAN	16125 4	61/25	7.8
ORIGINAL HERMAN	16125 7	61/25	11
ORIGINAL HERMAN	16136 3	61/36	14.2
ORIGINAL HERMAN	16140 7	61/40	15.75
ORIGINAL HERMAN	16150 9	61/50	19.7
ORIGINAL HERMANN	06220 1		7.9
ORIGINAL HERMANN	06220 2		7.9
ORIGINAL HERMANN	06230 1		11.8
ORIGINAL HERMANN	16114 1	61/14	4.7
ORIGINAL TEDDYBEAR	16230 8	62/30	11.8
OUTFIT, HIKING BOY	97020 0		FOR 7.9
OUTFIT, HIKING BOY	97021 7		
OUTFIT, HIKING GIRL	97120 7		
OVERALLS	96630 2		FOR 11.8
OVERALLS	96641 1		FOR 15.8
OVERALLS	96650 0		FOR 19.7
OVERALLS	97620 2		
OWL	1000		
OWL	42016 3	196/16	6.3
OWL	42017 0	196/16K	6.3
OWL	42018 7	196/18	7
OWL	42019 4	196/18K	7
OWL	42022 4		8.7
OWL	42025 5	196/25	9.8
OWL	42036 1		13.8
OWL W/MUSIC	1487/18		7
OWL, MUSICAL	197/18		7
PALLI-TEDDY	01523 2		11.8
PANDA	16014 4		5.5
PANDA	16030 4		11.8
PANDA	18618 2	86/18	7
PANDA	18625 0	86/25	10.2
PANDA	18630 4	86/30	11.8
PANDA BEAR	08635 2		15
PANDA BEAR	31540 7	82000/40	15.75
PANDA BEAR	31660 2	82006/60	23.6
PANDA BEAR	82006/28 31628 2		11
PANDA BEAR "PIEPE"	31628 2	82006/28	11
PANDA BEAR CROUCHING	31755 5	82007/55	19L X 12H
PANDA BEAR SITTING	31855 2	84090/55	22
PANDA BEAR SITTING	31875 0	84090/75	29.5
PANDA BEAR SITTING	31897 2	84090/110	43
PANDA BEAR "SCHNURZ"	31725 8	82007/25	10.2
PANDA BEAR, 4 LEGGED		MRF "M"	8.25LX7.5H
PANDA CIRCA 1950			9.5
PANDA CIRCA 1957			11.8
PANDA W/GROWLER	86/35		14.2
PANTHER	37543 5	2019/42	16.5
PANTHER, BLACK	2000/58		22.8
PANTHER, BLACK	37033 8	2000/33	13
PANTHER, LYING	37135 9	2018/35	13.8
PANTHER, LYING	37160 1	2018/60	23.6
PANTHER, SITTING	37542 5	2019/42	16.5
PANTHER, SITTING	37560 9	2019/60	23.6
PANTS	96730 9		FOR 11.8
PANTS	96740 8		FOR 15.8
PANTS	96750 7		FOR 19.7
PARROT	192/45		17.7
PARROT	200/35		13.8
PARROT	200/40		15.75
PARROT	200/50		19.8
PARROT	200/60		23.75
PARROT W/MUSIC	1490/40		15.75
PARROT, BLUE	42225 9	199/25	9.8
PARROT, GREEN	42125 2	198/25	9.8
PAUL	11935 7		13.4
PAULY	11930 2		11.8
"PAYNE" TOOTHACHE BEAR			11.8
PEACH FUZZ	01493 5		13.9
PENDANT	95005 9		1.57
PENDANT	95051 6		1.57
PENGUIN	46023 7	571/23	9.5
PENGUIN	46030 5	571/30	11.8
PENGUIN	46123 4	572/23	9.5
PENGUIN	46130 2	572/30	11.8
PENGUIN	46148 7	572/48	18.9
PENGUIN	46170 8	572/70	27.6
PENGUIN	46230 9		11.8
PENGUIN	46240 8		15.75
PENGUIN	46250 7		19.7
PETER	19845 1		18.1
PETER PAN	NO#		7.87
PETZI	10/28		14
PETZI	11/35		14.2
PHILLIPP	15630 7	DUPL. #	11.8
PIANIST AT PIANO	10525 1		6
PICNIC BASKET	95021 9		
PICNIC, MUSICAL SET	62/35 SU140		11.8
PIERRE	15440 2		15.75
PIGGY BANK	95007 3		
PIGGY BANK	95027 1		
PIGGY BANK, 1930 REPLICA	95017 2		

NAME	EAN/ OLD#	ALSO SEE	INCHES TALL
PIGLET	02016 5	02015 8	7.9
PIGLET	80740/30		11.8
PIGLET, CROUCHING	44530 2	80742/30	11.8
PIGLET, CROUCHING	44540 1	80742/40	15.75
PIGLET, CROUCHING	44550 0	80742/50	19.7
PIGLET, SITTING	80745/18		7
PIN	95053 0		1.57
PINCUSHION, BULLDOG	500/1		
PINCUSHION, BULLDOG	510/1		
PINCUSHION, PEKINGESE	500/2		
PINCUSHION, PEKINGESE	510/2		
PINCUSHION, SPORTING DOG	500/4		
PINCUSHION, SPORTING DOG	510/4		
PINCUSHION, TERRIER	500/3		
PINCUSHION, TERRIER	510/3		
PINGO	20/28		11.8
PINK BLOSSOM	05235 7		14.2
PIN, BEAR LABEL	95043 1		0.375
PIN, TEDDY	95043 9		
PIN, WOODEN	95052 3		
PLATE, BEAR	95005 9		6.7 DIA
PLATE, BEAR	95006 6		4 DIA
PLAY ROOM	10042 3		7.8L X 6W X 5.1H
POLAR BEAR	20250 9	80002/50	19.7
POLAR BEAR	20285 1	80002/85	33
POLAR BEAR	32728 8	590/28	8H X 11L
POLAR BEAR	3700/30		11.8
POLAR BEAR	80002/20		7.9
POLAR BEAR	80002/30		11.8
POLAR BEAR LYING	32635 9	3705/35	14.2
POLAR BEAR ON WHEELS	70017 3		5H X 6.5L
POLAR BEAR SITTING	32532 1	3701/32	12.6
POLAR BEAR, ACRYLIC		MRF "J"	4H X 7L
POLAR BEAR, LYING DOWN	32845 2	80001/45	17.7
POLAR BEAR, LYING DOWN	32860 5	80001/60	23.6
POLAR BEAR, LYING DOWN	32875 9	80001/75	29.5
POLDI BEAR	01512 3		8.7
POPPO	15832 5		4.7
POSTCARD	99008 6		
POSTCARD	99009 3		
POSTCARD	99010 7		
POSTCARD	99011 4		
POSTCARDS, STAND. BEARS	99002 4		
POSTCARD, ASS'TD	99016 1		
POSTCARD, IN BAMBERG	99013 8		
POSTCARD, CHEF OTTO	99003 1		
POSTCARD, FOR YOU	99014 5		
POSTCARD, FRIENDS	99015 2		
POSTCARD, GARDEN PARTY	99012 1		
POSTCARD, SAILOR	99006 2		
POSTCARD, SHEPHERD	99005 5		
POSTCARD, SIR ARTHUR	99007 9		
POSTCARD, SWEET ROSE	99004 8		
POSTER, ALASKA BEARS	98012 4		
POSTER, BEAR W/CUB	98013 1		
POSTER, BEARS IN DESERT	98014 8		
POSTER, BENJAMIN	98011 7		
POSTER, BIRTHDAY CHARLIE	98009 4		
POSTER, DEN OF BEARS	98008 7		
POSTER, JUBILEE BEARS	98003 2	9000.3	
POSTER, MINIATURES	98010 0		
POSTER, RIDING A HORSE	98001 8	9000.1	
POSTER, ROMANCE IN ROTH.	98007 0		
POSTER, SAILOR	98005 6		
POSTER, SIR ARTUR	98006 3		
POSTER, STANDING BEARS	98004 9	9000.4	
POSTER, TEDDYHEAD	98002 5	9000.2	
PRINCESS, CIRCA 1980			18.9
PRINCE, CIRCA 1980			18.1
PROFESSOR BERNHARD	11555 7	67/55	21.6
PUNCH	76226 3	1200/12	10.2
PUPIL AT BENCH	10522 0		7.9
PUPIL AT DESK	10514 5		5.5
RABBIT	1410/26		10.2
RABBIT	403/40		15.75
RABBIT	403/55		21.7
RABBIT	404/33		13
RABBIT	610/35		13.8
RABBIT	615/21		8.7
RABBIT	616/26		10.2
RABBIT	616/33		12.6
RABBIT	655/35		13.78
RABBIT	660/48		18.9
RABBIT	665/50		19.7
RABBIT	710/21		8.3
RABBIT	711/20		7.9
RABBIT	715/25		9.8
RABBIT	719/35		13.8
RABBIT	75328 5		11
RABBIT	80625/35		13.8
RABBIT	80640/35		13.8
RABBIT	80640/40		15.75
RABBIT	80642/35		13.8
RABBIT	82135 9	80626/35	13.8
RABBIT	82520 3	80715/20	10.2
RABBIT	82620 0	80716/20	10.2
RABBIT	84442 6		16.5
RABBIT ASST'D COLORS	83221 8	712/21	8.3
RABBIT POUNCING, SMALL	600/14		5.5
RABBIT POUNCING, SMALL	600/17		6.7
RABBIT WITH APRON	635/50		19.69
RABBIT WITH APRON	635/60		23.6
RABBIT W/PACKBACK	85025 0		9.8
RABBIT, ANGORA	80620/25		9.8
RABBIT, ANGORA	80620/35		13.8
RABBIT, ANGORA	80621/35		13.8
RABBIT, ANGORA	80622/25		9.8
RABBIT, ANGORA	80622/35		13.8
RABBIT, ANGORA	82025 3	80622/25	9.8
RABBIT, ANGORA	82035 2	80622/35	13.8
RABBIT, BABY	80022 4	101/22	8.7
RABBIT, BABY	80122 1	102/22	8.7
RABBIT, BROWN	80651/35		13.8
RABBIT, BUFFY	15740 3		2.8
RABBIT, CROUCHING	607/21		8.3
RABBIT, CROUCHING	607/28		11
RABBIT, CROUCHING	607/42		16.5
RABBIT, CROUCHING	645/30		11.8
RABBIT, CROUCHING	645/40		15.75
RABBIT, CROUCHING	645/60		23.6
RABBIT, CROUCHING	80630 1	646/30	11.8
RABBIT, CROUCHING	80650/30		11.8
RABBIT, CROUCHING	80650/50		19.7
RABBIT, CROUCHING	80652/30		11.8
RABBIT, CROUCHING	80740 7	647/40	15.75
RABBIT, DANGLING	720/52		20.5
RABBIT, DANGLING	80536 6	80660/35/1	13.8
RABBIT, DWARF	555/24		9.5
RABBIT, DWARF	555/32		12.6
RABBIT, DWARF	555/55		21.7
RABBIT, DWARF	780/20		7.9
RABBIT, FIELD, BLK & WHT	625/25/1		9.84
RABBIT, FIELD, BRN & WHT	625/25/2		9.84
RABBIT, FLUFFY	15741 0		2.8
RABBIT, GRAY	80650/35		13.8
RABBIT, LYING	718/35		13.8
RABBIT, LYING	80607/21		8.3
RABBIT, LYING	80607/28		11
RABBIT, LYING	80607/42		16.5
RABBIT, LYING	80608/21		8.3
RABBIT, LYING	82420 6	80714/20	10.2
RABBIT, LYING	84028 2	80600/28	11
RABBIT, LYING	84128 9	80601/28	11
RABBIT, LYING	84242 2	80608/42	16.5
RABBIT, LYING	84321 4	80609/21	8.3
RABBIT, MOTHER	80032 3	100/32	12.6
RABBIT, POUNCING	714/18		6.7
RABBIT, SITTING	708/28		11
RABBIT, SITTING	709/28		11
RABBIT, SITTING	796/32		12.6
RABBIT, SITTING	80709/28		11
RABBIT, SITTING	83028 3	80709/28	11
RABBIT, STANDING	630/28		11
RABBIT, STANDING	630/33		13
RABBIT, STANDING	630/40		15.75
RABBIT, STANDING	647/40	80740 7	15.75
RABBIT, STANDING	647/45		17.72
RABBIT, STANDING	67413 9	80538/13	5.1
RABBIT, STANDING	80550 2	80660/50	19.7
RABBIT, STANDING	85023 6	604/23	9.5
RACCOON	2500/25		9.8
RACCOON	2500/35		13.8
RACCOON	33515 3	2500/15	5.9
RACCOON	33625 9	2550/25	9.8
RATSKELLAR	10050 8		7.75 X 8 X 10
RAVEN	2200/25		9.8
RAVEN	42330 0	81350/30	11.8
RAVEN	74528 0	870/28	11
REUNIFICATION BEAR	15145 2		18.1
RHINOCEROS	550/24		9.5
RICHARD	12630 0		11.8
ROBIN HOOD	15345 0		18.1
ROBIN HOOD, LITTLE	15322 1		8.5
ROBIN HOOD, ORIGINAL	62/60	CA 240	
ROSA	12042 1		15.75
ROSABELLE	01014 0		15.75
ROSALLIE	15229 3		11.8
ROSAMUNDE	11323 2		7
ROSE	01204 1		15.75
ROSE	13617 0		6.5
ROSE QUARTZ	11622 6		6.3
ROSENKAVALIER	01421 4	14214 0	5
ROSENKAVALIER	01423 2		11.8
RUCKSACK FOR 7.9" BEAR	95203 9		
RUDY	12820 5		7.9
RUGGED REGGIE BEAR	16830 0		11.8
RUGGED REGGIE BEAR	16840 9		15.75
RUGGED REGGIE BEAR	16850 8		19.7
RUGGED REGGIE BEAR	16860 ?		23.6
RUGGED REGGIE BEAR	16880 5		31
RUGGED REGGIE BEAR	16880 ?		31
RUHRLI 1991/92	15217 0		7
RUNNING BEAR	70020		7.9
SADIE	15742 7		2.8
SAILOR BEAR SCHOOL	10011 9		7.9
SAILOR BOY	10321 9		7.9
SAILOR BOY	11121 1		7.9
SAILOR BOY	11121 4		7.9
SAILOR BOY	11123 8		7.9
SAILOR BOY	11221 1		7.9
SAILOR BOY	11231 0		11.8
SAILOR BOY	11515 1M		6.69
SAILOR BOY 1994	10421 6		7.9
SAILOR DRESS	97420 8		
SAILOR FATHER	11241 9		15.75
SAILOR GIRL	10221 2		7.9
SAILOR GIRL	10222 9		7.9
SAILOR GIRL	11120 7		7.9
SAILOR GIRL	11122 1		7.9
SAILOR GIRL	11200 4		7.9
SAILOR GIRL	11220 4		7.9
SAILOR GIRL	11230 3		11.8
SAILOR MOTHER	11240 2		15.75
SAILOR OUTFIT	96530 5		
SAILOR OUTFIT	96540 4		
SAILOR OUTFIT	96550 3		
SAILOR OUTFIT	97520 5		
SAILOR SUIT	96531 2		FOR 11.8
SAILOR SUIT	96541 1		FOR 15.8
SAILOR SUIT	96551 0		FOR 19.7
SALLY	15325 2		10.2
SAM	11840 4		15.75
SANDBOX W/2 BEARS	S 0003	6225HW	8 & 10
SANTA CLAUS 1927			16.5
SANTA CLAUS 1927 ??		MRF "G"	17.5
SANTA CLAUS	15940 7		4
SANTA W/MUSIC 1996	15135 3		14.2
SASSIE	15933 9		3.2
SATCHEL LEATHER FOR 7.9" BR	95201 5		
SCHNAUZER	70002 9		4
SCHOOL BABY	10420 9	63/20/4K	7.9
SCHOOL BOY	10320 2	63/20/3K	7.9
SCHOOL GIRL @ DESK	10520 6	63/20/5K	7.9
SCHOOL SET			7.9 & 14.2
SCHOOL SET COMPLETE	10001 0	63/01	47X21.6X12.5
SCHOOL SET (NO ROOM)	10001 0	274/100	47X21.6X12.5
SCHOOLGIRL	10223 6		7.9
SCHOOLGIRL PLASTIC BOX	10220 5	63/20/2K	7.9
SCHOOLHOUSE, 2 STORY	01009 0		
SCOOTERIST "ROLFI"	10085 0		7.5
SEAL	46524 9	736/24	9.5
SEAL	46532 4	736/32	12.6
SEAL	46542 3	736/42	16.5
SEA LION	736/65		25.6
SEA LION	737/32		12.6
SEA LION, BABY	46624 6	739/24	9.5
SEA LION, BABY	46632 1	739/32	12.6
SEA LION, BABY	46642 0	739/42	16.5
SEA LION, BABY	46665 9	739/65	25.6
SEA LION, BABY	735/28		11
SEA LION, BABY'S	76020 7	1200/10	7.9
SEA LION, BABY'S	76120 4	1200/11	7.9

NAME	EAN/OLD#	ALSO SEE	INCHES TALL
SEPPL	101246		7.9
SEPPL	256359	55/35/2	14.2
SETTEE	95522 1		
SHADOW	136309		11.5
SHEEP, GRAZING	861607	420/60	23.6
SHEPHERD SET	120353	62/35/5	14.2
SHOP FOR TEDDIES	955030		
SHOPPING BAG, 6 PCS	990055		
SILVER	159179		2.8
SILVER FOX	83025/85		33.5
SIMON	158332		4.7
SINGAPORE LION BEAR	016336		14.2
SIR ARTHUR	118459		18.1
SKIER	173205		10.2
SLED	951063		7.9
SNAIL	395256		9.8
SNAIL	777250		9.8
SNAIL	778257		9.8
SNOWMAN W/MUSIC	1365/16		6.3
SOCCER PLAYER	141303		11.8
SONNENBERG	122500		19.7
SPANKY	159230		2.8
SPECIAL BEAR FOR UK	144311		11.8
SPECIAL BEAR FOR UK	144410		15.75
·SQUIRREL	670179	80512/17	6.7
SQUIRREL	710103	512/10	4
SQUIRREL	710172	512/17	6.7
SQUIRREL	710240	512/24	9.5
SQUIRREL	80510/35		13.8
SQUIRREL	80510/50		19.7
SQUIRREL	80512/24		9.5
STANDING GOAT	1452/25		9.8
STANDING PANDA	700050		6
STAND, BEAR 18-30 CM	953029		
STAND, BEAR 26-46 CM	953036		
STAND, BEAR 9-15 CM	953111		
STAND, BEAR 9-15CM	953012		
STICKER, TEDDY SIGN	982302	12 DIA,	
STICKER, TEDDY SIGN 5" DIA	982128		
STRATFORD UPON AVON	016231		15.75
STRATFORD UPON AVON	016241		11.8
STRAWBEARY	148401		15.75
STUDENT	63205K		8
SUMMER JOY	052307		11.8
SUN W/MUSIC	773252	1484/25	9.8
SUNBEAM	136316		12.6
SUNNY	152262		8.5
SWAN	890553		21.6
SWAN, OLD ROSE	891246	1331/24	9.5
SWAN, WHITE	890249	1330/24	9.5
SWEATER & PANTS	962304		
SWEATER & PANTS	962311		FOR 11.8
SWEATER & PANTS	962403		
SWEATER & PANTS	962410		
SWEATER & PANTS	962502		
SWEATER & PANTS	962519		FOR 19.7
SWEATER + CAP	964308		
SWEATER + CAP	964315		FOR 11.8
SWEATER + CAP	964407		
SWEATER + CAP	964414		FOR 15.8
SWEATER + CAP	964506		
SWEATER + CAP	964513		FOR 19.7
SWEET ROSE	130352		14.2
SWEET TEDDY	62/50NWB		16.5
SWEET TEDDY	CA 330		33
SWEET TEDDYS	CA 40		4
SWEET TEDDYS	CA 55		5.5
SWEET TEDDYS	CA 140		14
SWEET TEDDYS	CH 40		4
SWEET TEDDYS	CH 80		8
SWEET TEDDYS	CH 140	62/35/1	14
SWEET TEDDYS	CI 40		4
SWEET TEDDYS	CI 80		8
SWEET TEDDYS	CI 140		14
SWEET TEDDYS	CO 40		4
SWEET TEDDYS	GO 80		8
SWEET TEDDYS	LI 40		4
SWEET TEDDYS	LI 140		14
SWEET TEDDYS	LI 140N		14
SWEET TEDDYS	LI 55 OR 62/14		5.5
SWEET TEDDYS	SU 40		4
SWEET TEDDYS	SU 55		5.5
SWEET TEDDYS	SU 70		7
SWEET TEDDYS	SU 75		5H X 6L
SWEET TEDDYS	SU 100		10
SWEET TEDDYS	SU 190		19
SWEET TEDDYS	SU 240		24
SWEET TEDDYS	SU 80		8
SWEET TEDDYS	SU120		12
SWEET TEDDYS	SU140	62/35NWR	14
SWEET THING	NO 70		7
SWEET THING	NO 140N		14
SWEETHEART BEAR	04025	040/25	7.75
SWEETHEART BEAR	136347		11.8
SWEETHEART BEAR	70062/20		7.9
TABATHA W/BASE	157335		2.8
TABLE	955214		
TB W/TRICYCLE C. 1970			11
TEA PARTY TEDDYS	114017		4.7
TEA PARTY TEDDYS	114024		4.7
TEA PARTY TEDDYS	114031		4.7
TEA PARTY TEDDYS	114048		4.7
TEA SET, MINI PORCELAIN	950011	9002.4	
TEA SET, MINI PORCELAIN	950011	9000.4	
TEA SET, MINI PORCELAIN	950110		
TEA SET, MINI PORCELAIN	950134		
TEDDY 2000	900283		11
TEDDY 2000	900504		19.7
TEDDY 2000	900656		25.6
TEDDY 2000	900856		33.5
TEDDY 2000	901150		5.9
TEDDY 2000	901228		8.7
TEDDY 2000	901556		21.7
TEDDY 2000	902508		19.7
TEDDY 2000	903208		7.87
TEDDY 2000	903500		19.7
TEDDY 2000	904601		23.6
TEDDY 2000	905202		7.87
TEDDY 2000	905226		8.66
TEDDY 2000	906247		9.45
TEDDY 2000	906353		13.8
TEDDY 2000	907307		11.8
TEDDY 2000	908258		9.84
TEDDY 2000	910220		5H X 7L
TEDDY 2000	910220		8.66
TEDDY 2000	910305		11.8
TEDDY 2000	911302		11.8
TEDDY 2000	912408		15.75
TEDDY 2000	912507		19.7
TEDDY 2000	912705		27.6
TEDDY 2000	913252		9.8
TEDDY 2000	913283		11
TEDDY 2000	913306		11.8
TEDDY 2000	913351		13.8
TEDDY 2000	914259		9.84
TEDDY 2000	914303		11.8
TEDDY 2000	915232		9
TEDDY 2000	915362		14.2
TEDDY 2000	915560		22
TEDDY 2000	916406		15.75
TEDDY 2000	917205		7.9
TEDDY 2000	917359		13.8
TEDDY 2000	918202		1.9
TEDDY 2000	91/30		11.8
TEDDY 2000	91/38		15
TEDDY 2000	91/42		16.5
TEDDY 2000	921141		5.5
TEDDY 2000	921202		7.9
TEDDY 2000	922254		9.8
TEDDY 2000	923206		7.9
TEDDY 2000	923206		7.9
TEDDY 2000	923220		8.7
TEDDY 2000	924302		11.8
TEDDY 2000	925255		9.8
TEDDY 2000	926306		11.8
TEDDY 2000	926351		13.8
TEDDY 2000	926504		19.7
TEDDY 2000	927150		5.9
TEDDY 2000	928409		15.75
TEDDY 2000	929239		9.5
TEDDY 2000	930204		7.9
TEDDY 2000	930358		13.8
TEDDY 2000	931140		5.5
TEDDY 2000	931355 1		13.8
TEDDY 2000	932260		10.2
TEDDY 2000	932451		17.7
TEDDY 2000	932451		17.8
TEDDY 2000	932468		18.1
TEDDY 2000	932505		19.7
TEDDY 2000	932703		27.6
TEDDY 2000	933175		6.7
TEDDY 2000	933304		11.8
TEDDY 2000	933403		15.75
TEDDY 2000	934172		6.7
TEDDY 2000	935188		7
TEDDY 2000	935409		15.75
TEDDY 2000	936206		7.9
TEDDY 2000	936350		13.8
TEDDY 2000, FOAL	902300		11.8
TEDDY 2000, XMAS	910251		9.84
TEDDY 2000, XMAS	910305		11.8
TEDDY 2000, XMAS	911081		3.9
TEDDY BEAR			10.2
TEDDY BEAR		MRF "AL"	12.6
TEDDY BEAR	011825		9.84
TEDDY BEAR	011931		11.8
TEDDY BEAR	013025		9.8
TEDDY BEAR	013031		11.8
TEDDY BEAR	013617		7.87
TEDDY BEAR	014732		11.8
TEDDY BEAR	014830		11.8
TEDDY BEAR	014936		13.8
TEDDY BEAR	014950		11.8
TEDDY BEAR	016280	70007/45	31.5
TEDDY BEAR	016331		11.8
TEDDY BEAR	016351	016330	14.2
TEDDY BEAR	052609	052357	23.6
TEDDY BEAR	062400		15.8
TEDDY BEAR	063801	163800	31.5
TEDDY BEAR	06755		22
TEDDY BEAR	07223		7.9
TEDDY BEAR	095408		11.8
TEDDY BEAR	100/40/1		15.75
TEDDY BEAR	144304		118
TEDDY BEAR	144403		15.75
TEDDY BEAR	144502		19.7
TEDDY BEAR	148302		11.8
TEDDY BEAR	157441		4.3
TEDDY BEAR	157809		1.6
TEDDY BEAR	157816		1.6
TEDDY BEAR	157823		1.6
TEDDY BEAR	157915		2
TEDDY BEAR	157922		2
TEDDY BEAR	157939		2
TEDDY BEAR	157946		2
TEDDY BEAR	157953		2
TEDDY BEAR	157960		2.4
TEDDY BEAR	157977		2.4
TEDDY BEAR	157984		2
TEDDY BEAR	157991		2
TEDDY BEAR	176305	76/30	11.8
TEDDY BEAR	176404	76/40	15.75
TEDDY BEAR	176503	76/50	19.7
TEDDY BEAR	176800	76/80	31LE
TEDDY BEAR	176985	76/120	47
TEDDY BEAR	176992	76/150	60
TEDDY BEAR	177302	77/30	11.8
TEDDY BEAR	177319		11.8
TEDDY BEAR	177401	77/40	15.75
TEDDY BEAR	177500	77/50	19.7
TEDDY BEAR	177807	77/80	31
TEDDY BEAR	178309		11.8
TEDDY BEAR	178408		15.75
TEDDY BEAR	178507		19.7
TEDDY BEAR	181354		14.2
TEDDY BEAR	181408	81/40	15.75
TEDDY BEAR	204251	80004/25	10.2
TEDDY BEAR	204305	80004/30	11.8
TEDDY BEAR	204487	80005/48	18.9
TEDDY BEAR	205517		19.7
TEDDY BEAR	205609	80005/60	23.6
TEDDY BEAR	205616		23.6
TEDDY BEAR	205708	80005/70B	27.5
TEDDY BEAR	205715		27.5
TEDDY BEAR	205906	80005/90	35
TEDDY BEAR	208504		19.7
TEDDY BEAR	208603		23.6
TEDDY BEAR	208702		28.3
TEDDY BEAR	209501		19.7
TEDDY BEAR	209600		23.6
TEDDY BEAR	220310		11.8
TEDDY BEAR	220327		11.8

NAME	EAN/OLD#	ALSO SEE	INCHES TALL
TEDDY BEAR	23128 8	80031/28	11
TEDDY BEAR	23133 2	80031/33	12.6
TEDDY BEAR	23142 4	80031/42	16.5
TEDDY BEAR	23228 5	80032/28	11
TEDDY BEAR	23233 9	80032/33	12.6
TEDDY BEAR	23242 1	80032/42	16.5
TEDDY BEAR	23328 2	80033/28	11
TEDDY BEAR	23333 6	80033/33	12.6
TEDDY BEAR	23342 8	80033/42	16.5
TEDDY BEAR	23440 2	80034/30	11.8
TEDDY BEAR	23442 5	80034/42	16.5
TEDDY BEAR	23530 9		11.8
TEDDY BEAR	23540 8		15.75
TEDDY BEAR	23639 9		15.7
TEDDY BEAR	24540 4	80046/40	15.75
TEDDY BEAR	24640 4	80046/40	15.75
TEDDY BEAR	24740 1	80047/40	15.75
TEDDY BEAR	4/30		11.8
TEDDY BEAR	4/35		14.2
TEDDY BEAR	58/30/1		11.8
TEDDY BEAR	58/30/2		11.8
TEDDY BEAR	61/36/1		14.2
TEDDY BEAR	61/40		15.75
TEDDY BEAR	6225NSO		10
TEDDY BEAR	6230		12
TEDDY BEAR	6230NSO		12
TEDDY BEAR	6235NSB		14
TEDDY BEAR	6235NWB		14
TEDDY BEAR	6240		16
TEDDY BEAR	6240MW		16
TEDDY BEAR	6280C		32
TEDDY BEAR	62/17/1		6.5
TEDDY BEAR	62/20/4		
TEDDY BEAR	62/20/?		7.9
TEDDY BEAR	62/25LA		11
TEDDY BEAR	62/30		11.8
TEDDY BEAR	62/30 OLD		11.8
TEDDY BEAR	62/35/1		14.2
TEDDY BEAR	62/40 MAIS		15.75
TEDDY BEAR	62/40 OLD		15.75
TEDDY BEAR	62/40/3/O		16.5
TEDDY BEAR	62/45		18.1
TEDDY BEAR	62/50NSB		19.6
TEDDY BEAR	62/85	CA 330	33
TEDDY BEAR	62/90		35.5
TEDDY BEAR	66/35		14
TEDDY BEAR	66/42		17
TEDDY BEAR	70007/45	7007/45 ERROR	15.75
TEDDY BEAR	70061/36		14.2
TEDDY BEAR	70062/25		9.5
TEDDY BEAR	70062/40		15.75
TEDDY BEAR	70062/40/3		15.75
TEDDY BEAR	70076 8		?
TEDDY BEAR	70084/18		7.5
TEDDY BEAR	70084/35		14.2
TEDDY BEAR	7040		15.75
TEDDY BEAR	70/28 OLD		11
TEDDY BEAR	70/38		15
TEDDY BEAR	70/50 OLD		19.6
TEDDY BEAR	70/50 ?		19.6
TEDDY BEAR	70/50 ?		19.6
TEDDY BEAR	70/60 OLD		23.5
TEDDY BEAR	75526 5		10.2
TEDDY BEAR	76235W		13.75
TEDDY BEAR	7630W		11.8
TEDDY BEAR	7650B		19.6
TEDDY BEAR	76/150W		59
TEDDY BEAR	76/30W		11.8
TEDDY BEAR	76/40B		15.75
TEDDY BEAR	76/50W		19.6
TEDDY BEAR	76/80W		32
TEDDY BEAR	77/50H		19.6
TEDDY BEAR	78/30		11.8
TEDDY BEAR	78/40		15.75
TEDDY BEAR	80005/60B		23.6
TEDDY BEAR	80005/90B		35
TEDDY BEAR	80006/62H		23.6
TEDDY BEAR	80006/72H		28.3
TEDDY BEAR	80028/28		11
TEDDY BEAR	80028/33		12.6
TEDDY BEAR	80029/33		12.6
TEDDY BEAR	80560B		23.6
TEDDY BEAR	80672H		28.3
TEDDY BEAR	80785C		33
TEDDY BEAR	80850B		19.7
TEDDY BEAR	80885B		33
TEDDY BEAR	81/50		19.7
TEDDY BEAR	82/26 MW		10.2
TEDDY BEAR	83042H		16.5
TEDDY BEAR	83133		12.6
TEDDY BEAR	83233		13.5
TEDDY BEAR	83242		16.5
TEDDY BEAR	84/24		9.5
TEDDY BEAR	84/28		11
TEDDY BEAR	84/42		16.5
TEDDY BEAR	925/40		11.8
TEDDY BEAR	925/60B		23.6
TEDDY BEAR	CO 180		18
TEDDY BEAR MISTAKE	15233 0	SPECIAL	11.8
TEDDY BEAR 1985 CONF	02035	020/35	11
TEDDY BEAR 2000 SIGN	98210 4		
TEDDY BEAR CIRCA 1930	61/60 OLD		23.6
TEDDY BEAR CIRCA '94	07225		7.9
TEDDY BEAR GREY	16430 2	64/30	11.8
TEDDY BEAR GREY	16425 8	64/25	10.2
TEDDY BEAR GREY CUB	16414 2	64/14	4.7
TEDDY BEAR GREY CUB	16420 3	64/20	7.9
TEDDY BEAR PAPA GREY	16440 1	64/40	15.75
TEDDY BEAR WASHABLE	20025 3	4/25	10.2
TEDDY BEAR WASHABLE	20026 0	4/25K	10.2
TEDDY BEAR WASHABLE	20030 7	4/30	11.8
TEDDY BEAR WASHABLE	20035 2	4/35	14.2
TEDDY BEAR WASHABLE	80012/26		9.6
TEDDY BEAR WASHABLE	80013/26		9.6
TEDDY BEARS	71 SERIES		VARIOUS
TEDDY BEAR, BABY'S	75525 8	1200/5	9.8
TEDDY BEAR, BLACK	16614 6	62/14s	5.6
TEDDY BEAR, BLACK	16620 7	62/20s	7.9
TEDDY BEAR, BLACK	16625 ?	62/25s	10.2
TEDDY BEAR, BLACK	16630 6	62/30s	11.8
TEDDY BEAR, CIRCA '18			29.1
TEDDY BEAR, CIRCA '24			19.6
TEDDY BEAR, CIRCA '25			19.6
TEDDY BEAR, CIRCA '27			14.2
TEDDY BEAR, CIRCA '27		MRF "P"	25.6
TEDDY BEAR, CIRCA '30			12.6
TEDDY BEAR, CIRCA '30			12.6
TEDDY BEAR, CIRCA '30			14.2
TEDDY BEAR, CIRCA '30		MRF "Z"	15
TEDDY BEAR, CIRCA '30			15.75
TEDDY BEAR, CIRCA '30		MRF "F"	16.5
TEDDY BEAR, CIRCA '30			18.1
TEDDY BEAR, CIRCA '30		MRF "S"	18.1
TEDDY BEAR, CIRCA '35		MRF "Q"	19.6
TEDDY BEAR, CIRCA '40		MRF "AB"	11.8
TEDDY BEAR, CIRCA '40			15
TEDDY BEAR, CIRCA '40			16.5
TEDDY BEAR, CIRCA '40			19.6
TEDDY BEAR, CIRCA '40			23.6
TEDDY BEAR, CIRCA '40			23.6
TEDDY BEAR, CIRCA '45			18.9
TEDDY BEAR, CIRCA '45			22
TEDDY BEAR, CIRCA '48			22.8
TEDDY BEAR, CIRCA '48		MRF "L"	23.6
TEDDY BEAR, CIRCA '48			23.6
TEDDY BEAR, CIRCA '49			15.75
TEDDY BEAR, CIRCA '49			26.8
TEDDY BEAR, CIRCA '50			10.2
TEDDY BEAR, CIRCA '50		MRF "AG"	10.2
TEDDY BEAR, CIRCA '50			10.2
TEDDY BEAR, CIRCA '50			11
TEDDY BEAR, CIRCA '50			11
TEDDY BEAR, CIRCA '50			11.8
TEDDY BEAR, CIRCA '50			12.6
TEDDY BEAR, CIRCA '50			15
TEDDY BEAR, CIRCA '50			15
TEDDY BEAR, CIRCA '50		MRF "AO"	15.75
TEDDY BEAR, CIRCA '50			15.75
TEDDY BEAR, CIRCA '50			15.75
TEDDY BEAR, CIRCA '50			15.75
TEDDY BEAR, CIRCA '50			16.5
TEDDY BEAR, CIRCA '50			18.1
TEDDY BEAR, CIRCA '50			18.9
TEDDY BEAR, CIRCA '50			19.6
TEDDY BEAR, CIRCA '50			19.6
TEDDY BEAR, CIRCA '50		MRF "AA"	21.3
TEDDY BEAR, CIRCA '50		MRF "H"	21.3
TEDDY BEAR, CIRCA '50			22.8
TEDDY BEAR, CIRCA '50			22.8
TEDDY BEAR, CIRCA '50		MRF "AN"	23.6
TEDDY BEAR, CIRCA '53			14.2
TEDDY BEAR, CIRCA '53			23.6
TEDDY BEAR, CIRCA '53		MRF "D"	26.8
TEDDY BEAR, CIRCA '55			9.5
TEDDY BEAR, CIRCA '55			11
TEDDY BEAR, CIRCA '55			14.2
TEDDY BEAR, CIRCA '55			14.2
TEDDY BEAR, CIRCA '55			16.5
TEDDY BEAR, CIRCA '55			18.1
TEDDY BEAR, CIRCA '55			19.6
TEDDY BEAR, CIRCA '57			11
TEDDY BEAR, CIRCA '57			14.2
TEDDY BEAR, CIRCA '57			15
TEDDY BEAR, CIRCA '59			9.5
TEDDY BEAR, CIRCA '59			9.5
TEDDY BEAR, CIRCA '59			11.8
TEDDY BEAR, CIRCA '60			9.5
TEDDY BEAR, CIRCA '60			9.5
TEDDY BEAR, CIRCA '60			10.2
TEDDY BEAR, CIRCA '60			11.5
TEDDY BEAR, CIRCA '60			14.2
TEDDY BEAR, CIRCA '60		MRF "T"	15.75
TEDDY BEAR, CIRCA '60			15.75
TEDDY BEAR, CIRCA '60			16.5
TEDDY BEAR, CIRCA '60			18.1
TEDDY BEAR, CIRCA '60			22.8
TEDDY BEAR, CIRCA '65			11
TEDDY BEAR, CIRCA '70			5 X ?
TEDDY BEAR, CIRCA '70			9.5
TEDDY BEAR, CIRCA '70			11
TEDDY BEAR, CIRCA '70			11.8
TEDDY BEAR, CIRCA '70			18.1
TEDDY BEAR, CIRCA '72			14.2
TEDDY BEAR, CIRCA '78			11.8
TEDDY BEAR, CIRCA '78			15
TEDDY BEAR, CIRCA '79			5.5
TEDDY BEAR, CIRCA '79			7
TEDDY BEAR, CIRCA '79			7.9
TEDDY BEAR, CIRCA '79			10.2
TEDDY BEAR, CIRCA '79			11.8
TEDDY BEAR, CIRCA '80			15.75
TEDDY BEAR, CIRCA '82			10.2
TEDDY BEAR, CIRCA '82			11
TEDDY BEAR, CIRCA '84			7.9
TEDDY BEAR, CIRCA '85		MRF "AI"	12.6
TEDDY BEAR, GREY CUB	GR 55		5.5
TEDDY BEAR, GREY CUB	GR 80		8
TEDDY BEAR, GREY CUB	GR 100		10
TEDDY BEAR, GREY CUB	GR 140		14
TEDDY BEAR, IRISH	01150 1		5.9
TEDDY BEAR, MUSICAL	01230 6		12
TEDDY BEAR, MUSICAL	10931 0		11.8
TEDDY BEAR, MUSICAL	10932 7		11.8
TEDDY BEAR, MUSICAL	10940 2		15.8
TEDDY BEAR, NO JOINTS			15
TEDDY BEAR, NOSTALGIC	10930 3	63/30/3	11.8
TEDDY BEAR, NOSTALGIC	11420 8		7.9
TEDDY BEAR, NOSTALGIC	11429 1		11.8
TEDDY BEAR, NOSTALGIC	11430 7		11.8
TEDDY BEAR, NOSTALGIC	11431 4		11.8
TEDDY BEAR, NOSTALGIC	11432 1		11.8
TEDDY BEAR, NOSTALGIC	11433 8		11.8
TEDDY BEAR, NOSTALGIC	11434 5		11.8
TEDDY BEAR, NOSTALGIC	11435 2		11.8
TEDDY BEAR, NOSTALGIC	11436 9		11.8
TEDDY BEAR, NOSTALGIC	12430 6		11.8
TEDDY BEAR, NOSTALGIC	12450 4		21.2
TEDDY BEAR, NOSTALGIC	14732 9		12.6
TEDDY BEAR, NOSTALGIC	14740 4		15.75
TEDDY BEAR, NOSTALGIC	15030 5		11.8
TEDDY BEAR, NOSTALGIC	15040 4		15.75
TEDDY BEAR, NOSTALGIC	15050 3		19.7
TEDDY BEAR, NOSTALGIC	15221 7		8.5
TEDDY BEAR, NOSTALGIC	15222 4		8.5
TEDDY BEAR, NOSTALGIC	15223 1		8.5
TEDDY BEAR, NOSTALGIC	15224 8		8.5
TEDDY BEAR, NOSTALGIC	15225 5		8.5
TEDDY BEAR, NOSTALGIC	15230 4		11.5
TEDDY BEAR, NOSTALGIC	15231 1/6?		11.8
TEDDY BEAR, NOSTALGIC	15232 8/3?		11.8
TEDDY BEAR, NOSTALGIC	15233 0		11.8

NAME	EAN/OLD#	ALSO SEE	INCHES TALL
TEDDY BEAR, NOSTALGIC	15233 5/0?		11.8
TEDDY BEAR, NOSTALGIC	15245 8		18.1
TEDDY BEAR, NOSTALGIC	16214 8	62/14	4.7
TEDDY BEAR, NOSTALGIC	16214 8	62/14	4.7
TEDDY BEAR, NOSTALGIC	16214 8	62/14 OLD	5
TEDDY BEAR, NOSTALGIC	16217 9	62/17/1	6.6
TEDDY BEAR, NOSTALGIC	16217 9	62/17	6.6
TEDDY BEAR, NOSTALGIC	16217 ?	62/17w	4.7
TEDDY BEAR, NOSTALGIC	16220 9	62/20	8.1
TEDDY BEAR, NOSTALGIC	16225 4	62/25	10.2
TEDDY BEAR, NOSTALGIC	16230 8 ?	62/30NSO	11.8
TEDDY BEAR, NOSTALGIC	16230 8 ?	?62/30NSO ?	11.8
TEDDY BEAR, NOSTALGIC	16235 3	62/35	13.7
TEDDY BEAR, NOSTALGIC	16235 ?	62/35/1	13.7
TEDDY BEAR, NOSTALGIC	16240 7	62/40	15.75
TEDDY BEAR, NOSTALGIC	16250 6	62/50	19.7
TEDDY BEAR, NOSTALGIC	16250 ?	62/50 LI	19.7
TEDDY BEAR, NOSTALGIC	16308 4	63/8	3.15
TEDDY BEAR, NOSTALGIC	16314 5	63/14	5.5
TEDDY BEAR, NOSTALGIC	16317 6	63/17	7
TEDDY BEAR, NOSTALGIC	16320 6	63/20	7.9A
TEDDY BEAR, NOSTALGIC	16325 1	63/25	10.2A
TEDDY BEAR, NOSTALGIC	16330 5	63/30	11.8
TEDDY BEAR, NOSTALGIC	16335 0	63/35	14.2
TEDDY BEAR, NOSTALGIC	16340 4	63/40	15.75
TEDDY BEAR, NOSTALGIC	16350 3	63/50	18.1
TEDDY BEAR, NOSTALGIC	16360 2	63/60	23.6
TEDDY BEAR, NOSTALGIC	16380 0	06380 0 & 63/80	31.5
TEDDY BEAR, NOSTALGIC	16514 9	62/14 MAIS	5.6
TEDDY BEAR, NOSTALGIC	16517 0	62/17MAIS	6.6
TEDDY BEAR, NOSTALGIC	16530 3	62/30MAIS	11.8
TEDDY BEAR, NOSTALGIC	16714 3	62/14w	5.6
TEDDY BEAR, NOSTALGIC	16720 4	62/20w	7.9
TEDDY BEAR, NOSTALGIC	16730 3	62/30w	11.8
TEDDY BEAR, NOSTALGIC	19445 3		16.5
TEDDY BEAR, NOSTALGIC	63/35 OLD		13.8
TEDDY BEAR, PG 47	960/50		19.6
TEDDY BEAR, PG 47	960/60B		23.6
TEDDY BEAR, REPLICA '25	12350 7		18.9
TEDDY BEAR, SITTING	20750 4	80007/50	19.7
TEDDY BEAR, SITTING	20751 1		19.7
TEDDY BEAR, SITTING	20785 6	80007/85	33.5
TEDDY BEAR, SITTING	20786 3		33.5
TEDDY BEAR, SITTING	20798 6	80007/120	47
TEDDY BEAR, SITTING	20799 3		47
TEDDY BEAR, SITTING	20850 1		19.7
TEDDY BEAR, SITTING	20885 3		33
TEDDY BEAR, SOFT	20650 7	80006/50	19.7
TEDDY BEAR, SOFT	20660 6		23.6
TEDDY BEAR, SOFT	20662 0	80006/62	23.6
TEDDY BEAR, SOFT	20672 9	80006/72	27.6
TEDDY BEAR, SUPERSOFT	80003/21		8.3
TEDDY BEAR, SUPERSOFT	80003/30		11.8
TEDDY BEAR, WASHABLE	21026 9	80010/26	10.2
TEDDY BEAR, WASHABLE	21126 6	80011/26	10.2
TEDDY BEAR, WASHABLE	22035 0	80020/35	14.2
TEDDY BEAR, WASHABLE	22135 7	80021/35	13.8
TEDDY BEAR, WASHABLE	22235 4	80023/35	13.8
TEDDY BEAR, WASHABLE	22335 1	80022/35	13.8
TEDDY BEAR, WASHABLE	22740 3	80029/41	16.5
TEDDY BEAR, WASHABLE	22840 0	80029/42	16.5
TEDDY BEAR, WASHABLE	22940 7	80029/43	16.5
TEDDY BEAR, WASHABLE	23028 1	80030/28	11

NAME	EAN/OLD#	ALSO SEE	INCHES TALL
TEDDY BEAR, WASHABLE	23033 5	80030/33	12.6
TEDDY BEAR, WASHABLE	23042 7	80030/42	16.5
TEDDY BEAR, WHITE	08419 8		7.5
TEDDY BEAR, ZOTTY	85/23		9.5
TEDDY BEAR, ZOTTY	85/24		9.5
TEDDY BEAR, FLEXIBLE	19155 1		21.7
TEDDY BEAR, FLEXIBLE	19156 8		21.7
TEDDY COUGAR	01954 1		15.75
TEDDY FOR AUCTION	01769 9		59
TEDDY GREY BENDABLE	16408 1	64/8	3.3
TEDDY LEOPARD	01954 36		15.75
TEDDY ON SCOOTER	10080 5		3
TEDDY PUPIL W/DESK	10508 4		4
TEDDY SCHOOL	10044 7	1	5.7 X 8.5 X 9.5
TEDDY TIGER	01954 29		15.75
TEDDY TREND COLLECTION	15815 8		5.5
TEDDY TREND COLLECTION	15826 4		10
TEDDY TREND COLLECTION	15833 2		13.8
TEDDY TREND COLLECTION	15835 6		13.8
TEDDY @ DESK	10521 3		7.9
TEDDYBAR TOTAL 95	01611 7		6.5
TEDDY-BEAR	925/100		39.4
TEDDY-BEAR	925/30		11.8
TEDDY-BEAR	925/35		14.2
TEDDY-BEAR	925/40		15.75
TEDDY-BEAR	925/50		19.6
TEDDY-BEAR	925/60		23.6
TEDDY-BEAR	925/70		28.3
TEDDY-BEAR	925/80		31
TEDDY-BEAR	925/90		35
TEDDY-BEARS	900/10		3.9
TEDDY-BEARS	900/20		7.9
TEDDY-BEARS	900/25		9.8
TEDDY-BEARS	900/30		11.8
TEDDY-BEARS	900/35		13.8
TEDDY-BEARS	900/40	"LORD FAUNTLEROY"	15.8
TEDDY-BEARS	900/50		19.7
TEDDY-BEARS	900/60		23.6
TEDDY-BEARS	900/70		27.6
TEDDY-BEARS	900/80		31.8
TEDDY-BEAR, DRESSED	60/30/1		11.8
TEDDY-BEAR, DRESSED	60/30/2		11.8
TEDDY-BEAR, NO-NO	925/30B		11.8
TEDDY-BEAR, NO-NO	925/35B		14.2
TEDDY-BEAR, NO-NO	925/40B		15.75
TEDDY-BEAR, NO-NO	925/50B		19.6
TEDDY-BEAR, NO-NO	925/60B		23.6
TEDDY-HAMSTER	72518 3		7
TEDDY, LARGE	5/50		19.7
TEDDY, LARGE	5/60		23.6
TEDDY, LARGE	5/70		27.6
TEDDY, LARGE	5/90		35.5
TEDDY, LARGE	5/90/2		35.5
TEDDY, SOFT	50/42		16.5
TEDDY, SOFT	51/42		16.5
TEDDY, SOFT	52/42		16.5
TEDDY, SOFT	5/50		19.7
TEDDY, SOFT	5/60		23.6
TEDDY, SOFT	5/70		28.3
TEDDY, SOFT	5/90		35
TEDDY, SOFT	5/90/2		35
TEDDY, SOFT	79/25		9.6

NAME	EAN/OLD#	ALSO SEE	INCHES TALL
TEDDY, SOFT	79/30		11.8
TEDDY, SOFT	79/36		14.2
TEDDY, SOFT	79/45		18.1
TEDDY, SOFT	79/55		21.7
TEDDY, SOFT	80008/45		18.1
TEDDY, SOFT	80008/48		18.9
TEDDY, SOFT	80008/50		19.6
TEDDY, SOFT	80008/61		23.6
TEDDY, SOFT	80008/62		24.5
TEDDY, SOFT	80008/72		28.3
TEDDY, SOFT	80009/40		15.75
TEDDY, SOFT	80030/28H		11
TEDDY, SOFT	80035/28		11
TEDDY, SOFT	80035/33		12.6
TEDDY, SOFT	80035/42		16.5
TEDDY, SOFT	80036/35		14.2
TEDDY, SOFT	80036/42		16.5
TEDDY, SOFT	80040/42		16.5
TEDDY, SOFT	80041/42		16.5
TEDDY, SOFT	80045/42		16.5
TEDDY, SOFT	80083/40		15.75
TEDDY, SOFT	80164/35		13.8
TIGER EYE	11620 2		6.3
TIGER, GOLD	36570 9		27.6
TIGER, WHITE	36571 6		27.6
TING PANDA	15743 4		2.8
TO GRANDMOTHERS HOUSE	H 0001		4
TOM	19540 5		15.75
TOOTH ACHE BEAR	13625 5		9.8
TOPSY	15776 2		3.1
TORO W/BASE	15734 2		2.8
TORTOISE	39020 6	890/20	7.9
TORTOISE	39120 3	892/20	7.9
TORTOISE	39240 8	84095/40	15.75
TORTOISE	39255 2	84095/55	21.7
TORTOISE	39275 0	84095/75	29.5
TORTOISE	39320 7	894/20	7.9
TORTOISE	39420 4	802416/40	15.75
TOUGH RUDY	06235 6		13.8
TREFF, GROTESQUE	600/5		8.7
TREVOR	15234 7		11.8
TURTLE	890/30		11.8
TURTLE W/MUSIC	1489/20		7.9
TURTLE W/MUSIC	77522 5	1488/22	8.7
VAGABOND	13745 0		15.75
VAGABOND, HOBO, SCAMP?	80450/35		13.8
VASE 1930 REPLICA	95018 9		
VIOLET	13417 6		6.75
WALDGEIST	13230 1		11.8
WALL CASE W/MINI BEARS	15750 2		LARGE
WANDSBEKER HUSAR	01333 4		11.8
WASTL	13530 2		11
WEINBRANDT	01514 0		15.75
WHALE	49035 7	84100/35	13.8
WHALE	49045 6	84100/45	17.7
WHALE	49065 4	84100/65	25.6
WHALE	49565 9	84120/65	25.6
WILLY	13135 9		14.2
WILLYUM	15830 1		4.7
WINNIE	02010		11.8
WINNIE THE STUDENT	02002 8		9.84
WINNIE, THE SAILOR	O2015 8	02016 5	12.6
WINTER DREAM	01633 0		11.8

NAME	EAN/OLD#	ALSO SEE	INCHES TALL
WRIST WATCH	95030 1		
WRIST WATCH	95031 8		
WRIST WATCH	95032 5		
WRIST WATCH	95033 2		
WRIST WATCH	95034 9		
WRIST WATCH	95035 6		
XAVER	15631 4		11.8
XMAS BEAR	15140 1		14
XMAS BEAR W/SLED	15120 3		7.9
XMAS BEAR W/HORSE	15125 8		10.2
XMAS BEAR W/MUSIC	15130 2		11.8
XMAS CHILDREN	16210 0		4
XMAS CHILDREN	16211 7		4
XMAS ELF, OLD GOLD	15114 2		5.5
XMAS ELF, WHITE	15115 9		5.5
XMAS JESTER	15943 8		3.1
YOUNG BEAR	18025 8		10.2
YOUNG BEAR	18030 2		11.8
YOUNG BEAR	18040 1	80/40	15.75
YOUNG BEAR	18418 8	84/18	8.5
YOUNG BEAR	18425 6	84/25	10.2
YOUNG BEAR	18430 0	84/30	11.8
YOUNG BEAR	18435 5	84/35	14.2
YOUNG BEAR	18440 9	84/40	15.75
YOUNG BEAR	18450 8	84/50	19.7
YOUNG BEAR	18528 4		11
YOUNG BEAR	6/23		9
YOUNG BEAR	6/26		10.3
YOUNG BEAR	6/30		11.8
YOUNG BEAR	6/40		12.6
YOUNG BEAR	85/55		19.7
YOUNG BEAR	87/24		9.5
YOUNG BEAR	87/28		11
YOUNG BEAR	88/30		11.8
YOUNG BEAR	88/38		14.9
YOUNG BEAR	88/42		16.5
YOUNG BEAR FAMILY	85/18		7
YOUNG BEAR FAMILY	85/28		11
YOUNG BEAR FAMILY	85/28('60)		11
YOUNG BEAR FAMILY	85/28('70)		11
YOUNG BEAR FAMILY	85/35		14.2
YOUNG BEAR FAMILY	85/42		15.75
YOUNG BEAR FAMILY	85/50		19.7
YOUNG BEAR REPLICA	18535 2		14.2
YOUNG BEAR, LYING	166/18		7
YOUNG BEAR, LYING	166/25		9.8
YOUNG BEAR, SLEEPING	166/28		11
YOUNGBEAR	5/23		8.66
YOUNGBEAR	5/26		10.2
YOUNGBEAR	5/30		11.8
YOUNGBEAR	5/34		12.6
YOUNGBEAR	6/23		8.8
YOUNGBEAR	6/23		9.8
YOUNGBEAR	6/23		11.8
YOUNGBEAR	6/23		13.4
ZEBRA	48130 0	560/30	11.8
ZEKE	15931 5		2
ZOTTY CIRCA 1930		MRF "R"	21.3
ZOTTY CIRCA 1950			14.2
ZOTTY CIRCA 1965			14.2
ZOTTY, USA EXCLUSIVE	04035 4	70084/35	14.2

Bibliography

Brewer and Waught. *Antique & Modern Teddy Bears*. New York: Random House, 1988.

Bialosky, Peggy, and Alan Bialosky. *The Teddy Bear Catalog*. New York: Workman Publishing, 1980.

Brooks, Jacki. *The Complete Encyclopedia of Teddy Bears*. Colburn, Australia: Australian Doll Digest, 1990.

Cockrill, Pauline. *The Ultimate Teddy Bear Book*. New York: Dorling Kindersley, Inc., 1991.

———. *The Teddy Bear Encyclopedia*. Dorling Kindersley, Inc., 1993.

Dent, Nicola. *Collectable Teddy Bears*. Edison, NJ: Chartwell Books, 1995.

Friedberg, Milton R. "Hooked by Hermann." *Teddy Bear and Friends Magazine*, August 1997, page 130.

Grey, Margeret, and Gerry Grey. *Teddy Bears*. Philadelphia, PA: Running Press Book Publishers, 1994.

Hermann, Dr. Ursla. *A Teddy Bear Comes Home*. Coburg, Germany: Hermann Spielwaren, Gmbh, 1990.

Hermann Teddy Original. *Catalogs*. Hirschaid, Germany: Hermann Teddy Original, 1982-1998.

Hockenberry, Dee. *Collectible German Animals Value Guide 1948-68*. Cumberland, MD: Hobby House Press, Inc., 1990.

———. *The Teddy Bear Companion, Vol I*. Stamford, CT: Cowles Magazine Inc., 1995.

———. *The Teddy Bear Companion, Vol II*. Stamford, CT: Cowles Magazine Inc., 1996.

———. *The Big Bear Book*. Atglen, PA: Schiffer Publishing Ltd., 1996.

Maanen, James Van. "All in the Family." *Teddy Bear Review Magazine*, July/August 1996, page 62.

Mandel, Margaret Fox. *Teddy Bears & Steiff Animals*. Paducah, KY: Collector Books, 1993.

Manolis, Argie. *The Teddy Bear Sourcebook for Collectors and Artists*. Atglen, PA: Schiffer Publishing Ltd., 1995.

Menten, Ted. *Teddy's Bearzaar*. Philadelphia, PA: Running Press Book Publishers, 1988.

———. *The Teddy Bear Lover's Companion*. Philadelphia, PA: Running Press Book Publishers, 1989.

Michaud, Terry, and Doris Michaud. *Contemporary Teddy Bear Price Guide, Artists to Manufacturers*. Cumberland, MD: Hobby House Press, Inc., 1992.

Mullins, Linda. *4th Teddy Bear & Friends Price Guide*. Cumberland, MD: Hobby House Press, Inc., 1993.

Pearson & Ayers. *Teddy Bears, a Complete Guide to History, Collecting and Care*. New York: Macmillan, 1995.

Pistorius, Rolf, and Cristal Pistorius. *Tales of Teddy Hermann*. Germany: Weingarten, 1994.

Ruddell, Gary R. "Hermann, Original Teddy Bears." *Teddy Bear & Friends Magazine*, Fall 1984, page 38.

Schoonmaker, Patricia N. *A Collector's History of the Teddy Bear*. Cumberland, MD: Hobby House Press, Inc., 1981.

Severin, Gustav. *Teddy Bear, A Loving History of The Classic Childhood Companion*. Philadelphia, PA: Running Press Book Publishers, 1992.

Sieverling, Helen. *2nd Teddy Bear & Friends Price Guide*. 1985

———. *3rd Teddy Bear & Friends Price Guide*. 1988

Slider, Mark. "Behind the Red Seal, Gebrüder Hermann." *Teddy Bear & Friends Magazine*, Jan/Feb 1993.

Sparrow, Judy. *Teddy Bears*. New York: Smithmark Publishers, Inc., 1993.

Teddy Bear & Friends, Various Issues, American Magazine

Teddy Bear Review, Various Issues, American Magazine.

Teddy Bear Times, Various Issues, English Magazine.